D1570158

Mexico in the WTO and NAFTA

Global Trade Law Series

VOLUME 24

Series Editor

ROSS BUCKLEY
Professor, Faculty of Law, University of New South Wales, Sydney, Australia.

Associate Series Editor

ANDREAS ZIEGLER
Professor, Faculty of Law and Criminal Sciences, University of Lausanne, Lausanne, Switzerland.

Advisory Board

KLUWER LAW INTERNATIONAL

Mexico in the WTO and NAFTA

Litigating International Trade Disputes

Jorge Alberto Huerta-Goldman

Wolters Kluwer
Law & Business

AUSTIN   BOSTON   CHICAGO   NEW YORK   THE NETHERLANDS

Published by:
Kluwer Law International
PO Box 316
2400 AH Alphen aan den Rijn
The Netherlands
Website: www.kluwerlaw.com

Sold and distributed in North, Central and South America by:
Aspen Publishers, Inc.
7201 McKinney Circle
Frederick, MD 21704
United States of America
Email: customer.service@aspenpublishers.com

Sold and distributed in all other countries by:
Turpin Distribution Services Ltd.
Stratton Business Park
Pegasus Drive, Biggleswade
Bedfordshire SG18 8TQ
United Kingdom
Email: kluwerlaw@turpin-distribution.com

Printed on acid-free paper.

ISBN 978-90-411-3169-0

Printed in Great Britain.

To:

Ana María Serafín Chavez
Carlota Serafín Chavez
Herman Goldman Wagner
Ana Elda Goldman Serafín
Marco Antonio Huerta Wilde

... because we are the result of endless efforts...

Table of Contents

Chapter 5
Interpretations of the Data 163

About the Author

Jorge A. Huerta-Goldman, born in Guadalajara, Mexico, is a WTO law practitioner and researcher. He is currently working for the Permanent Mexican Mission to the WTO in Geneva.

With almost ten years of experience as a government official, he has been a Doha negotiator (NAMA, Dispute Settlement reforms, Trade Remedies, and Development among others) as well as a WTO litigator (litigating several cases as a member of the Mexican team). He started his career at the trade remedies investigating authority (UPCI) in Mexico City. Mr. Huerta-Goldman also litigated civil and commercial law cases before Mexican courts.

Mr. Huerta-Goldman was a visiting scholar at Columbia Law School, New York, during the Fall 2006. He has spoken at different universities in Mexico, Europe and the US. He received a *doctorat en droit* (Ph.D.) at the University of Neuchâtel with *Magna Cum Laude*, in Switzerland. He received the LLM in European Law from the College of Europe, Bruges, Belgium, in 2001, and the LLM in International Trade Law from the University of Arizona in 1998. He was admitted to practice law in Mexico in 1996, after completing his law studies at ITESO, in Guadalajara.

The opinions expressed in this work are entirely those of the author.

You may contact him at jahg@mexico-wto.org or Jorge.huerta@unine.ch

Preface

This volume by Jorge Alberto Huerta-Goldman fills a vacuum in the specialized literature available to us both in respect of his analysis of Mexico's practice and record in international economic disputes, and, more generally, in the field of investigation country by country into the use of such litigation.

Mexico is in this respect an interesting case. Though not one of the economic super-powers, it is an important middle size player and one of the largest from the developing world. Moreover, Mexico is party to an almost unique web of regional and bilateral agreements with dispute settlement mechanisms. Finally, it has been a frequent user of these proceedings, even to the point of finding itself arguing or defending substantially the same case, or related cases, in different fora. Thus, Mexico is an excellent example of how a country can sort out, and make the best use of, the ever growing multiplicity of third-party adjudication mechanisms. On the one hand, such mechanisms expand internationally the application of the rule of law in the interests of the security of cross border economic exchange. On the other hand, their very multiplicity presents the risk of fragmentation as different sets of international norms are developed and applied, to the point that a country may be faced with conflicting obligations and real difficulties in managing the 'spaghetti bowl' of the array of options.

Jorge's research is of great interest for those who wish to know in detail the disputes to which Mexico has been a party in the first place. The accuracy of the examination of individual cases, the supporting statistical data and his personal insight into many of the disputes render the work invaluable in this respect and a model for similar research into the practice of other economies.

As noted above, more generally, this work makes a valuable contribution to the knowledge and evaluation of the functioning of trade dispute settlement mechanisms in various contexts – global, regional and bilateral – and under different sets of procedural rules.

I am pleased, therefore, to recommend highly this work to all those interested in this growing and fascinating field at the cross roads of international law and economics.

Giorgio Sacerdoti
Bocconi University, Milano, and Appellate Body of the WTO, Geneva
October 2009.

Acknowledgements

The first person to be acknowledged in this work is Professor Petros C. Mavroidis, a mentor, a friend and a natural-born builder. Thank you very much for your time, for your knowledge and for showing confidence in me.

The analysis of Mexico's experience in International Trade Litigation was made possible by observing and working with my colleagues at the *Secretaría de Economía* (the *Consultoría Jurídica,* the *UPCI*, and the Mexican Mission to the World Trade Organization (WTO)). Each member of the team encouraged me, directly or indirectly, to finish the book. Pablo Klein Bernard contributed enormously through the whole process with his suggestions and discussions. Also, discussions with Soledad Leal Campos were very useful for this work. Nora Oviedo Muñoz and Linda Pasquel guided me through the labyrinth of Mexican cases when I was lost in the information. Dora Rodriguez Romero also led me through the southern agreements. I learned a lot by working with Aristeo Lopez Sanchez, Luis Alberto González García, Guillermo Malpica Soto, Beatriz Leycegui Gardoqui, Adriana Díaz Ortiz, Alejandro Sanchez Arriaga, Hugo Perezcano Díaz, Fernando de Mateo, Ricardo Ramirez Hernandez, José Manuel Vargas Menchaca, Rodrigo Orozco Galvez, Mariano Gomezperalta Casali, Gustavo Adolfo Baez Lopez, Orlando Perez Garate, Mateo Diego Fernandez, Carlos Vejar Borrego and the rest of the team. Eduardo Perez Motta and Angel Lopez Hoher inspired me when we were working on the diagnosis of the WTO Understanding on Rules and Procedures Governing the Settlement of Disputes (DSU) and the old DSU proposal. Finally, Roberta Cervantes García, Alejandra Berlanga and Samuel Chio del Angel helped enormously with their research. I would also like to thank Diego Carrillo Santoscoy and Misael Romero.

I would like to thank the professors at Columbia University in the United States for the very generous invitation they gave me as a visiting scholar at a crucial time for this book. I learned a lot from Prof. Jagdish Bhagwati and Prof. George A. Bermann. I thank Prof. Kyle Bagwell, currently at Stanford University, for his time and suggestions during my period in New York.

The PhD Panel at the *Université de Neuchâtel*, Switzerland, gave me excellent feedback and allowed me to test my work. My thanks go to Prof. Olivier Guillod, Prof. Evelyne Clerc, Prof. Robert Kolb and Prof. Werner Zdouc from the WTO secretariat. The advice from Prof. Pascal Mahon was very welcome, and the guidance from the UNINE kindly given by Ms Viviane Perratone could not have been more valuable.

Prof. David Gantz from the University of Arizona, one of my *almae matres*, prepared me some years ago for the challenge of this book and was always there to discuss a variety of technical issues. When facing a dead end, whether real or imagined, I got help from Prof. Jacques Bourgeois of the College of Europe in Bruges, another of my *almae matres*. The help and support received from Dr Peter Bennett was invaluable and essential for the completion of the book.

Finally, I am enormously grateful to my beloved Ilaria Accorsi, not only for her technical input and comments, but also for her always being there and for her enormous patience when I was focusing my energy on the book.

Jorge A. Huerta-Goldman
Carouge, Switzerland, June 2009

Introduction

This work is about the conduct of Mexico's international trade litigation from 1986 to 2007. My research is limited to the multilateral and bilateral[1] forums and is set in the context of the specificities of these legal regimes – I do not aim to advance ideas on how such regimes should be modified to better address Mexico's concerns. Mexico operated within these parameters and I have taken them for granted. Chapter I explains the various (multi- and bilateral) options for trade litigation available to Mexico.

Throughout the research, I have sought to analyse the data from three distinct perspectives: administrative capacity, bargaining power and political economy considerations. These three areas provide support for my conclusions regarding Mexico's conduct of its trade disputes. In a nutshell, Mexico's participation is constrained by its administrative capacity, which in turn imposes a need to prioritize which disputes to pursue and how far, in light of political economy considerations. Bargaining power is a vital element in explaining the use of legal remedies.

The cases adjudicated through the multilateral dispute settlement mechanisms include those under the General Agreement on Tariffs and Trade (GATT) and the World Trade Organization (WTO). Mexico participated in these cases either as a main Party to the dispute (complainant or defendant) or as a Third Party under both jurisdictions. Chapter II describes these cases.

In Chapter III, I move to discuss cases under Preferential Trade Agreements (PTAs). They are Free Trade Agreements, plus ALADI, that Mexico is Party to – essentially cases under the North American Free Trade Agreement (NAFTA). I distinguish between country versus country cases and private party versus country cases. All of the PTAs where Mexico is a Party contain country versus country

---

1. Twelve PTAs plus the *Asociación Latinoamericana de la Integración,* or Latin American Integration Association (ALADI).

dispute settlement mechanisms,[2] but only three have been used. The private party versus country dispute settlement mechanism is included in Chapter 19 of NAFTA.

Chapter IV presents a comparison of key data drawn from the WTO cases, using specific variables.

Finally, I present my interpretation of the data in Chapter V. My main findings are reflected in this chapter. It presents conclusions regarding Mexico's administrative capacity with respect to the initiation and litigation of disputes. There is an analysis of cases negotiated versus cases litigated. The lobbying power of Mexican economic interests is discussed, both when Mexico acts as complainant and when it acts as defendant. The utilization of legal remedies and issues of double forums are also covered.

---

2.   This is not the case for ALADI, where the parties have to negotiate specific dispute settlement mechanisms.

Summary of Findings

When litigating trade disputes, Mexico must work within a specific regulatory frame-work that is both multilateral (WTO) and bilateral (PTAs).[3] Its involvement is con-strained domestically by its administrative capacity, which in turn imposes a need to prioritize, in the light of political economy, which disputes to pursue and how far. Bargaining power is a vital element in explaining Mexico's use of legal remedies.

I.   THE MULTILATERAL AND BILATERAL FORUMS

Mexico has access to country versus country dispute settlement procedures and to procedures triggered by private parties against countries (private party versus coun-try). The WTO Understanding on Rules and Procedures Governing the Settlement of Disputes (DSU) and Chapter 20 of NAFTA deal with disputes among countries, whereas Chapter 19 of NAFTA (Article 1904 Panel) deals with antidumping/ countervailing duties (AD/CVD) disputes between a private party and a country. Each procedure has its jurisdictional limitations, but there can be some concurrent jurisdiction.

At the end of the day, the WTO and Chapter 20 of NAFTA require compliance with the Panel report – temporary compensation or retaliation are transitional options. A dispute can, of course, always be settled through a mutually agreed solution (MAS). Compliance, and to some extent MAS, are usually referred to as 'property rules', where the author of an illegal act must change its behaviour so as to eliminate the illegality. Compensation and retaliation are 'liability rules' – the author of an illegal act can pay and compensate those affected by the illegality without, however, incur-ring the obligation to change its behaviour. The WTO DSU takes an unambiguous stance in favour of 'property rules' (compliance). For instance, if a 'liability rule' such

---

3.   Twelve PTAs plus ALADI.

as compensation has been agreed, but the illegality persists, the author of the illegal measure may face new complaints by other WTO Members.

An Article 1904 Panel, usually triggered by a private party, revises final AD/CVDs imposed by one of the three NAFTA Parties. It is a substitute for domestic legal procedures challenging those final AD/CVDs. A given Article 1904 Panel may remand or affirm the final determination subject to review. There may be several remands with respect to the same final determination, and there may be several 1904 Panels reviewing different final determinations within the same AD/CVD order. Data on these cases is a good means of measuring the power of lobbies. The main legal remedies in an Article 1904 Panel – to uphold or to remand the final determination – are 'property rules'. But if a NAFTA Party considers that an Article 1904 Panel has been undermined, it can trigger the Special Committee. This procedure may lead to the suspension of NAFTA benefits or the suspension of Article 1904 procedures – 'liability rules'.

II.   THE CASES

Mexico has used the multilateral forum (thirty-three cases under GATT/WTO) significantly more than the regional country versus country forums (four cases under NAFTA/other PTAs). Exporters have several times used the procedures under Article 1904 of NAFTA (sixteen AD/CVD orders with several 1904 Panels).

This study classifies cases into three categories: abandoned, implemented and pending. The factors used to evaluate Mexico's conduct of its international trade disputes are: subject matter; identity of the Parties involved; products; adjudicators; procedural stage at which the litigation stopped or was pending at the cut-off date; number of findings won/lost by Mexico; implementation (*ex ante* and *ex post*); and legal remedies used.

III.   THE GATT

Even though Mexico won most of the claims in its three cases under the GATT (50% of the findings in two cases and 100% in the third case), it did not manage to secure implementation – only one case was adopted and implemented, and this one was initiated by Mexico, Canada and the EC, not by Mexico alone. Mexico could have been a free rider in this single adopted case, by not participating as complainant, since implementation was on a most-favoured-nation (MFN) basis. This MFN implementation also benefited non-parties to the dispute. The other reports remain unadopted and are hence of limited legal value.

IV.   THE WTO PROCEDURAL STAGES

Mexico litigated its WTO cases beyond the original Panel/Appellate Body (Panel/AB) stage only against the US/EC: to the retaliation stage, one case as complainant;

to the Article 21.5 Panel/AB stage, two cases as complainant and one case as defendant; and to the reasonable period of time under Article 21.3 of the DSU (which could be in practice determined by agreement or by binding arbitration), or RPT, stage, three cases as complainant. Cases against Parties which were not Members of the Organisation for Economic Co-operation and Development were implemented, abandoned or pending at an earlier stage.

V. THE WTO FINDINGS WON

As complainant, Mexico won the highest number of Panel/AB findings when it cooperated with other complainants. In *US – Offset Act* (217/234) the co-complainants won 71% of the Panel findings and 64% of the AB findings, whereas in *EC – Bananas III* (27) the co-complainants won 100% of the Panel findings and 82% of the AB findings. As a single litigant before the AB, Mexico did not win any finding in two cases as complainant. As defendant, it did not win any finding in two cases and won 13% of the AB findings in another case.

Mexico as a single complainant won a higher number of findings when the defendant was not an OECD Member – 95% of the Panel findings against Guatemala in one case, and 75% of the Panel findings, though subsequently revoked by the AB, against Guatemala in another case. It won fewer findings when the defendant was the US/EC – 20% at Panel stage and none before the AB. As defendant, the only cases that Mexico litigated within the period of observation were initiated by the US/EC, and Mexico won very few findings.

Administrative capacity may have contributed to the low number of findings won by Mexico.

VI. THE WTO IMPLEMENTATION

As defendant, Mexico implemented more cases initiated by the US/EC (four out of nine total) than the US/EC did in cases initiated by Mexico (two of ten). For cases with non-Members of OECD, the rate of implementation is more balanced: four of six total as complainant and three of five as defendant. The defendant's bargaining power seems to have a strong influence on whether a case is implemented. But Mexico is more disposed to agree to comply *ex ante* when the complainant is a non-Member of OECD.

When Mexico does not have bargaining power as complainant to press for legal remedies it litigates to an advanced stage in sensitive cases, such as those against US/EC (three cases). It seems to seek to use loss of reputation as a lever against defendants with stronger bargaining power. But as defendant, it also litigates to an Article 21.5 Panel/AB stage against US/EC on sensitive issues (one case on sweeteners) and holds off until the end of the RPT before implementing (three cases initiated by the US).

Within the period of observation, when the complainant was more powerful than the defendant[4] (one case of Mexico as complainant and four cases as defendant), successful litigation was always followed by implementation. When the US/EC defended against Mexico, successful litigation was not followed by implementation by the US/EC in three cases. These are the only cases where Mexico as complainant won findings against the US/EC. No cases involving Mexico as defendant against non-Members of OECD were litigated, and Mexico complied *ex ante* in three cases but did not in two cases (one abandoned by Brazil and the other pending by Guatemala). This shows that bargaining power matters for implementation, regardless of the results of the Panel/AB findings. But Mexico did not use it when defending against weaker Members and used it only to a limited extent when defending against US/EC.

VII.   THE POWER OF LOBBYING

When cement and steel exports have faced antidumping (AD) measures, the respective industries have used their lobbying power. Mexico initiated as complainant one of three cases in the GATT era and five of sixteen cases under the WTO to address illegalities obstructing its exports of cement. From 1990 to 2006, exports of cement from Mexico did not represent more than 0.3% of its total exports per year. The cement lobby, however, remains a very powerful lobby in the domestic setting. Turning to cases on steel products, Mexico initiated five of sixteen cases to defend the export interests of its steel producers. Between 1995 and 1997, its exports of steel products represented 1% of total exports, and from 1998 to 2006 less than 0.8%. In sum, Mexico initiated as complainant eleven of nineteen GATT/WTO cases (from 1986 to 2006) relating to products that represented less than 2% of its yearly exports, demonstrating that the cement and steel products industries have strong lobbying power and have used that power in support of their export interests.

The Mexican sugar industry has not achieved substantive results when Mexico has acted as complainant. The opposite is true when Mexico was defending its domestic market. From 1997 to 2006 there was a significant decrease in Mexico's sugar exports at the same time as imports and production of high fructose corn syrup – a sugar substitute – appeared on the domestic market. The sugar industry is highly sensitive/labour intensive, even if it does not contribute significantly to gross domestic product (GDP). Agriculture, sugar included, represented less than 6.3% of Mexico's GDP per year from 1995 to 2007. The government responded to this situation with two measures: first, an administrative AD measure which was challenged twice in the WTO and once under Article 1904 of NAFTA; and second, a measure involving a discriminatory 20% tax on high fructose corn syrup which was challenged through the WTO and the investor-State dispute settlement mechanism under NAFTA.

---

4. Two combinations appear in Mexico's data: (a) US/EC vs Mexico and (b) Mexico vs non-
     Members of the OECD.

VIII.   THE STRENGTH OF WTO LEGAL REMEDIES

A mutually agreed solution (MAS) and compliance may appear either before or after the adoption of a Panel/AB report. Hence, we distinguish *ex ante* compliance or MAS from *ex post* compliance or MAS. The two other legal remedies – compensation and retaliation – may only appear after the adoption of a Panel/AB report with a finding of WTO violation.

Each of the remedies requires a degree of activity by the defendant which is of inverse relationship to the level of activity by the defendant. For instance, compliance requires a very active role by the defendant, but the complainant can be very passive. Compensation and MAS require almost the same level of activity from both Parties, and retaliation requires an active role by the complainant while the defendant may rest passive. This makes it easier for the complainant to achieve a legal remedy, regardless of the level of passivity or activity by the defendant.

The defendant is, however, able to some extent to postpone the appearance of WTO legal remedies, regardless of which remedy is used – but there can be political and financial costs if it holds off for too long. It is very difficult to measure these costs. For instance, the US as defendant agreed to a MAS *ex ante* 4.10 months after the request for consultations in the *US – Tomatoes* (49) case, whereas in *US – Cement* (281) it allowed the same legal remedy, but 36.03 months after the request for consultations.[5]

The possibility of postponing the appearance of the legal remedies is present regardless of the initial bargaining power of the Parties. But, generally speaking, delaying the legal remedy is more common when the defendant has stronger bargaining power, as shown in the following table. Perhaps if the bargaining power is stronger it is easier to bear the cost of litigation.

Table 1. Cases with the Latest Appearance of Legal Remedies

	Mexico as Complainant	**Mexico as Defendant**
Stronger vs weaker bargaining power	Mx vs Non-OECD: 21.27 months to compliance *ex post* (*Guatemala – Cement II* [156])	US/EC vs Mx: 60.70 months to MAS *ex post* (*Mexico – Telecoms* [204])
Weaker vs stronger bargaining power	Mx vs US/EC: 68.37 months from consultations to cut-off date (*US – Offset Act* [217/234])[6]	Non-OECD vs Mx: 33.03 months to MAS *ex ante* (*Mexico – Matches* [232])

---

5. For our calculation, a month has thirty days.
6. This case was initiated by Mexico with several co-complainants, including the EC. Retaliation took place earlier than the cut-off date, but the case was still pending at that time.

When a given defendant uses its option to postpone the appearance of a legal remedy, the complainant's bargaining power is markedly diminished. This diminishment of bargaining power affected the terms of the MAS signed between Mexico and the US on *US – Cement* (281). For the complainant, there was little legal certainty, but it did not have much choice.

IX.   JURISDICTIONAL ISSUES AND DOUBLE FORUMS

There are three possible scenarios for potential forum-shopping between NAFTA and the WTO:

(1)   The relationship between the Article 1904 Panel (final AD/CVD determinations) and the general dispute settlement mechanisms of NAFTA is solved within the NAFTA, and merits no further analysis.

(2)   The relationship between the Article 1904 Panel and the DSU of the WTO should not create double-forum concerns. 1904 Panels are substitutes for domestic tribunals, and they rule based on domestic laws. WTO case law suggests that a WTO Panel should continue its work regardless of any domestic litigation on the same measure (AD/CVD determination). This rule should also apply to Article 1904 Panel procedures, since they are substitutes for domestic tribunals. Moreover, the Parties to the dispute are different, even if a NAFTA Party may participate in an Article 1904 Panel. The law is also different (domestic versus WTO law), although in Mexico's case, WTO law has been incorporated into domestic law. The measure may be the same, since both WTO and NAFTA may deal with final AD/CVD determinations.

(3)   The relationship between Chapter 20 of NAFTA and the DSU may raise concerns about double forums. The only rules that exist are set out in NAFTA, but they are far from perfect. Work still needs to be done to differentiate WTO law from NAFTA law and to define what is meant by identity of measures. The rules, moreover, do not cover the scenario where a second case is taken by the other NAFTA Party, if that case is initiated at a different time from the first one.

List of Acronyms and Definitions

Acronym/Word	Definition
AB	The WTO Appellate Body.
Abandoned case	A case which is not procedurally active due to: (a) inactivity for more than three years (because after three years one cannot reasonably expect a renaissance); or (b) the presentation of a new request for consultation challenging the original measure or its modified version, such as provisional and definitive antidumping measures;[7] we further classify the abandoned cases by declaration or no declaration of abandonment by the complainant.
ACE	*Acuerdo de Complementación Económica,* or Economic Complementation Agreement under ALADI.
AD	Antidumping.
AD/CVD orders	The AD/CVD investigations and procedures towards the imposition of duties; they may contain original investigations, yearly reviews and sunset reviews, among others.
ADA	The WTO Agreement on Implementation of Article VI of the General Agreement on Tariffs and Trade (GATT) 1994, or Antidumping Agreement.

---

7. We count these reformulated cases – e.g., provisional and definitive AD measures – as a single case per each request for consultations. This is important for our analysis of legal remedies in Ch. 5, 'Interpretations of the Data'.

ADD   Antidumping duty.

Adoption of GATT   Under the GATT rules, Panel reports were not
Panel reports   automatically adopted. They were adopted only
                             if there was consensus.[8] Hence, any Contracting
                             Party had a veto power. The current WTO rules
                             allow for adoption of a Panel/AB report unless
                             there is a consensus not to adopt it – i.e., the nega-
                             tive consensus rule.[9] A report not adopted means
                             no legal obligation with respect to implementation.

ALADI   *Asociación Latinoamericana de la Integración*
                             (Latin American Integration Association).

Case   A dispute settlement number provided by the WTO
                             when a Member files a request for consultations;[10]
                             we count one case per request for consultations
                             even if one request challenges a provisional AD
                             measure and another challenges a definitive AD
                             measure.[11]

Claim   The legal basis for a request for consultations;
                             since we compare all WTO cases at the same level,
                             we do not take into account the evolution of the
                             claim at subsequent stages (i.e., Panel request or
                             notice of appeal). We do not distinguish claims
                             entered from claims actually litigated.

Complainant   The WTO/PTA Member that initiates a case.

Consultations   The first procedural stage of WTO Dispute Settle-
                             ment as set out in Article 4 of the DSU; general
                             dispute settlement provisions in PTAs also allow
                             for consultations.

Country versus   Those cases adjudicated through jurisdictions
country cases   allowing exclusive standing to WTO Members or
                             to Parties to a PTA; for PTAs, these are usually the
                             general dispute settlement mechanisms, such as in
                             Chapter 20 of NAFTA.

Customs Valuation   The WTO Agreement on Customs Valuation.

---

8. There is consensus if no Member, present at the meeting when the decision is taken, formally
    objects to the proposed decision. See n. 1 of the WTO Agreement for the WTO description of
    consensus.
9. See Arts 16.4 and 17.14 of the DSU.
10. For a full list see <www.wto.org/english/tratop_e/dispu_e/dispu_status_e.htm>, August 2009.
11. We count these individual requests for consultations as separate cases. Counting them as one
    could affect our analysis of legal remedies.

Cut-off date	1 January 2007 for Mexico's cases under the WTO or 1 January 2008 for those under the PTAs; all the factual information used in this work is correct as of those dates.
CVD	Countervailing duties.
Defendant	The WTO/PTA Member to which the request for consultations is addressed.
DG	Director General of the WTO.
DOC	The United States Department of Commerce.
DSB	The WTO Dispute Settlement Body.
DSU	The WTO Understanding on Rules and Procedures Governing the Settlement of Disputes.
EC	European Communities, or the European Union as Member of the WTO.
ECA	Economic complementation agreements under ALADI.
Ex ante compliance or MAS	Compliance or MAS achieved before a Panel/ AB ruling on the legality of a measure; here, the obligation derives from Article XVI:4 of the WTO Agreement, which is designed to ensure the conformity of its measures with the obligations provided in the WTO covered agreements, regardless of any ruling on the legality of a particular measure.
Ex post compliance or MAS	Compliance or MAS achieved after a Panel/ AB has ruled that a measure is WTO inconsistent; here, there is an obligation to modify or withdraw the measure in light of the Panel/AB analysis and findings. Compensation and suspension of concessions may be triggered after this stage.[12]
Finding won/ lost by Mexico	Any successful finding by a GATT Panel, PTA Panel, WTO Panel/AB (original or Article 21.5 of the DSU) or arbitrator (Articles 21.3 or 22.6 of the DSU).[13] We use findings as a unit of account. We

---

12. See Ch. 1, 'Mexico's Options for Settlement of International Trade Disputes', where we explain the DSU process.
13. We determine success in findings by the arbitrator under Arts 21.3 or 22.6 of the DSU by comparing them with the position sustained by each party to the arbitration. As an example, assume that a finding on RPT of two months and one party's position was one month and the

do not pronounce on overall win/loss, which is a very difficult issue to tackle.[14]

For WTO cases, we distinguish the Panel findings from the AB findings by counting them separately. We do not count findings under Article 3.8 of the DSU – although we do take them into account if the Article was the legal base of a defence. Nor do we count absence of findings through judicial economy.

The findings from the Panel, as amended by the AB, may come from two sources: claims that were the basis of the complaint (Article 6.2 of the DSU) or defences presented by the defendant (such as Article XX of the GATT).

FTAs	Free trade agreements.
GATS	The WTO General Agreement on Trade in Services.
GATT	General Agreement on Tariffs and Trade.
GDP	Gross domestic product.
Goods, agricultural	The goods covered by Article 2 of the Agreement on Agriculture.
Goods, general	General Goods, in cases that do not specify particular goods; the measure challenged in these cases affects several goods. It is not possible to differentiate the product using the industrial goods/agricultural goods classification.
Goods, industrial	All the goods not covered by Article 2 of the Agreement on Agriculture.
Hit-and-run measures	Those measures that affect concessions or other obligations for a short period of time.
Implementation or measure amended	A measure is deemed to be amended or implemented when: (a) the complainant is satisfied with the amendment; or (b) the measure has been withdrawn no later than one year from the last communication of a disputing Party or an

---

other party's position was three months. Here we would allocate a one-half finding of success to each party.

14. For instance, even when the findings were in favour of the US in the *Mexico – Telecoms* (204) case, there were internal interests in Mexico that wanted to amend the domestic regulations, and some government officials used the Panel report as a leverage to do so.

	adjudicative body, and the complainant does not oppose the modification or elimination of the measure; or (c) there is a MAS. Under WTO law, one finding of violation is sufficient to trigger the obligation to implement, unless the measure is no longer in force when the Panel/AB issues the finding. Article 19.1 of the DSU obliges Panels to recommend that the measure be brought into conformity, if a violation is found.
LDCs	Least developed countries, as defined by the United Nations, that are WTO Members.
Legal remedies	The means to solve a wrongful act; we found three main legal remedies in the DSU: compliance, compensation pending compliance, and suspension of concessions or other obligations. We count a MAS as a secondary legal remedy.
Licensing Agreement	The Agreement on Import Licensing Procedures.
MAS	Mutually agreed solution, including: (a) notified agreements or agreements publicly available; (b) a unilateral manifestation of compliance not followed by opposition by the complainant; (c) requests for suspension under Article 12.12 of the DSU; and (d) implemented cases.
Measure	The challenged act or omission performed or omitted by a WTO Member or a Party to a PTA; the measure would be the facts or omissions to be examined in the light of the rights and obligations of the WTO covered Agreements or the substantive law of a PTA.
Ministerial decision on declared value	The WTO Ministerial Decision regarding cases where customs administrations have reasons to doubt the truth or accuracy of the declared value.
N. or I.	Nullification or impairment as used in the WTO covered agreements.
NAFTA	The North American Free Trade Agreement.
NAFTA Party	Canada, the US or Mexico.
OECD	The Organization for Economic Cooperation and Development with thirty Members.

Other Party involved	When Mexico is attacking, the other Party involved is the defendant. When Mexico is defending, the other Party involved is the complainant. We further classify the other Party involved – the 153 WTO Members[15] – in accordance with their economic development as (a) US/EC (29 Members),[16] (b) other OECD Members (10 Members including Mexico),[17] (c) non-Members of OECD (80 non-Members)[18] and (d) LDCs or least developed countries (32 Members).[19]
Other OECD Members	All the Members of the OECD except for the US/EC; the remaining Members, without counting Mexico, are Australia, Canada, Iceland, Japan, Korea, New Zealand, Norway, Switzerland and Turkey.
Panel/AB	The procedural stage where the Panel and the Appellate Body are judging the case; it starts from the establishment of the Panel and ends with the adoption of the Panel/AB report.
Panel, Article 21.5	The Panel under Article 21.5 of the DSU, this may include consultations and appeal under Article 21.5 of the DSU. This provision in fact contemplates

---

15. See <www.wto.org/english/thewto_e/whatis_e/tif_e/org6_e.htm>, August 2009.

16. This classification includes the twenty-seven Member States from the EC, the EC itself, and the US. In addition to its Member States, the EC is also a WTO Member. However, as n. 2 of the WTO Agreement indicates with respect to the decision-making process of the WTO, 'the number of votes of the European Communities and their Member States shall in no case exceed the number of the Member States of the European Communities'.

17. Excluding the US and the EC, they are: Australia, Canada, Iceland, Japan, Korea, New Zealand, Norway, Switzerland, and Turkey (and, of course, Mexico).

18. These are the WTO Members that are neither OECD Members nor LDCs: Albania; Antigua and Barbuda; Argentina; Armenia; Kingdom of Bahrain; Barbados; Belize; Bolivia; Botswana; Brazil; Brunei Darussalam; Cameroon; Chile; China; Colombia; Costa Rica; Côte d'Ivoire; Croatia; Cuba; the Democratic Republic of the Congo; Dominica; Dominican Republic; Ecuador; Egypt; El Salvador; Fiji; the Former Yugoslav Republic of Macedonia; Gabon; Georgia; Ghana; Grenada; Guatemala; Guyana; Honduras; Hong Kong, China; India; Indonesia; Israel; Jamaica; Jordan; Kenya; Kuwait; the Kyrgyz Republic; Liechtenstein; Macao; Malaysia; Mauritius; Moldova; Mongolia; Morocco; Namibia; Nicaragua; Nigeria; Oman; Pakistan; Panama; Papua New Guinea; Paraguay; Peru; the Philippines; Qatar; Saint Kitts and Nevis; Saint Lucia; Saint Vincent and the Grenadines; Saudi Arabia; Singapore; South Africa; Sri Lanka; Suriname; Swaziland; Chinese Taipei; Thailand; Tonga; Trinidad and Tobago; Tunisia; United Arab Emirates; Uruguay; Venezuela; Viet Nam; and Zimbabwe.

19. Those that are Members of the WTO are: Angola, Bangladesh, Benin, Burkina Faso, Burundi, Cambodia, the Central African Republic, Chad, the Democratic Republic of the Congo, Djibouti, Gambia, Guinea, Guinea Bissau, Haiti, Lesotho, Madagascar, Malawi, Maldives, Mali, Mauritania, Mozambique, Myanmar, Nepal, Niger, Rwanda, Senegal, Sierra Leone, the Solomon Islands, Tanzania, Togo, Uganda, and Zambia. See <www.wto.org/english/thewto_e/whatis_e/tif_e/org7_htm/>, August 2007.

	neither consultations nor appeal, but in practice they are covered in this stage.
Pending Case	A procedurally active case, as opposed to abandoned or implemented cases.
Product	The good, service or intellectual property right subject to the dispute settlement mechanism; we classify them under four clusters: (a) industrial goods; (b) agricultural goods; (c) general goods; and (d) services (Mexico has had no TRIPS cases). There are some cases covering two products at the same time – e.g., *EC – Bananas III* (27), which dealt with agricultural goods and services. Those cases have been recorded by half units for each product (i.e., 0.5 for agricultural product and 0.5 for services).[20]
PTAs	Preferential trade agreements, as in Article XXIV of the GATT; they could be customs unions or free trade agreements. Other forms of economic integrations, such as ALADI, are allowed in the WTO through the so-called Enabling Clause.[21]
Request for consultations/Panel	The date of the request for consultations/ establishment of a Panel; the date refers to the date of the communication, not the date of distribution by the WTO.
Retaliation	The suspension of concessions or other obligations, or the adoption of appropriate countermeasures.
RPT	Reasonable period of time under Article 21.3 of the DSU, which in practice could be determined by agreement or by binding arbitration.
S&D	Special and differential treatment; the principle in the WTO whereby developing countries, including least developed countries, are entitled to treatment different from developed countries.
SCM Agreement	The WTO Agreement on Subsidies and Countervailing Duties.
SECOFI	*Secretaría de Comercio y Fomento Industrial*, now *Secretaría de Economía* (Mexican Ministry of Trade).

---

20. There is one NAFTA case dealing with services and investment at the same time.
21. See WTO decision of 28 Nov. 1979 (L/4903) agreed under the GATT on differential and more favourable treatment reciprocity and fuller participation of developing countries.

Service	A service as presented by the GATS.
SPS Agreement	The Agreement on the Application of Sanitary and Phytosanitary Measures.
Stage	Refers to the procedural phase of the DSU: consultations, Panel/AB, RPT, Article 21.5 Panel/AB, and retaliation.
Status of a case	All the country versus country cases are in one of the following clusters: implemented, pending or abandoned.
Subject matter	The WTO covered agreement under which the case in question has been adjudicated; in more detail, subject matter also includes the article or provision of the covered agreement related to the case. We only cover the claims set out at the request for consultations. Findings under adjudicative procedures are covered in findings won/lost by Mexico.
TBT Agreement	The Agreement on Technical Barriers to Trade.
Times cited	The number of times an agreement or a specific provision of an agreement has been cited as part of the WTO documents WT/DS series relating to the request for consultations. If an article or an agreement has been cited several times within a particular WT/DS series, it would count as one citation.
TRIMS	The Agreement on Trade Related Investment Measures.
US	The United States.
US/EC	The United States and the European Communities; usually used to identify them separately from other WTO Members – i.e., other OECD Members, non-Members of OECD, and LDCs.
USITC	The US International Trade Commission.
WTO	The World Trade Organization.

List of Cases

B.   WTO Cases with Mexico as a Party

C.   *PTA Country versus Country Cases with Mexico as a Party*

- *US – Safeguard on Broom Corn Brooms* (NAFTA 20)
- *US – Cross-Border Trucking* (NAFTA 20)
- *Peru – Origin of Computers from Mexico* (ALADI)
- *Mexico – Sanitarian Registry and Access for Medicines* (FTA among Mexico, El Salvador, Guatemala and Honduras)

D.   *AD/CVD Orders Subject to Article 1904 NAFTA Panel Procedures*

(1) AD/CVD Orders Imposed by the US against Exports from Mexico
   (a) CVD – Investigation on Leather Wearing Apparel
   (b) AD – Investigation on Cement
   (c) AD – Investigation on Fresh Cut Flowers
   (d) AD – Investigation on Non-Alloy Steel Pipe and Tube
   (e) AD – Investigation on OCTG
   (f) AD – Investigation on Porcelain-on-Steel Cookware

(2) AD/CVD Orders Imposed by Canada against Exports from Mexico
   (a) AD Investigation on Certain Hot-Rolled Carbon Steel Plate

(3) AD/CVD Orders Imposed by Mexico against Exports from the US and Canada
   (a) AD – Investigation on Bovine Carcasses and Half Carcasses, Fresh or Chilled, from the US
   (b) AD – Investigation on Sodium Hydroxide (caustic soda) from the US
   (c) AD – Investigation on Cut-to-Length Plate Products from the US
   (d) AD – Investigation on High-Fructose Corn Syrup from the US
   (e) AD – Investigation on Polystyrene and Impact Crystal from the US
   (f) AD – Investigation on Flat Coated Steel Plate from the US
   (g) AD – Investigation on Urea from the US
   (h) AD – Investigation on Rolled Steel Plate from Canada
   (i) AD – Investigation on Hot-Rolled Steel Sheet from Canada

List of Tables

Chapter 1

Mexico's Options for Settlement of International Trade Disputes

Tengo miedo del encuentro con el pasado que vuelve a enfrentarse con mi vida ... pero el viajero que huye, tarde o temprano detiene su andar ...

Volver con la frente marchita las nieves del tiempo, platearon mi sien ... sentir que es un soplo la vida, que 20 años no es nada ...[1]

('Interpretation of the song Volver'), by Carlos Gardel with lyrics by
Alfredo Le Pera

Mexico has been litigating disputes under international trade law in different forums for almost twenty years. Gardel and Le Pera in their verse suggest that travellers in life should take time to look back. The aim of this book is to do just that and analyse Mexico's experience, not of love, but of trade dispute litigation over the past two decades ('that twenty years is nothing').

Mexico became a Contracting Party to the General Agreement on Tariffs and Trade (GATT) – and subsequently a Member of the World Trade Organization (WTO) – through its Protocol of Accession signed on 17 July 1986.[2] This was the first major step towards opening up its economy to international trade. Later, Mexico entered into several Preferential Trade Agreements (PTAs). Currently, it is Party to eleven Free Trade Agreements (FTAs), and one Agreement on Economic Partnership.[3] There are additional PTAs negotiated under the umbrella of

---

1. I am afraid of the encounter with the past that returns to confront my life ... but the traveller that flees sooner or later stops his walking ...
   To return, with withered face, the snows of time have whitened my temples ... to feel that life is a puff of wind, that twenty years is nothing ...
2. See GATT document L/6010.
3. NAFTA; FTA with Colombia (originally also with Venezuela); FTA with Costa Rica; FTA with Bolivia; FTA with Nicaragua; FTA with Chile; FTA with the European Union; FTA with Israel;

Asociación Latinoamericana de Integración (Latin American Integration Association (ALADI)[4] that have dispute settlement mechanisms (three Economic Complementation Agreements(ECAs)).[5]

Through its policy of actively seeking to become Party to a number of International Trade Agreements, Mexico now has at its disposal not only a series of different instruments containing substantive law and concessions, but also a set of various forums for solving international trade disputes, each having its own jurisdiction. The PTAs and the WTO provide Mexico with mechanisms to solve trade disputes at different levels of trade: country versus country, as well as private party versus country.

I.   MEXICO'S INTERNATIONAL TRADE DISPUTE
           CASES AT A GLANCE

This work covers the history of Mexico's international trade disputes over the period from 1986 – the date of Mexico's accession to the GATT – until 1 January 2007 for WTO cases and 1 January 2008 for PTA cases.

Mexico participated in three cases under the GATT as a Party and four cases as a Third Party. Using the Dispute Settlement Understanding of the WTO (DSU), it has participated in thirty cases as a Party and thirty cases as a Third Party.

Turning to PTAs: Mexico has been very active in North American Free Trade Agreement (NAFTA) dispute settlement issues. Within the country versus country category, it has participated in two cases as a Party and one as a Third Party based on Chapter 20 of NAFTA (country versus country panel on NAFTA general disputes). Also, Mexico has participated in one dispute in the context of the FTA with El Salvador, Guatemala and Honduras (this case was country versus country). In addition it participated in one case under the ECA with Peru, negotiated under the umbrella of ALADI. Finally, there has been heavy involvement in country/ private party versus country dispute settlement mechanisms: Mexico, or at least one of its nationals,[6] has participated in forty-five cases based on Chapter 19 of NAFTA (Panels to deal with antidumping/countervailing duties (AD/CVD).

FTA with El Salvador, Guatemala and Honduras; FTA with Iceland, Norway, Liechtenstein and Switzerland; FTA with Uruguay; and Agreement on Economic Partnership with Japan.

4.   ALADI comprises: Argentina; Bolivia; Brazil; Chile; Colombia; Cuba; Ecuador; Mexico; Paraguay; Peru; Uruguay; and Venezuela.

5.   Mexico has ECAs on market access – with dispute settlement mechanisms – with Argentina, Brazil and Peru.

6.   One of the dispute settlement mechanisms in Ch. 19 of NAFTA provides standing to private parties. See s. C.1.2., 'Chapter 19 – Review and Dispute Settlement in AD and CVD Matters', below.

Table 1.1 All cases litigated by Mexico in GATT/WTO and PTAs

	As a Party	As a Third Party
GATT	3 cases	4 cases
WTO	30 cases	30 cases
NAFTA		
Chapter 19	45 cases	n/a
Chapter 20	2 cases	1 case
FTA with El Salvador,	1 case	0 cases
Honduras and Guatemala		
ALADI (ECA Mexico – Peru)	1 case	0 cases

Source: WTO, NAFTA and Secretaría de Economía.[7]

II.   THE MULTILATERAL FORUM

The only multilateral forum for solving international trade disputes is the WTO, formerly the GATT.

A.   THE GENERAL AGREEMENT ON TARIFFS AND TRADE

The history of GATT dispute settlement covers experiences over almost fifty years.[8] The GATT Agreement was negotiated with the intention that a handful of countries would apply it provisionally and that it would later be replaced by an International Trade Organization. That provisional period lasted from 1947 until 1995.

The dispute settlement mechanism was only one of the many elements included in the original text of the GATT. The Contracting Parties, the highest organ of the GATT, had the power to take the decisions needed to implement the rights and obligations of the GATT. It was they who solved disputes arising from the GATT: Article XXIII of the GATT, entitled Nullification or Impairment, provided that the Contracting Parties could rule on claims of legal violation and non-violation situations, make recommendations for correction, and authorize the withdrawal of concessions when needed. Hudec noted that this provision created a dispute settlement system that was broader and shallower than other enforcement procedures. As he explained, 'It was broader in that it also allowed … to rule on [non-violation cases, and] … shallower, on the other hand, in that the ultimate remedy, for both legal violations and for other impairment of benefits, was simply the withdrawal of equivalent concessions by the aggrieved Party'. (Hudec 1993, §1.01).

---

7. See <www.wto.org>, <www.nafta-sec-alena.org>, and <www.economia.gob.mx> (all consulted in August 2009).
8. For an analysis of the dispute settlement system of the GATT, see Hudec (1993).

At a certain point, the GATT was wavering between two different paths: a system of diplomatic negotiations for dispute settlement (Article XXII of the GATT)[9] and a system of more formal legal procedures (Article XXIII.2 of the GATT).[10] As disputes became more complicated, the Contracting Parties decided to establish Panel procedures. Yet, they were the ultimate decision makers: Panel reports would be submitted to them for approval. The Contracting Parties kept the consensus rule of decision making for three key steps: establishment of Panels, adoption of Panel reports and authorization to suspend concessions or other obligations. This provided a veto power to any contracting party, which meant the losing Party could block decisions on any of the three steps.

As we can see from the following table, there were 207 complaints from 1948 to 1989. There were rulings in 43% of the total complaints, 31% were settled or conceded, and 27% were withdrawn or abandoned. Hence, it took many GATT cases to get agreement on the 1989 Montreal Rules.

Table 1.2 Procedural Outcomes in the GATT Cases from 1948–1989
(HUDEC 1993, §11.05)

Total Complaints	Rulings		Settled or Conceded by Defendant		Withdrawn or Abandoned	
	Number	Total (%)	Number	Total (%)	Number	Total (%)
207	88	43	64	31	55	27

B.   THE 1989: ADOPTION OF THE MONTREAL RULES

In April 1989, the Montreal Rules were adopted by the GATT Contracting Parties. This constituted the basis for the current WTO dispute settlement rules – e.g., time

---

9. Article XXII of the GATT ('Consultation') provides two or more contracting Parties with a negotiation forum aimed at solving any matter affecting the operation of the GATT. Also, it provides for consultation with the Contracting Parties. The procedures in this article are more diplomatic in nature and aim at solving the matters using negotiation and/or conciliation or mediation.

10. Article XXIII of the GATT ('Nullification or Impairment') provides for written representations or proposals to another contracting party when a benefit is nullified or impaired or when any objective of the GATT is being impeded by violation, non-violation, or any other situation. The matter may be referred to the Contracting Parties, they then investigate it and make recommendations to the contracting party concerned or give a ruling on the matter. They may authorize a contracting party to suspend concessions or other obligations under the GATT as they determine to be appropriate in the circumstances. The contracting party facing the retaliatory measures may withdraw from the GATT. Certainly the procedures in this article are more adjudicatory in nature (governing action by the Contracting Parties) and aim at solving the matter by convincing the Contracting Parties of the seriousness of the situation.

frames, steps in the procedures, automatic establishment of Panels – since they applied provisionally until the end of the Uruguay Round and the creation of the WTO (Palmeter and Mavroidis 2004, 10). In the course of the Brussels Ministerial meeting in December 1990, the Uruguay Round negotiations agreed on the main elements to reform the dispute settlement mechanism. Those elements were further refined in the 'Dunkel Draft' of December 1990, which consolidated all the earlier GATT Agreements on dispute settlement.

The end of the Uruguay Round, or 1 January 1995 to be more precise, brought two key elements: first, the elimination of the veto power on Panel establishment, thus codifying Montreal Rules, adoption of reports, and authorization for suspension of concessions or other obligations by inserting the negative consensus rule – i.e., the decision is automatically adopted unless all of the Members present at the meeting agree otherwise. The second key element was to give greater legal form to the process by including an Appellate Body (AB) (Palmeter and Mavroidis 2004, at §1.4 and 1.5).

C.   THE DISPUTE SETTLEMENT MECHANISM OF THE WTO

A WTO Member can file a complaint against another WTO Member. This is a dispute in the sense of Article 1 of the DSU. The DSU process has a variety of procedural steps.[11] The following table shows the sequence of these procedures and the questions they need to address at each stage.[12]

Table 1.3 Procedural Stages of the DSU with Their Questions To Be Solved

Procedure	Question To Be Solved
Consultations[13]	Can the Parties negotiate a solution by themselves?
Panel procedure[14]	Are the facts in violation of WTO law?[15]

---

11. For further reading on the work of the DSU, see the comprehensive and detailed work by Palmeter and Mavroidis (2004). Further research on the DSU process has been developed by the following authors: Bhala (2008); on AD cases, Czako, Human & Miranda (2003) and Vermulst & Graafsma (2002); Mavroidis (2007); Jackson, Davey & Sykes (2001) and Jackson (2000).
12. Since they are not necessarily used in the whole DSU process (they are not part of the sequence of procedures), we do not include two procedures in this chart: good offices, conciliation and mediation (Art. 5 of the DSU) and arbitration as an alternative dispute settlement mechanism (Art. 25 of the DSU).
13. See Art. 4 of the DSU.
14. See Arts 6 to 16 and 19 of the DSU.
15. Two basic and simple questions must be answered in order to tackle the main issue: What are the facts, and what are the WTO obligations?

Table 1.3 (contd)

Procedure	Question To Be Solved
AB procedure[16]	Are the legal interpretations and issues of law correctly applied and assessed by the Panel?[17]
Reasonable period of time (RPT) (by negotiation or arbitration)[18]	What is the time the defendant has to comply with the Panel/AB recommendations?
Panel/AB under Article 21.5 of the DSU[19]	Is the measure taken to comply with the Panel/AB report: (a) existent, and/ or (b) consistent with the Covered Agreements?
Arbitration under Article 22.6 of the DSU[20]	What is the impact caused by the illegal measure?[21] Or what is the level of countermeasures?[22]

1.   The Procedures in More Detail

The consultation process and the dispute itself are triggered upon the presentation of a request for consultations, which serves as a notification document. It identifies 'the measure at issue and … [indicates] … the legal basis for the complaint'.[23] The consultations stage does not have any fundamental rule of proceedings, except for the requirement that it has to take place within sixty days from the request for consultations.[24]

The Panel procedure, AB procedure, Article 21.5 Panel/AB procedure, arbitration under Article 21.3, and arbitration under Article 22.6 contain some common procedural steps. First, all of these procedures allow the disputing Parties to present written submissions followed by a hearing with oral discussions. Then the adjudicating body and the Parties may ask questions (except during the appeal process). Finally, the adjudicating body issues its report or award.[25]

---

16. See Arts 17 to 19 of the DSU.
17. See Art. 17.6 of the DSU.
18. See Art. 21.3 of the DSU.
19. See Art. 21.5 of the DSU. In practice, the provisions for consultations, Panel and AB procedure may apply *mutatis mutandis*.
20. Articles 22.6 and 22.7 contain most of the procedural guidance for this arbitration. Yet most of the paragraphs under Art. 22 of the DSU may be relevant for the substance of the arbitration.
21. The arbitrator may have to answer the following specific issues: (a) Is the level of suspension equivalent to the level of nullification or impairment? (b) Is the suspension allowed by the Covered Agreements? and (c) Have the principles of Art. 22.3 of the DSU been followed?
22. See Arts 4.11 and 7.9 of the SCM Agreement.
23. See Art. 4.4 of the DSU.
24. See Art. 4.7 of the DSU.
25. Commonly, the word 'report' refers to the resolution by a Panel or the AB, whereas the word 'award' refers to the resolution of arbitrators under Arts 21.3, 22.6, or 25 of the DSU.

Nonetheless, each procedure has its own particularities. First, in the case of the Panel procedures there is an organizational meeting with the Parties which is designed to deal with the timetable and procedural matters. Then the Parties may present a first and second written submission, each followed by an oral hearing. Before and after each hearing, the Panel and the Parties may submit written questions and answers.[26] Later, the Panel issues the descriptive part of the report, where it summarizes the claims and arguments of the Parties, followed by an interim report with the findings and conclusions of the Panel. The interim report becomes the definitive report unless a Party requests a review.[27] Finally, the report is adopted – based on the negative consensus rule – unless a Party files an appeal.[28]

The AB procedure is triggered by a notice of appeal where a Party requests the AB to review certain issues of law covered in the appeal.[29] It is followed by a written submission (called appellant's submission), which expands on the notice of appeal.[30] In a unique procedural issue on appeals, the counterpart may cross-appeal citing other issues of law not covered in the original notice of appeal. The cross-appeal is expanded in the subsequent written submission.[31] Then, the Party or Parties, depending on whether there is a cross-appeal, present their response to each other's appeal: these are the appellee's submissions. Third Parties may file a written submission at this stage.[32] Finally, there is a hearing with the AB, the Parties and the Third Parties[33] followed by the report of the AB to be adopted by the WTO Dispute Settlement Body (DSB).[34]

Panels and appeals under Article 21.5 of the DSU work in the same way as the ordinary procedures. Yet, case law suggests that Parties are not required to consult before an Article 21.5 procedure.[35] Article 21.5 of the DSU does not provide clear guidance on the procedures to be followed. Hence, Panels and the AB have followed the standard procedures of ordinary Panel procedures and appeals.

Arbitration under Articles 21.3(c) and 22.6 of the DSU allows for a written submission followed by a hearing with oral submissions. The arbitrator may ask questions after the hearing, then the award is issued.

However, Article 22.6 arbitrations have a difference with respect to the rest of the adjudicative procedures: the original defendant becomes the complainant

---

26. See Arts 8 and 13 and Appendix 3 of the DSU.
27. See Art. 15 of the DSU.
28. See Art. 16 of the DSU.
29. See Arts 16.4 and 17.4 of the DSU and Rule 20 of the Working Procedures of the AB.
30. See Rule 21 of the Working Procedures of the AB.
31. See Rule 23 of the Working Procedures of the AB.
32. See Rules 22 and 23 of the Working Procedures of the AB. Rule 24(i) deals with Third-Parties submissions.
33. See Rule 27 of the Working Procedures of the AB.
34. See Art. 17.4 of the DSU.
35. See Report of the AB, *Mexico – HFCS (21.5)*, WT/DS132/AB/RW, para. 65. The AB said '… *even if* the general obligations in the DSU regarding prior consultations were applicable [in 21.5 procedures] … non-compliance with those obligations would not [deprive the Panel of its duty to deal with the matter]'.

and vice versa, due to the fact that the original complainant has previously requested authorization to suspend concessions or other obligations before the original defendant challenges that request by submitting the issue to arbitration. Therefore, the original defendant becomes a complainant in this arbitration by challenging the level of suspension requested by the original complainant.[36] This swap affects the burden of proof – an issue not clearly resolved by the jurisprudence even when the complainant carries the original burden of proof.[37] It also requires the original complainant – now the defendant in the arbitration – to present an explanatory note, subject to scrutiny by the arbitrator, on how it calculated the level of suspension requested. Hence, the procedure starts with a submission from the original complainant (defendant for the purpose of the arbitration) explaining the basis for its calculation of the level of nullification or impairment.[38]

Finally, if at any procedural stage, the Parties are able to reach a mutually agreed solution (MAS) to the dispute, it has to be WTO-consistent and also notified to the membership.[39]

a.   Some Horizontal Issues

i.   Jurisdiction
The DSU does not contain a specific article dealing with Panel's jurisdiction, unlike Article 36 of the Statute of the International Court of Justice. Nonetheless, different DSU provisions deal tacitly with the jurisdiction of Panels/AB/arbitrators.[40] These provisions provide the WTO with the capacity for compulsory jurisdiction depending on the subject matter (*ratione materiae*), and the Parties to the dispute (*ratione personae*) (Palmeter and Mavroidis 2004, 17 et seq.).

---

36.   It could be argued that the same situation occurs in the cases of appeals because they can be triggered by the original defendant. However, appeals aim at reviewing the report of the Panel – with both Parties analyzing what the Panel issued – rather than a request for retaliatory rights by the complainant.

37.   See the award of the arbitrator under 22.6 of the DSU, *US – Offset Act (217/234)* (WT/DS234/ARB/MEX), paras 2.25 and 2.28. The arbitrator concluded that 'while it is for the US to prove that Mexico's request for suspension exceeds the level of nullification or impairment, Mexico must also sufficiently support its allegations that its request meets the requirement for equivalence of Art. 22.4 of the DSU'. The arbitrator also mentioned that he was of the view that 'if a Party makes a particular claim but fails to cooperate and provide evidence sufficiently supporting its claim, we may reach a conclusion on the basis of the evidence available, including evidence submitted by the other Party or data publicly available'.

38.   *Ibid.,* para. 1.12.

39.   See Art. 3.6 of the DSU.

40.   See, for instance, the following provisions of the DSU: Art. 1 (coverage and application), Art. 2 (establishment of a Dispute Settlement Body), Art. 3.1 (member's adherence to the principles applied by the GATT), Art. 6 (establishment of Panels), Art. 7 (terms of references), Art. 17.6 (issues of law on appeals), Art. 17.13 (authorizing the AB to uphold, modify or reverse the legal findings of the Panel).

ii.   Third Parties

A WTO Member may participate as a Third Party in the DSU procedures. However, there are some procedural stages where the DSU does not provide any rule for Third Party participation. First, non-consulting WTO Members may not request to be joined in consultations if the request for consultations was based on Article XXIII of the GATT or Article XXIII of the General Agreement on Trade in Services (GATS).[41] Also, the DSU does not cover rights for Third Parties after the first hearing of the Panel procedure.[42] Finally, neither Article 21.3(c) nor Article 22.6 of the DSU contains rules on Third Party participation in arbitration.[43]

iii.   Legal Remedies

The DSU includes four main legal remedies – i.e., ways to solve the negative effects of a measure that is not WTO-consistent. The first legal remedy is a MAS, which can take any form as long as it is WTO-consistent.[44] It is completely voluntary in nature and may appear at any procedural stage of the dispute. The second is compliance with the Panel report as modified by the AB.[45] The defendant has to withdraw the measure or put it into conformity.[46] The third is temporary compensation pending compliance, which is also voluntary.[47] Finally, the last legal remedy is suspension of concessions or other obligations on a discriminatory basis vis-à-vis the other member, subject to authorization by the DSB.[48]

There is a legislative hierarchy among these legal remedies. The preferred option is a MAS or compliance[49] with the Panel/AB report. When compliance cannot be achieved within the RPT, compensation may be used. Only if

---

41. See Art. 4.11 of the DSU. A Member may request to be joined in consultations provided that the request for consultations is based on Art. XXII of the GATT. XXII of the GATS or the corresponding provisions of the Covered Agreements. The requested Party may decide on a case by case basis whether to accept the request to be joined in the consultations.

42. See Art. 10 of the DSU.

43. Article 22.6 does not cover Third Parties. The arbitration under Art. 22.6 in *US – Offset Act* (217/234) allowed all requesting Members to participate simultaneously in that procedure. Under the procedures before the Panel in the same case, the Panel allowed through Third Party rights other co-complainants to participate in all the hearings. However, the arbitration in *US – Offset Act* (217/234) case is silent on Third Parties, notwithstanding the fact that in practice it provided such rights. See the award of the Arbitrator under 22.6 of the DSU, *US – Offset Act* (217/234) (WT/DS234/ARB/MEX), para. 10.10 et seq.

44. See Arts 3.6 and 3.7 of the DSU.

45. See Arts 3.7 and 21.1 of the DSU.

46. Article 3.7 of the DSU states that the illegal measure has to be withdrawn, whereas Art. 22.1 of the DSU states that the Member concerned has to bring the measure into conformity. This lack of clarity has enormous consequences in practice, since correcting the challenged measure is not the same as withdrawing it.

47. See Arts 3.7 and 22.2 of the DSU.

48. See Arts 3.7 and 22.2 of the DSU.

49. The importance of compliance can be confirmed by Art. XVI:4 of the WTO Agreement, which states that every WTO Member 'shall ensure the conformity of its laws, regulations and administrative procedures with its [WTO] obligations'.

compensation has not been agreed may suspension of concessions or other obligations be imposed; this is subject to authorization by the DSB.

Mavroidis (2007, §4.9) presents a classification of legal remedies in *property rules* – which captures the idea that the Parties to a contract must always perform the contract – and *liability rules* – which provides the Parties to the contract with the possibility of compensating in lieu of performing the contract. Compliance (and for us, to some extent, a MAS) would be property rules, whereas compensation and suspension of concessions would be liability rules. Mavroidis presents two viewpoints on the ambiguity of the legislative wording saying that compliance (property rule) is the main objective of the DSU. First, suspension of concessions (liability rule) is the interim measure until compliance (property rule) occurs. However, because suspension of concessions can stay in place, in principle, forever, it becomes some sort of permanent solution. Second, the liability rule has not been created with enough persuasive force to ensure that it will indeed be temporary and will lead to compliance (the defendant knows that in a worst-case scenario it could pay back for the damaged caused). We note, in addition, that a system with no retrospective remedies would worsen this scenario.

Schwartz and Sykes (2002) advocate legal remedies that provide 'efficient breach' of WTO law – i.e., the defendant would give to the victorious complainant something of equal value in exchange for what it would have been obliged to give by WTO law had the contract been fulfilled. We believe that a system with this option in force would be more efficient. However, this requires an evolution of benchmarks to calculate equivalence. Perhaps, as Mavroidis sustains, we need to know the system better, and there is a need for further analysis of what has in practice happened so far.

Table 1.4 Legal Remedies in the WTO Broken Up into Property/Liability Rule, Procedural Stages and the Member Implementing the Legal Remedy

	MAS	Compliance	Compensation	Retaliation
Property rules versus liability rules	Property rules and/or liability rules[50]	Property rules	Liability rules	Liability rules
Procedural stage	Any procedural stage	The end of the RPT	The end of the RPT[51]	De jure: the end of the RPT;

---

50. A MAS may include steps to comply, terms of compensation and even characteristics of retaliatory measures.

51. De jure, negotiations on compensation start at the end of the RPT. However, the so-called 'sequencing agreement' contains a de facto lacuna on when the negotiations have to take place. Because, according to this agreement, Art. 21.5 of the DSU takes effect before any retaliatory measures are authorized, the negotiations on compensation are omitted.

Table 1.4 (contd)

	MAS	Compliance	Compensation	Retaliation
				De facto: after a possible Article 21.5 Panel/AB
Member imple-menting the legal remedy	Complainant and defendant	Defendant	Complainant and defendant	Complainant

When Panels and the AB find a violation, they shall recommend that the violating Member bring the measure into conformity. In addition, they may suggest ways to implement this recommendation.[52]

The following table shows the whole DSU process and the point at which the legal remedies cut in (assuming Article 5 on conciliation, mediation and good offices and Article 25 on arbitration have not been triggered). The process is presented in accordance with the agreed sequencing practice, since the Article 21.5 appears before Article 22.6 arbitration on nullification or impairment.

Table 1.5   DSU Legal Remedies within DSU Procedural Stages

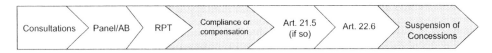

Consultations > Panel/AB > RPT > Compliance or compensation > Art. 21.5 (if so) > Art. 22.6 > Suspension of Concessions

III.   THE REGIONAL FORUMS

Mexico has signed 11 FTAs and one Agreement on Economic Partnership since 1993. These PTAs provide Mexico with different dispute settlement forums to adjudicate international trade disputes. NAFTA is the most significant FTA for Mexico.

Mexico's first FTA was NAFTA, and it influenced all other subsequent PTAs: the main changes to Mexico's internal legislation were made as a result of NAFTA negotiations. Moreover, of all the PTA dispute settlement mechanisms it is those in NAFTA that Mexico has used the most. On only two occasions have mechanisms other than NAFTA been used.[53]

The importance of NAFTA for Mexico is further confirmed by its total trade in 2006 – i.e., imports plus exports. NAFTA partners accounted for 70.1% of Mexico's total trade. The share of the European Union – the second largest PTA – was 7.89%. Japan – another PTA partner – accounted for 3.34%, while the share of remaining partners was less than1% of Mexico's total trade.

---

52. See Art. 19.1 of the DSU.
53. It is difficult to draw substantive conclusions from just two cases.

Table 1.6 Mexico's Total Trade per PTA Partner

PTA	Partners	Entry into Force	Percentage of Total Trade (Imports plus exports) in 2006 in millions of US Dollars (USD)[54]
1. NAFTA	US and Canada	1 January 1994	70.10% (USD 354,806)
2. FTA Mexico – EU	European Union	1 July 2000	7.89% (USD 39,945)
3. EPA Mexico – Japan	Japan	1 April 2005	3.34% (USD 16,889)
4. FTA Mexico – Chile	Chile	1 August 1999	0.67% (USD 3,375)
5. FTA–G3	Colombia (formerly Venezuela)[55]	1 January 1995	0.57% (USD 2,876)
6. FTA Mexico – *Triángulo del Norte*	El Salvador, Guatemala and Honduras	15 March 2001 with El Salvador and Guatemala; 1 June 2001 with Honduras.	0.45% (USD 2,255)
7. FTA Mexico – European Free Trade Association	Norway, Iceland, Switzerland and Liechtenstein	1 July 2001	0.33% (USD 1,653)
8. FTA Mexico – Costa Rica	Costa Rica	1 January 1995	0.26% (USD 1,311)
9. FTA Mexico – Nicaragua	Nicaragua	1 July 1998	0.12% (USD 600)
10. FTA Mexico – Israel	Israel	1 July 2000	0.10% (USD 520)
11. FTA Mexico – Uruguay	Uruguay	15 July 2004	0.07% (USD 329)
12. FTA Mexico – Bolivia	Bolivia	1 January 1995	0.01% (USD 74)
Rest of the World	N/A	N/A	16.10% (USD 81,495)
Total	N/A	N/A	100% (USD 506,128)

54. Data from Mexican Ministry of Economy (*Secretaría de Economía*) at <www.economia.gob. mx/?P=226>, August 2009.
55. As of 19 Nov. 2006, the FTA among the G-3 became a FTA between Mexico and Colombia.

A.   NAFTA DISPUTE SETTLEMENT MECHANISMS AT A GLANCE

NAFTA has three main chapters on dispute settlement. Chapter 20 addresses the disputes among NAFTA Parties on the interpretation and application of the Agreement. Chapter 19 addresses the antidumping (AD) and countervailing duties (CVD) determinations and the issues on legislations relating to trade remedies applied by each NAFTA Party.[56] Specific disputes in other NAFTA chapters such as financial services and safeguards are adjudicated under Chapter 20.[57] Finally, Chapter 11 addresses arbitrations on investor-State issues within the NAFTA region. It contains procedural and substantial law on investor-State matters.[58]

1.   **Chapter 20: General Dispute Settlement Mechanisms**

Section A of Chapter 20 of NAFTA refers to the Free Trade Commission – made up of cabinet-level representatives of the Parties or their designated officials – which has the task of supervising the implementation of NAFTA, overseeing its further elaboration, resolving disputes, supervising the NAFTA committees and working groups, and considering other matters when needed.[59]

Section B of Chapter 20 of NAFTA deals with the general dispute settlement mechanism of NAFTA under this heading, and section C covers domestic procedures and private commercial dispute settlement, which are not the subject of this work.

The general dispute settlement mechanism applies to all disputes between the NAFTA Parties regarding the interpretation and application of NAFTA. It also applies with respect to actual or proposed measures that may be NAFTA-inconsistent or cause nullification or impairment.[60] The cases of nullification or impairment are limited in scope to certain sections of NAFTA only.[61]

The dispute settlement in Chapter 20 of NAFTA is the default option. If a dispute does not go under Chapter 19 (Review and Dispute Settlement in

---

56. For further discussion on the development of Chs 19 and 20 of NAFTA, see Gantz (1999). The following scholars and practitioners have also developed some work on these issues: Bhala (2008); Perezcano-Diaz (1997); on the dispute settlement mechanisms of some of PTAs, Enders (1993); Clyde-Hufbauer & Goodrich (2004) and Appleton (1994).

57. See Art. 1414.1 of NAFTA dealing with disputes on financial services. Also, see Ch. 8 of NAFTA for safeguards.

58. Our research addresses Chs 20 and 19 because they are directly related to International Trade Law and hence the WTO. We are leaving Ch 11 out of the scope of this work because it covers issues not included within the current WTO mandate.

59. The Free Trade Commission establishes its rules and procedures and takes decisions by consensus (unless otherwise agreed). It convenes at least once a year and is chaired successively by each Party. See Art. 2001 of NAFTA.

60. See Art. 2004 of NAFTA.

61. See Annex 2004 of NAFTA on nullification and impairment. Note that NAFTA refers to nullification and impairment, whereas the WTO refers to nullification or impairment.

Antidumping and Countervailing Duty Matters) or Chapter 11(Investor-State disputes), it falls under Chapter 20.[62] Nonetheless, questions relating to the interpretation or application of those chapters may be adjudicated through Chapter 20.[63]

Chapter 20, contrary to Chapters 11 and 19, contains some rules relating to overlapping jurisdictions. The general rule is that disputes regarding any matter arising under both NAFTA and the WTO[64] may be settled in either forum at the discretion of the complainant.

Yet, there are three cases where NAFTA prevails over the WTO, regardless of the choice by the complainant:

(1) Before initiating a WTO case, the complainant is required to notify the NAFTA Parties if the matter may also be covered by NAFTA. If there is a third Party wishing to have recourse to dispute settlement under NAFTA regarding the same matter, the Parties must try to agree on a single forum. If there is no agreement, NAFTA normally is the proper forum.

(2) If the respondent Party claims that the action is subject to Article 104 of NAFTA (Relation to Environmental and Conservation Agreements) and requests that the matter be solved under NAFTA, the complaining Party may only use NAFTA for that matter.

(3) If any dispute arises under Section B of Chapter 7 of NAFTA (Sanitary or Phytosanitary Measures) or Chapter 9 (Standards-Related Measures), and the responding Party requests that the matter be solved under NAFTA, the complaining Party may only use NAFTA for that matter.[65]

According to Gantz (1999 p. 1091), the issue of overlapping jurisdictions (Chapters 19 and 20 of NAFTA and WTO) could be presented as follows:

(1) There are cases with *no effective choice of forum*, where the Parties may adjudicate the issue in only one forum and have no discretion to choose – for instance, a case where the substantive law applicable to the measure is only NAFTA, but not WTO law or vice versa.

(2) There are cases *with effective choice of forum*, where the complainant may choose either WTO or Chapter 20 of NAFTA but may not choose both, applying the rules on double forums (Article 2005 of NAFTA) – for instance, a case where the substantive law applicable to the measures is covered by both NAFTA and WTO (the *US – Safeguard on Broom Corn Brooms* case is a good example because the US safeguard could have

---

62. Article 2004 of NAFTA specifically provides for the exception from Ch. 20 with respect to Ch. 19 of NAFTA. Furthermore, Art. 2004 also exempts 'as otherwise provided in this Agreement', which includes Ch. 11 B on investor-State cases.
63. See Gantz (1999), 1034.
64. The text of NAFTA refers to GATT or any subsequent Agreement.
65. See Art. 2005 of NAFTA.

been challenged through the WTO, but Mexico decided to initiate a Panel under Chapter 20 of NAFTA).[66]

(3) There are cases with *availability of parallel forums*, where the government may take a WTO case and one of its exporters may initiate a Panel under Chapter 19 of NAFTA, both challenging the same measure – for instance, an AD case adjudicated through Chapter 19 of NAFTA and the WTO. The AD measure on cement imposed by the US against Mexican exports would be a good example, because Mexico took a WTO case, whereas the exporter initiated several Panels under Chapter 19 of NAFTA.[67]

Coming back to Chapter 20 of NAFTA: Any NAFTA Party may request consultations with another NAFTA Party. If there is no agreement between the Parties within thirty days of the request for consultations (fifteen days for perishable goods and forty-five days if another Party wants to participate), a meeting with the Commission may be requested.[68] Unless otherwise agreed, if the matter has not been resolved within thirty days of the meeting with the Commission, a Panel may be requested, to be established by the Commission upon receipt of the request. A third Party with substantial interest may join as a complaining Party.

Panels comprise five Members, and the disputing Parties are required to agree on the chair within fifteen days of the request for a Panel. The rest of the selection process varies depending on the number of disputing NAFTA Parties in the Panel. In cases where only two NAFTA Parties are involved:

(1) If there is no agreement on the chair within fifteen days of the request for a Panel, a disputing NAFTA Party is selected by lot to choose the chair within five days. The chair cannot be a citizen of that Party – it could choose a national of one of the other two NAFTA Parties.

(2) Each disputing Party then selects, within fifteen days, two panellists who are citizens of the other disputing Party. The defendant selects two nationals from the complainant and vice versa.

(3) If a Party fails to select its panellists within such period, the remaining panellists are selected by lot from the roster Members. They must be citizens of the other disputing Party.

In cases where more than two NAFTA Parties are involved in the process, the selection process is as follows:

(1) If there is no agreement on the chair within fifteen days of the request for a Panel, a Party or Parties from one side of the dispute is/are chosen by lot.

---

66. See the *US – Safeguard on Broom Corn Brooms* (USA-97-2008-01) case below in Ch. 3, 'Mexico's Cases under Preferential Trade Agreements'.
67. For the WTO case on cement with the US, see the *US – Cement* (281) case in Ch. 2, 'Mexico's GATT and WTO Cases'. For a NAFTA Ch. 19 case on cement with the US, see Ch. 3, 'Mexico's Cases under Preferential Trade Agreements'.
68. See Arts 2006 and 2007 of NAFTA.

Within ten days, this Party or Parties selects the chair, who cannot be a citizen of such Party or Parties.

(2) The defending Party selects two panellists, one who is a citizen of a complaining Party and the other who is a citizen of another complaining Party.

(3) The complaining Parties select two panellists who are citizens of the defending Party.

(4) If a Party fails to select its panellists within such period, the remaining panellists are selected by lot from the roster, observing the established citizenship criteria for Panels with more than two disputing Parties.

The NAFTA Parties are required to establish a roster of panellists comprising up to thirty individuals with technical knowledge and experience, independent from any Party, and subject to a code of conduct established by the Commission.[69] There is nothing on public record indicating that the formal roster has been agreed.[70] It appears, however, that it may well exist, but that it has not yet been made public. In the absence of a roster, the disputing Parties must agree on the composition of the Panel (in accordance with the process explained above), since there is no default roster to rely upon when a Party fails to appoint its panellists.

The NAFTA Chapter 20 Panel procedure is governed by the Model Rules of Procedures:[71] there should be at least one hearing, with initial and rebuttal written submissions; the procedures are confidential; the terms of reference are standard, but may be amended to include the degree of adverse trade effects and claims of nullification or impairment.[72] The rules allow for third Party participation.[73] Panels may seek information and advice from experts and scientific review boards in certain cases.[74]

A Panel presents an initial report to the disputing Parties within ninety days of the selection of the last panellist. The report includes its findings of fact, its findings of law, its findings on nullification or impairment (or other findings

---

69. See Art. 2009 of NAFTA.
70. Mexico alleged in the case of *Mexico – Soft Drinks* (308) that the US did not appoint its panellist for a NAFTA Ch. 20 Panel. If a roster were to be established, a problem regarding a decision by a defendant under Ch. 20 of NAFTA not to appoint the panellist would be resolved by selecting the remaining members from the roster; see para. 4.223 of the Panel report and n. 106 of the AB report. The website of the NAFTA secretariat does not contain a roster of panellists under Ch. 20 of NAFTA; <www.nafta-sec-alena.org/en/view.aspx?x=279>, August 2009.
71. For the text of the Model Rules of Procedures, see <www.nafta-sec-alena.org/en/view. aspx?x=344>, August 2009. The rules develop the following topics: Application; Definitions; Terms of Reference; Written Submissions; Operation of Panels; Hearings; Supplementary Written Submissions; Burden of Proof Regarding Inconsistent Measures and Exceptions; Availability of Information; Ex Parte Contacts; Scientific Review Boards; Translation and Interpretation; Computation of Time; Suspension of Benefits; Panels Regarding Investment Disputes in Financial Services; Responsible Section of the Secretariat; and Maintenance of Rosters.
72. See Art. 2012 of NAFTA.
73. See Art. 2013 of NAFTA.
74. See Arts 2014 and 2015 of NAFTA.

requested under the terms of references), and its recommendation for solving the dispute (if any). The disputing Parties may present their comments on the report. Within thirty days of its initial report, a Panel must present its final report to the Parties and send it to the Commission as well. The report is published fifteen days after receipt by the Commission.[75]

The disputing Parties must agree on the means of resolving the dispute, taking into account the Panel's report. Whenever possible, the resolution must involve the implementation or removal of the NAFTA-inconsistent measure or the measure causing nullification or impairment. If this does not happen, the disputing Parties may revert to compensation. However, if the Parties do not agree on a resolution within thirty days of receipt of the report, the complaining Party may suspend benefits of equivalent effect until the Parties have reached agreement on the resolution of the dispute. The suspension has to take place in the same sector or sectors, unless the complaining Party considers that it is not practicable or effective to do so. Finally, the Commission may establish a Panel, upon request, to determine whether the level of benefits suspended by a Party is manifestly excessive.[76] It is not clear if this Panel would be able to order the suspension of the countermeasures, because its mandate is limited to whether the level of suspension is manifestly excessive and countermeasures may last until such time as the disputing Parties have reached agreement on a resolution of the dispute. Experience of the application of this mechanism does not offer any guidance on this question.

The same analysis on WTO legal remedies developed above (property versus liability rules) would apply to the legal remedies of NAFTA Chapter 20 dispute settlement mechanism.[77]

2.	**Chapter 19: Review and Dispute Settlement in AD and CVD Matters**

Chapter 19 provides for the dispute settlement mechanism to review final AD and CVD determinations imposed by one of the NAFTA Parties,[78] and AD and CVD legislative amendments by one of the NAFTA Parties.[79]

NAFTA Parties are allowed to apply their domestic AD/CVD laws to goods imported from the territory of any other NAFTA Party. Furthermore, the NAFTA Parties reserve their right to amend such domestic AD/CVD laws. But an amendment may apply to other NAFTA Parties only if the following conditions have been fulfilled: it specifically states that it applies to NAFTA Parties; the NAFTA Parties have been notified accordingly; if requested, NAFTA Parties are consulted before the enactment; and it is not WTO/Chapter 19-inconsistent.

---

75. See Arts 2016 and 2017 of NAFTA.
76. See Arts 2018 and 2019 of NAFTA.
77. See our discussion of WTO legal remedies in ss II.C.1.a, 'Some Horizontal Issues,' and III.A.2.a.iii, Legal Remedies.
78. See Art. 1904 of NAFTA.
79. See Art. 1903 of NAFTA.

Chapter 19 includes four procedures: the Article 1904 Panel (review of AD/CVD final determinations); the Extraordinary Challenge Committee (hereinafter 'the Committee') procedure covering review of possible behaviour by the Panel (i.e., misconduct, conflict of interest, due process, jurisdiction); the review of AD/CVD statutory amendments; and involvement of the Special Committee safeguarding the functioning of the system, whose role is to avoid obstruction in the establishment of Panels and to monitor the implementation of its decisions.

a.   *The Article 1904: Panel Review of AD/CVD Final*
                  Determinations

This Panel procedure replaces the judicial review of final AD/CVD determinations. The Panel's mandate is to determine whether such determinations are in accordance with the AD/CVD law of the importing Party. The Article 1904 Panel decision is based on the domestic laws of the importing Member, rather than on International Trade Law (regional as in Chapter 20 of NAFTA or multilateral as in the WTO). The AD/CVD law for the purposes of NAFTA Chapter 19 consists of the relevant statutes, legislative history, regulations, administrative practice and judicial precedents to the extent that a court of the importing Party would rely on such materials in reviewing a final determination of the competent investigating authority.[80] This raises the question of whether a 1904 Panel may rule basing itself on the WTO Agreements: the WTO Agreement on Implementation of Article VI of the GATT 1994, or Antidumping Agreement (ADA); and the WTO Agreement on Subsidies and Countervailing Duties (SCM Agreement). This depends, among other things, upon the hierarchy of international law and domestic law, monistic or dualistic,[81] in each NAFTA Party.[82]

---

80. See Arts 1904.1 to 1904.3 of NAFTA.
81. When a country uses international law and domestic law as one whole legal system, it is considered to have a monist system. International treaties are generally self-executed in monist systems. When a country uses one system for domestic law and another for international law, it is considered to have a dualist system. Under a dualist system, an international obligation usually requires a transposition into the domestic legal system to become national law.
82. For instance, it could be argued that for Mexico the ADA is part of its internal laws based on Art. 133 of the Constitution of the United Mexican States. A similar argument can be used in the US based on Art. VI of the US Constitution, 'the supreme Law of the Land'. However, the US implements many International Trade Agreements by enacting domestic legislation as executive agreements. The Uruguay Round Agreements Act of 1994 (the US internal law implementing the Uruguay Round Agreements, 19 USC §3512) says that no provision of the Uruguay Round Agreement, or its application to any person or circumstance, that is inconsistent with US law shall have effect. Therefore, whether the WTO Agreements are part of domestic law of a WTO Member is a question of enormous complexity and requires careful analysis. It depends, among other things, on the nature of the constitutional law of each WTO Member. Case law suggests that Article 1904 Panels reviewing Mexican AC/CVD orders apply the ADA or SCM Agreement as Mexican domestic law. See Ch. 3, 'Mexico's Cases under Preferential Trade Agreements'.

The NAFTA Parties determined specific standards of review for each Party. An Article 1904 Panel has a specific standard of review depending on the importing Party. The NAFTA Parties kept the same standard of review that a domestic judge would use in reviewing the final AD/CVD determination in Mexico, the US or Canada (Annex 1911 of NAFTA).

A request for a Panel must be presented to the other Party involved in the process within thirty days of the date of publication of the final determination, or the date of its notification in cases where the determination is not published. A NAFTA Party on its own initiative may, or on request of a person otherwise entitled to initiate internal judicial procedures must, request the review by the Panel. Both the NAFTA Party and the person entitled to trigger the procedure have the right to appear and be represented by counsel before the Panel.[83] The Panel is composed of five Members.[84]

The NAFTA Parties are required to adopt Rules of Procedure for Article 1904 bi-national Panel Reviews.[85] The whole procedure must last less than 315 days and allow for:

(1) thirty days for filing the complaint;
(2) thirty days for filing a certified copy of the record;
(3) sixty days for the complainant to file its brief;
(4) sixty days for the respondent to file its brief;
(5) fifteen days for the filing of reply briefs;
(6) fifteen to thirty days for the Panel to convene an oral hearing; and
(7) ninety days for the Panel to issue its decision.[86]

The Panel may uphold the final determination or remand it to the investigating authority for action consistent with the Panel's decision. These remedies are property rules, since they are designed to perform the contract.[87] If the determination is remanded, the Panel will determine a reasonable time for compliance. The same Panel may review within ninety days the action taken by the investigating authority to comply with the remand. The decision of the Panel is binding on the Parties involved. The Article 1904 Panel may not be combined with internal judicial procedures. The legislation of the NAFTA Parties must be amended to allow the

---

83. See Arts 1904.4 to 1904.7 of NAFTA.
84. See Art. 1901 and Annex 1901.2 of NAFTA.
85. The rules of procedure entered into force on the same day as NAFTA. For the text of the Rules of Procedure for Art. 1904 Bi-national Panel Reviews, see <www.nafta-sec-alena.org/en/view.aspx?x=344>, August 2009. The rules have eight parts: General, Commencement of Panel Review Rules; Panels; Proprietary Information and Privileged Information; Written Proceedings; Oral Proceedings; Decisions and Completions of Panel Reviews; and Completion of Panel Review.
86. See Art. 1904.14 of NAFTA.
87. See the discussion of property/liability rules in Section III.A.2.d. 'The Article 1905 Special Committee', below.

Article 1904 Panel process to take place.[88] Also, the NAFTA Parties are required to amend their legislation to ensure that they allow for the refund, with interest, of AD/CVD duties paid when a Panel decides this should be done; and their legislation must ensure that sanctions can be imposed pursuant to the laws of the other Parties to enforce provisions of any protective order or undertaking on access to confidential information.[89]

b.   *The Extraordinary Challenge Committee*

An involved NAFTA Party may trigger Committee procedures when it considers that the behaviour of a Member of the Panel is not consistent with the standards expected in conducting legal processes. A NAFTA Party may avail itself of this procedure if it believes that any of the following acts 'has materially affected the Panel's decision':

(1) A panellist was guilty of gross transgression, bias, or a serious conflict of interest, or materially violated the rules of conduct.
(2) The Panel seriously departed from a fundamental rule of procedure.
(3) The Panel manifestly exceeded its powers, authority or jurisdiction.[90]

The Committee is made up of three Members selected from a roster within fifteen days of the request.[91] Each NAFTA Party involved selects one Member, and the Party selecting the third Member is determined by lot. The Rules of Procedure for the Committee regulate the procedure.[92] The decision of the Committee is issued within ninety days of its establishment. Committee decisions are binding on the Parties. If the Committee finds that one of the claims has been established, it dissolves the 1904 Panel and a new 1904 Panel is established. Alternatively, the issue may be remanded to the original 1904 Panel for action not inconsistent with the Committee's decisions. However, if the Committee does not find that at least one claim has been established, the original Panel decision stands affirmed.[93]

---

88. See Arts 1904.8 to 1904.12 of NAFTA.
89. See Art. 1904.15 of NAFTA.
90. See Art. 1904.13 of NAFTA.
91. The website of the NAFTA secretariat only contains the roster drawn up by Canada and the US. Apparently, Mexico has not selected its Members. (See <www.nafta-sec-alena.org/en/view.aspx?x=279>, August 2009.
92. For the text of the Rules of Procedures for the Article 1904 Extraordinary Challenge Committees, see <www.nafta-sec-alena.org/en/view.aspx?x=344>, August 2009. The rules have six parts: General; Written Proceedings; Conduct of Oral Proceedings; Responsibilities of the Secretary; Orders and Decisions; and Completion of Extraordinary Challenges.
93. See Annex 1904.13 of NAFTA.

c.   *The Statutory Amendments*

A NAFTA Party may request that a statutory amendment on AD/CVD laws be referred to a Panel for a declaratory opinion. Through this procedure a Panel may decide whether the amendment:

(1) is WTO-inconsistent[94] or inconsistent with the object or purpose of NAFTA/Chapter 19 of NAFTA;[95] or
(2) has the function and effect of overturning a prior 1904 Panel and is inconsistent with WTO or NAFTA/Chapter 19 of NAFTA.[96]

The Panel procedures are contained in Annex 1903.2 of NAFTA. The Panel sets its own rules of procedures, unless the Parties have otherwise agreed before its establishment. The procedure is confidential, unless otherwise agreed, and must include at least one hearing, as well as written submissions and rebuttals by each Party. The Panel bases its decision only on the arguments and submissions by the Parties. The Panel must present an initial written declaratory opinion within ninety days of the appointment of the chair. The opinion may include, in the case of positive determination, the means by which the amending opinion could be brought into conformity with Article 1902(2)(d) of NAFTA (i.e., the WTO, NAFTA or Chapter 19 of NAFTA). The initial written declaratory opinion becomes final unless one Party presents a written statement of its objections within fourteen days of the initial opinion's issuance. Then the Panel hears both Parties, conducts any examination that it deems appropriate and issues its final opinion within thirty days of the request for reconsideration.

When the Panel recommends modifications to the amending legislation, both Parties must consult to seek a mutually satisfactory solution within ninety days. If corrective legislation is not enacted within nine months from the end of the ninety days period and there is no other agreement, the Party that requested the Panel may:

(1) take comparable or equivalent executive action; or
(2) within sixty days notice, terminate the Agreement (i.e., NAFTA) with regard to the amending Party.[97]

d.   *The Article 1905 Special Committee*

A NAFTA Party may request consultations with another Party, to be initiated within fifteen days of the date of the request, if it considers that the application of the other Party's domestic law has:

(1) prevented the establishment of a Panel;
(2) prevented the Panel from rendering its final decision;

---

94.   As provided in Art. 1902.2(d)(i) of NAFTA.
95.   As provided in Art. 1902.2(d)(ii) of NAFTA.
96.   See Art. 1903.1 of NAFTA.
97.   See Art. 1903.3 of NAFTA.

    (3) prevented the implementation of a Panel decision or denied its binding force; or

    (4) resulted in a failure to allow for review of the final AD/CVD determination by a Panel or internal court independent from the investigating authority.[98]

The complaining NAFTA Party may request the establishment of a Special Committee if the issue has not been resolved within forty-five days of the request for consultations. The roster for the composition of the Special Committee is the same roster as for the Committee referred to above.

    Annex 1905.6 of NAFTA provides that the NAFTA Parties are to establish rules of procedure[99] in accordance with the following principles:

    (1) at least one hearing, and one set of written submissions/rebuttals;

    (2) issuance of an initial report within sixty days of the appointment of its last Member, with the final report being issued after the Parties have had an opportunity to comment;

    (3) confidentiality of the procedures; and

    (4) a decision published after it has been handed to the Parties.

When the Special Committee issues an affirmative determination of the claims, both Parties must engage in consultations aimed at a mutually satisfactory solution within sixty days. If that is not achieved or the Party complained against has not demonstrated to the satisfaction of the Special Committee that it has corrected the failure established by the Special Committee's original determination, the complaining Party may suspend:

    (1) the operation of Article 1904 of NAFTA with respect to the defendant; or

    (2) the application, with respect to the defendant, of benefits of NAFTA as appropriate under the circumstances.[100]

The Party complained against may request a new determination by the Special Committee to determine whether the suspension of benefits is excessive or that the violation has been addressed.[101] Finally, there are some provisions accommodating situations arising when the Special Committee has been triggered: the parallel

---

98. See Art. 1905.1 of NAFTA.

99. For the text of the Rules of Procedure for the Art. 1905 Special Committees, see <www. nafta-sec-alena.org/DefaultSite/index_een/view.aspx?DetailID=232>.x=344>, August 2009. The rules cover the following topics: Statement of General Intent; Interpretation; Operation of the Special Committee; Service of Documents; Written Submissions; Hearings; Language of Proceedings; Special Committee Deliberations; Reports; Reconvening of Special Committee; Completion of Special Committee Proceedings; Confidentiality; Ex Parte Contacts; Extension and Computation of Time; Responsibilities of the Responsible Secretary; Death or Incapacity; and Translation and Interpretation.

100. See Arts 1905.7 and 1905.8 of NAFTA.

101. See Art. 1905.10 of NAFTA.

suspension of Article 1904, the timing for suspension of pending 1904 Panels, and the availability of domestic judicial reviews, among others.[102]

As we have seen above, an Article 1904 Panel may uphold or remand the files back to the investigating authority. These legal remedies would be property rules, since they aim at performing the contract. If the Special Committee is triggered, the suspension of Article 1904 Panels or NAFTA benefits may be granted. These two legal remedies would be liability rules, but the suspension of Article 1904 Panels may not be appealing to a complainant who has triggered the Special Committee claiming its rights to a functioning Article 1904 Panel system.[103]

Table 1.7 The Legal Remedies of Article 1904 Panels and the Special Committee

	Through the 1904 Panel		Through the Special Committee:
	Upheld	**Remand (time)**	**(a) Suspension of Article 1904 Panels (b) Suspension of NAFTA benefits**
Property rules versus liability rules	Property rules	Property rules	Liability rules

B.   Non-NAFTA PTAs Signed by Mexico

As mentioned above, Mexico is a Party to 11 FTAs and one Agreement on Economic Partnership.[104] Also, there are three additional PTAs negotiated under the umbrella of ALADI (ECAs), with Brazil, Argentina and Peru, that have dispute settlement mechanisms.

1.   PTAs: The General Dispute Settlement Mechanisms

All eleven other PTAs to which Mexico is a Party – excluding NAFTA – contain general provisions on dispute settlement to solve disagreements on the application

---

102. See Art. 1905.11 et seq.
103. See our discussion of WTO legal remedies in ss. II.C.1.a, 'Some Horizontal Issues,' and III.A.2.a.iii, Legal Remedies.
104. NAFTA; FTA with Colombia (originally also with Venezuela); FTA with Costa Rica; FTA with Bolivia; FTA with Nicaragua; FTA with Chile; FTA with the European Union; FTA with Israel; FTA with El Salvador, Guatemala and Honduras; FTA with Iceland, Norway, Liechtenstein, and Switzerland; FTA with Uruguay; and Agreement on Economic Partnership with Japan.

and interpretation of the Treaty.[105] These mechanisms are very similar to NAFTA Chapter 20, which was explained above. Most set out rules on the following: consultations; Panel selection; interim report; final report; compliance; and suspension of benefits. The jurisdiction of the mechanisms is limited to disputes regarding the rights and obligations of the Parties to the PTA in question.

Some of the Agreements contain special disciplines – for instance, sanitary and phytosanitary measures or short-term entry for business people – which may be reviewed through the general dispute settlement mechanism of the PTA.[106]

There is nothing in the other PTAs signed by Mexico similar to NAFTA Chapter 19 (Panels dealing with legislation and final determinations on AD/CVD). But some PTAs[107] contain requirements regarding the actual development of AD/CVD investigations undertaken by one of the Parties: public notice of determinations, time frames, hearings, technical meetings, content of resolutions, and special procedures (such as new shipment), among other substantive and procedural rights and obligations. These provisions were included in some of the PTAs despite the fact that all the Parties to them are WTO Members. Violations of these provisions may be resolved through the general dispute settlement mechanism of the PTA in question. For instance, in the FTA with Bolivia, the general chapter of dispute settlement also addresses those provisions relating to the investigation of unfair trade practices.[108] Finally, the PTAs with the European Union[109] and with Israel[110] reaffirm the commitment of the Parties to their WTO obligations on the ADA, the SCM Agreement and the GATT. So, for practical purposes, the issues relating to unfair trade practices in the PTAs mentioned would be adjudicated in the WTO forum.

Finally, some of the PTAs also contain a dispute settlement mechanism and substantive law on investment, such as NAFTA Chapter 11. However, investor-State disputes are not part of our work in this book, as mentioned at the beginning of this chapter.

2.   **The PTAs under ALADI**

The 1980 Montevideo Treaty created, and still constitutes, ALADI. It promotes the creation of a trade and economic preference area in the region, aimed at a Latin American common market. There are two fundamental tools for achieving this: regional Agreement among all Member countries and partial Agreements between two or more countries of the area. In sum, ALADI works as a forum to negotiate

---

105.   For the text of the PTAs, see <www.economia.gob.mx/work/snci/negociaciones/ficha_publica_tlcs.htm>, August 2009.
106.   For instance, see Arts 8-11 and 12-07 of the FTA Mexico – Uruguay.
107.   FTA-G3 (Colombia); FTA Mexico – Triangulo del Norte (El Salvador, Guatemala, and Honduras); FTA Mexico – Costa Rica; FTA Mexico – Nicaragua; FTA Mexico – Uruguay; and FTA Mexico – Bolivia.
108.   See Art. 8.20 of the Mexico – Bolivia FTA.
109.   See Art. 14 of the Mexico – European Union FTA.
110.   See Art. 7-01 of the Mexico – Israel FTA.

regional Agreements in different areas – trade among them – at different levels of integration.[111] Some of these Agreements have evolved to become FTAs.[112]

Neither the Montevideo Treaty nor the regional Agreements – i.e., those including all ALADI Members – contains sections on dispute settlement. Only some ECAs contain such mechanisms. Besides those Agreements that became FTAs – which were covered in the previous section – there are three ECAs containing dispute settlement mechanisms: the ECA between Mexico and Brazil (AAP.CE N° 53), the ECA between Mexico and Peru (AAP.CE N° 8), and the ECA between Mexico and Argentina (AAP.CE N° 6). Indeed, as mentioned above, Mexico participated in one case against Peru that was adjudicated through the ECA forum.

The dispute settlement mechanisms of these three ECAs are similar to the NAFTA Chapter 20 mechanism: consultations, Panel, and suspension of concessions, among others. The mechanisms were negotiated after the Agreement on the ECAs. Hence, they take the form of additional protocols.

---

111. The Agreements cover different areas (e.g., technology, culture, trade) and have different levels of integration (e.g., total trade or some products).
112. See <www.aladi.org>, August 2009.

Chapter 2
Mexico's GATT and WTO Cases

We discuss here Mexico's cases (as complainant, defendant and third party) from the time of its accession to the GATT in 1986 until the cut-off date of our WTO data on 1 January 2007. Given the creation of the WTO in 1995, we have divided the discussion into two: Part A, 'Mexico's GATT Cases', dealing with the cases during GATT era; and Part B, 'Mexico's WTO Cases', covering those under the WTO.

The following clarifications may be useful to understand the variables used in this chapter:[1]

Abandoned case	A case which is not procedurally active due to: (a) inactivity for more than three years (because after three years one cannot reasonably expect a renaissance); or (b) the presentation of a new request for consultation challenging the original measure or its modified version, such as provisional and definitive antidumping measures;[2] we further classify the abandoned cases by declaration or no declaration of abandonment by the complainant.
Adoption of GATT Panel reports	Under the GATT rules, Panel reports were not automatically adopted. They were

---

1. These definitions refer to both the GATT era and the WTO. Hence, those definitions for the cases taken under GATT have to be read without the additional and later WTO elements, and vice versa.
2. We count these reformulated cases – e.g., provisional and definitive AD measures – as a single case per each request for consultations. This is important for our analysis of legal remedies in Ch. 5, 'Interpretations of the Data'.

adopted only if there was consensus.[3] Hence, any Contracting Party had veto power. The current WTO rules allow for adoption of a Panel/AB report unless there is a consensus not to adopt it – i.e., the negative consensus rule.[4] A report not adopted means no legal obligation with respect to implementation.

Finding won/lost by Mexico

Any successful finding by a GATT Panel, PTA Panel, WTO Panel/AB (original or Article 21.5 of the DSU) or arbitrator (Articles 21.3 or 22.6 of the DSU).[5] We use findings as a unit of account. We do not pronounce on overall win/ loss, which is a very difficult issue to tackle.[6]

For WTO cases, we distinguish the Panel findings from the AB findings by counting them separately. We do not count findings under Article 3.8 of the DSU – although we do take them into account if the Article was the legal base of a defence. Nor do we count absence of findings through judicial economy.

The findings from the Panel, as amended by the AB, may come from two sources: claims that were the basis of the complaint (Article 6.2 of the DSU) or defences presented by the defendant (such as Article XX of the GATT).

Implementation or measure amended

A measure is deemed to be amended or implemented when: (a) the complainant is satisfied with the amendment; or (b) the measure has been withdrawn no later than one year from the last communication of a disputing Party or an adjudicative body, and the complainant does not oppose the modifi- cation or elimination of the measure; or (c) there is a MAS.

---

3. There is consensus if no Member, present at the meeting when the decision is taken, formally objects to the proposed decision. See n. 1 of the WTO Agreement for the WTO description of consensus.
4. See Arts 16.4 and 17.14 of the DSU.
5. We determine success in findings by the arbitrator under Arts 21.3 or 22.6 of the DSU by com- paring them with the position sustained by each party to the arbitration. As an example, assume that a finding on RPT of two months and one party's position was one month and the other party's position was three months. Here we would allocate a one-half finding of success to each party.
6. For instance, even when the findings were in favour of the US in the *Mexico – Telecoms* (204) case, there were internal interests in Mexico that wanted to amend the domestic regulations, and some government officials used the Panel report as a leverage to do so.

	Under WTO law, one finding of violation is sufficient to trigger the obligation to implement, unless the measure is no longer in force when the Panel/AB issues the finding. Article 19.1 of the DSU obliges Panels to recommend that the measure be brought into conformity, if a violation is found.
Other Party involved	When Mexico is attacking, the other Party involved is the defendant. When Mexico is defending, the other Party involved is the complainant. We further classify the other Party involved – the 153 WTO Members[7] – in accordance with their economic development as (a) US/EC (29 Members),[8] (b) other OECD Members (10 Members including Mexico),[9] (c) non-Members of OECD (80 non-Members)[10] and (d) LDCs or least developed countries (32 Members).[11]
Pending Case	A procedurally active case, as opposed to abandoned or implemented cases.
Product	The good, service or intellectual property right subject to the dispute settlement

---

7. See <www.wto.org/english/thewto_e/whatis_e/tif_e/org6_e.htm>, August 2009.
8. This classification includes the twenty-seven Member States from the EC, the EC itself, and the US. In addition to its Member States, the EC is also a WTO Member. However, as n. 2 of the WTO Agreement indicates with respect to the decision-making process of the WTO, 'the number of votes of the European Communities and their Member States shall in no case exceed the number of the Member States of the European Communities'.
9. Excluding the US and the EC, they are: Australia, Canada, Iceland, Japan, Korea, New Zealand, Norway, Switzerland, and Turkey (and, of course, Mexico).
10. These are the WTO Members that are neither OECD Members nor LDCs: Albania; Antigua and Barbuda; Argentina; Armenia; Kingdom of Bahrain; Barbados; Belize; Bolivia; Botswana; Brazil; Brunei Darussalam; Cameroon; Chile; China; Colombia; Costa Rica; Côte d'Ivoire; Croatia; Cuba; the Democratic Republic of the Congo; Dominica; Dominican Republic; Ecuador; Egypt; El Salvador; Fiji; the Former Yugoslav Republic of Macedonia; Gabon; Georgia; Ghana; Grenada; Guatemala; Guyana; Honduras; Hong Kong, China; India; Indonesia; Israel; Jamaica; Jordan; Kenya; Kuwait; the Kyrgyz Republic; Liechtenstein; Macao; Malaysia; Mauritius; Moldova; Mongolia; Morocco; Namibia; Nicaragua; Nigeria; Oman; Pakistan; Panama; Papua New Guinea; Paraguay; Peru; the Philippines; Qatar; Saint Kitts and Nevis; Saint Lucia; Saint Vincent and the Grenadines; Saudi Arabia; Singapore; South Africa; Sri Lanka; Suriname; Swaziland; Chinese Taipei; Thailand; Tonga; Trinidad and Tobago; Tunisia; United Arab Emirates; Uruguay; Venezuela; Vietnam; and Zimbabwe.
11. Those that are Members of the WTO are: Angola, Bangladesh, Benin, Burkina Faso, Burundi, Cambodia, the Central African Republic, Chad, the Democratic Republic of the Congo, Djibouti, Gambia, Guinea, Guinea Bissau, Haiti, Lesotho, Madagascar, Malawi, Maldives, Mali, Mauritania, Mozambique, Myanmar, Nepal, Niger, Rwanda, Senegal, Sierra Leone, the Solomon Islands, Tanzania, Togo, Uganda, and Zambia. See <www.wto.org/english/thewto_e/whatis_e/tif_e/org7_e.htm>, August 2007.

mechanism; we classify them under four clusters: (a) industrial goods; (b) agricultural goods; (c) general goods; and (d) services (Mexico has had no TRIPS cases). There are some cases covering two products at the same time – e.g., *EC – Bananas III* (27), which dealt with agricultural goods and services. Those cases have been recorded by half units for each product (i.e., 0.5 for agricultural product and 0.5 for services).[12]

Stage
Refers to the procedural phases of the DSU: consultations, Panel/AB, RPT, Article 21.5 Panel/AB, and retaliation.

Subject matter
The WTO covered Agreement under which the case in question has been adjudicated. In more detail, subject matter also includes the article or provision of the covered Agreement related to the case. We only cover the claims set out at the request for consultations. Findings under adjudicative procedures are covered in Findings won/lost by Mexico.

I.   MEXICO'S GATT CASES

Mexico participated in three cases as a complainant under the GATT (it was never a defendant):

(1) The first is *US – Superfund*. It was initiated by Canada, the European Economic Community (EEC)[13] and Mexico against the US. The complainants challenged the US tax regime relating to petroleum and certain chemical products (US Superfund Amendments and Reauthorization Act of 1986). Mexico's request for consultations was issued on 10 November 1986.[14]

(2) The second case is *US – Tuna (Mexico)*. It was initiated by Mexico on 5 November 1990 when it filed its request for consultations.[15] Mexico claimed that two US internal laws were GATT-inconsistent: the Marine

---

12. There is one NAFTA case dealing with services and investment at the same time.
13. In the GATT section, we make references to the EEC, whereas in the WTO section EC means the European Communities. This accommodates the evolution and the different names of the current European Union.
14. See L/6093.
15. See C/M/246/27.

Mammal Protection Act and the Dolphin Protection Consumer Information Act.[16]

(3) The third case is *US – Cement*. Mexico initiated it on 24 October 1990 by requesting consultations with the US on the imposition of AD duties on imports of gray Portland cement and cement clinker from Mexico.[17]

Mexico also participated in four cases as a Third Party in the GATT era: *EEC – Bananas 1* (32/R), *EEC – Parts and Components* (BISD 37S/132 L/6657), *US – Customs User Fee* (BISD 35S/245 L/6264), and *Japan – Semi-Conductors* (BISD 35S/116 L/6309).

A.   GATT CASES: THE SUBJECT MATTER

As complainant,[18] Mexico has cited GATT provisions in two cases,[19] citing Article I of the GATT ('Most-Favoured-Nation Treatment') once and the provisions of the GATT relating to national treatment (Article III) twice. It has also cited Article IX of the GATT (Marks of Origin), Article XI of the GATT (General Elimination of Quantitative Restrictions) and Article XIII of the GATT (Non-discriminatory Administration of Quantitative Restrictions) one time each.

Table 2.1 Mexico's GATT Cases by Subject Matter: The GATT Agreement

	I	III	IX	XI	XIII
As Complainant	1	2	1	1	1
As Defendant	0	0	0	0	0

There is one case under the GATT where Mexico cited the Agreement on Implementation of Article VI of the General Agreement (Tokyo AD Code, which

---

16. See Panel report, *US – Tuna (Mexico)*, (39S/155), paras 2.3–2.12.
17. See ADP/51.
18. There is no case of Mexico as defendant during the time of the GATT.
19. See the Report of the GATT Panel, *US – Superfund*, para. 3.1.1, and the Report of the GATT Panel, *US – Tuna (Mexico)*, paras 3.1 to 3.5.

was the predecessor of the ADA). That was *US – Cement*,[20] where it cited Article 1 (Principles), Article 3 (Injury), Article 4 (Definition of Industry), Article 5 (Initiation and Subsequent Investigation), and Article 6 (Evidence) of the AD Code.

Table 2.2 Mexico's GATT Cases by Subject Matter: The AD Code

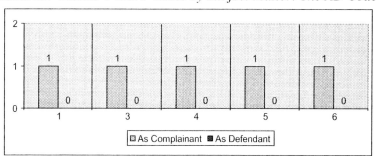

B.   GATT CASES: THE NUMBER OF COMPLAINANTS

All of the GATT cases initiated by Mexico were against the US. Two were taken by Mexico alone:

    (1) *US – Tuna (Mexico)*; and
    (2) *US – Cement.*

The third case was initiated by Mexico together with Canada and the EEC:

    (3) *US – Superfund*

Table 2.3 Mexico's GATT Cases against the US by Number
of Complainants

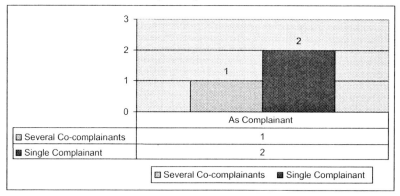

20.   See the Report of the GATT Panel, *US – Cement*, paras 3.3.1 to 3.4.88.

C.   GATT CASES: THE PRODUCT INVOLVED

All of Mexico's cases under the GATT relate to trade in industrial goods:

    (1) *US – Superfund*, relating to petroleum and feedstock chemicals;
    (2) *US – Cement*, relating to cement; and
    (3) *US – Tuna (Mexico)*, relating to tuna. Fish, and hence tuna, has been
        classified as industrial goods under the Uruguay Round.[21]

Table 2.4 Mexico's GATT Cases by Product Involved

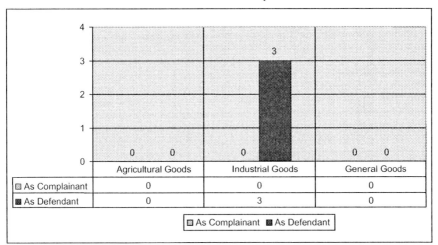

	Agricultural Goods	Industrial Goods	General Goods
As Complainant	0	0	0
As Defendant	0	3	0

D.   GATT CASES: ADOPTION AND IMPLEMENTATION

Out of the three cases where Mexico was a complainant under the GATT, one was
adopted and implemented:[22]

    (1) *US – Superfund*, initiated by Mexico together with Canada and the EEC.

The remaining two cases were neither adopted nor implemented. In the GATT, if
a report was not adopted there was no obligation to implement. But implementation could still happen. Mexico was the sole complainant in these two cases:

    (1) *US – Tuna (Mexico);* and
    (2) *US – Cement.*

---

21. Article 2 and Annex 1 of the Agreement on Agriculture classify fish as non-agricultural market
    access (NAMA) products by not including them in the list of agricultural products. Moreover,
    Mexico's goods schedule (*Lista LXXVII, Parte I, Sección I – A*) under the Uruguay Round does
    not consider that tuna fish is an exception to the general rule for NAMA products. Hence, tuna
    has been classified as a NAMA product for Mexico.
22. As mentioned in Ch. 1 above, in the GATT era adoption was not semiautomatic as in the WTO
    where there is the negative consensus rule. Hence, GATT cases had to be adopted by positive
    consensus.

Table 2.5 Mexico's GATT Cases by Adoption,
Implementation and Number of Complainants

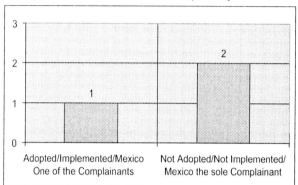

The adopted/implemented case of Mexico under the GATT is:

(1) *US – Superfund*: On 22 November 1989, the US Congress passed the Steel Trade Liberalization Program Implementation Act, which put in place a new tax which was the same for both foreign and domestic oil. This eliminated the tax discrimination that had applied previously between the domestic and the imported products.[23] The Panel report was adopted on 17 June 1998. Even though it took more than one year from adoption of the report to its implementation, we consider this case to be implemented.

The cases not adopted/implemented are:

(2) *US – Cement*: Mexico challenged under the WTO the original AD order by the US which imposed antidumping duty (ADD) on exports of cement from Mexico. Duties stayed in place even beyond five years, as the existence of a WTO case challenging the same order demonstrates.[24]

(3) *US – Tuna (Mexico)*: The US National Marine Fisheries Services (a division of the Department of Commerce) exempted Mexico from the embargo on yellowfin tuna from 1 April 2005 until 31 March 2010. This exemption does not mean that Mexico can export using dolphin-free labels.[25] It is subject to annual review and the US Department of Commerce (DOC) published the last affirmative review for Mexico on

---

23. See the archives of American University at <www.american.edu/TED/sfund.htm>, August 2009.
24. The WTO case on *US – Cement* (281) challenges the sunset reviews and yearly reviews of the original AD order, among other things. This shows that Mexico did not consider the US to be in compliance with the un-adopted GATT Panel report on cement. See the information on the WTO case *US – Cement* (281) below.
25. See <swr.nmfs.noaa.gov/psd/embargo2.htm>, August 2009.

23 July 2007.[26] Mexico is still trying to gain approval to use the 'Dolphin Safe' label. But on 27 April 2007 a Federal Appeals Court refused to allow the weakening of the 'Dolphin Safe' tuna label on the grounds that the DOC based its findings on political considerations, not on science.[27] Hence, we classify this GATT Panel report as not implemented.[28]

E.   GATT: FINDINGS WON

1.   The Findings Won by Mexico, at a Glance

Mexico won at least half of the findings in the three GATT cases it initiated. In two cases it won 50% of the findings and the US won the remaining 50%:

(1) *US – Superfund*; and
(2) *US – Tuna (Mexico)*;

and in one case it won 100% of the findings: *US – Cement*

Table 2.6 GATT Cases: Percentage of Findings Won by Mexico

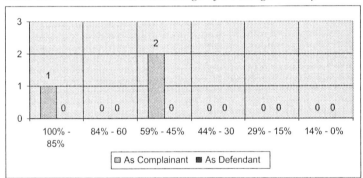

The following table sets out in greater detail aspects of the implementation of each GATT case initiated by Mexico. It shows that the case initiated by Mexico with other complainants was adopted and implemented by the US. Mexico won 50% of the findings in that case. The other two cases, initiated by Mexico alone, were, however, not implemented by the US and were not adopted, despite the fact that Mexico won 50% of the findings in one and 100% in the other.

---

26.   See Federal Register/Vol. 72, No. 140/Monday, 23 Jul. 2007/Notices, 40118.
27.   See <www.earthisland.org/journal/index.php/eij/article/international_marine_mammal_project/>, August 2009.
28.   Note that Mexico requested consultations on 24 Oct. 2008 with respect to its tuna exports to the US, but this dispute is outside our scope of analysis. See United States – Measures Concerning the Importation, Marketing and Sale of Tuna and Tuna Products (381).

Table 2.7 GATT Cases: Findings Won and Lost/
Adoption/Implementation

Case	Won/Lost		Adoption/ Implementation
US – Superfund	Total Findings	2	Adopted/ Implemented
Defendant: US	The US won	1 (50%)	
Other Complainant: Canada and EEC	Mexico won	1 (50%)	
Product: industrial Goods (petroleum and feedstock chemicals)			
US – Tuna (Mexico)	Total Findings	4	Not adopted/Not implemented
Defendant: US	The US won	2 (50%)	
Product: industrial Goods (Tuna)	Mexico won	2 (50%)	
US – Cement	Total Findings	1	Not adopted/Not implemented
Defendant: US	The US won	0 (0%)	
Product: industrial Goods (Cement)	Mexico and other complainants won	1 (100%)	

2.   The Findings Won by Mexico: Detailed Presentation

This section presents the outcome of Mexico's GATT cases in more detail, specifying the Panel's findings. After each of the findings we indicate, in parentheses, who won it.

a.   US – Superfund

This case was initiated by Canada, the EEC and Mexico against some US taxes relating to chemicals and petroleum. Mexico's request for consultations was presented on 10 November 1986.[29] The products protected by the US were industrial

---

29. See Panel report, *US – Superfund*, para. 1.

goods (petroleum and feedstock chemicals). The measure was eliminated on 22 November 1989 as mentioned above.

(A)   *Measures Challenged by Mexico*
The US Superfund Amendments and Reauthorization Act of 1986 of 17 October 1986. The law:

    (1) re-imposed an excise tax on petroleum at higher rates;
    (2) re-imposed a tax on certain chemicals (feedstock chemicals); and
    (3) imposed a new tax on certain imported substances produced or manufac-
        tured from taxable feedstock chemicals.

(B)   *Mexico's Claims*
Article III.2 of the GATT.

(C)   *The Findings of the Panel*
The Panel issued two findings. Mexico, along with Canada and the EEC, won one. The US won the other. *The Panel*:

    (1) *found* that the tax on petroleum was inconsistent with Article III.2, first
        sentence, of the GATT (the rate of tax applied to the imported products
        was 3.5 cents per barrel higher than the rate applied to the like domestic
        product);[30] *(MX)* and
    (2) *found* that the tax on certain imported substances constituted a tax adjust-
        ment corresponding to the tax on certain chemicals that was consistent
        with Article III.2, first sentence, of the GATT; and, the exaction of the
        penalty rate provisions as such did not constitute an infringement of
        Article III.2, first sentence, because the tax authorities had regulatory
        power to eliminate the need for imposing the penalty rate. *(US)*

b.   *US – Tuna (Mexico)*

This case was initiated by Mexico against the US embargo, based on environmental considerations, on tuna imports from Mexico. The request for consultations
was presented on 5 November 1990.[31] The products protected by the US were
industrial goods (tuna). The Panel report was neither adopted nor implemented,
but Mexico was temporarily exempted from the embargo from 1 April 2005 until
31 March 2010, as mentioned above.

(A)   *Measures Challenged by Mexico*

    (1) The Marine Mammal Protection Act of the US:

---

30.   See the report of the Panel, *US – Superfund*, paras 5.1.1 and 5.1.12.
31.   See Panel report, *US – Tuna (Mexico)*, para. 1.

(a) measures on imports from Mexico (embargo on tuna from Mexico subject to fishing practices); and

(b) measures on intermediary country imports (embargo on tuna imported from a third country if that country had imported tuna from Mexico).

(2) Dolphin Protection Consumer Information Act (labelling requirements for 'dolphin safe').[32]

(B)   *Mexico's Claims*

Mexico claimed that:

(1) The US embargo on tuna from Mexico was inconsistent with Arts III, XI and XIII of the GATT.

(2) The US intermediary nations embargo was inconsistent with Article XI of the GATT.

(3) The US Dolphin Protection Consumer Act was inconsistent with Articles I and IX of the GATT.

(C)   *The Findings of the Panel*

The Panel issued four findings. Mexico won two and the US the other two. *The Panel:*

(1) *found* the prohibition on tuna imports from Mexico and the provisions of the Maritime Mammal Protection Act under which it is imposed to be contrary to Article XI.1 and not justified under Articles XX(b) or XX(g) of the GATT; *(MX)*

(2) *found* the prohibition on tuna imports from 'intermediary nations' and the provisions of the Maritime Mammal Protection Act under which it is imposed to be contrary to Article XI.1 and not justified under Articles XX(b), XX(d) or XX(g) of the GATT; *(MX)*

(3) *found* that the provisions of the Fishermen's Protective Act (allowing the president at his or her discretion to prohibit imports of all fish or wildlife products from the country in question) were not inconsistent with the General Agreement (discretionary/mandatory principle); *(US)* and

(4) *found* the labelling provisions of the Dolphin Protection Consumer Information Act relating to tuna caught in the Eastern Tropical Pacific Ocean were not inconsistent with Article I.1 of the GATT. *(US)*

c.   *US – Cement*

This case was initiated by Mexico against the US AD measure on cement from Mexico. Mexico's request for consultations was presented on 24 October 1990.[33] The products protected by the US were industrial goods (cement).

---

32. See Panel report, *US – Tuna (Mexico)*, paras 2.3 to 2.12.
33. See Panel report, *US – Cement*, para. 1.

(A)   *Measures Challenged by Mexico*
The imposition by the US on 30 August 1990 of an AD duty order on imports of cement from Mexico.

(B)   *Mexico's Claims*
Articles 1, 3, 4, 5 and 6 of the Agreement on Implementation of Article VI of the General Agreement (Tokyo AD Code).[34]

(C)   *The Findings of the Panel*
The Panel issued one finding. Mexico won it. The *Panel found* the US initiation of the investigation on cement from Mexico inconsistent with Article 5.1 of the Agreement on Implementation of Article VI of the GATT (Tokyo AD Code).[35] *(MX)*

F.   GATT CASES WHERE MEXICO PARTICIPATED AS A
            THIRD PARTY

Mexico participated as a Third Party in four GATT cases. Three of the four cases were initiated by a developed country, or countries, against a developed country, and all three were adopted:

(1) *EEC – Parts and Components*;
(2) *US – Customs User Fee*; and
(3) *Japan – Semi-Conductors*.

Mexico participated as a Third Party in one case, initiated by developing countries against a developed country, which was not adopted: *EEC – Bananas I.*[36]

*Table 2.8 GATT Cases: Mexico as a Third Party,
Classified by Disputing Parties*

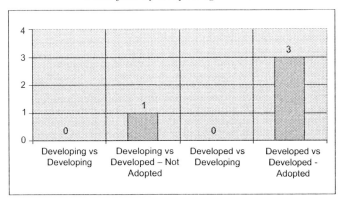

---

34. The Agreement on Implementation of Art. VI of the General Agreement is the predecessor to the current ADA. See the Report of the GATT Panel, *US – Cement*, paras 3.3.1 to 3.4.88.
35. See the report of the Panel, *US – Cement*, paras 6.1 and 6.2.
36. For a compilation of the elements of GATT cases where Mexico participated as a Third Party, see the Appendix, Table 2, 'GATT Cases Where Mexico Participated as Third Party'.

One GATT case where Mexico participated as a Third Party relates to trade in industrial goods: *Japan – Semi-Conductors*

Two relate to trade in general goods:

(1) *EEC – Parts and Components*; and
(2) *US – Customs User Fee*;

and one relates to trade in agricultural goods: *EEC – Bananas I*.

*Table 2.9 GATT Cases: Mexico as a Third Party,
Product by Product*

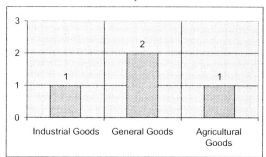

Mexico made a written or oral statement in one case: *EEC – Bananas I*. In its statement Mexico supported one of the claims of the complainant (Article XI:1 on elimination of quantitative restrictions) which was found GATT inconsistent by the Panel.

In three cases Mexico decided not to make any written or oral intervention:

(1) *EEC – Parts and Components*;
(2) *US – Customs User Fee*; and
(3) *Japan – Semi-Conductors*.

*Table 2.10 GATT Cases: Interventions
as a Third Party*

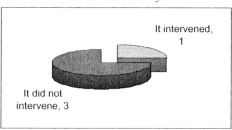

II.   MEXICO'S WTO CASES

There are three main sections in this chapter. Section A presents cases where there was a final resolution – i.e., cases terminated either by abandonment or by implementation. Section B covers pending cases (cases still active as at the closing date of this work),[37] and Section C deals with WTO cases where Mexico was a Third Party.[38] For the glossary used in this section refer to the beginning of this chapter.

A.   WTO CASES WITH FINAL RESOLUTION
      (COMPLAINANT/DEFENDANT)

This section presents the cases involving Mexico which are not procedurally active. We distinguish between: (a) cases abandoned by the complainant, and (b) cases implemented by the defendant to the satisfaction of the complainant.[39]

1.   Abandoned Cases

We now turn to abandoned cases.[40] As a complainant, Mexico has abandoned seven cases:

(1) *US – AD on Steel Zeroing I* (325). Consultations were requested on 5 January 2005. Mexico initiated *US – AD on Steel Zeroing II* (344) on 26 May 2005.
(2) *US – CVD on Steel* (280). Consultations were requested on 21 January 2003. The Panel was established by the WTO Dispute Settlement Body (B) on 29 August 2003 but was never composed.
(3) *Ecuador – Cement I* (182). Consultations were requested on 5 October 1999. Mexico initiated *Ecuador – Cement II* (191) on 15 March 2000.
(4) *EC – Bananas III New Request* (158). Consultations were requested on 20 January 1999. Their aim was to discuss with the EC its measures to comply with *EC – Bananas III* (27). There is no further record of this new request for consultations.
(5) *Guatemala – Cement I* (60). Consultations were requested on 15 October 1996. Mexico initiated a new case, *Guatemala – Cement II* (156), on 5 January 1999.
(6) *EC – Bananas III* (27). Consultations were requested on 5 February 1996. Mexico requested consultations under Article 21.5 of the DSU (18 August 1998), as its last procedural step. But it abandoned the case at that stage even though Ecuador and the US went further in the DSU process.

---

37. Sections 1 and 2 represent the totality of cases where Mexico was Party to the dispute either as complainant or defendant.
38. The observations are based on DS series from 1 Jan. 1995 to 1 Jan. 2007 for WTO cases.
39. We interpret satisfaction of complainant as being sufficient for classifying those cases as finally resolved. Arts 3.5 and 3.6 of the DSU deal with MAS and the notification to the WTO. However, if the complainant is not satisfied with the implementation steps taken by the defendant, it may start a new dispute.
40. For more detail on the abandoned cases when Mexico acts as a Party, see the Appendix Table 3, 'Mexico's abandoned cases in WTO' and Table 11, 'WTO cases: Measures, claims and implementation'.

(7) *EC – Bananas III Old Request* (16). Consultations were requested on 28 September 1995. Mexico and the other co-complainants subsequently initiated *EC – Bananas III* (27).

In cases where Mexico has been the defendant, complainants have abandoned their challenges on five occasions:

(1) *Mexico – Olive Oil I* (314). Consultations were requested on 18 August 2004. The EC initiated *Mexico – Olive Oil II* (341) on 31 March 2006.
(2) *Mexico – Transformers* (216). The date of the request for consultations is 20 December 2000. Mexico eliminated the measure three months after the request. But we classify this measure as a 'hit and run' violation – i.e., one designed to violate for a short period. Accordingly, we do not consider it implemented.
(3) *Mexico – Swine* (203). The request for consultations was made on 10 July 2000. The US did not withdraw the complaint, and Mexico eliminated the AD measure almost three years after the request for consultations.
(4) *Mexico – Corn Syrup I* (101). Consultations were requested on 4 September 1997. The US initiated *Mexico – Corn Syrup II* (132) on 8 May 1998.
(5) *Mexico – Customs Valuation from EC* (53). The request for consultations was made on 27 August 1996. The EC did not withdraw the complaint, and Mexico did not present any information on implementation. For NAFTA products, Mexico used free on board (FOB) value, whereas it used cost, insurance and freight (CIF) value for most-favoured-nation (MFN) products. This discrimination was automatically eliminated when NAFTA tariffs reached zero because there was no longer any need to value NAFTA goods. Valuation was necessary only for MFN products.

Table 2.11 Mexico's Abandoned Cases

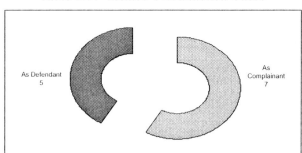

a.   Abandoned Cases: Explicit and Implicit Abandonment

Declaration of abandonment may be explicit or implicit. A declaration is explicit when the complainant states it has abandoned the case – for example, when the complainant challenges a reformed measure and not the measure it originally challenged. An implicit declaration is when the complainant's actions imply that it has abandoned the case.

Out of the seven abandoned cases where Mexico acted as complainant, three of them are implicit cases:

(1) *EC – Bananas III New Request* (158);
(2) *EC – Bananas III* (27); and
(3) *US – CVD on Steel* (280);

The other four cases are explicit:

(4) *US – AD on Steel Zeroing I* (325);
(5) *EC – Bananas III Old Request* (16).
(6) *Ecuador – Cement I* (182); and
(7) *Guatemala – Cement I* (60).

Out of the five abandoned cases against Mexico, three were implicit:

(1) *Mexico – Transformers* (216);
(2) *Mexico – Swine* (203); and
(3) *Mexico – Customs Valuation from the EC* (53).

The remaining two cases were explicit:

(4) *Mexico – Olive Oil I* (314); and
(5) *Mexico – Corn Syrup I* (101).

Table 2.12 Mexico's Cases: Declaration of Abandonment

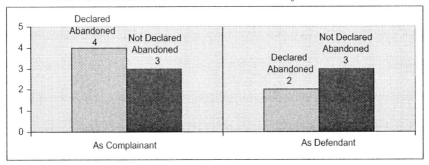

b.   *Abandoned Cases by Subject Matter*

Examining the abandoned cases, we observe the following: four cases relating to the GATT were abandoned with Mexico as complainant and two when it was the defendant. In its abandoned cases as complainant Mexico cited the Antidumping Agreement (ADA) three times, and three times complainants cited it against Mexico. As complainant in such cases, Mexico cited the WTO General Agreement on Trade in Services (GATS) and the Import Licensing Agreement twice each and the WTO Agreement and the Agreement on Subsidies and Countervailing Duties

(SCM) once each. Once, a complainant cited the latter once against Mexico. The Agreement on Agriculture has been cited once by Mexico as complainant and twice against it. Still on the theme of abandoned cases, Mexico as complainant has claimed violation of the Agreement on Trade Related Investment Measures (TRIMS) once, and in another similar case it made no claim of violation.[41] Finally, charges of violation of the Agreement on Technical Barriers to Trade (TBT) and the Agreement on the Application of Sanitary and Phytosanitary Measures (SPS Agreement) have been recorded only in the case of complainants against Mexico at the rate of one abandoned case per agreement.[42]

Table 2.13 WTO Cases: Abandoned Cases by Subject Matter (Agreements)

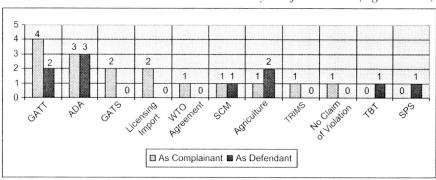

c.   *Abandoned Cases: Identity of the Other Party Involved*

We observe that Mexico as complainant has abandoned a total of seven cases, five of which were against the US/EC. On the other hand, when Mexico has been the defendant five cases have been abandoned by the complainants against Mexico, four of which by the US/EC.[43] Mexico has also abandoned two cases as

41. See *EC – Bananas III New Request* (158), where Mexico and the other co-complainants did not specify any violation, but wanted to consult with the EC on the RPT of *EC – Bananas III* (27).
42. For a disaggregated picture of all Mexico's cases by subject matter, refer to Ch. 4, 'Mexico's Conduct of Its Cases: An Explanation of the WTO Experience'. There, we present the subject matter by covered agreement and by each provision of the covered agreement.
43. Mexico as complainant has abandoned three cases against the EC:

(1) *EC – Bananas III New Request* (158);
(2) *EC – Bananas III* (27); and
(3) *EC – Bananas III Old Request* (16).

The EC has abandoned two cases against Mexico:

(1) *Mexico – Olive Oil I* (314) and
(2) *Mexico – Customs Valuation from EC* (53).

Mexico has abandoned two cases against the US:

(1) *US – AD on Steel Zeroing I* (325); and
(2) *US – CVD on Steel* (280).

The US has abandoned two cases initiated against Mexico:

complainant, initiated against non-Members of OECD. Out of a total of five cases against Mexico that were abandoned, one was initiated and subsequently abandoned by a non-Member of OECD.[44]

Table 2.14 WTO Cases: Party That Abandoned, Classified by Its Economic Development

	US/EC	Other OECD	Non- OECD	LDCs
As Complainant	5	0	2	0
As Defendant	4	0	1	0

The following table disaggregates this information. Mexico when acting as complainant abandoned cases against the EC, the US, Guatemala and Ecuador. The EC, the US and Brazil have all abandoned cases where Mexico was the defendant.

Table 2.15 WTO Cases: Abandonment Classified by the Other Party Involved

	EC	US	Guatemala	Ecuador	Brazil
As Complainant	3	2	1	1	0
As Defendant	2	2	0	0	1

---

(1) *Mexico – Swine* (203); and

(2) *Mexico – Corn Syrup I* (101).

44. Mexico as complainant has abandoned one case against Guatemala and one against Ecuador:

(1) *Guatemala – Cement I* (60) and

(2) *Ecuador – Cement I* (182).

Brazil has abandoned one case against Mexico:

(1) *Mexico – Transformers* (216).

d.   *Abandoned Cases: The Product Involved*

Mexico as complainant has abandoned four cases relating to trade in industrial goods:

(1) *US – AD on Steel Zeroing I* (325);
(2) *US – CVD on Steel* (280);
(3) *Ecuador – Cement I* (182); and
(4) *Guatemala – Cement I* (60);

and one complainant attacking Mexico (Brazil) abandoned one case, also relating to industrial goods: *Mexico – Transformers* (216)

On agricultural goods, Mexico has abandoned 1.5 cases:

(1) *EC – Bananas III New Request* (158);
(2) *EC – Bananas III* (27); and
(3) EC – *Bananas III Old Request* (16);[45]

while complainants against Mexico have abandoned three cases relating to trade in agricultural goods:

(1) *Mexico – Olive Oil I* (314);
(2) *Mexico – Swine* (203); and
(3) *Mexico – Corn Syrup I* (101).

One complainant against Mexico (the EC) abandoned its case relating to trade in general goods: *Mexico – Customs Valuation from EC* (53)

Finally, only Mexico as complainant has abandoned cases relating to trade in services (1.5 cases):

(1) *EC – Bananas III New Request* (158);
(2) *EC – Bananas III* (27); and
(3) *EC – Bananas III Old Request* (16).[46]

Table 2.16 WTO Cases: Abandonment by Product

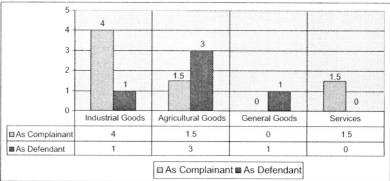

	Industrial Goods	Agricultural Goods	General Goods	Services
As Complainant	4	1.5	0	1.5
As Defendant	1	3	1	0

As Complainant As Defendant

45. All the *EC – Bananas III* cases (*Old Request, New Request, and III*) deal with trade in both agricultural goods and services. Hence, we classify each case as 0.5 relating to trade in agricultural goods and 0.5 to trade in services.
46. See the previous note.

e.   *Abandoned Cases Classified by Procedural Stage Where*
            Abandonment Occurred

Mexico abandoned four cases at consultations when acting as complainant (three
of them against the US/EC):

(1) *US – AD on Steel Zeroing I* (325);
(2) *Ecuador – Cement I* (182);
(3) *EC – Bananas III New Request* (158); and
(4) *EC – Bananas III Old Request* (16).

Complainants which abandoned cases against Mexico (four by the US/EC and one
by Brazil) dropped all (five) cases at the consultations stage:

(1) *Mexico – Olive Oil I* (314);
(2) *Mexico – Transformers* (216);
(3) *Mexico – Swine* (203);
(4) *Mexico – Corn Syrup I* (101); and
(5) *Mexico – Customs Valuation from EC* (53).

Mexico abandoned two cases at the Panel/AB stage. In the first case the Panel was
established, but did not issue a report; and in the second the Panel and the
AB issued a report:

(1) *US – CVD on Steel* (280); and
(2) *Guatemala – Cement I* (60).

Finally, Mexico abandoned one case (against the US/EC) at the Article 21.5 Panel/
AB stage:[47] *EC – Bananas III* (27).[48]

Table 2.17 WTO Cases: Abandonment by Procedural Stage

	Consultations	Panel/AB	RPT	21.5 Panel/AB	Retaliation
As Complainant	4	2	0	1	0
As Defendant	5	0	0	0	0

As Complainant · As Defendant

---

47. This case went from consultations to the Art. 21.5 Panel/AB, passing through the Panel/AB and
    RPT stages.
48. Mexico presented its last DS document in this case on 8 Aug. 1998, when it made the request
    for the establishment of an Art. 21.5 Panel. Its role after that was passive, even though other
    complainants continued the process.

i   Cases Litigated But Subsequently Abandoned

We now turn to litigated cases, with or without a report issued by the Panel/AB, that were subsequently abandoned. Mexico as complainant dropped three such cases. Of the cases where Mexico abandoned at the Panel/AB stage, one was dropped before any ruling by the Panel: *US – CVD on Steel* (280).

Another case was abandoned after the ruling by the AB:

(1) *Guatemala – Cement I* (60)
     (a) at the Panel stage Mexico won three findings and Guatemala won one; and
     (b) at the AB stage, Mexico did not win any findings and Guatemala won three. Based on these findings the AB concluded that there were no recommendations for Guatemala.

Finally, Mexico abandoned one case, as complainant, at the Article 21.5 Panel/AB stage:

(1) *EC – Bananas III* (27)
     (a) at the Panel stage Mexico and the co-complainants won six findings and the EC won none;
     (b) at the AB stage, Mexico and the co-complainants won twenty-three findings and the EC won five;
     (c) at the arbitration to define the reasonable period of time under Article 21.3 of the DSU (RPT), Mexico and the co-complainants did not win any findings and the EC won one.[49]

Table 2.18 WTO Cases: Findings in Abandoned Cases

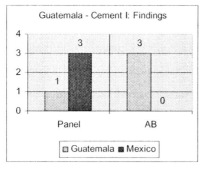
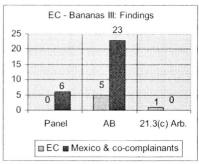

f.   *Abandoned Cases Presented According to a Combination of Variables*

This section presents abandoned cases based on a combination of variables: the product, the other Party involved and the procedural stage where abandonment took place.

---

49. For a full presentation of the findings won and lost in the totality of Mexico's cases, refer to Ch. 4, 'Mexico's Conduct of Its Cases: An Explanation of the WTO Experience'.

Mexico, as complainant, abandoned four cases relating to trade in industrial goods. Two were against the US. One was dropped at the consultations stage (*US – AD on Steel Zeroing I* (325)) and the other at the Panel/AB stage (*US – CVD on Steel* (280)). Mexico abandoned one case against Guatemala at the Panel/AB stage (*Guatemala – Cement I* (60)) and another against Ecuador at the consultations stage (*Ecuador – Cement I* (182)).

Again as complainant, Mexico abandoned 1.5 cases against the EC relating to agricultural goods[50] – two halves of a case at the consultations stage (*EC – Bananas III Old Request* (16), and *EC – Bananas III New Request* (158)) and the remaining half of a case at the Article 21.5 Panel/AB stage (*EC – Bananas III* (27)). The same occurred with the 1.5 cases relating to trade in services against the EC: two halves were abandoned at consultations (*EC – Bananas III Old Request* (16), and *EC – Bananas III New Request* (158)) and one half at the Article 21.5 Panel/AB stage (*EC – Bananas III* (27)).

Table 2.19 Mexico as Complainant: Abandoned Cases by Combination of Variables

	Industrial Goods			Agricultural Goods	Services
	US	Guat.	Ecu.	EC	EC
Consultations	1		1	1	1
Panel/AB	1	1			
RPT					
Article 21.5				0.5	0.5
Panel/AB					
Retaliation					

All of the cases abandoned by complainants against Mexico were dropped at the consultations stage. One taken by Brazil relates to industrial goods (*Mexico – Transformers* (216)). Three cases relate to trade in agricultural goods: the US abandoned two of them (*Mexico – Swine* (203) and *Mexico – Corn Syrup I* (101)), and the EC the third (*Mexico – Olive Oil I* (314)). Finally, one case abandoned by the EC against Mexico relates to trade in general goods (*Mexico – Customs Valuation from EC* (53)).

---

50. As mentioned above, three cases initiated against the EC relate not only to agricultural goods but also to trade in services. Hence, we decided to split the unit of account with regard to products: one-half for agricultural goods and one-half for services.

Table 2.20 Mexico as Defendant: Implemented Cases by
Combination of Variables

	Industrial Goods	Agricultural Goods		General Goods
	Brazil	**US**	**EC**	**EC**
Consultations	1	2	1	1
Panel/AB RPT				
Article 21.5				
Panel/AB				
Retaliation				

2.   WTO Implemented Cases (Complainant/Defendant)

Defendants implemented six cases where Mexico was the complainant:

(1) *Panama – Milk* (329). Following a MAS, Panama amended its tariff sched-
    ule for milk. It set a new tariff of 5% taking into account its bound tariff.
(2) *US – Cement* (281). Following a MAS, the parties agreed to gradually
    (over three years) resolve the litigation on the AD duties, to enhance
    market access, and to revoke the AD duties.
(3) *Ecuador – Cement II* (191). The AD definitive measure expired six
    months after its publication, as indicated in the public notice of the final
    determination.
(4) *Guatemala – Cement II* (156). Guatemala withdrew the measure on
    4 October 2000.
(5) *US – Tomatoes* (49). The Mexican exporter of tomatoes signed a price
    undertaking with the US investigating authority. There are no further
    documents after the request for consultations.
(6) *Venezuela – OCTG* (23). Mexico notified its intention to put an end to
    the procedure on 6 May 1997, even though Venezuela had closed the
    investigation earlier, on 12 December 1995.

Mexico has implemented seven cases initiated against it:

(1) *Mexico – Soft Drinks* (308). Implementation was published in Mexico's
    Official Journal on 27 December 2006 and subsequently notified to
    the WTO.
(2) *Mexico – Customs Valuation from Guatemala* (298). On 29 August 2005
    Guatemala notified a MAS and requested closure of the case.
(3) *Mexico – Beef and Rice* (295). Mexico eliminated the final AD determina-
    tion on 11 September 2006 and amended the Foreign Trade Act on 21
    December 2006.

(4) *Mexico – Beans* (284). Nicaragua notified a MAS and withdrew its complaint on 8 March 2004.

(5) *Mexico – Matches* (232). Chile withdrew its complaint on 2 February 2004.

(6) *Mexico – Telecoms* (204). Based on an RPT agreement, Mexico complied on 12 August 2005 and made a spontaneous declaration of full compliance on 19 August 2005.

(7) *Mexico – Corn Syrup II* (132). Mexico withdrew the measure on 20 May 2002, but we could not find any reference in the WTO to its implementation.[51]

Table 2.21 WTO Implemented Cases

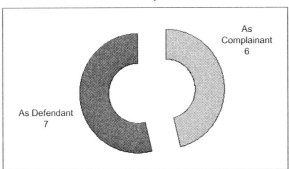

a.   *Implemented Cases: Subject Matter*

Six cases claiming violation of the GATT were implemented when Mexico was the complainant and another six when it was the defendant. Mexico claimed violation of the ADA in five cases as complainant and in two cases claims of violation of the same agreement were made against it. Mexico has defended two cases claiming violation of the Import Licensing Agreement. As complainant, it has claimed violation one time each of the Agreement on Agriculture and the WTO Agreement, and it has had to defend similar claims of violation of the same agreements one time each. Complainants against Mexico have claimed one case of violation each of the GATS, the SCM, the SPS, the TBT, the Customs Valuation Agreement and a Ministerial Decision.[52] Finally, Mexico claimed violation of the Principle of Non-discrimination in one case – but it cited the principle without reference to any particular WTO provision (*US – Tomatoes* (49)).[53]

---

51. For more detail on the implemented cases where Mexico acts as a Party, see the Appendix, Table 4, 'Mexico's Implemented Cases in WTO' and Table 11, 'WTO Cases: Measures, Claims and Implementation'.

52. A complainant against Mexico claimed violation of the ministerial decision regarding cases where customs administrations have reasons to doubt the truth or accuracy of the declared value. See *Mexico – Customs Valuation from Guatemala* (298).

53. For a disaggregated presentation of all Mexico's cases by subject matter, refer to Ch. 4, 'Mexico's Conduct of Its Cases: An Explanation of the WTO Experience'. There we present the subject matter by covered agreement and by each provision of the covered agreements.

Table 2.22 WTO Cases: Implemented Cases
by Subject Matter (Agreements)

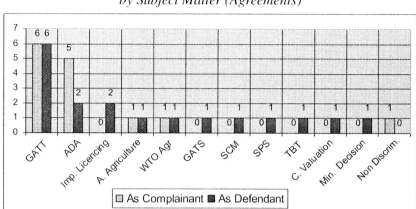

b.   *Implemented Cases: The Other Party Involved*

When acting as complainant, Mexico achieved implementation by the US/EC in
two cases, whereas it has implemented four cases when defending against the
US/EC. Also, when it has attacked non-Members of OECD, it has achieved implementation in four cases; it has implemented its measures in three cases where
Non-members of OECD have initiated cases against it.

Table 2.23 WTO Cases: Implementation by the Other Party Classified
According to Its Economic Development

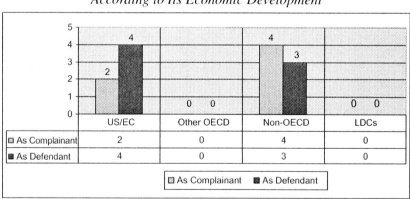

	US/EC	Other OECD	Non-OECD	LDCs
As Complainant	2	0	4	0
As Defendant	4	0	3	0

We now further disaggregate the implemented cases classified in accordance with
the other Party involved. The US has implemented 2 cases where Mexico was the
complainant:

(1) *US – Cement* (281); and
(2) *US – Tomatoes* (49);

and Mexico has implemented four cases brought by the US:

(1) *Mexico – Soft Drinks* (308);
(2) *Mexico – Beef and Rice* (295);
(3) *Mexico – Telecoms* (204); and
(4) *Mexico – Corn Syrup II* (132).

Guatemala and Mexico have each implemented one case initiated by the other:

(1) *Guatemala – Cement II* (156); and
(2) *Mexico – Customs Valuation from Guatemala* (298).

Venezuela, Panama and Ecuador have implemented one case each when Mexico has attacked them:

(1) *Venezuela – OCTG* (23);
(2) *Panama – Milk* (329); and
(3) *Ecuador – Cement II* (191).

Finally, Mexico has implemented one case initiated by Nicaragua and one by Chile:

(1) *Mexico – Beans* (284) (Nicaragua); and
(2) *Mexico – Matches* (232) (Chile).

Table 2.24 WTO Cases: Implementation by the Other Party Involved

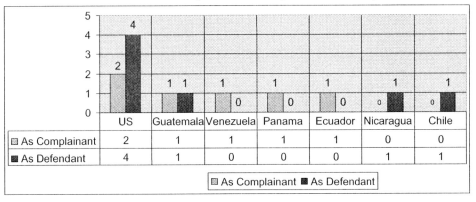

	US	Guatemala	Venezuela	Panama	Ecuador	Nicaragua	Chile
As Complainant	2	1	1	1	1	0	0
As Defendant	4	1	0	0	0	1	1

As Complainant   As Defendant

c.   *Implemented Cases: The Product Involved*

In cases of Mexico as complainant, implementation has occurred in four cases relating to trade in industrial goods:

(1) *US – Cement* (281);
(2) *Ecuador – Cement II* (191);
(3) *Guatemala – Cement II* (156); and
(4) *Venezuela – OCTG* (23);

and as defendant it has implemented one case relating to industrial goods:

(1) *Mexico – Matches* (232)

With regard to trade in agricultural goods, implementation occurred in two cases as complainant:

(1) *Panama – Milk* (329); and
(2) *US – Tomatoes* (49);

and as defendant it has implemented four cases relating to agricultural goods:

(1) *Mexico – Soft Drinks* (308);
(2) *Mexico – Beef and Rice* (295);
(3) *Mexico – Beans* (284); and
(4) *Mexico – Corn Syrup II* (132).

Mexico as defendant has implemented one case relating to trade in general goods: *Mexico – Customs Valuation from Guatemala* (298) and one case relating to trade in services: *Mexico – Telecoms* (204)

Table 2.25 WTO Cases: Implementation by Product

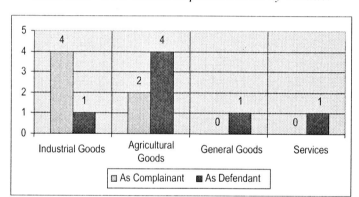

d.   *Implemented Cases: The Procedural Stage*

With Mexico as complainant, implementation occurred in four cases at the consultations stage:

(1) *Panama – Milk* (329);
(2) *Ecuador – Cement* (191);
(3) *US – Tomatoes* (49); and
(4) *Venezuela – OCTG* (23);

and as defendant it implemented three cases at consultations:

(1) *Mexico – Customs Valuation from Guatemala* (298);
(2) *Mexico – Beans* (284); and
(3) *Mexico – Matches* (232).

Two cases where Mexico was the complainant were implemented at the Panel/AB stage, after going through consultations:

(1) *US – Cement* (281); and
(2) *Guatemala – Cement II* (156).

As defendant Mexico has implemented three cases at the RPT stage:[54]

(1) *Mexico – Soft Drinks* (308);
(2) *Mexico – Beef and Rice* (295); and
(3) *Mexico – Telecoms* (204).

Finally, Mexico implemented one case at the Article 21.5 Panel/AB stage: *Mexico – Corn Syrup II* (132).[55]

Table 2.26 WTO Cases: Implementation by Procedural Stage

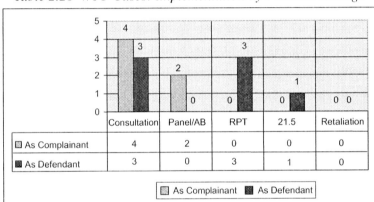

	Consultation	Panel/AB	RPT	21.5	Retaliation
As Complainant	4	2	0	0	0
As Defendant	3	0	3	1	0

i   Cases Litigated and Subsequently Implemented

When Mexico was the complainant, two litigated cases were implemented at the Panel/AB stage. Only one ended with a report by the Panel (not appealed), because the other one was suspended with a MAS. As defendant Mexico implemented three cases at the RPT stage and one at the Article 21.5 Panel/AB stage.

First, the implemented cases with Mexico as complainant:

(1) *US – Cement* (281). The Panel did not produce a report because the parties agreed on a MAS.
(2) *Guatemala – Cement II* (156). Mexico won eighteen findings and lost one. The Panel report in this case was not appealed – Guatemala withdrew the measure.

---

54. These cases went through the consultations and Panel/AB stages before being implemented at the RPT stage.
55. The US took this case through all the procedural stages up to the Art. 21.5 Panel/AB stage, when Mexico implemented.

Table 2.27 WTO Implemented Cases:
Findings Won by Mexico as Complainant

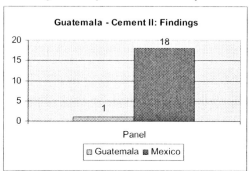

We now turn to the cases with Mexico as defendant. First, those implemented by Mexico at the RPT stage:

(1) *Mexico – Soft Drinks* (308):
 (a) at the Panel stage Mexico did not win any findings because the US won all eight;
 (b) at the AB stage, Mexico did not win any findings; the US won all three.
(2) *Mexico – Beef and Rice* (295):
 (a) at the Panel stage, Mexico won two findings and the US won thirteen.
 (b) at the AB stage, Mexico won one finding and the US sixteen.

Table 2.28 WTO Implemented Cases: Findings Won by Mexico as Defendant (a)

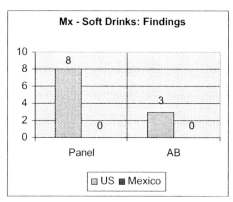
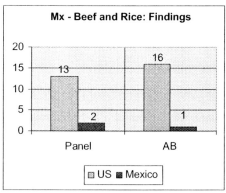

(3) *Mexico – Telecoms* (204). Mexico won three Panel findings and the US four.

Finally, the only case implemented at the Article 21.5 Panel/AB stage:

(1) *Mexico – Corn Syrup II* (132)

(a) at the Panel stage, Mexico won five findings and the US one (the Panel report was not appealed);

(b) at the Article 21.5 Panel stage, Mexico did not win any findings, and the US won two;

(c) at the Article 21.5 AB stage, Mexico did not win any findings; the US won all five.[56]

Table 2.29 WTO Implemented Cases: Findings Won by Mexico as Defendant (b)

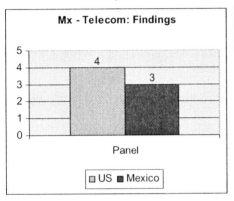
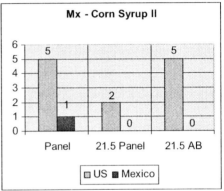

e.   *Implemented Cases Presented According to a Combination of Variables*

This section concludes the presentation of implemented cases by classifying them based on a combination of variables: the product, the other Party involved and the procedural stage.

Implementation occurred in four cases relating to industrial goods when Mexico was the complainant. When the US was the defendant, it implemented one case at the Panel/AB stage (*US – Cement* (281)). Venezuela implemented one case at the consultations stage (*Venezuela – OCTG* (23)); Guatemala one case at the Panel/AB Stage (*Guatemala – Cement II* (156)); and Ecuador one case at the consultations stage (*Ecuador – Cement II* (191)).

Two cases relating to agricultural goods were implemented when Mexico was the complainant, both at the consultations stage. The US implemented one (*US – Tomatoes* (49)) and Panama the other (*Panama – Milk* (329)).

---

56. For a full presentation of the findings won and lost in the totality of Mexico's cases, refer to Ch. 4, 'Mexico's Conduct of Its cases: An Explanation of the WTO Experience'.

Table 2.30 Mexico as Complainant: Implemented Cases Presented in a Combination of Variables

	Industrial Goods				Agricultural Goods	
	US	Vene.	Guat.	Ecu.	US	Panama
Consultations		I		I	I	I
Panel/AB	I		I			
RPT						
Article 21.5						
Panel/AB						
Retaliation						

Mexico as defendant implemented one case initiated by Chile relating to industrial goods (*Mexico – Matches* (232)) at the consultations stage.

Also as defendant, Mexico implemented four cases related to trade in agricultural goods, three of them initiated by the US. Two were at the RPT stage (*Mexico – Soft Drinks* (308) and *Mexico – Beef and Rice* (295)), one at the Article 21.5 Panel/AB stage (*Mexico – Corn Syrup II* (132)) and the fourth case, initiated by Nicaragua, at the consultations stage (*Mexico – Beans* (284)).

Mexico implemented one case related to general goods, initiated by Guatemala, at the consultations stage (*Mexico – Customs Valuation from Guatemala* (298)) and one case relating to trade in services, initiated by the US, at the RPT stage (*Mexico – Telecoms* (204)).

Table 2.31 Mexico as Defendant: Implemented Cases Presented in a Combination of Variables

	Industrial Goods	Agricultural Goods		General Goods	Services
	Chile	US	Nicaragua	Guatemala	US
Consultations	I		I	I	
Panel/AB					
RPT		2			I
Article 21.5		I			
Panel/AB					
Retaliation					

B.   WTO Pending Cases (Complainant/Defendant)

There are three pending cases involving Mexico as complainant:[57]

(1) *US – AD on Steel Zeroing II* (344). The Panel was composed by the Director General of the WTO (DG) on 22 December 2006.
(2) *US – OCTG* (282). Mexico requested consultations under Article 21.5 of the DSU on 21 August 2006.
(3) *US – Offset Act* (217/234). On 17 February 2006 the US gave notification that it had taken steps to repeal the Byrd Amendment. However, duties imposed on goods imported into the US up to 30 September 2007 will still be distributed after their collection.

Mexico as defendant has two cases pending:

(1) *Mexico – Olive Oil II* (341). The EC requested the establishment of a Panel on 7 December 2006; and
(2) *Mexico – AD on Tubes* (331). On 8 January 2007, the Chairman of the Panel advised that the latter hoped to complete the report by the end of March 2007.

Because all these cases are pending, none of them has been implemented. There are two cases, however, where the defendants have declared compliance but Mexico (as complainant) has not acquiesced: *US – OCTG* (282) and *US – Offset Act* (217/234). Because the matters were still under dispute as of the closing date of this work, we classify them as pending.

Table 2.32 WTO Cases: Mexico's Pending Cases

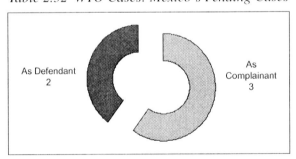

As Defendant
2

As Complainant
3

---

57. The cut-off date of this work is 1 Jan. 2007 for WTO cases, as indicated in 'Acronyms and Definitions'. For more detail on the pending cases where Mexico is involved as a Party, see the Appendix, Table 5, 'Mexico's Pending Cases in WTO' and Table 11, 'WTO Cases: Measures, Claims and Implementation'.

1.   Pending Cases: The Subject Matter

Mexico, as complainant, has cited the GATT in three pending cases, and the GATT
has been cited twice by complainants against Mexico. The ADA was the legal basis
of three cases with Mexico as complainant and one case where Mexico was the
defendant. The WTO Agreement has been cited by Mexico as complainant in three
pending cases, the SCM once by Mexico as complainant and once by a complainant
against Mexico, and the A. Agriculture once by a complainant against Mexico.[58]

Table 2.33 WTO Cases: Pending Cases by Subject Matter (WTO Agreements)

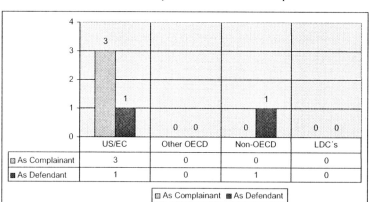

2.   Pending Cases: The Other Party Involved

Mexico is the complainant in three pending cases against the US/EC, while there
is one case, initiated by the US/EC, pending against Mexico. The other remaining
pending case against Mexico was initiated by a non-Member of OECD.

*Table 2.34 WTO Cases: Pending Cases Classified in Accordance
with the Other Party's Economic Development*

	US/EC	Other OECD	Non-OECD	LDC´s
As Complainant	3	0	0	0
As Defendant	1	0	1	0

As Complainant ■ As Defendant

---

58. For a disaggregated presentation of all Mexico's cases by subject matter, refer to Ch. 4,
     'Mexico's Conduct of Its Cases: An Explanation of the WTO Experience'. There we present
     the subject matter by covered agreement and by each provision of the covered agreements.

As complainant, it has three cases against the US:

    (1) *US – AD on Steel Zeroing II* (344);
    (2) *US – OCTG* (282); and
    (3) *US – Offset Act* (217/234);

and, as defendant there are two pending cases, one initiated by the EC and the other by Guatemala:

    (1) *Mexico – Olive Oil II* (341); and
    (2) *Mexico – AD on Tubes* (331).

Table 2.35 WTO Cases: Pending Cases Classified in Accordance with the Other Party Involved

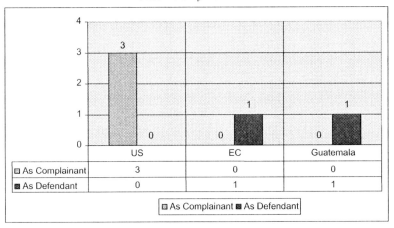

3.   Pending Cases: The Product Involved

We now turn to pending cases classified by the product involved. There are two cases relating to trade in industrial goods where Mexico is the complainant:

    (1) *US – AD on Steel Zeroing II* (344); and
    (2) *US – OCTG* (282);

and one case pending relating to trade in industrial goods where Mexico is the defendant:

    (1) *Mexico – AD on Tubes* (331).

In one case relating to trade in agricultural goods, Mexico is the defendant:

    (1) *Mexico – Olive Oil II* (341);

and in one case, relating to trade in general goods, it is the complainant:

(1) *US – Offset Act* (217/234).[59]

Table 2.36 WTO Cases: Pending Cases by Product

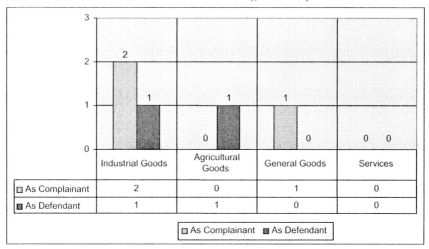

4.   Pending Cases: The Procedural Stage

There is one case with Mexico as complainant which is pending at the Panel/AB stage:

(1) *US – AD on Steel Zeroing* (344);

and two cases pending where Mexico is the defendant:

(1) *Mexico – Olive Oil II* (341); and
(2) *Mexico – AD on Tubes* (331).

There is one pending case with Mexico as complainant at the Article 21.5 Panel/AB stage:

(1) *US – OCTG* (282).[60]

---

59. We consider that the case *US – Offset Act* (217/234) had not been implemented at the cut-off date for WTO cases (1 Jan. 2007). On 17 Feb. 2006, the US notified the DSB that it had taken the steps to repeal the Byrd Amendment (WT/DSB/M/205). The Deficit Reduction Act repealing the Continued Dumping and Subsidy Offset Act of 2000 (CDSOA) provides that duties imposed on goods imported into the US up to 30 Sep. 2007 will still be distributed after their collection. See the Library of Congress at <http://thomas.loc.gov/home/c111query.html>, August 2009. See also Appendix, Table 11, 'WTO cases: Measures, claims and implementation'.
60. Mexico has gone through all the preceding procedural stages in order to challenge a reformulated measure before an Art. 21.5 Panel.

Finally, there is one case where Mexico has gone through the consultations, Panel/AB and RPT stages which is currently pending at retaliation, after Article 22.6 arbitration: *US – Offset Act* (217/234).

Table 2.37 WTO Cases: Pending Cases by Procedural Stage

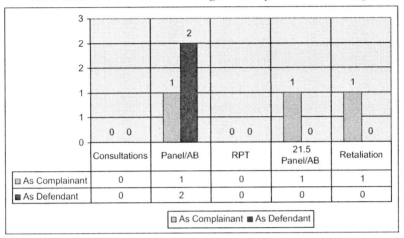

	Consultations	Panel/AB	RPT	21.5 Panel/AB	Retaliation
As Complainant	0	1	0	1	1
As Defendant	0	2	0	0	0

As Complainant   As Defendant

a.   *Litigated Cases that Are Pending*

A case is litigated if, after going through the stage of consultations, it enters into a subsequent stage of an adjudicative nature. Out of Mexico's three pending cases as complainant, a Panel/AB report has already been issued on two. One of them also has had the award on the RPT (Article 21.3 of the DSU) and the award on the level of nullification or impairment (Article 22.6 of the DSU). As of the closing date of this work, no Panel/AB report had been issued with respect to either of the two pending cases at the Panel/AB stage with Mexico as defendant. The two litigated cases as complainant with a Panel/AB report are:

(1) US – Offset Act (217/234):
   (a) Mexico and the co-complainants won four findings and the US ten at the Panel stage.
   (b) At the AB stage, Mexico and the co-complainants won four findings and the US seven.
   (c) At the Article 21.3(c) arbitration, Mexico and the co-complainants won 0.5 findings and the US won the other 0.5; and
   (d) At the Article 22.6 arbitration, Mexico and the co-complainants won 0.5 findings and the US won the other 0.5.[61]

---

61. Both arbitrators – i.e., Arts 21.3(c) and 22.6 – issued the awards using Salomonic judgment by ruling halfway between the two Parties' argumentations. Hence, we allocate half of the unit of account (finding) to each Party in both arbitrations.

Table 2.38   Mexico as Complainant: Findings Won by Mexico in Pending Case (US – Offset Act (217/234))

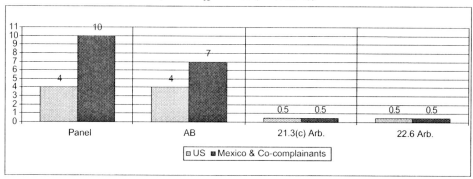

(2) *US – OCTG (282)*

   (a) at the Panel stage, Mexico won two findings and the US won eight; and

   (b) At the AB stage, Mexico did not win any findings and the US won eleven.[62]

Table 2.39 Mexico as Complainant: Findings Won by Mexico in Pending Case (US – OCTG (282))

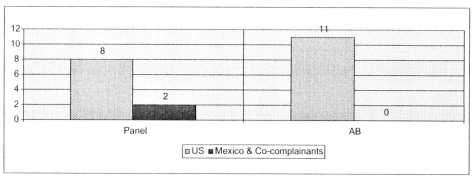

5.   Pending Cases Presented According to a Combination of Variables

To conclude, this section presents the pending cases based on a combination of variables: the product, the other Party involved and the procedural stage.

---

62. For a full presentation of the findings won and lost in the totality of Mexico's cases, refer to Ch. 4, 'Mexico's Conduct of its Cases: An Explanation of the WTO Experience'.

As of the closing date of this work, there were three pending cases with Mexico as complainant, all against the US. Two relate to trade in industrial goods: one was pending at the Panel/AB stage (*US – AD on Steel Zeroing II* (344)), and the other at the Article 21.5 Panel/AB stage (*US – OCTG* (282)). The third case relating to trade in general goods was pending at the retaliation stage (*US – Offset Act* (217/234)).

Table 2.40 Mexico as Complainant: Abandoned Cases by Different Variables

	Industrial Goods	General Goods
	US	US
Consultations		
Panel/AB	1	
RPT		
Article 21.5 Panel/AB	1	
Retaliation		1

We found two cases pending with Mexico as defendant, both at the Panel/AB stage. One, initiated by Guatemala (*Mexico – AD on Tubes* (331)), relates to trade in industrial goods. The other was initiated by the EC (*Mexico – Olive Oil II* (341)) and relates to trade in agricultural goods.

Table 2.41 Mexico as Defendant: Implemented Cases by Different Variables

	Industrial Goods	Agricultural Goods
	Guatemala	EC
Consultations		
Panel/AB	1	1
RPT		
Article 21.5		
Panel/AB		
Retaliation		

C.   WTO CASES WHERE MEXICO PARTICIPATED AS A
                        THIRD PARTY

Mexico has participated in thirty cases as a Third Party.[63] This final section
presents those cases, classifying them by the parties involved in the dispute,
the product involved and Mexico's intervention in the adjudicative
procedures.

We classify the parties involved in the cases in accordance with their economic
development, as set out above. In twenty cases, the complainant is a US/EC
Member: eleven were against other US/EC Members (US versus EC or vice
versa), six against other-OECD Members, and three against non-Members of
OECD. Three cases were initiated by other-OECD Members against US/EC
Members. Finally, Mexico was a Third Party in seven cases initiated by
non-Members of OECD: six were against US/EC Members and one against a non-
Member of OECD.[64]

*Table 2.42 Cases as Third Party Classified by Economic
Development of the Parties to the Dispute*

	Defendants			
	US/EC	**Other OECD**	**Non-OECD**	**LDCs**
Complainants				
US/EC	11	6	3	
Other OECD	3			
Non-OECD	6		1	
LDCs				

We note that Mexico participated as a Third Party in fifteen cases (51% of the
total) involving trade in industrial goods, seven cases (23%) involving trade in
agricultural goods, seven cases (23%) involving trade in general goods, and in one
case (3%) involving trade in services.

---

63.   We merge the DS numbers where a single Panel was composed for adjudicating the cases. For
      further details on the cases where Mexico participated as Third Party see Appendix, Table 6,
      'WTO Cases Where Mexico Participated as Third Party'.
64.   For an explanation of the categories used in classifying WTO Members, see 'Acronyms and
      Definitions'.

Table 2.43 WTO Cases with Mexico as Third Party
by Product Involved

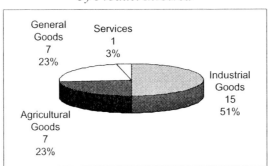

We note that 30% of the cases where Mexico participated as a Third Party had not produced a Panel report within the period of observation of our work.[65] In 50% of the cases where it was a Third Party, it intervened arguing either in favour or against one of the disputing parties. But in 20% of the cases it decided not to intervene and instead played a passive role as observer.

Table 2.44 WTO Cases of Mexico as Third Party
Classified in Accordance with Type of Intervention
by Mexico

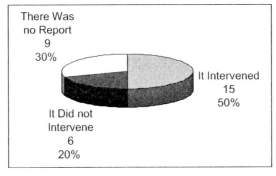

---

65. Some of the cases could have been abandoned. In some other cases the Panel report was issued outside our period of observation for WTO cases.

Chapter 3
Mexico's Cases under Preferential Trade Agreements

The cut-off date for this discussion is 1 January 2008.[1] Part A deals with the cases between Mexico and other sovereign states. Part B deals with Mexico's trade remedy cases under Article 1904 of NAFTA – that is, cases where individuals have standing.[2]

The following definitions are relevant to this chapter. They apply *mutatis mutandis*.

Finding won/lost by Mexico	Any successful finding by a GATT Panel, PTA Panel, WTO Panel/AB (original or Article 21.5 of the DSU) or Arbitrator (Articles 21.3 or 22.6 of the DSU).[3] We use findings as a unit of account. We do not pronounce on overall win/loss, which is a very difficult issue to tackle.[4]

---

1. The cut-off date for Mexico's cases under PTAs is 1 Jan. 2008, while for those under the WTO it is 1 Jan. 2007.
2. For more information on the PTAs, and their dispute settlement mechanisms, where Mexico is a Party see Ch. 1, 'Mexico's Options for Settlement of International Trade Disputes'. As we explain there, we do not cover Mexico's investor-State cases.
3. We determine success in findings by the Arbitrator under Arts 21.3 or 22.6 of the DSU by comparing them with the position sustained by each party to the arbitration. As an example, assume that a finding on RPT of two months and one party's position was one month and the other party's position was three months. Here we would allocate a one-half finding of success to each party.
4. For instance, even when the findings were in favour of the US in the *Mexico – Telecoms* (204) case, there were internal interests in Mexico that wanted to amend the domestic regulations, and some government officials used the Panel report as a leverage to do so.

For WTO cases, we distinguish the Panel findings from the AB findings by counting them separately. We do not count findings under Article 3.8 of the DSU – although we do take them into account if the Article was the legal base of a defence. Nor do we count absence of findings through judicial economy.

The findings from the Panel, as amended by the AB, may come from two sources: claims that were the basis of the complaint (Article 6.2 of the DSU) or defences presented by the defendant (such as Article XX of the GATT).

Implementation or measure amended

A measure is deemed to be amended or implemented when: (a) the complainant is satisfied with the amendment; or (b) the measure has been withdrawn no later than one year from the last communication of a disputing Party or an adjudicative body, and the complainant does not oppose the modification or elimination of the measure; or (c) there is a MAS.

Under WTO law, one finding of violation is sufficient to trigger the obligation to implement, unless the measure is no longer in force when the Panel/AB issues the finding. Article 19.1 of the DSU obliges Panels to recommend that the measure be brought into conformity, if a violation is found.

Other Party involved

When Mexico is attacking, the other Party involved is the defendant. When Mexico is defending, the other Party involved is the complainant. We further classify the other Party involved – the 153 WTO Members[5] – in accordance with their economic development

	as (a) US/EC (29 Members),[6] (b) other OECD Members (10 Members including Mexico),[7] (c) non-Members of OECD (80 non-Members)[8] and (d) LDCs or least developed countries (32 Members).[9]
Product	The good, service or intellectual property right subject to the dispute settlement mechanism; we classify them under four clusters: (a) industrial goods; (b) agricultural goods; (c) general goods; and (d) services (Mexico has had no TRIPS cases). There are some cases covering two products at the same time – e.g., *EC – Bananas III* (27), which dealt with agricultural goods and services. Those cases have been recorded by half units for each product (i.e., 0.5 for agricultural product and 0.5 for services).[10]
Subject matter	The WTO covered agreement under which the case in question has been adjudicated; in more detail, subject

---

6. This classification includes the twenty-seven Members States from the EC, the EC itself and the US. In addition to its Member States, the EC is also a WTO Member. However, as n. 2 of the WTO Agreement indicates with respect to the decision-making process of the WTO 'the number of votes of the European Communities and their Member States shall in no case exceed the number of the Member States of the European Communities'.

7. Excluding US and the EC; they are: Australia; Canada; Iceland; Japan; Korea; New Zealand; Norway; Switzerland; and Turkey (and, of course, Mexico).

8. These are the WTO Members that are neither OECD Members nor LDCs: Albania; Antigua and Barbuda; Argentina; Armenia; Kingdom of Bahrain; Barbados; Belize; Bolivia; Botswana; Brazil; Brunei Darussalam; Cameroon; Chile; China; Colombia; Costa Rica; Côte d'Ivoire; Croatia; Cuba; the Democratic Republic of the Congo; Dominica; Dominican Republic; Ecuador; Egypt; El Salvador; Fiji; the Former Yugoslav Republic of Macedonia; Gabon; Georgia; Ghana; Grenada; Guatemala; Guyana; Honduras; Hong Kong; India; Indonesia; Israel; Jamaica; Jordan; Kenya; Kuwait; Kyrgyz Republic; Liechtenstein; Macao; Malaysia; Mauritius; Moldova; Mongolia; Morocco; Namibia; Nicaragua; Nigeria; Oman; Pakistan; Panama; Papua New Guinea; Paraguay; Peru; the Philippines; Qatar; Saint Kitts and Nevis; Saint Lucia; Saint Vincent and the Grenadines; Saudi Arabia; Singapore; South Africa; Sri Lanka; Suriname; Swaziland; Chinese Taipei; Thailand; Tonga; Trinidad and Tobago; Tunisia; United Arab Emirates; Uruguay; Venezuela; Viet Nam; and Zimbabwe.

9. Those that are Members of the WTO are: Angola; Bangladesh; Benin; Burkina Faso; Burundi; Cambodia; Central African Republic; Chad; Democratic Republic of the Congo; Djibouti; Gambia; Guinea; Guinea Bissau; Haiti; Lesotho; Madagascar; Malawi; Maldives; Mali; Mauritania; Mozambique; Myanmar; Nepal; Niger; Rwanda; Senegal; Sierra Leone; the Solomon Islands; Tanzania; Togo; Uganda; and Zambia. See <www.wto.org/english/thewto_e/whatis_e/tif_e/org7_e.>, August 2007.

10. There is one NAFTA case dealing with services and investment at the same time.

matter also includes the article or provision of the covered agreement related to
the case. We only cover the claims set
out at the request for consultations.
Findings under adjudicative procedures
are covered in findings won/lost by
Mexico.

I.   COUNTRY VERSUS COUNTRY PTA CASES

Mexico participated in four country versus country cases[11] (three as complaint
and one as defendant). The following is a brief summary of the cases before we
go into more detail:

- *US – Safeguard on Broom Corn Brooms (NAFTA 20)* was initiated by
  Mexico against the imposition of a safeguard measure on broom corn
  brooms by the US. It submitted a request for consultations to the US under
  NAFTA Chapter 20 on 21 August 1996. The US withdrew the safeguard
  measure some time after the report of the Panel that found NAFTA violations by the US to Mexico's detriment.
- *US – Cross-Border Trucking (NAFTA 20)* was initiated by Mexico against
  the US on its moratorium on market access and investment on cross-border
  trucking. Mexico submitted a request for consultations to the US under
  NAFTA Chapter 20 on 18 December 1995. The Panel found against the
  US. The US did not, however, comply and maintained the moratorium.
- *Peru – Origin of Computers from Mexico (ALADI)* was initiated by Mexico
  against Peru's refusal to grant preferential treatment to computers from
  Mexico as agreed under ALADI. Mexico submitted a request for consultations to Peru under the dispute settlement mechanism of the ACE No. 8
  between Mexico and Peru under ALADI on 16 January 2002. The Panel
  supported the main claims presented by Mexico. Peru amended its most-
  favoured nation (MFN) applied tariff to zero for the products subject to
  dispute. This eroded Mexico's preference.
- *Mexico – Sanitarian Registry and Access for Medicines (FTA among Mexico,
  El Salvador, Guatemala and Honduras)* was initiated by El Salvador against

---

11. Country versus country PTA cases present additional difficulties for researchers. It is not pos-
    sible to find reliable sources of information with respect to requests for consultations, and the
    transparency and organization of the data is far more obscure than in WTO cases. At the WTO,
    publicly available information is compiled by the WTO Secretariat – e.g., claims, measures,
    dates of request – even when consultations under the DSU are kept confidential. For our work,
    we only cover those country versus country cases under PTAs that produced a Panel report. See
    Gantz (1999), 1057, for a compilation of information on all cases, even if they did not produce
    a Panel report. The author used news reports on international trade matters to compile the
    information regarding requests for consultations.

Mexico's phytosanitary procedures for registering medicines. In July 2006, El Salvador requested consultations under the general dispute settlement mechanism chapter of the FTA. The Panel supported the main arguments presented by El Salvador and Mexico implemented the report.[12]

A.   COUNTRY VERSUS COUNTRY PTA CASES: THE SUBJECT MATTER

One of the three cases with Mexico as complainant dealt with safeguard rules under NAFTA and WTO. The second covered national treatment and MFN treatment for services and investment in NAFTA; and the last one dealt with preferential rules of origin under ALADI. The only case with Mexico as defendant related to the sanitarian rules included in the relevant FTA.

Table 3.1 Country versus Country by Subject Matter

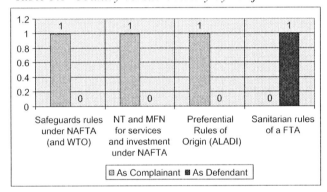

The three cases of Mexico as complainant dealt with the following subject matter:

(1) *US – Safeguard Broom Corn Brooms from Mexico (NAFTA Chapter 20).* The Panel ruled on Articles 801(1) and 805 of NAFTA, or Article 4 of the WTO Agreement on Safeguards[13] on the exclusion of plastic brooms from the determination of 'domestic industry'. Mexico considered them to be 'like or directly competitive goods'.

(2) *US – Cross-Border Trucking (NAFTA Chapter 20).* The Panel ruled on Article 1202 (national treatment for cross-border services) and/or

---

12. For more information on these cases, see the Appendix, Table 13, 'Country versus country (NAFTA Chapter 20 and like mechanisms of other PTAs)'.
13. Consultations were requested on 21 Aug. 1996 – i.e., after the Uruguay Round had concluded. The Panel report, however, refers to the Safeguards Code rather than the Agreement on Safeguards.

Article 1203 (MFN treatment for cross-border services) of NAFTA. It also ruled on Article 1102 (national treatment) and/or Article 1103 (MFN treatment) on the refusal to permit Mexican investment in companies in the US that provide transportation of international cargo. The Panel also analysed some possible exceptions in this case: Articles 1202 or 1203, or other provisions of NAFTA, such as those found in Chapter 9 (standards) or Article 2101 (general exceptions).[14]

(3) *Peru – Origin of Computers from Mexico (ALADI).* The Panel ruled on Articles 2, 9 and 15 of the Economic Complementation Agreement (ECA) No. 8, Article First and Tenth of Resolution 78, and Article First and Fifteenth of the Resolution 252 on Rules of Origin for Preferential Treatment.

Finally, the country versus country case with Mexico as defendant dealt with the following subject matter: *Mexico – Sanitarian Registry and Access for Medicines (FTA among Mexico, El Salvador, Guatemala and Honduras)*, El Salvador claimed violation of Articles 3-03, 15-05 and 15-10 of the FTA. It also wanted to know the extent to which the measure affected trade. It alleged that Mexico lacked proper procedures for registering medicines.

B.   COUNTRY VERSUS COUNTRY PTA CASES: IDENTITY OF THE OTHER PARTY INVOLVED

Mexico complained twice against the US and once against Peru, and it responded to claims by El Salvador once.

Table 3.2 Country versus Country: The Other Party Involved

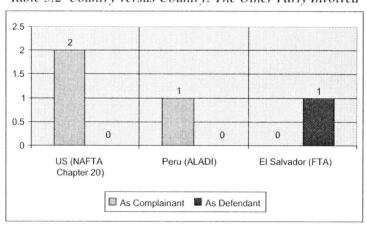

---

14. Contrary to our practice with respect to WTO cases, we include here defences in the subject matter of the dispute since Mexico included them in its first written submission after lodging its claims in the case, even though it was the complainant.

C.   COUNTRY VERSUS COUNTRY PTA CASES:
              THE PRODUCT INVOLVED

Out of the three cases of Mexico as complainant, two related to trade in industrial goods (*US – Safeguard on Broom Corn Brooms* (NAFTA 20) and *Peru – Origin of Computers from Mexico* (ALADI)), and one to trade in services and investment (*US – Cross-Border Trucking* (NAFTA 20)). The case where Mexico was involved as defendant related to trade in industrial goods (*Mexico – Sanitarian Registry and Access for Medicines* (FTA)).

Table 3.3 Country versus Country Cases: Product Involved

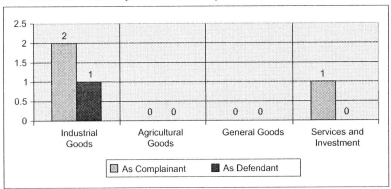

D.   COUNTRY VERSUS COUNTRY PTA CASES:
              THE FINDINGS WON

In two cases as complainant Mexico won 100% of the findings and in the remaining case it won between 60% and 84%. As defendant, it won 15%–29% of the findings.

Table 3.4 Country versus Country: Percentage of Findings Won by Mexico

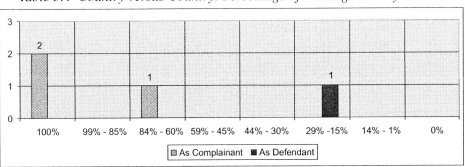

1.   Findings in Cases of Mexico as Complainant

a.   US – Safeguard Action Taken on Broom Corn Brooms (NAFTA 20)

Mexico challenged the imposition of safeguard measures by the US on broom corn brooms (industrial goods).[15] It initiated this procedure based on the dispute settlement mechanism of NAFTA Chapter 20. Consultations were requested on 21 August 1996. It instituted retaliatory tariffs against the US on 12 December 1996. The Panel report was issued on 30 January 1998 and the safeguard measure was withdrawn on 8 December 1998.[16]

(A)   *Measure Challenged by Mexico*
The safeguard measure on broom corn brooms (Proclamation No. 6961, 61 Fed. Reg. 64431-33 (4 December 1996) (To Facilitate Positive Adjustment to Competition from Imports of Broom Corn Brooms)).

(B)   *Mexico's Claims*
The US 'domestic industry' determination included only the production of broom corn brooms and not that of plastic brooms; Mexico argued that the two products are 'like or directly competitive goods'. It claimed violation of:
    (1) Article 801(1) and 805 NAFTA; or
    (2) Article 4 of the WTO Agreement on Safeguards.

(C)   *The Findings of the Adjudicating Body*
Mexico won four findings and the US none.

    The *Panel*:

    (1) *found* that the safeguard, based on an ITC determination that failed to provide 'reasoned conclusions on all pertinent issues of law and fact', constituted a continuing violation of NAFTA (*MX*); and

---

15.   The safeguard measure can be summarized as follows, as descried by the Panel in its report, para 13:

      Broom corn brooms (other than whisk brooms) from Mexico valued at no more than 96 US Cents remained free if imported in quantities within the global tariff quota of 121,478 dozen, but if imported in quantities over 121,478 dozen they became subject to an over-quota tariff rate of 33 US Cents in the first year, reduced to 32.5 US Cents in the second year, to 32.1 US Cents in the third year, and then back to zero; and
          Broom corn brooms (other than whisk brooms) from Mexico valued at more than 96 US Cents, formerly free of duty if imported in quantities within a tariff quota of 100,000 dozen but subject to a over-quota tariff rate of 22.4%, remained free if imported in quantities within the quota, but became subject to an over-quota tariff rate of 33% for the first year, reduced to 32.5% in the second year, to 32.1% in the third year; and then to the rate of 16%.

16.   On 28 Apr. 1997 Colombia challenged the same measure (Presidential Proclamation 6961) under the WTO dispute settlement mechanism. It claimed violation of Arts 2, 4, 5, 9 and 12 of the Safeguards Agreement and Arts II, XI, XIII and XIX of the GATT. The case did not go beyond the consultations stage in the WTO and never went to a Panel. Mexico did not seek to be joined in those DSU consultations. See WTO Dispute Settlement Database by Horn and Mavroidis <go.worldbank.org/X5EZPHXJY0>, August 2009.

(2) *recommended* that the US bring its conduct into compliance with NAFTA at the earliest possible time. (*MX*)

The *Panel* issued some intermediary findings:

(1) Since the NAFTA (Annex 803.3(12)) and WTO versions of the rule (3.1 of the WTO Agreement on Safeguards) are substantially identical, application of the WTO version of the rule would have in no way changed the legal conclusion reached under NAFTA. We rely on NAFTA substantive law. (*MX*)

(2) The claims were properly presented by Mexico and in a timely fashion. (*MX*)

b.   *US – Cross-Border Trucking (NAFTA 20)*

Mexico challenged the US moratorium on the processing of applications by Mexican-owned trucking firms for authority to operate in the US border states – i.e., market access for trucking services, and investment (services and investment). Mexico initiated this procedures based on the dispute settlement mechanism of NAFTA Chapter 20. Consultations were requested on 18 December 1995, and the Panel report was issued on 6 February 2001. The measure was not implemented by the US. As discussed below, on 23 February 2007, the US and Mexico started implementing a provisional programme aimed at opening the border to cross-border trucking services. The programme is ongoing at the time of this writing.

(A)   *Measure Challenged by Mexico*
Failure to lift the moratorium on the processing of applications by Mexican-owned trucking firms for authority to operate in the US Border States.

(B)   *Mexico's Claims*
(1) Article 1202 of NAFTA (national treatment for cross-border services) and/or Article 1203 of NAFTA (MFN treatment for cross-border services); and
(2) Article 1102 of NAFTA (national treatment) and/or Article 1103 of NAFTA (MFN treatment) by refusing to permit Mexican investment in companies in the US that provide transportation of international cargo.
(3) In its first written submission Mexico also contested possible exceptions to the rules that the US might seek to use in order to justify its case, including Article 1202 and 1203, as well as some other provisions of NAFTA, such as those found in Chapter 9 (standards) and Article 2101 (general exceptions).

(C)   *The Findings of the Adjudicating Body*
Mexico won four findings and the US none.
    The *Panel* unanimously found that:

(1) The US refusal to review and consider for approval any application by a Mexican-owned carrier for trucking services violated NAFTA:

(a) Annex I (reservations);

(b) Article 1202 (national treatment for services), and Article 1203 (MFN treatment for services); and

(c) an exception to these obligations is not authorized by Article 1202 and 1203 or by the exceptions set out in Chapter 9 or under Article 2101 (*MX*).

(2) The inadequacies of the Mexican regulatory system did not provide sufficient legal basis for the US to maintain a moratorium (*MX*).

(3) The US refusal to permit Mexican nationals to invest violated:

(a) Annex I (reservations);

(b) Article 1102 (national treatment – investment); and

(c) Article 1103 (MFN treatment – investment) (*MX*).

The Panel issued the following intermediary finding: there was no need for a Scientific Review Board (*MX*).

The Panel recommended that the US bring its practices into compliance:

(1) in doing so the US could require compliance with US regulations and require different Procedures in certain cases; and

(2) the issue of investment did not raise issues of safety as both Parties agreed.

c.   *Peru – Origin of Computers from Mexico (ALADI)*

Mexico challenged Peru's refusal to grant preferential treatment to Mexican computers (industrial goods). It initiated this case based on the dispute settlement mechanism of the ACE No. 8 between Mexico and Peru under ALADI.[17] Consultations were requested on 16 January 2002, and the Panel report was issued on 11 March 2004. With respect to implementation, we note that the MFN applied tariff used by Peru as of 2007 for the goods subject to dispute was zero. Hence, Mexico's preferential tariff was eroded. But we do not have information on whether Mexican exports between 2004 and 2007 were ultimately given preference.

(A)   *Measure Challenged by Mexico*
The refusal by Peru to grant the preferences to Mexican-origin computers.

(B)   *Mexico's Claims*

(1) Articles 2, 9 and 15 of the *Acuerdo de Complementación Económica,* or Economic Complementation Agreement (ACE) No. 8;

(2) Article First and Tenth of Resolution 78; and

(3) Article First and Fifteenth of Resolution 252.

---

17. See <www.aladi.org/nsfaladi/textacdos.nsf/inicio2004?OpenFrameSet&Frame=basefrm&Src=%2Fnsfaladi%2Ftextacdos.nsf%2Ftextacdos2004%3FOpenPage%26AutoFramed>, August 2009.

(C)   *The Findings of the Adjudicating Body*
Mexico won two findings and Peru won one.
   The *Panel* unanimously found that:

(1) Peru's failure to inform Mexico that the certificates of origin for computers were not in conformity with the rules for the establishment of origin was in conflict with its obligations relating to rules of origin set out in the ACE No. 8 signed by Peru and Mexico. Those obligations are contained in Article Tenth of Resolution 78 and Article Fifteenth of Resolution 252 (*MX*); and
(2) the measure adopted by Peru that required the payment of import tariffs on computers from Mexico was compatible with the rules of origin in the Partial Agreement on Economic Complementation concluded between Peru and Mexico. They are contained in Article Tenth of Resolution 78 and Article Fifteenth of Resolution 252 (*Peru*).

The Panel by majority found that the computers subject to dispute were of Mexican origin. Hence, Peru's failure to recognize that fact was incompatible with Article First of ALADI's Resolution 78, Resolution 252, and Articles 2 and 9 of the ACE No. 8 (*MX*).

2.   Findings in Cases of Mexico as Defendant

a.   *Mexico – Sanitarian Registry and Access for Medicines (FTA among Mexico, El Salvador, Guatemala and Honduras)*

El Salvador challenged phytosanitary issues relating to trade in medicines (industrial goods). It initiated this case based on the dispute settlement mechanism of the FTA among Mexico and El Salvador, Guatemala and Honduras. Consultations were requested on 18 July 2006, and the Panel report was dated 14 August 2006. As mentioned below, the measure appears to have been implemented for El Salvador:

(A)   *Measures Challenged by El Salvador*
Absence of procedures in Mexico's phytosanitary system for registering medicines.

(B)   *El Salvador's Claims*
   (1) Articles 3-03, 15-05 and 15-10 of the FTA (Mexico, El Salvador, Guatemala and Honduras).
   (2) The trade distortion effects of the measure.

(C)   *The Findings of the Adjudicating Body*
Mexico won one finding and El Salvador won five.
   The *Panel* found that:

(1) the parallel letters exchanged between the FTA Parties granted Mexico a waiver of two years in its obligations under Chapter XV of the FTA (national treatment) (*MX*);

(2) Mexico did not modify its measure to grant national treatment to producers, traders and distributors (nationals from an FTA Party) for the registration of medicines after the waiver of two years had expired (*El Salvador*); and

(3) the requirement by Mexico that the factory or laboratory be located in Mexico violated national treatment, 3-03, 15-05, and 15-10 of the FTA (*El Salvador*).

The Panel issued some intermediary findings:

(1) the claims were not extended by the complainant (*El Salvador*);

(2) the measure was not justified under XX(b) of GATT (incorporated into the FTA through 20-02 of the FTA). The parallel letters provided for registration but at the same time aimed to protect human life and health (*El Salvador*); and

(3) even though the complainant did not present evidence of adverse trade effects, a violation caused nullification or impairment (*El Salvador*).

E.   COUNTRY VERSUS COUNTRY PTA CASES:
            IMPLEMENTATION ISSUES

We start with those cases where Mexico is the complainant:

(1) *US – Safeguard on Broom Corn Brooms* (NAFTA Chapter 20): The measure was implemented, not immediately, as the Panel recommended, but ten months after the Panel report. On 8 December 1998, the presidential proclamation to terminate the safeguard measure was published.[18] Mexico had imposed retaliatory tariffs on the US on 12 December 1996. According to Mexico, the US measure affected trade to the value of approximately 1.4 million US Dollars (USD) in the first year.[19] The retaliatory tariffs imposed by Mexico affected: fructose, wine, wine coolers, brandy, Tennessee whiskey, notebooks, flat glass and wooden furniture.[20] The decree does not have a date of expiration, and we did not find information on when Mexico stopped the retaliatory tariffs.

(2) *US – Cross-Border Trucking* (NAFTA Chapter 20): The measure has not been implemented. On 23 February 2007, the US and Mexico started a

---

18. See 'Termination of the Safeguard Measure: Presidential Proclamation 7154, to Terminate Temporary Duties on Imports of Broom Corn Brooms', 63 Fed. Reg. 67761 (8 December 1998).

19. See 'US Safeguard Action Taken on Broom Corn Brooms from Mexico', USA-97-2008-01, para. 16.

20. These goods are classified under the following HS numbers in Mexican law: 1702.40.01 12.5; 1702.40.99 12.5; 1702.50.01 12.5; 1702.60.01 12.5; 2204.10.01 20.0; 2204.21.01 20.0; 2204.21.02 20.0; 2204.21.03 20.0; 2204.21.04 20.0; 2204.29.99 20.0; 2206.00.01 20.0; 2208.20.02 20.0; 2208.30.04 20.0; 4820.20.01 10.0; 7005.29.02 20.0; 7005.29.03 20.0; 7005.29.99 20.0; 9403.30.01 12.0; and 9403.50.01 14.0.

provisional programme aimed at opening the border to cross-border trucking services from Mexico.[21] The programme was scheduled to last for one year, and the first consignment by a Mexican company was made in September 2007.[22]

(3) *Peru – Origin of Computers from Mexico* (ALADI): Peru's applied MFN tariff as of 2007 was zero with respect to the goods subject to dispute. Hence, Mexico's preferential tariff has been eroded ever since. There is no information whether Mexican exports between 2004 (the date of the Panel report) and 2007 were given any preference. Mexico continued to export to Peru after 2004.

We now present material on the implementation of cases where Mexico is the defendant:

(1) *Mexico – Sanitarian Registry and Access for Medicines* (FTA among Mexico, El Salvador, Guatemala and Honduras): The measure has been implemented. The press in El Salvador reported that, based on an agreement between both Parties, Mexican legislation on the requirement for companies importing medicines to have a factory or a laboratory in Mexico would not be applied to El Salvador.[23] On 2 January 2008, Mexico added new requirements to its legislation which already required the presence of a factory or a laboratory in Mexico.[24]

II.   PRIVATE PARTY VERSUS COUNTRY (CHAPTER 19 OF NAFTA)

As explained in Chapter I, Panels under Article 1904 of NAFTA substitute domestic tribunals when challenging AD/CVD final determinations relating to the NAFTA region. The following is a hypothetical example of an AD order that has been challenged through a 1904 Panel:

For example assume that the investigating authority of a NAFTA Party has an AD order and issues different final AD determinations: final determination, first administrative review, second administrative review, third administrative review, fourth administrative review and a sunset review.

---

21. See <www.dot.gov/affairs/cbtsip/dot2107.htm>, August 2009.
22. See '*Continuará EE.UU. implementando el programa piloto de transporte transfronterizo terrestre con México*' dated 7 Jan. 2008. This information was published by *Inteligencia Comercial* (IQOM) <www.iqom.com.mx>, August 2009. Furthermore, in January 2008 the US Department of Transportation referred to the provisional programme to allow Mexican trucks to make international deliveries to and from the US; see 'DOT To Continue Mexican Truck Project despite Spending Prohibition', *Inside US Trade*, 4 Jan. 2008.
23. See '*Publica Secretaría de Salud requisitos adicionales para importar medicamentos producidos en el extranjero*', *Inteligencia Comercial* (IQOM) <www.iqom.com.mx>, August 2009.
24. *Ibid.*

The following table shows such a case where a given exporter, for instance, challenged three final decisions (within the same AD order) through the 1904 Panel: the definitive AD determination, the first administrative review and the third administrative review.

In our example, the Panel dealing with the final AD determination remanded the determination to the investigating authority for corrections. The investigating authority then sent back its re-determination to the Panel, which was sent it back again (remanded) for further amendments. Finally, the investigating authority sent its second re-determination back and the Article 1904 Panel affirmed it. The same situation occurred in our example, with respect to the third administrative review where we have three Procedures under a Article 1904 Panel. Still in our hypothetical example, the Panel affirmed the investigating authority's determination on the first administrative review. Hence, there were no further Panels with respect to the final determination of the first review.[25]

Table 3.5 Timeline of Article 1904 Panels under NAFTA

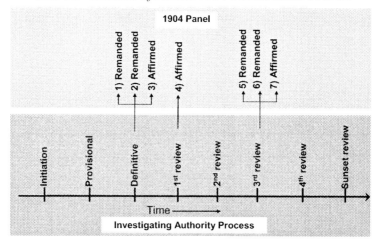

25. As noted below, the Art. 1904 Panel dealing with the AD order imposed by Mexico on sodium hydroxide (caustic soda) from the US found that under Mexican and NAFTA law Sunset Reviews are not final determinations in terms of Mexico's specific definitions. Hence, the Panel concluded that it was not competent to rule on a review of a Mexican Sunset Review. However, Sunset Reviews by the US have been subject to Art. 1904 Panels in AD orders like Cement from Mexico or OCTG from Mexico.

A.   THE AD/CVD ORDERS SUBJECT TO NAFTA ARTICLE 1904
PANELS AT A GLANCE

The CVD/AD orders related to Mexico that were subject to at least one challenge through an Article 1904 Panel can be divided into two categories. The first contain those where the Article 1904 Panel produced a report. We present these cases in detail. The other is made up of those where no Panel report was issued.[26] Following is a general overview:

(1) The US investigating authority issued ten AD/CVD orders that were subject to an Article 1904 Panel challenge. Six of them produced Panel reports. The other four did not.[27]

(2) The Canadian investigating authority issued two AD/CVD orders that were subject to an Article 1904 Panel challenge. One of them produced a Panel report. The other did not.[28]

(3) The Mexican investigating authority issued seventeen AD/CVD orders that were subject to an Article 1904 Panel challenge. Nine of them produced Panel reports and eight did not.[29]

We now present the AD/CVD orders subject to an Article 1904 challenge which produced at least one Panel report. Seven AD/CVD orders were imposed against Mexican exports, six by the US and one by Canada. Mexico imposed nine AD/CVD orders, seven against US exports and two against Canadian exports.

---

26. We do not present these orders in any detail. The reasons why an Art. 1904 Panel procedure may not produce a report are not very clear. Rule 77(1) of the 'Rules of Procedure for Article 1904 Bi-national Panel Reviews' provides that upon termination, a notice of final action shall be issued. However, we did not find any reference to it in many Art. 1904 Panel Procedures. This lack of clarity affects the cases with an Art. 1904 Panel requested and composed but without any panel report; and the cases where, after several remands/re-determinations, there is no information on the termination of the procedure. The reason why many cases do not have notices of final action might be lack of resources devoted by NAFTA Parties to the handling of these procedures.

27. The US AD/CVD orders subject to Art. 1904 Panel that did not produce a report are: AD Investigation on Certain Welded Large Diameter Line Pipe from Mexico (USA-MEX-2007-1904-03); AD Investigation on Carbon and Certain Alloy Steel Wire Rod (USA-MEX-2002-1904-10); AD Investigation on Purified Carboxymethylcellulose (USA-MEX-2005-1904-05); and AD Investigation on Stainless Steel Sheet and Strip in Coils (USA-MEX-2005-1904-06 and USA-MEX-2007-1904-01).

28. The Canadian AD/CVD order subject to an Art. 1904 Panel that did not produce a report is: AD Investigation on Wood Venetian blinds and slats (CDA-MEX-2004-1904-01).

29. The Mexican AD/CVD orders subject to Art. 1904 Panel that did not produce a report are: Investigation on Fresh Red Delicious and Golden Delicious Apples Originating in the US (MEX-USA-2003-1904-02); Investigation on Apples Originating in the US (MEX-USA-2006-1904-02); Investigation on Bovine Carcasses and Half Carcasses, Fresh or Chilled, Originating in the US (MEX-USA-2002-1904-01); Investigation on Imports of Carbon Steel Tubing with Straight Longitudinal Seam from the US (MEX-USA-2005-1904-01); Investigation on Hydrogen Peroxide Originating in the US (MEX-97-1904-01); Investigation on Pork Originating in the US (MEX-USA-2006-1904-01); Investigation on Seamless Line Pipe Originating in the US (MEX-95-1904-01); and Investigation on Cold-Rolled Steel Sheet Originating in, or Exported from, Canada (MEX-96-1904-01).

Table 3.6 AD/CVD Orders Imposed by/against Mexico That Were Challenged

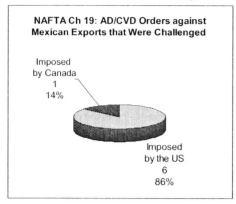

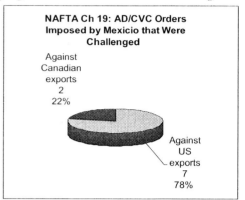

B.   THE AD/CVD ORDERS SUBJECT TO NAFTA ARTICLE 1904
            PANEL IN MORE DETAIL

We will break down the information into three sections. The first and second sections present the AD/CVD orders imposed by Canada and the US against Mexican exports. This is equivalent to cases with Mexico as complainant. The third section presents the AD/CVD orders imposed by Mexico against US and Canadian exports. This is equivalent to cases where Mexico is the defendant. Finally, the fourth section presents the only case we found relating to Mexico based on the Extraordinary Challenge Committee of NAFTA Chapter 19.[30]

**1.   The Orders Imposed by the US against Mexican
             Exports**

a.   CVD on Leather Wearing Apparel

On 10 April 1981 the US imposed final CVDs against Mexican exports of leather wearing apparel. The order was in effect until 9 August 1995 when it was revoked. Later, the revocation was amended to apply retroactively from 23 April 1985. From that date all unliquidated entries were to be liquidated without CVD collection, and any CVD collected after that date was to be refunded with interest. The amendment was made in light of another CVD decision (Ceramica) with similar facts which also lacked the injury determination, as described by the US investigating authority.[31]

---

30. For more information on these cases, see the Appendix, Table 14, 'NAFTA Chapter 19 Cases
     (Private Party versus Country on Trade Remedies)'.
31. See Federal Register: 24 May 1996 (Volume 61, Number 102), DOC [C-201-001], Leather
     Wearing Apparel From Mexico; Notice of Termination of the Countervailing Duty Administrative
     Review and Amendment to the Revocation of the Countervailing Duty Order.

The Article 1904 Panel Procedures:
An Article 1904 Panel dealing with the US Department of Commerce (DOC) final CVD administrative review (USA-94-1904-02) issued its report on 20 October 1995. It affirmed the determination because no written submissions relating to the determination had been received.

b.   *AD on Cement*

On 30 August 1990, the US imposed final AD duties against Mexican exports of cement ranging from 3.69% to 58.38%.[32] The order is still in effect but subject to a MAS, which provided for a gradual elimination of the AD duties and the settlement of NAFTA Chapter 19 cases and the WTO case.[33] The AD order on cement from Mexico was challenged sixteen times under NAFTA Chapter 19, contesting different final determinations within the same order. Some of them were remanded several times.

The Article 1904 Panel Procedures
We found ten challenges against final determinations within the AD order on cement that did not produce a Panel report:

(1)   Cement from Mexico: DOC Final Results of the 8th AD Duty Administrative Review (USA-MEX-2000-1904-03);
(2)   Cement from Mexico: DOC Final Results of the Full Sunset Review of the AD Duty Order (USA-MEX-2000-1904-05);
(3)   Cement from Mexico: DOC Final Results of the 9th AD Duty Administrative Review (USA-MEX-2001-1904-04);
(4)   Cement from Mexico: The US International Trade Commission (USITC) Final Results of the Five-Year Review of the AD Duty Order and USITC Dismissal of a Request to Institute a Section 751(b) Investigation (USA-MEX-2002-1904-01);
(5)   Cement from Mexico: DOC Final Results of the 10th AD Duty Administrative Review (USA-MEX-2002-1904-05);
(6)   Cement from Mexico: DOC Final Results of the 11th AD Duty Administrative Review (USA-MEX-2003-1904-01);
(7)   Cement from Mexico: DOC Final Results of the 12th AD Duty Administrative Review (USA-MEX-2003-1904-03);
(8)   Cement from Mexico: DOC Final Results of the 13th AD Duty Administrative Review (USA-MEX-2004-1904-03);

---

32. These NAFTA Panels have one parallel Panel procedure under the GATT and one under the WTO. See Ch. 2, 'Mexico's GATT and WTO Cases'.
33. For the text of the MAS relating to the US AD order on cement, see <ia.ita.doc.gov/cement-agreement/cement-final-agreement.pdf>, August 2009.

(9) Cement from Mexico: DOC Final Results of the 14th AD Duty Administrative Review (USA-MEX-2006-1904-03); and

(10) Cement from Mexico: DOC Final Results of the AD Duty Administrative Review (USA-MEX-2007-1904-02).

The other six Panel reports are set below. Some did not finish with a Panel report affirming the re-determination by the investigating authority. There is no clear information on whether they are active or terminated, as explained above. The only clear reference would be that there is a MAS with respect to the AD order on cement from Mexico.

Article 1904 Panel Number One
The Article 1904 Panel dealing with the third administrative review (USA-95-1904-02) issued one report on 13 September 1996. It found that the US final determination in the third administrative review (60 Fed. Reg. 26,865 (19 May 1995)) had been based upon substantial evidence on the record and was in accordance with the law.

Article 1904 Panel Number Two
The Article 1904 Panel dealing with the fourth administrative review (USA-97-1904-02) issued its report on 4 December 1998 affirming the DOC's determination.

Article 1904 Panel Number Three
The Article 1904 Panel dealing with the fifth administrative review (USA-97-1904-01) issued its report on 18 June 1999 ordering that the matter be remanded. It affirmed several issues: the refusal to revoke the order, the adjustments and the products in the course of trade, among others. It also remanded some issues: the determination of like product, the constructed export price, the differences in merchandise and the ministerial errors. On 10 February 2000, the Panel affirmed the re-determination on remand.

Article 1904 Panel Number Four
The Article 1904 Panel dealing with the five-year review (USA-MEX-2000-1904-10) issued its report on 24 June 2005. It affirmed some issues: the reasonable foreseeable time, the regional industry, the duty absorption, and cumulation. It remanded other issues: the standard of 'probable' or 'more likely than not'; the further explanation of the likely volume of subject imports, their likely price effects and the likely impact on the domestic industry if the order were revoked; the conclusion that all, or almost all, of the production in the Southern Tier region was likely to suffer material injury if the order were revoked; and the full evaluation of the Southdown acquisition.

Article 1904 Panel Number Five
The Article 1904 Panel dealing with the sixth administrative review (USA-MEX-98-1904-02) issued its report on 26 May 2005 ordering a remand. It affirmed some

issues: the refusal to revoke the order and the use of partial adverse facts, among others. It also remanded some issues to the investigating authority: the determination that certain home market sales were outside the ordinary course of trade, the calculation of differences in merchandise, and the constructed export price. On 3 November 2005, the Panel issued its report dealing with the re-determination by the investigating authority. It affirmed some issues and remanded those of ordinary course of trade and differences in merchandise adjustments.

Article 1904 Panel Number Six

The Article 1904 Panel dealing with the seventh administrative review (USA-MEX-99-1904-03) issued its report on 30 May 2002 ordering the matter to be remanded. It affirmed some issues: part of the home market sales and the ordinary course of trade, the adjustments, the partial adverse facts available, and the refusal to revoke the order. It also remanded other issues: part of home market sales and the ordinary course of trade, assessment of duties on a nationwide basis, bulk and bagged cement as like products, warehousing expenses and differences in merchandise, among others. The Panel issued the second report on the first re-determination by the investigating authority on 11 April 2003. It affirmed some issues: the part of home market sales and the ordinary course of trade that had been remanded, the partial facts available, the assessment on a nationwide basis, and the issue of bulk and bagged cement. It also further remanded the issue of whether under US law the sales by one company should be compared with the home market sales of another company. On 4 September 2003, the Panel issued the third report dealing with the second re-determination by the investigating authority. After affirming some issues, it remanded the decision to apply adverse facts available to a company that fully cooperated in calculating *Cementos de Chihuahua*'s importer-specific rate. On 25 November 2003, the Panel issued the fourth report dealing with the third re-determination by the investigating authority. It further remanded the issue of adverse facts available and instructed the investigating authority to use non-adverse facts available. The Panel made the pointed comment that it found particularly disturbing DOC's decision to deliberately disobey its instructions.

c.   AD on Fresh Cut Flowers

On 23 April 1987, the US imposed final AD duties on certain fresh cut flowers from Mexico. The order was revoked for an exporter on 14 May 1998 based on an administrative review. The rest of the order was revoked on 3 September 1999 because DOC found that the domestic interested Parties had withdrawn in full their participation in the ongoing Sunset Reviews. The AD order on fresh cut flowers from Mexico was challenged once under NAFTA Chapter 19.

The Article 1904 Panel Procedures

The Article 1904 Panel dealing with the administrative review (USA-95-1904-05) issued its report on 16 December 1996. It affirmed the determination on two issues: first, that Mexican exporters had made evasive and misleading statements on their obligations relating to tax returns in Mexico; and second, the issue of best information available. It remanded the file with instructions to assess the second-tier best information available rate of 18.20% for each Mexican complainant (Mexican exporters), since they had made efforts to cooperate with the investigation.

d.   *AD on Non-Alloy Steel Pipe and Tube*

On 2 November 1992, the US imposed final AD duties on non-alloy steel pipe and tube from Mexico. The order was still in effect as of 1 January 2008. It was challenged twice under NAFTA Chapter 19.

The Article 1904 Panel Procedures

Article 1904 Panel Number One
The Article 1904 Panel dealing with the administrative review (USA-97-1904-06) did not issue any decision. The Panel was requested in 1997, but we were not able to find any further information.

Article 1904 Panel Number Two
The Article 1904 Panel dealing with the final scope ruling of the AD order (USA-MEX-98-1904-05) issued four reports, the first on 19 November 2002. It remanded the issue of the refutable presumption. The correct presumption, according to the Panel, was that the merchandise subject to the scope ruling was outside the scope of the order, and the investigating authority should have considered any on-record evidence that might have demonstrated that the products were covered by the order (the US had taken the opposite presumption at the review). The Panel issued its second report with respect to the re-determination by the investigating authority on 16 March 2003. It remanded the file with instructions to use on-record evidence to determine whether the order applied to products intended for export. The Panel issued its third report with respect to the second re-determination by the investigating authority on 18 December 2003. It remanded the file with instructions to apply the definition of mechanical tubing when assessing the record evidence and to include the exporter's submission. It also asked the investigating authority to explain fully the reasoning behind its conclusions. Finally, the Article 1904 Panel issued the fourth report with respect to the third re-determination by the investigating authority on 7 June 2004. It affirmed the re-determination on remand, because it found it reasonable and adequately supported by evidence in the administrative record.

e.   *AD on Oil Country Tubular Goods*

On 11 August 1995, the US imposed final AD duties on oil country tubular goods (OCTG) from Mexico. The final AD duty in the original investigation was 23.79%. The order expired on 25 July 2006 through the second Sunset Review determination published on 22 June 2007. In that review, the US found likelihood of dumping but did not find likelihood of injury and withdrew the order. The AD order on OCTG from Mexico was challenged five times under NAFTA Chapter 19.[34]

The Article 1904 Panel Procedures

Article 1904 Panel Number One
The Article 1904 Panel dealing with the final determination of sales at less than fair value (USA-95-1904-04) issued its decision on 31 July 1996. It upheld some issues: the best information available in the calculation of financial expense and the rejection of the non-standard cost allocation method. It remanded the file for a detailed explanation of the reasons for the rejection of certain financial data.

Article 1904 Panel Number Two
The Article 1904 Panel dealing with the full Sunset Review of the order[35] (USA-MEX-2001-1904-03) issued five reports:

(1) Its first report was issued on 11 February 2005. The Panel remanded the file to determine whether the 'other factors' raised by the exporter in its 'substantive response' to the initiation of the Sunset Review were 'relevant' to the DOC's 'likelihood' determination; and to reopen the record for fact-finding on the exporter's 'other factors' regarding the determination of likelihood of dumping.

(2) The Article 1904 Panel issued the second report regarding the first re-determination by the investigating authority on 8 February 2006. It remanded the file with instructions to determine whether the decrease in the magnitude of the exporter's foreign currency-denominated debt in the Sunset Review period outweighed the 'likelihood'. If that were not the case, the investigating authority was directed to explain its determination. Alternatively, the investigating authority was directed to find no likelihood of continuation or recurrence of dumping.

(3) The Article 1904 Panel issued the third report dealing with the second re-determination by the investigating authority on 28 July 2006. It remanded the file, directing the relevant authority to reconsider its likelihood determination and either issue a determination of no likelihood or give a reasoned analysis to support a conclusion.

---

34. There are two parallel cases in the WTO. One of them was initiated by Mexico against the US (US – OCTG (282) and the other by Argentina against the US with Mexico as a Third Party (US – Sunset Reviews of AD Measures on Oil Country Tubular Goods from Argentina (268). The latter case later became US – AD Administrative Review of Oil Country Tubular Goods from Argentina (346), but this it is outside our period of observation for WTO cases.
35. This determination, 'Oil Country Tubular Goods ('OCTG') from Mexico: Final Results of Sunset Review of AD Duty Order', was published on 9 Mar. 2001 in 66 Federal Register 14131.

(4) The Article 1904 Panel issued the fourth report dealing with the third re-determination by the investigating authority on 17 January 2007. It remanded the file for either a determination of no likelihood to be issued or else a reasoned analysis to support the conclusion. It emphasized that it would not affirm the re-determination if the investigating authority continued to be disrespectful of the Panel's review authority under Chapter 19 of the NAFTA.

(5) The Article 1904 Panel issued the fifth report dealing with the fourth re-determination on 1 June 2007. It remanded the file, ordering the investigating authority to make a determination that the evidence on the record did not support a finding of likelihood of recurrence or continuation of dumping upon revocation of the AD duty order – i.e., the investigating authority could not prolong the AD order beyond the Sunset Review. The Panel added that, based on the evidence and the evasive attitude of the investigating authority, it assumed that the latter was not in a position to issue a reasonable affirmative likelihood determination. We were not able to find any further information on this Panel.[36]

Article 1904 Panel Number Three
The Article 1904 Panel dealing with the fourth administrative review and the determination not to revoke the order (USA-MEX-2001-1904-05) issued three reports:

(1) Its first report was issued on 27 January 2006. The Panel upheld some issues: the commercial quantity threshold for revocation of the AD order; the zeroing under US law; and the cost of export credit insurance as a direct cost of sale. It also remanded the file to recalculate the cost of production of the two sizes of pipe and the packing costs in the constructed value.

(2) The Panel issued the second report dealing with the re-determination by the investigating authority on 11 August 2006. The Panel remanded the file for reconsideration of the determination that an exporter did not ship in commercial quantities. It explained that the investigating authority acted in an arbitrary and capricious fashion by failing to justify its determination in relation to that exporter. It added that the result of the ninth administrative review could not be taken into account in the decision of the fourth administrative review.

---

36. As mentioned above, the order expired on 25 Jul. 2006 through the second Sunset Review determination published on 22 Jun. 2007. The finding of the Panel on the first Sunset Review was that there was no likelihood of dumping. However, the US found with respect to the second Sunset Review that there was likelihood of dumping but not of injury. The case was withdrawn by the US in the second Sunset Review.

(3) The Panel issued the third report dealing with the second re-determination by the investigating authority on 16 January 2007. The Panel affirmed the determination that the exporter did not ship in commercial quantities and upheld the determination not to revoke the order.

Article 1904 Panel Number Four
The Article 1904 Panel dealing with the final results of the administrative review (USA-MEX-2006-1904-06) did not issue a report. We found no further information on this Panel.

Article 1904 Panel Number Five
The 1904 Panel dealing with the 'USITC Dismissal of a Request to Institute a Section 751(B) Investigation' (USA-MEX-2001-1904-06) issued its report on 22 March 2007. It affirmed the determination.

f.   *AD on Porcelain-on-Steel Cookware*

On 2 December 1986, the US imposed final AD duties on Porcelain-on-steel cookware from Mexico. On 22 April 2002 it published a determination revoking the order as of 1 December 1995. From that date, all unliquidated entries were to be liquidated without AD collection and any duty collected was to be refunded with interest. The AD order on Porcelain-on-steel cookware from Mexico was challenged eight times under NAFTA Chapter 19.

The Article 1904 Panel Procedures

Article 1904 Panel Number One
The Article 1904 Panel dealing with the administrative review (USA-95-1904-01) issued its report on 30 April 1996. The Panel supported the investigating authority on the majority of issues involved. It remanded the file on the error associated with product number 10158 for further proceedings not inconsistent with its opinion. It also remanded the appropriate adjustment for rebated or uncollected value-added taxes with instructions for the DOC to apply the tax neutral methodology approved by the US tribunals. We have no further information on this first Panel.

Article 1904 Panel Numbers Two and Three
The Article 1904 Panels dealing with the sixth and eighth administrative reviews (USA-96-1904-01 and USA-97-1904-05) did not issue reports.

Article 1904 Panel Number Four
The Article 1904 Panel dealing with the ninth administrative review (USA-97-1904-07) issued its report on 30 April 1999. It affirmed almost all of the issues. It remanded the use of the global ratio in calculating Yamaka's indirect selling expense in order to determine whether its calculation was in fact a clerical error.

If so, the error was to be corrected and the basis of the correction explained in detail with comment specifically related to the proper calculation. We found no further information on this issue.

Article 1904 Panel Number Five et seq.
Finally, we found four Panels that did not issue reports. Those Panels, which dealt with different final determinations within the same order, are:

(1) The Article 1904 Panel dealing with the tenth administrative review (USA-MEX-98-1904-04).
(2) The Article 1904 Panel dealing with the eleventh administrative review (USA-MEX-99-1904-05).
(3) The Article 1904 Panel dealing with the twelfth administrative review (USA-MEX-2000-1904-04).
(4) The Article 1904 Panel dealing with the thirteenth administrative review (USA-MEX-2001-1904-02).

2.   The AD/CVD Orders Imposed by Canada against Mexican Exports

a.   AD on Certain Hot-Rolled Carbon Steel Plate

On 27 October 1997, Canada imposed final AD duties on certain hot-rolled carbon steel plate from Mexico. The original margin of dumping at the final determination was 26.2%. On 18 January 2003, Canada published in its Official Gazette a decision dated 10 January 2003 revoking the order. The AD order on certain hot-rolled carbon steel plate from Mexico was challenged twice under NAFTA Chapter 19.

The Article 1904 Panel Procedures

Article 1904 Panel Number One
The Article 1904 Panel dealing with the injury finding by the investigating authority (CDA-97-1904-02) issued its report on 19 May 1999. It remanded the file to determine whether, under Canadian law, a separate order was required with respect to Mexico and whether separate reasons were also needed. The same Panel issued the second report on 15 December 1999 dealing with the re-determination. It affirmed the allowance on the late disclosure or non-disclosure of certain material, given the tribunal's broad powers and the complainant's inability to specify the resultant prejudice; the decision not to issue separate reasons for an exporter; the determination with respect to cumulation; and the determination covering the non-exclusion of AHMSA (an exporter).

Article 1904 Panel Number Two
Finally, the Article 1904 Panel (CDA-MEX-99-1904-01) dealing with the new injury finding by the investigating authority, corrigendum to the finding of 27 October 1997, did not issue any report.

3.   The AD/CVD Orders Imposed by Mexico on Exports from its NAFTA Partners

We now turn to cases where AD/CVD orders imposed by Mexico against exports from the US or Canada were subject to a review by an Article 1904 Panel, and the Panel produced a report. We found nine AD orders: seven against US exports and two against Canadian exports.

a.   AD on Bovine Carcasses, Fresh or Chilled, from the US

On 28 April 2000, Mexico imposed final AD duties on bovine carcasses and half carcasses, fresh or chilled, from the US. The original margin of dumping in the final determination went from USD 0.03 to USD 0.80 per kg. The order is still in effect, because it was extended for five more years from 28 April 2005 through the Sunset Review's final determination published on 24 April 2006. The AD order on bovine carcasses and half carcasses, fresh or chilled, from the US was challenged once under NAFTA Chapter 19.[37]

The Article 1904 Panel Procedures
The Article 1904 Panel dealing with the final AD determination (MEX-USA-00-1904-02) issued its report on 15 March 2004 remanding the file. It upheld almost all the determinations. It dismissed some issues – the claims relating to the competence of certain authorities of the Ministry of Economy, and those on question-naires, evidence and arguments presented beyond the legal time limit. The Panel remanded the following general issues: the determination of a relevant market, the determination of an AD duty greater than the margin of dumping and the method-ology for calculating the margin of dumping for broker companies. Some specific issues were also remanded. The panel sent back the issue relating to the national production of meat in carcasses, fresh, chilled or frozen, with instructions not to include the totality of imports in the consideration of the rate of increase and to analyse properly the available and unused capacity of all exporters from the US following this Resolution. With respect to the national production of meat in bone-in and boneless cuts, fresh, chilled or frozen it remanded the file with an instruction to reach a finding of injury, carrying out the causality analysis required by Article 41 of the Foreign Trade Act. Finally, the Panel did not rule on the exten-sion of the deadline for the preliminary AD duties, because it considered that it did not have jurisdiction on the preliminary measures.

Finally, on 11 May 2007 the same Panel issued its second report on the re-determination. It affirmed the remanded determination by the investigating authority.

---

37.   The same AD order was challenged by the US at the WTO (*Mexico – Beef and Rice* (295)) but the challenge was not pursued at the Panel/AB stage – i.e., the US only challenged the beef AD order at consultations even though it pursued the complaint with respect to rice and some pro-visions of the Mexican Foreign Trade Act.

b.   *AD on Sodium Hydroxide (Caustic Soda) from the US*

On 12 July 1995, Mexico imposed final AD duties on Sodium Hydroxide (caustic soda) from the US. The original margin of dumping in the final determination was as follows: when the product was below the reference 'normal value' of USD 147.43 per metric ton, there was a requirement to pay the difference between the export price (ex-works) and the reference normal value. The maximum price payable was USD 38.89 per ton. The order is still in effect, because it was extended for five more years from 13 July 2005 through the Sunset Review's final determination published on 6 June 2006. The AD order on Sodium Hydroxide from the US was challenged once under NAFTA Chapter 19.

The Article 1904 Panel Procedures
The Article 1904 Panel dealing with the final AD determination of the Sunset Review (MEX-USA-2003-1904-01) issued its report on 13 July 2006. It decided, by majority (as opposed to in unanimity), that it lacked competence based on Mexican law to review the final determination of the Sunset Review. It explained that Sunset Reviews are not included in Mexico's list of final determinations subject to bi-national Panel review. It found no ambiguity, obscurity, or absurdity in this plain reading of the literal language of the Treaty.

c.   *AD on Cut-to-Length Plate Products from the US*

On 2 August 1994, Mexico imposed final AD duties on cut-to-length plate products from the US. The original margin of dumping in the final determination was from 3.86% to 78.46%. The order was revoked on 22 October 1999 through the Sunset Review's final determination published on 21 October 1999. The AD order was challenged once under NAFTA Chapter 19.

The Article 1904 Panel Procedures
The Article 1904 Panel dealing with the final AD determination (MEX-94-1904-02) issued its report on 30 August 1995. It remanded the file with the instruction to recalculate or clarify the calculations of freight adjustments and to determine injury without the use of the expert consultant's report on injury, unless opposing counsel had the opportunity to comment on the report as well as on the possible bias of the consultant.

d.   *AD on High-Fructose Corn Syrup from the US*

On 23 January 1998, Mexico imposed final AD duties on high-fructose corn syrup from the US. The original margin of dumping at the final determination was from USD 55.37 to USD 175.85 per metric ton. The order was withdrawn on 21 May 2002 in the Resolution passed to comply with the bi-national NAFTA Panel report published on 20 May 2002. The AD order was challenged once under NAFTA Chapter 19.[38]

The Article 1904 Panel Procedures
The Article 1904 Panel dealing with the final AD determination (MEX-USA-98-1904-01) issued its report on 3 August 2001. Having found that the investigating authority had failed to prove threat of injury, it remanded the file with two options: either to promptly terminate the order and refund the duties; or to re-evaluate the justification of threat of injury in light of the multiple proceedings already completed. The Panel noted that the investigating authority had expressly revised its reasoning in response to a WTO Panel that found violation on the threat of injury analysis and issued two essentially identical determinations of threat of injury.

On 15 April 2002, the same Article 1904 Panel issued a second report on the re-determination by the investigating authority. It remanded the file ordering the investigating authority to take action, no later than thirty days following the entry into force of this decision, consistent with the Panel's decision that the duties had been illegally imposed and collected. It noted that the investigating authority had had multiple opportunities to review the material and expand upon it as a result of the first WTO Panel and that there existed no support in the combined record for a conclusion of threat of injury.

e.   *AD on Polystyrene and Impact Crystal from the US*

On 11 November 1994, Mexico imposed final AD duties on polystyrene and impact crystal from the US. The original margin of dumping in the final determination was from 11.82% to 44.32%. The order was revoked as of 11 November 1999 through a Resolution published on 23 March 2001. The AD order was challenged once under NAFTA Chapter 19.

The Article 1904 Panel Procedures
The Article 1904 Panel dealing with the final AD determination (MEX-94-1904-03) issued its report on 12 September 1996. It affirmed the final determination.

f.   *AD on Flat Coated Steel Plate from the US*

On 2 August 1994, Mexico imposed final AD duties on flat coated steel products from the US. The original margin of dumping in the final determination was 38.21%. The order was withdrawn as of 2 August 1999 through the Resolution dated 27 October 1999. The AD order was challenged once under NAFTA Chapter 19.

---

38.   The same AD order was challenged through the DSU of the WTO in *Mexico – Corn Syrup I* (101) and *Mexico – Corn Syrup II* (132).

The Article 1904 Panel Procedures

The Article 1904 Panel dealing with the final AD determination (MEX-94-1904-01) issued its report on 27 September 1996. The Panel affirmed most of the issues. It remanded the file with respect to the company Inland and for further rights for evidence to be considered. With respect to dumping, it remanded the file for standard values to be determined for exports by New Process (another company), using the cost data it had submitted; for new price discrimination margins for that exporter to be computed; and for a new determination of injury to be made. In the case of the company USX, it ordered the recalculation of the export price based on specific instructions, with the determination of whether it caused injury. Also, it declared illegal under Mexican law the freight adjustments to export prices and the inclusion of expenses in the calculation of the reconstructed value for the company Bethlehem. On the injury side, the Panel remanded the file for the technical diagnosis to be considered, while maintaining confidentiality; for additional views to be considered on whether to exclude some products in the determination of threat of injury; for a new determination of threat of injury to be made in the light of these considerations; for comments on certain data used for the injury determination; for interested Parties to be allowed to comment on the data relating to the period after 1992; and for consideration to be given to whether the 'product mix' methodology used distorted price comparison.

The same Article 1904 Panel issued its second report on 15 September 1997 relating to the re-determination by the investigating authority. The Panel affirmed the issue of allocation of cost for New Process. It remanded the file for information and clarification of evidence used with respect to the New Process calculation and product exclusion; for New Process to be allowed to provide additional information and clarification of the evidence; and for a new dumping calculation for New Process and Inland to be made.

The same Article 1904 Panel issued its third report on 13 April 1998 relating to the second re-determination by the investigating authority. It affirmed the re-determination.

g.   *AD on Urea from the US*

The final determination was published on 17 April 2000 without imposing AD duties on imports of urea from the US. The petitioner, AGROMEX, challenged this final determination through an Article 1904 Panel. The re-determination by the investigating authority dated 18 October 2002 imposed AD duties subject to the resumption of domestic production by AGROMEX. The AD duties were designed as follows.

For urea from the US:

imports below 160 USD per metric ton would pay the difference between the import value and the reference price with a ceiling of 52.75 USD per metric tonne if they are from the US. If the import price is over this reference price, there is no AD duty payable.

The petitioner stated that it would recommence production on 15 January 2003. Hence, the AD duties would start on 16 April 2003 if 'AGROMEX' had resumed domestic production by then, or three months after domestic production had recommenced. 'AGROMEX' had until October 2003 to restart domestic production.

In a communication published on 18 March 2004, Mexico advised that the petitioner had not resumed domestic production by 31 October 2003. This was a prerequisite for the application of AD duties. Hence, AD duties were never applied.

The AD order on urea from the US was challenged once under NAFTA Chapter 19.

The Article 1904 Panel Procedures
The Article 1904 Panel dealing with the final AD determination (MEX-USA-00-1904-01) issued its report on 23 May 2002. It remanded the file to the investigating authority with two main issues for consideration:

(1) With respect to the legal standing of the complainant (the petitioner AGROMEX), the Panel found that the final determination lacked factual and legal analysis. The investigating authority concluded that the petitioner had not legal standing since it did not produce urea during the investigation.
(2) The Panel noted the issues of lack of analysis, allegations and evidence submitted by the complainant (the petitioner AGROMEX) were linked to the determination of legal standing. Consequently, the investigating authority's decision would be subject to the decision on that issue.

On 29 January 2004, the same Article 1904 Panel issued its second report dealing with the re-determination by the investigating authority, which it affirmed.

h.   *AD on Rolled Steel Plate from Canada*

On 28 December 1995, Mexico imposed final AD duties on Rolled Steel Plate from Canada. The original margin of dumping in the final determination was 31.08%. The order was withdrawn as of 29 December 2000 in a Resolution published on 30 January 2001. The AD order was challenged once under NAFTA Chapter 19.

The Article 1904 Panel Procedures
The Article 1904 Panel dealing with the final AD determination (MEX-96-1904-02) issued its report on 17 December 1997. It remanded the file with the following instructions:

(1) To establish from the record whether the company Titan was the sole Canadian exporter to Mexico in 1992; to establish the volume of exports attributed to Titan in 1992; to assess the significance of the exports for accumulation under Mexican law; to evaluate Titan's injurious impact in

1992; to substantiate the conclusion with the new evidence; and, to establish, if appropriate, a specific margin of price discrimination.

(2) With respect to Canadian exporters other than Titan, to reassess the countrywide price discrimination margin against Canada, since evidence suggested that only Titan had exported.

The same Article 1904 Panel issued its second report dealing with the re-determination by the investigating authority on 3 August 1998. The Panel upheld the re-determination except that the following was remanded:

(1) With respect to Titan, it ordered that no legal effect be given to the margin of 108% applied to Titan; that Titan be allowed to present evidence and comment on the analysis as an independent trading company; and that a new margin for Titan be calculated.

(2) It ordered that no legal effect be given to the margin of 108% applied to all other Canadian exporters and that a new margin based on the record and not higher than 31.08% be determined for Canadian exporters other than Titan.

i.   *AD on Hot-Rolled Steel Sheet from Canada*

On 30 December 1995, Mexico imposed final AD duties on hot-rolled steel sheet from Canada. The original margin of dumping in the final determination was from 15.37% to 45.86%. The order was withdrawn as of 16 August 1997 by a Resolution published on 15 August 1997. The AD order was challenged once under NAFTA Chapter 19.

The Article 1904 Panel Procedures
The Article 1904 Panel dealing with the final AD determination (MEX-96-1904-03) issued its report on 16 June 1997. It remanded the file with the following instructions:

(1) With respect to Titan, to allow imports coming from Titan and supplied by the company Dofasco the same treatment as imports coming from Dofasco; to assess specific duties *by supplier* for imports from Titan supplied by manufacturers other than Dofasco, and in so doing evaluate the impact of excluding the imports coming from Dofasco from the countrywide determination and assess whether they were still significant for the purpose of accumulation with imports from other countries. It also instructed that if the imports were significant, injury and causation for each supplier of Titan other than Dofasco should be analysed. Finally, it instructed that the AD duty be calculated for each Titan supplier other than Dofasco.

(2) With respect to the companies Algoma and Stelco, it said that the investigating authority should act on the basis that the legal requirements for imposition of AD duties for injury had not been met. This view was based

on the fact that the case was on injury and not threat of injury; that the two companies did not export the product during the period of investigation; and that both cooperated with the investigation.

4.   Extraordinary Challenge Committee of NAFTA Chapter 19

As explained in Chapter I above, the procedure of an Extraordinary Challenge Committee is designed to review possible Panel misbehaviour – i.e., misconduct, conflict of interest, due process, and jurisdiction. Mexico was involved in one report by a Committee dealing with Article 1904 Panels.

a.   AD Investigation on Cement

The Committee Procedures in the case (ECC-2000-1904-01USA) related to the Article 1904 Panel proceedings (USA-97-1904-01) reviewing the AD order on cement from Mexico imposed by the US. The Committee unanimously denied the petition and affirmed the 18 June 1999 report by the Article 1904 Panel.

The Petitioners of the Committee Procedures were the US and the Southern Tier Cement Committee. The Committee issued its report on 30 October 2003. It concluded that the petitioners had failed to demonstrate either that the Article 1904 Panel 'manifestly exceeded its powers, authority or jurisdiction' or that its determination on the single issue raised in the petition 'threaten[ed] the integrity of the Bi-national Panel review process'. The petition was accordingly denied and the 18 June 1999 decision of the Article 1904 Panel was maintained unaltered.

Chapter 4

Mexico's Conduct of Its Cases: An Explanation of the WTO Experience

I.   THE SUBJECT MATTER

A.   THE ALLEGED VIOLATIONS: AGREEMENT BY AGREEMENT

For the purpose of assessing the subject matter agreement by agreement, our unit of account is the WTO covered agreement cited in Mexico's cases at the consultations stage.[1] When Mexico has been the complainant (sixteen cases), the General Agreement on Tariffs and Trade (GATT) has been the most cited covered agreement. Mexico has argued violations of the GATT in thirteen cases. After the GATT, the Antidumping Agreement (ADA) is the agreement cited second most often by Mexico. Mexico has claimed a violation of the ADA in eleven cases. The WTO Agreement has been used as a legal basis for the complaint four times. Mexico has claimed that the Agreement on Subsidies and Countervailing Duties (SCM), the General Agreement on Trade in Services (GATS), the Import Licensing Agreement, and the Agreement on Agriculture have each been violated twice. It has argued a violation of the Agreement on Trade Related Investment Measures (TRIMS) once and the principle of non-discrimination once.[2] Finally, in one case Mexico made no claim at all.[3]

---

1. The sum of the covered Agreements cited will not be equal to the total number of cases, since one case may cite several covered Agreements.
2. In the case *US – Tomatoes (49)* Mexico claimed a violation of the principle of non-discriminatory treatment in international trade. It did not specify any particular provision of the WTO agreements. See the Appendix, Table 11, 'WTO Cases: Measures, Claims and Implementation'.
3. In the case *EC – Bananas (158)* Mexico did not present any claim of violation. The aim of the requesting parties in that case was to explore and consult with the EC on the evolution of its banana regime. See the Appendix, Table 11, 'WTO cases: Measures, claims and implementation'.

Table 4.1 Mexico as Complainant: Agreement by Agreement

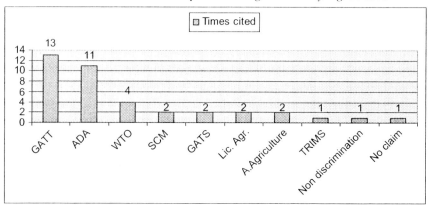

When Mexico has been the defendant (fourteen cases), the GATT has been the most cited agreement. The complainants have claimed violation by Mexico of the GATT in nine cases. The ADA is the second most cited agreement when Mexico is a defendant (six cases). Violations by Mexico of the Agreement on Agriculture have been claimed in four cases. Then, the SCM Agreement has been cited in three cases against Mexico; the SPS, the Licensing Agreement and the Agreement on Technical Barriers to Trade (TBT) in two cases each; and finally, there has been one case each of alleged violation by Mexico of the following agreements: the WTO Agreement, the GATS, a Ministerial Decision[4] and the Agreement on Customs Valuation.

Table 4.2 Mexico as Defendant: Agreement by Agreement

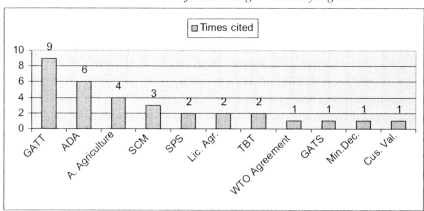

---

4. They claimed violation of the ministerial decision regarding cases where customs administrations have reasons to doubt the truth or accuracy of the declared value. Ministerial declarations
are not formally part of the covered agreements. Yet jurisprudence suggests that decisions may
even serve as an exception to basic WTO principles, such as the MFN obligations. (See the AB
in *EC – Tariff Preferences*, paras 101–102, WT/DS246/AB/R.)

B.   THE ALLEGED VIOLATIONS: PROVISIONS OF THE COVERED
       AGREEMENTS

For purpose of assessing the subject matter by provision of the covered agreement, our unit of account is the number of times a provision of a covered agreement has been cited in Mexico's cases. We count a case as one citation regardless of how many times a provision has been cited it.[5]

1.   The GATT

The MFN provision (Article I) has served as the basis for three cases when Mexico was the complainant and two cases when defending. Mexico has challenged the obligations with respect to the schedules of concessions (Article II) in three cases and has been challenged once on this score. On national treatment (Article III), Mexico has requested consultations based on this obligation three times and has been requested to consult three times as well. The antidumping (AD) provisions of the GATT (Article VI) have been challenged by Mexico ten times, and three times complainants have challenged Mexico. There has been one claim against Mexico for violations of the provision relating to valuation for customs purposes (Article VII). Mexico has claimed violation of the provision on transparency and administration (Article X) seven times, and other countries have used similar claims twice against Mexico. Mexico has made one claim of violation of the provisions on the elimination of quantitative restrictions (Article XI) and this claim has been used twice against Mexico. The consistency of measures with the provision on administration of quantitative restrictions (Article XIII) has been the subject matter of challenges by Mexico in two cases and of one case against it. Mexico has claimed violations of the provision on subsidies (Article XVI) in one case. In addition it has twice challenged the provision on nullification or impairment (Article XXIII) and has had to respond once on this score. One claim has been made that its practices were inconsistent with the provision on Preferential Trade Agreements (PTAs) (Article XXIV). Finally, Mexico has challenged once as complainant the consistency of practices of its trading partners with the provision relating to the modification of schedules (Article XXVIII).

Table 4.3 GATT Articles: The Times Cited

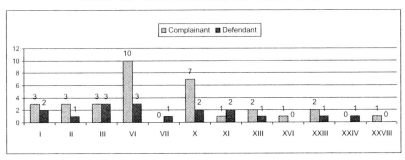

---

5.   For instance, if Art. 5 of the ADA were the legal basis of five claims in a given case, we would count it as one appearance in that case.

2.   The WTO Agreement

Under the WTO Agreement, Article XVI ('Miscellaneous Provisions') has been the only provision cited.[6] Mexico referred to this provision four times when attacking and has had to defend its practices once under this provision.

Table 4.4 WTO Agreement: The Times Cited

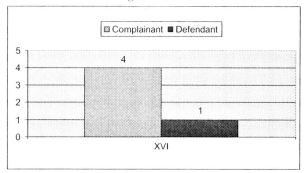

3.   The ADA

Turning to the ADA, the second most cited agreement, Mexico as complainant has cited a total of sixteen different provisions – Article 1 (Principles), Article 2 (Determination of Dumping), Article 3 (Determination of Injury), Article 4 (Definition of Domestic Industry), Article 5 (Initiation and Subsequent Investigation), Article 6 (Evidence), Article 7 (Provisional Measures), Article 8 (Price Undertakings), Article 9 (Imposition and Collection of ADD), Article 10 (Retroactivity), Article 11 (Duration and Review of ADD and Price Undertakings), Article 12 (Public Notice and Explanation of Determinations), Article 16 (Committee on AD Practices), Article 18 (Final Provisions), the Annex I (On-the-Spot Investigations) and the Annex II (Best Information Available). Fourteen provisions of the ADA have been cited against Mexico when defending – Article 1 (Principles), Article 2 (Determination of Dumping), Article 3 (Determination of Injury), Article 4 (Definition of Domestic Industry), Article 5 (Initiation and Subsequent Investigation), Article 6 (Evidence), Article 7 (Provisional Measures), Article 9 (Imposition and Collection of ADD), Article 10 (Retroactivity), Article 11 (Duration and Review of ADD and Price Undertakings), Article 12 (Public Notice and Explanation of Determinations), Article 18 (Final Provisions) and the Annex II (Best Information Available).

---

6.   The specific provision cited was Art. XVI:4 of the WTO Agreement, which relates to the conformity of internal measures with the WTO covered agreements.

Table 4.5 ADA Articles: The Times Cited

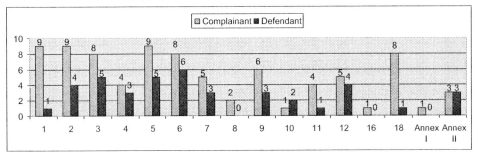

4.   The Agreement on Agriculture

Three provisions of the Agreement on Agriculture have been cited: Mexico has cited Article 4 (Market Access) once, and on two occasions it has been cited against Mexico. Article 13 (the 'peace clause') has been cited twice against Mexico. Finally, Article 21 (Final Provisions) has been cited twice against Mexico as well.

Table 4.6 Agreement on Agriculture: The Times Cited

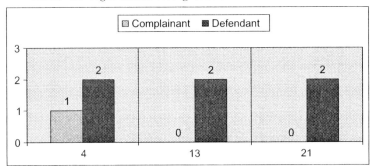

5.   The SCM Agreement

Seventeen provisions of the SCM Agreement have been cited in Mexico's cases (both as complainant and as defendant). As complainant, Mexico has cited ten provisions – Article 1 (Definition of a Subsidy), Article 5 (Adverse Effect), Article 6 (Serious Prejudice), Article 10 (Application of Article VI of the GATT), Article 11 (Initiation and Subsequent Investigation), Article 14 (Amount of the Subsidy in Terms of the Benefit), Article 18 (Undertaking of Countervailing Measures), Article 19 (Impositions and Collection of Countervailing Duties), Article 21 (Duration, Review of Duties and Undertakings), and Article 32 (Other Final Provisions). A total of fourteen provisions of the SCM Agreement have been cited against Mexico – Article 1 (Definition of a Subsidy), Article 10 (Application of Article VI of the GATT), Article 11 (Initiation and Subsequent Investigation), Article 12 (Evidence), Article 13 (Consultations), Article 14 (Amount of the Subsidy in terms of the Benefit), Article 15 (Determination of

Injury), Article 16 (Definitions of Domestic Industry), Article 17 (Provisional Measures), Article 19 (Impositions and Collection of Countervailing Duties), Article 20 (Retroactivity), Article 21 (Duration, Review of Duties and Undertakings), Article 22 (Public Notice and Explanation of Determinations), and Article 32 (Other Final Provisions).

Table 4.7 SCM Agreement: The Times Cited

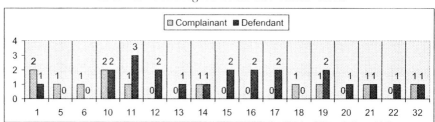

A further breakdown of the SCM Agreement based on its different parts would yield the following picture: first, the provisions of Part I of the SCM Agreement (General Provision) have been cited by Mexico twice and once against it. Part III (Actionable Subsidies) has been cited twice by Mexico but it has never been cited against it. Mexico has cited provisions on countervailing measures (Part V) seven times, and twenty times it has been cited against Mexico. Finally, Part XI of the SCM Agreement (Final Provisions) has been cited on one occasion by Mexico and cited by others against Mexico once.

Table 4.8 Parts of the SCM Agreement: The Times Cited

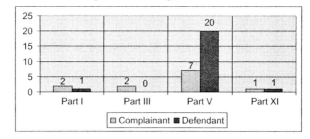

6.   The GATS

We turn now to the GATS. The provisions on MFN treatment in Article II of the GATS have been cited twice by Mexico as complainant. Article IV of the GATS, on the participation of developing countries, has been cited by Mexico as complainant once. Article VI on domestic regulations has been cited against Mexico in one case where it was defending its measures. The provisions on market access (Article XVI) have been cited by Mexico in two cases and by others against Mexico once. Mexico has cited the provisions on national treatment under Article XVII twice, and they have been cited once against Mexico. Finally, provisions in two additional instruments have been cited against Mexico one time each: those in Mexico's Reference Paper and in the Annex on Telecommunications.

Table 4.9 GATS Articles: The Times Cited

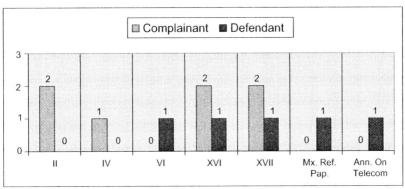

7. The Agreement on Import Licensing

Article 1 (General Provisions) of the Agreement on Import Licensing has been cited twice by Mexico and twice has been used against it. Article 2 (Automatic Import Licensing) has been cited once against Mexico. Furthermore, Mexico has claimed a violation of Article 3 (Non-automatic Import Licensing) in two cases, whereas it has had to respond to claims on Article 3 once. Finally, Article 5 (Notifications) has been cited once against Mexico.

Table 4.10 Licensing Agreement Articles: The Times Cited

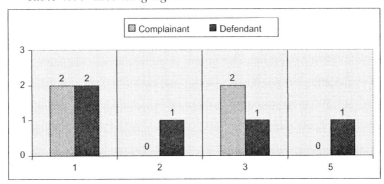

8. The TRIMS

Mexico has claimed violations of the following TRIMS articles one time each: Article 2 (National Treatment and Quantitative Restrictions) and Article 5

(Notifications and Transitional Arrangements). Mexico has not had to respond to claims based on the TRIMS.

Table 4.11 TRIMS Articles: The Times Cited

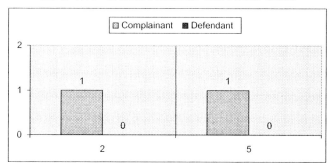

9.   The Agreement on Customs Valuation

The Agreement on Customs Valuation has been cited only against Mexico. Complainants claimed violation of fourteen provisions of this agreement, once each provision. Twelve of those provisions relate to 'Rules on Customs Valuation' in Part I of the agreement. One deals with national legislation ('Final Provisions' in Part IV). Annex I, relating to the Interpretative Notes, has also been cited once.

Table 4.12 Customs Valuation Agreement Articles: The Times Cited

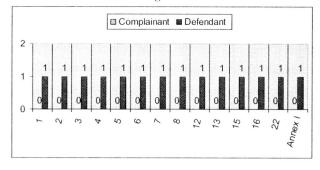

10.   The SPS Agreement

The SPS Agreement has been cited only against Mexico. Article 2 (Basic Rights and Obligations) has been cited twice; the provision on harmonization (Article 3) once; Article 5, 'Risk Assessment and the Level of SPS Protection', twice; the provision on transparency (Article 7) twice; and Article 8, 'Control, Inspection and Approval of Procedures' once. Finally, Annex B (Transparency on SPS Regulations) has been cited on one occasion against Mexico.

Table 4.13 SPS Agreement Articles: The Times Cited

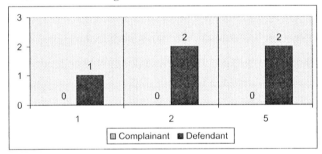

11. The TBT Agreement

The TBT Agreement has been cited only against Mexico. Complainants on one occasion argued a violation of Article 1 (General Provisions) and twice violations of each of the following provisions: Article 2 (Preparation, Adoption and Application of Technical Regulations) and Article 5 (Procedures for Assessment of Conformity by Central Government Bodies).

Table 4.14 TBT Agreement Articles: The Times Cited

12. Other

Mexico has argued a violation of the principle of non-discrimination in one case without referring to any specific provision of the WTO Agreement[7], and it requested consultations once without entering a specific claim in its request.[8] Violation of 'the Ministerial Decision regarding cases where Customs Administrations have reasons to doubt the truth or accuracy of the Declared Value' has been cited once against Mexico.[9]

---

7. See *US – Tomatoes* (49).
8. See *EC – Bananas III New Request* (158).
9. See *Mexico – Customs Valuation from Guatemala* (298).

Table 4.15 Other Provisions: The Times Cited

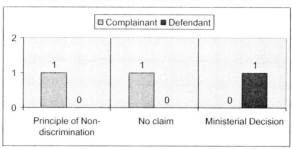

II.   THE IDENTITY OF THE OTHER PARTY

This section classifies defendants in cases where Mexico attacks and those where complainants attack Mexico. It does so using the economic development of both complainants and defendants as a yardstick. As mentioned above, we classify the WTO Members in four clusters: US/EC, other-OECD Members,[10] non-Members of OECD, and LDCs.[11]

Mexico has initiated ten cases against US/EC, and been requested to engage into consultations by US/EC nine times as defendant. It initiated six cases against non-OECD countries, whereas there have been five cases initiated by non-OECD countries against Mexico.

Table 4.16 Mexico's Cases: The Other Party Involved:
The Economic Development

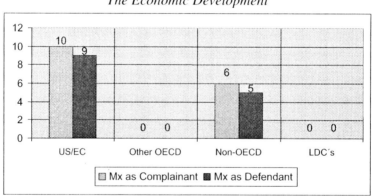

Disaggregating even further the disputes against US/EC, we note that Mexico has initiated seven of sixteen total cases against US,[12] and US has initiated six of fourteen total cases against Mexico.[13] On the other hand, Mexico has initiated three of sixteen cases against the EC,[14] and the EC has initiated three of fourteen cases against Mexico.[15]

Table 4.17 Mexico's Cases against US/EC

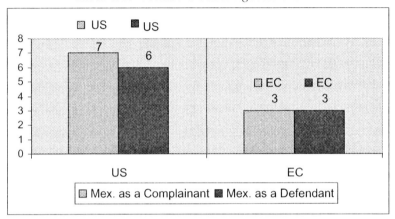

Regarding cases against non-Members of OECD, we note that Guatemala has been the most active counterpart. Mexico has initiated two of sixteen total cases against Guatemala,[16] and Guatemala has initiated two of fourteen cases against Mexico.[17] Mexico has also initiated two of sixteen cases against Ecuador.[18] Mexico has initiated one of the sixteen cases against Venezuela and one of the sixteen cases against Panama.[19] Finally, Nicaragua, Chile and Brazil have each initiated one of the sixteen cases against Mexico.[20]

---

12. *US – AD on Steel Zeroing II* (344); *US – AD on Steel Zeroing I* (325); *US – OCTG* (282); *US – Cement* (281); *US – CVD on Steel* (280); *US – Offset Act* (217/234); and *US – Tomatoes* (49).
13. *Mexico – Soft Drinks* (308); *Mexico – Beef and Rice* (295); *Mexico – Telecoms* (204); *Mexico – Swine* (203); *Mexico – Corn Syrup II* (132); and *Mexico – Corn Syrup I* (101).
14. *EC – Bananas III New Request* (158); *EC – Bananas III* (27); and *EC – Bananas III Old Request* (16).
15. *Mexico – Olive Oil II* (341); *Mexico – Olive Oil I* (314); and *Mexico – Customs Valuation from EC* (53).
16. *Guatemala – Cement II* (156) and *Guatemala – Cement I* (60).
17. *Mexico – AD on Tubes* (331) and *Mexico – Customs Valuation from Guatemala* (298).
18. Ecuador – Cement II (191) and Ecuador – Cement I (182).
19. *Venezuela – OCTG* (23) and *Panama – Milk* (329).
20. *Mexico – Beans* (284); *Mexico – Matches* (232); and *Mexico – Transformers* (216).

Table 4.18 Mexico's Cases against Non-Members of OECD

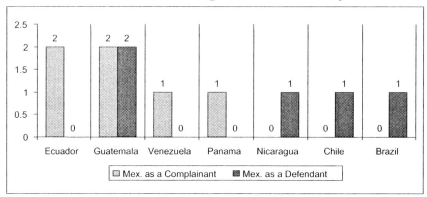

Finally, the US has been the target of Mexico's complaints in 43% of the cases, whereas the US has initiated 44% of the complaints against Mexico. Mexico has initiated 19% of its cases against the EC while the EC has initiated 21% of the cases against Mexico. Mexico has initiated 13% of the cases against Guatemala and Guatemala 14% of the cases against Mexico. Mexico has initiated 13% of its cases against Ecuador, 6% against Venezuela and 6% against Panama. Finally, Nicaragua, Chile and Brazil have initiated each 7% of the cases against Mexico.

Table 4.19 Mexico's Cases Classified by the Other Party Involved

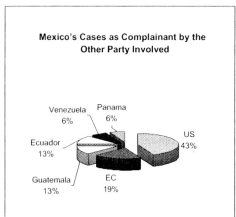
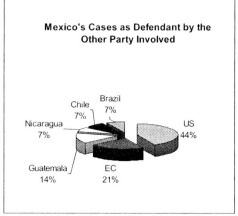

III.   THE PRODUCTS AT ISSUE IN CASES INVOLVING
                MEXICO: AS COMPLAINANT AND AS DEFENDANT

Mexico's cases, as both a complainant and a defendant, deal with trade in goods – agricultural, industrial or general – and services. Out of the sixteen cases where Mexico has been the complainant, 22% relate to trade in agricultural goods, 63%

to industrial goods, 6% to general goods and 9% to services. On the other hand, when Mexico has defended (fourteen cases), the disputes relating to agricultural goods represent 58% of the total disputes, while 21% have dealt with industrial goods, 14% general goods, and 7% services.

Table 4.20 Mexico's Cases by Product Percentage

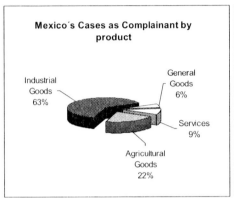
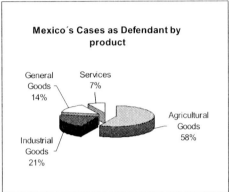

Disaggregating the material provided on Mexico's cases product by product, Mexico as complainant initiated 3.5 cases relating to trade in agriculture:

(1) *Panama – Milk* (329);
(2) *US – Tomatoes* (49);
(3) *EC – Bananas III New Request* (158);
(4) *EC – Bananas III* (27); and
(5) *EC – Bananas III Old Request* (16).[21]

As defendant, Mexico has had to respond to eight cases initiated against it on trade in agricultural products:

(1) *Mexico – Beef and Rice* (295);
(2) *Mexico – Beans* (284);
(3) *Mexico – Corn Syrup II* (132);
(4) *Mexico – Corn Syrup I* (101);
(5) *Mexico – Swine* (203);
(6) *Mexico – Olive Oil II* (341);
(7) *Mexico – Olive Oil I* (314); and
(8) *Mexico – Soft Drinks* (308).

As complainant Mexico has initiated ten cases relating to trade in industrial goods:

(1) *US – Cement* (281);
(2) *Ecuador – Cement II* (191);

---

21. All three *EC – Bananas* cases dealt with both trade in agricultural goods and trade in services. Hence, we classify each case as 0.5 relating to agricultural goods and 0.5 to services.

(3) *Ecuador – Cement I* (182);
(4) *Guatemala – Cement II* (156);
(5) *Guatemala – Cement I* (60);
(6) *US – AD on Steel Zeroing II* (344);
(7) *US – AD on Steel Zeroing I* (325);
(8) *US – OCTG* (282);
(9) *US – CVD on Steel* (280); and
(10)*Venezuela – OCTG* (23).

Complainants, on the other hand, have initiated three cases against Mexico relating to trade in industrial goods:

(1) *Mexico – Transformers* (216);
(2) *Mexico – Matches* (232); and
(3) *Mexico – AD on Tubes* (331).

Mexico as complainant has initiated one case relating to trade in general goods:
    US – Offset Act (217/234);
whereas Mexico has defended two cases relating to trade in general goods initiated against it:

(1) *Mexico – Customs Valuation from Guatemala* (298); and
(2) *Mexico – Customs Valuation from EC* (53).

Finally, Mexico has initiated as complainant 1.5 cases relating to trade in services:

(1) *EC – Bananas III New Request* (158);
(2) *EC – Bananas III* (27); and
(3) *EC – Bananas III Old* Request (16);[22]

whereas the complainants against Mexico have initiated one case against Mexico relating to trade in services: *Mexico – Telecoms* (204).

Table 4.21 Mexico's Cases by Product (Number of Cases)

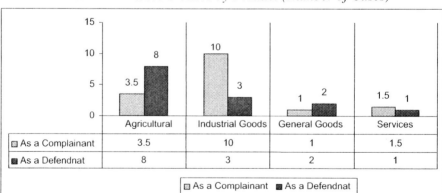

	Agricultural	Industrial Goods	General Goods	Services
As a Complainant	3.5	10	1	1.5
As a Defendnat	8	3	2	1

---

22. *Ibid.*

IV.   WHO RULED?

This section sets out the nationality of the decision makers in Mexico's cases. There is a fundamental distinction between the selection of Panel members and AB members. There is a standing AB of seven members working in divisions of three members, whereas Panel members were selected on a case-by-case basis by agreement of the Parties or by appointment by the WTO Director General. Hence, the Parties have significantly more influence in the selection of panellists than in the selection of AB members for a division.[23]

We observe that there were four Panel members from the US/EC when Mexico was the complainant and five when it was the defendant. There were seven Panel members from other-OECD countries when Mexico was the complainant, and six when it was the defendant. There were ten Panel members from non-OECD countries when Mexico was the complainant and also ten when it was the defendant.[24]

Table 4.22 Panellists (Ordinary Panel and 21.5 Panel) in WTO Cases: Nationality by Economic Development

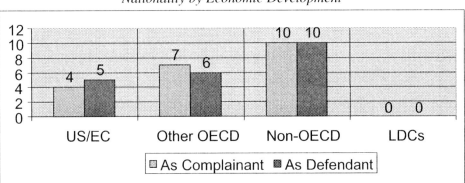

When Mexico was the complainant, there were two AB members with US/EC nationality, whereas there were three AB members with US/EC nationality when Mexico was the defendant. Five of AB members had other-OECD nationalities when Mexico was the complainant, whereas three were other-OECD when Mexico was the defendant. Finally, there were five AB members from non-OECD countries when Mexico was the complainant and three when Mexico was defending its measures.

---

23. See Ch. 1, 'Mexico's Options for Settlement of International Trade Disputes', for details on the process.
24. For an explanation of the groupings (US/EC; other OECD; non-OECD; and LDCs) see 'Acronyms and Definitions'.

Table 4.23 AB Members (Ordinary Appeal and 21.5 Appeal) in WTO Cases: Nationality by Economic Development

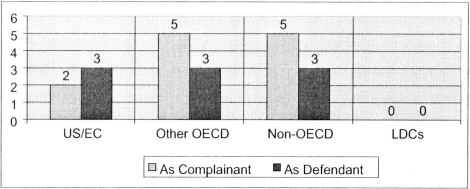

We found three cases where panellists did not issue a report. There was one panellist from the Czech Republic (Peter Palecka – Chair), one from New Zealand (Martin Garcia), and from South Africa (David Unterhalter) in a case where Mexico was the complainant (*US – Cement* (281)) and the Director General selected the panellists. This case was suspended by the MAS of Mexico and the US.

When Mexico was the defendant, there were two cases with no ruling issued by the Panel. In one pending case (*Mexico – AD on Tubes* (331)) the Parties agreed on the selection of the panellists: one from Uruguay, Julio Lacarte-Muro (Chair); one from Ecuador, Cristian Espinosa Cañizares; and one from Chile, Alvaro Espinoza. The other pending case with Mexico as defendant (*Mexico – Olive Oil II* (341)), which was composed by the WTO Director General, has one panellist from Canada, Debra Steger (Chair); one from Chile, Gloria Peña; and one from South Africa, Jan Heukelman.

Table 4.24 WTO Panellists in Cases without a Report

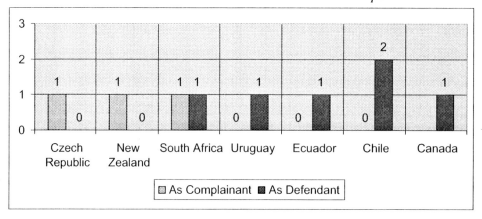

We now deal with the panellists, from ordinary Panels or Article 21.5 Panels, in Mexico's cases where a report has been issued – i.e., not only has a Panel been composed, but a report has been issued as well. We note that these panellists came from seventeen different nationalities, and we distinguish between cases where Mexico acted as complainant and those where it was a defendant. Unless specified, the panellists were selected by the Director General and not by agreement of the Parties:

(1) New Zealand: two panellists where Mexico was complainant (Bruce Cullen, *US* – AD *on Steel Zeroing II* (344), and William Falconer, *US* – *Offset Act* (217/234)) and two panellists where Mexico was defendant (David Walker, *Mexico* – *Soft Drinks* (308) (agreement by the Parties), and Crawford Falconer (Chair), *Mexico* – *Beef and Rice* (295));

(2) South Africa: two panellists where Mexico was complainant (Johannes Human (Chair), *Guatemala* – *Cement II* (156), and Leora Blumberg, *US* – *AD on Steel Zeroing II* (344));

(3) Venezuela: two panellists where Mexico was complainant (Oscar Hernández, *Guatemala* – *Cement II* (156), and Gerardo Teodoro Thielen Graterol, *Guatemala* – *Cement I* (60)) and one panellist where Mexico was defendant (Enie Neri de Ross, *Mexico* – *Beef and Rice* (295));

(4) Switzerland: two panellists where Mexico was complainant (Luzius Wasescha (Chair), *US* – *Offset Act* (217/234), and Christian Haberli, *EC* – *Bananas III* (27));

(5) Australia: two panellists where Mexico was complainant (Stephanie Sin Far Man, *US* – *OCTG* (282) (agreement by the Parties), and Kym Anderson, *EC* – *Bananas III* (27)) and one panellist where Mexico was defendant (Paul O'Connor, *Mexico* – *Corn Syrup II* (132) Article 21.5 Panel (agreement by the Parties));

(6) Philippines: two panellists where Mexico was complainant (Antonio Buencamino, *Guatemala* – *Cement II* (156), and Antonio S. Buencamino, *Guatemala* – *Cement I* (60));

(7) Sweden: one panellist where Mexico was complainant (Christer Manhusen (Chair) *US* – *OCTG* (282) (agreement by the Parties)) and two panellists where Mexico was defendant (Christer Manhusen (Chair), *Mexico* – *Corn Syrup II* (132) (agreement by the Parties) and Christer Manhusen (Chair), *Mexico* – *Corn Syrup II* (132) Article 21.5 Panel (agreement by the Parties));

(8) United Kingdom: one panellist where Mexico was complainant (Alistair James Stewart, *US* – *OCTG* (282) (agreement by the Parties)) and one panellist where Mexico was defendant (Edmond McGovern, *Mexico* – *Soft Drinks* (308) (agreement by the Parties));

(9) Egypt: one panellist where Mexico was complainant (Maamoun Abdel-Fattah, *US* – *Offset Act* (217/234));

(10) Argentina: one panellist where Mexico was complainant (Alberto Juan Dumont (Chair), *US* – *AD on Steel Zeroing II* (344));

(11) Germany: one panellist where Mexico was complainant (Klaus Kautzor-Schröder (Chair), *Guatemala – Cement I* (60)) and one panellist where Mexico was defendant (Ernst-Ulrich Petersmann (Chair), *Mexico – Telecoms* (204));

(12) Hong Kong: one panellist where Mexico was complainant (Stuart Harbinson (Chair), *EC – Bananas III* (27)) and one panellist where Mexico was defendant (Raymond Tam, *Mexico – Telecoms* (204));

(13) Costa Rica: one panellist where Mexico was defendant (Ronald Saborío Soto (Chair), *Mexico – Soft Drinks* (308) (agreement by the Parties));

(14) Brazil: one panellist where Mexico was defendant (Marta Calmon Lemme, *Mexico – Beef and Rice* (295));

(15) Chile: one panellist where Mexico was defendant (Björn Wellenius, *Mexico – Telecoms* (204));

(16) The Netherlands: one panellist where Mexico was defendant (Edwin Vermulst, *Mexico – Corn Syrup II* (132) (agreement by the Parties)); and

(17) Canada: two panellists where Mexico was defendant (Gerald Salembier, *Mexico – Corn Syrup II* (132) (agreement by the Parties), and Gerald Salembier, *Mexico – Corn Syrup II* (132) Article 21.5 panel (agreement by the Parties)).

Table 4.25 WTO Panellists in Cases with a Report

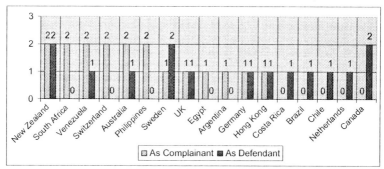

We now present further details on the selection process of panellists in Mexico's cases. Out of the eighteen panellists involved in the cases where Mexico was a complainant, three (17%) were selected by agreement of the Parties.[25] The remaining fifteen panellists (83%) were selected by the WTO Director General. On the other hand, out of the twenty-one panellists involved in the cases when Mexico has

---

25. From Australia: Stephanie Sin Far Man in *US – OCTG* (282) (agreement by the Parties); from Sweden: Christer Manhusen (Chair) in *US – OCTG* (282) (agreement by the Parties); from United Kingdom: Alistair James Stewart in *US – OCTG* (282) (agreement by the Parties).

defended its measures, twelve (57%) were selected by agreement of the Parties[26] and nine (43%) by the WTO Director General.

Table 4.26 Selection of WTO Panellists (DG versus Agreement of the Parties)

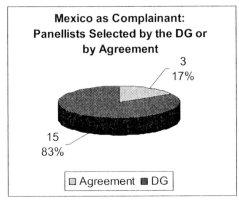

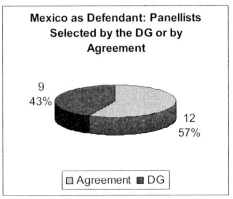

Next, we turn to the nationalities of the AB divisions[27] of Mexico's cases that were appealed. We do not show the names of the AB members, since the Parties do not have a role in selecting the AB division in charge of an appeal. Mexico has had an AB member from Australia twice when acting as complainant and once when acting as defendant. An AB member from Egypt served twice each in cases with Mexico as complainant and as defendant. Mexico has had an AB member from New Zealand twice when it was complainant. An AB member from India has ruled once in a case with Mexico as complainant. Once as complainant and twice as defendant, Mexico has had a ruling from a Japanese AB member. A member from Italy has ruled in one complainant and one defendant case. A Brazilian member has ruled once in a case with Mexico as complainant. An AB from the US has

---

26. From Uruguay: Julio Lacarte-Muro (Chair) in *Mexico – AD on Tubes* (331) (agreement by Parties); from Ecuador: Cristian Espinosa Cañizares in *Mexico – AD on Tubes* (331) (agreement by Parties); from Chile: Alvaro Espinoza in *Mexico – AD on Tubes* (331) (agreement by Parties); from Costa Rica: Ronald Saborío Soto (Chair) in *Mexico – Soft Drinks* (308) (agreement by Parties); from the United Kingdom: Edmond McGovern in *Mexico – Soft Drinks* (308) (agreement by Parties); from New Zealand: David Walker in *Mexico – Soft Drinks* (308) (agreement by Parties); from Sweden: Christer Manhusen (Chair) in *Mexico – Corn Syrup II* (132) (agreement by Parties); from Canada: Gerald Salembier in *Mexico – Corn Syrup II* (132) (agreement by Parties); from Netherlands: Edwin Vermulst in *Mexico – Corn Syrup II* (132) (agreement by Parties); from Sweden: Christer Manhusen (Chair) in *Mexico – Corn Syrup II* (132) Art. 21.5 Panel (agreement by Parties); from Canada: Gerald Salembier in *Mexico – Corn Syrup II* (132) Art. 21.5 Panel (agreement by Parties); and from Australia: Paul O'Connor in *Mexico – Corn Syrup II* Art. 21.5 Panel (agreement by Parties).
27. There are three AB members in each division. A division is in charge of an appeal.

ruled in one case with Mexico as complainant and one where Mexico was the defendant. The AB member from Uruguay ruled once in a case with Mexico as complainant. Finally, the AB members from Philippines and Germany have each ruled once where Mexico was the defendant.

Table 4.27 Nationality of WTO AB Members

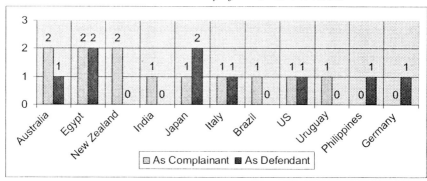

Mexico has twice participated as complainant in arbitrations to define the RPT. The arbitrator in one case was from Japan: Yasuhei Taniguchi in *US – Offset Act* (217/234); and in the other case was from Egypt: Said El-Naggar in *EC – Bananas III* (27).

Table 4.28 Nationality of Arbitrators on RPT

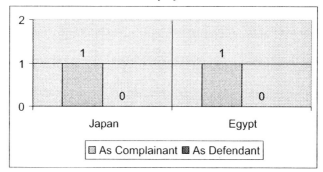

Finally, there is one case, *US – Offset Act* (217/234), where Mexico participated as complainant in arbitration to define the level of nullification or impairment (retaliation). The arbitrators were from Switzerland (Luzius Wasescha ,Chair), Egypt (Maamoun Abdel-Fattah) and New Zealand (William Falconer).[28]

---

28.   For more information on the decision makers (name, nationality, case and chairmanship when
      applicable), see the Appendix, Table 88 'Nationality of decision makers in WTO cases'.

Table 4.29 Nationality of Arbitrators on Retaliation

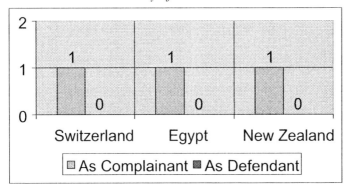

V.   LITIGATION: HOW MANY FINDINGS DID
            MEXICO WIN?

This section presents Mexico's results at litigation in the WTO by showing the findings won and lost on each and every adjudicating procedure – i.e., Panel, AB, Article 21.5 Panel, Article 21.5 AB, arbitration to define the RPT and arbitration to define the level of nullification or impairment (retaliation). We understand 'findings won by Mexico' to mean as follows:[29]

Finding won/lost by Mexico	Any successful finding by a GATT Panel, PTA Panel, WTO Panel/AB (original or Article 21.5 of the DSU) or arbitrator (Articles 21.3 or 22.6 of the DSU).[30] We use findings as a unit of account. We do not pronounce on overall win/loss, which is a very difficult issue to tackle.[31]
	For WTO cases, we distinguish the Panel findings from the AB findings by counting them separately. We do not count findings under Article 3.8 of the DSU – although we do take them into account if the Article was

---

29. Also included in 'Acronyms and Definitions'.
30. We determine success in findings by the arbitrator under Arts 21.3 or 22.6 of the DSU by comparing them with the position sustained by each party to the arbitration. As an example, assume that a finding on RPT of two months and one party's position was one month and the other party's position was three months. Here we would allocate a one-half finding of success to each party.
31. For instance, even when the findings were in favour of the US in the *Mexico – Telecoms* (204) case, there were internal interests in Mexico that wanted to amend the domestic regulations, and some government officials used the Panel report as a leverage to do so.

the legal base of a defence. Nor do we count absence of findings through judicial economy.

The findings from the Panel, as amended by the AB, may come from two sources: claims that were the basis of the complaint (Article 6.2 of the DSU) or defences presented by the defendant (such as Article XX of the GATT).

We use findings as the unit of account in this section, not DS numbers, as in other sections.

A.   FINDINGS WON BY MEXICO, AT A GLANCE

We start with the percentage of findings won by Mexico at the Panel and Article 21.5 Panel stages. As complainant, in one case Mexico won 100% of the claims and in another case it won 85%–99% of the findings. In both of these cases, Mexico was one of several co-complainants. There were two cases, still as complainant, where Mexico won 60%–84% of the findings. In the remaining cases as complainant, Mexico won 15%–29% of the findings. As defendant, in one case Mexico won 30%–44% of the findings. It won 15%–29% of the findings in another case and 1%–14% of the findings in a further case. Finally, it did not win any findings in two cases as defendant.

Table 4.30 Percentage of Findings Won by Mexico at Panel Stage
(Ordinary and Article 21.5)

	100%	99%–85%	84%–60%	59%–45%	44%–30%	29%–15%	14%–1%	0%
As Complainant	1	1	2			1		
As Defendant					1	1	1	2

Next, we turn to the percentage of findings won by Mexico at the AB and Article 21.5 stage. As complainant, in two cases Mexico won 60%–84% of the findings. In both cases, Mexico was one of several co-complainants. In another two cases as complainant Mexico did not win any findings at the AB and Article 21.5 AB stage. There was one case as defendant where Mexico won 1%–14% of the findings, and two cases where Mexico did not win any findings .

Table 4.31 Percentage of Findings Won by Mexico at Appeal Stage
(Ordinary and Article 21.5)

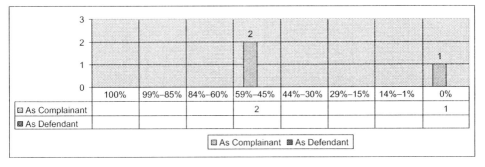

	100%	99%–85%	84%–60%	59%–45%	44%–30%	29%–15%	14%–1%	0%
As Complainant			2					2
As Defendant							1	2

Finally, we present the range of findings won by Mexico at Article 21.3(c) or Article 22.6 arbitration. We only found cases of Mexico as complainant, and in all three arbitrations Mexico was one of several co-complainants. There were two cases where Mexico won 45%–59% of the cases and one where it did not win any findings.

Table 4.32 Percentage of Findings Won by Mexico at Arbitrations
on RPT and Retaliation

	100%	99%–85%	84%–60%	59%–45%	44%–30%	29%–15%	14%–1%	0%
As Complainant				2				1
As Defendant								

Disaggregating the material on the findings case by case, we will discuss the implementation of each case, starting with those where Mexico was the complainant. Out of the five litigated cases, one was implemented:

(1) *Guatemala – Cement II* (156)
    (a) The Panel made nineteen findings. Mexico won eighteen (95%) of the findings, and Guatemala won one (5%).[32]

The remaining four litigated cases with Mexico as complainant had not been implemented as at the closing date of this work:

(1) *US – OCTG* (282)
    (a) The Panel made ten findings. Mexico won two (20%) of the findings, and the US won eight (80%).

---

32. The case was not appealed.

    (b) The AB made eleven findings. Mexico did not win any of them; the US won all eleven (100%).

(2) *US – Offset Act* (217/234)

    (a) The Panel made fourteen findings. Mexico and the co-complainants won ten (71%), and the US won four (29%).

    (b) The AB made eleven findings. Mexico and the co-complainants won seven (64%), and the US four (36%).

    (c) The arbitrator to define the RPT made one finding. Mexico and the co-complainants won one-half (50%) of the finding and the US won one-half (50%).

    (d) The arbitrator to define the nullification or impairment made one finding. Mexico and the co-complainants won one-half (50%) of the finding and the US won one-half (50%).[33]

(3) *Guatemala – Cement I* (60)

    (a) The Panel made four findings. Mexico won three (75%) of the findings and Guatemala won one (25%).

    (b) The AB made three findings. Mexico did not win any, and Guatemala won all (100%) – the AB concluded that there were no recommendations to be made to Guatemala.

(4) *EC – Bananas III* (27)

    (a) The Panel made six findings. Mexico and the co-complainants won six (100%), and the EC did not win any.

    (b) The AB made twenty-six findings. Mexico and the co-complainants won twenty-one (81%), and the EC won five (19%).

    (c) The arbitrator on RPT made one finding. Mexico and the other co-complainants did not win it; the EC did (100%).

Table 4.33 Cases of Mexico as Complainant: Findings Won and Lost/Implementation

Case	Won/Lost		Implementation
Guatemala – Cement II (156)	Total findings by the Panel	19	Implemented
Defendant: Guatemala	Guatemala won	1 (5%)	
Product: industrial goods (cement)	Mexico won	18 (95%)	

---

33. For the arbitrations, both under Arts 21.3(c) and 22.6 of the DSU, we allocate half of the unit of account (finding) to each Party. The arbitrators took a Solomonic decision.

Table 4.33 (contd)

Case	Won/Lost		Implementation
US – OCTG (282)	Total findings by the Panel	10	Not implemented
Defendant: US Product: industrial goods (steel)	The US won	8 (80%)	
	Mexico won	2 (20%)	
	Total findings by the AB	11	
	The US won	11 (100%)	
	Mexico won	0	
US – Offset Act (217/234)	Total findings by the Panel	14	Not implemented
Defendant: US Product: general goods (goods subject to AD duties)	The US won	4 (29%)	
	Mexico and other complainants won	10 (71%)	
	Total findings by the AB	11	
	The US won	4 (36%)	
	Mexico and other complainants won	7 (64%)	
	Total findings by the arbitrator on RPT	1	
	The US won	0.5 (50%)	
	Mexico and other complainants won	0.5 (50%)	
	Total findings by the arbitrator on N. or I.	1	
	The US won	0.5 (50%)	
	Mexico and other complainants won	0.5 (50%)	
Guatemala – Cement I (60)	Total findings by the Panel	4	Not implemented
Defendant: Guatemala	Guatemala won	1 (25%)	

Table 4.33 (contd)

Case	Won/Lost		Implementation
Product: industrial goods (Cement)	Mexico won	3 (75%)	
	Total findings by the AB	3	
	Guatemala won	3 (100%)[34]	
	Mexico won	0	
EC – Bananas III (27) **Req. cons.** 5 February 1996 Defendant: The EC	Total findings by the Panel	6	Not Implemented
	The EC won	0	
	Mexico and other complainants won	6 (100%)	
Product: agricultural goods and services (Bananas and distributions)	Total findings by the AB	28	
	The EC won	5 (18%)	
	Mexico and other complainants won	23 (82%)	
	Total Findings by the arbitrator on RPT	1	
	The EC won	1 (100%)	
	Mexico and other complainants won	0	

We now turn to the cases where Mexico acted as defendant. Four of them have been implemented by Mexico:

(1) *Mexico – Soft Drinks* (308)
   (a) The Panel made eight findings. Mexico did not win any, and the US won eight (100%).
   (b) The AB made three findings. Mexico did not win any, and the US won three (100%).
(2) *Mexico – Beef and Rice* (295)

---

34. Based on its findings, the AB concluded that there were no recommendations to Guatemala. Mexico lost all the claims presented to the Panel.

    (a) The Panel made 15 findings. Mexico won two (13%), and the US won thirteen (87%).
    (b) The AB made seventeen findings. Mexico won one (6%), and the US won sixteen (94%).
 (3) *Mexico – Telecoms* (204)
    (a) The Panel made seven findings. Mexico won three (43%), and the US won four (57%).
 (4) *Mexico – Corn Syrup II* (132)
    (a) The Panel made six findings. Mexico won one (17%), and the US won five (83%).
    (b) The Article 21.5 Panel made two findings. Mexico did not win any, and the US won two (100%).
    (c) The Article 21.5 AB made five findings. Mexico did not win any, and the US won five (100%).

*Table 4.34 Cases of Mexico as Defendant: Findings Won
and Lost/Implementation*

Case	Won/Lost		Implementation
***Mexico – Soft Drinks* (308)**	Total findings by the Panel	8	Implemented
Complainant: US	The US won	8 (100%)	
Product: agricultural goods (sweeteners, mainly sugar)	Mexico won	0	
	Total findings by the AB	3	
	The US won	3 (100%)	
	Mexico won	0	
***Mexico – Beef and Rice* (295)**	Total findings by the Panel	15	Implemented
Complainant: US	The US won	13 (87%)	
Product: agricultural goods (beef and rice)	Mexico won	2 (13%)	
	Total findings by the AB	17	
	The US won	16 (94%)	
	Mexico won	1 (6%)	
***Mexico – Telecoms* (204)**	Total findings by the Panel	7	Implemented

Table 4.34 (contd)

Case	Won/Lost		Implementation
Complainant: US Product: services (telecommunication services)	The US won Mexico won	4 (57%) 3 (43%)	
Mexico – Corn Syrup II (132)	Total findings by the Panel	6	Implemented
Complainant: US Product: agricultural goods (corn syrup sweet- ener and sugar)	The US won Mexico won	5 (83%) 1 (17%)	
	Total findings by the Article 21.5 Panel	2	
	The US won Mexico won	2 (100%) 0	
	Total findings by the Article 21.5 AB	5	
	The US won	5 (100%)	
	Mexico won	0	

B.   THE FINDINGS WON BY MEXICO: DETAILED PRESENTATION

This section presents the findings of Mexico's cases in more detail, specifying the findings at the different stages of litigation. We start with the cases of Mexico as complainant then proceed to the cases as defendant.

After each of the findings, we have indicated in parentheses who won the finding. This is the basis for our results on findings won by Mexico.

1.   Findings in the Cases of Mexico as Complainant

a.   EC – Bananas III (27)

This case was initiated by Mexico, Ecuador, Guatemala, Honduras and the US on 5 February 1996. The case related to trade in agricultural goods and in services (importation, sales and distribution of bananas). Mexico abandoned this case at the Article 21.5 Panel stage, after requesting the Panel's establishment. As of the closing date of this work some WTO Members were continuing to push the case forward. The EC first faced countermeasures by the US only. It then requested and obtained two waivers – one expired on 31 December 2005,[35] and the expiration of the other one[36] is being disputed in an ongoing Article 21.5 Panel at the moment of writing. In the view of the remaining complaining Parties, the EC has not complied with the original report:

(A)   *Measures Challenged by Mexico and its Co-complainants*
   (1) EC regime for the importation, sale and distribution of bananas established by Regulation 404/93 (OJ L 47 of 25 February 1993, 1).
   (2) The subsequent instruments, including the Framework Agreement on bananas, which implement, supplement and amend that regime.

(B)   *Mexico's Claims*
   (1) Articles I, II, III, X, XI and XIII of the GATT.
   (2) Articles 1 and 3 of the Agreement on Import Licensing Procedures.
   (3) The Agreement on Agriculture.
   (4) Articles II, IV, XVI and XVII of the GATS.
   (5) Articles 2 and 5 of the TRIMS.

(C)   *The Findings of the Adjudicating Bodies*

Mexico and the co-complainants won six of six total findings at the Panel stage, whereas the EC won none. Mexico and the co-complainants won twenty-three of twenty-eight findings made by the AB, and the EC won five. Finally, Mexico and the co-complainants did not win the finding made by the arbitrator under Article 21.3(c); the EC won it.

(1)   On GATT

There was one finding by the Panel on the GATT. Mexico and the co-complainants won it. The *Panel found* that the Banana Regime violated Articles I.1, III.4, X.3, and XIII.1 of the GATT (*MX* and the co-complainants won).

There were twelve findings by the AB on the GATT. Mexico and the co-complainants won ten and the EC won two. The *AB*:

   (1) *upheld* the conclusion that the Agreement on Agriculture does not permit the EC to act inconsistently with XIII of the GATT (*MX* and the co-complainants won);
   (2) *upheld* the finding that the allocation of tariff quota shares to some, but not to other, Members not having a substantial interest in supplying bananas to the EC was inconsistent with Article XIII:1 of the GATT (*MX* and the co-complainants won);

---

35. See waiver on Art. XIII of the GATT, EC – Transitional Regime for the EC Autonomous Tariff Rate Quotas on Imports of Bananas (WT/MIN(01)/16), 14 Nov. 2001.
36. See waiver on Art. I of the GATT, EC – The ACP-EC Partnership Agreement (WT/MIN(01)/15), 14 Nov. 2001.

(3) *upheld* the finding that the tariff quota reallocation rules of the Framework Agreement on Bananas were inconsistent with Article XIII:1 of the GATT, and *modified* the finding by concluding that the Framework Agreement on Bananas tariff quota reallocation rules were also inconsistent with the chapeau of Article XIII:2 of the GATT (*MX* and the co-complainants won);

(4) *concluded* that the EC was required under the relevant provisions of the Lomé Convention to provide duty-free access for bananas from traditional Africa, Caribbean, and Pacific States (ACP); provide duty-free access for 90,000 tonnes of non-traditional-ACP bananas; provide a margin of tariff preference in the amount of 100 ECU/tonne for all other non-traditional-ACP bananas; and allocate tariff quota shares to the traditional ACP States in the amount of their pre-1991 best-ever export volumes (*EC* won);

(5) *concluded* that the EC was not required under the relevant provisions of the Lomé Convention to allocate tariff quota shares to traditional ACP States in excess of their pre-1991 best-ever export volumes; allocate tariff quota shares to ACP States exporting non-traditional ACP bananas; or maintain the EC import licensing procedures that were applied to third-country and non-traditional ACP bananas (*MX* and the co-complainants won);

(6) *upheld* (based on the conclusions above) the findings that the EC:
    (a) was required under the relevant provisions of the Lomé Convention to provide preferential tariff treatment for non-traditional ACP bananas (*EC* won);
    (b) was not required to allocate tariff quota shares to traditional ACP States in excess of their pre-1991 best-ever export volumes (*MX* and the co-complainants won); and
    (c) was not required to maintain the EC import licensing procedures that were applied to third-country and non-traditional ACP bananas (*MX* and the co-complainants won);

(7) *reversed* the finding that the Lomé Waiver waived any inconsistency with XIII:1 of the GATT to the extent necessary to permit the EC to allocate tariff quota shares to traditional ACP States (*MX* and the co-complainants won);

(8) *upheld* the findings that the non-discrimination provisions of the GATT, specifically, Articles I:1 and XIII, applied to the relevant EC regulations, irrespective of whether there were one or more 'separate regimes' for the importation of bananas (*MX* and the co-complainants won);

(9) *upheld* the conclusions that the EC activity function rules and the Framework Agreement on Bananas export certificate requirement were inconsistent with Article I:1 of the GATT (*MX* and the co-complainants won); and

(10) *upheld* the findings that Article III:4 of the GATT applied to the EC import licensing procedures, and that the EC practice with respect to

hurricane licenses was inconsistent with Article III:4 of the GATT (*MX* and the co-complainants won).

(2)   On Import Licensing

There was one finding by the Panel regarding import licensing. Mexico and the co-complainants won it. The *Panel found* that the Banana Regime violated Articles 1.2 and 1.3 of the Agreement on Licensing (*MX* and the co-complainants won).

There were four findings by the AB regarding import licensing; Mexico and the co-complainants won two, and the EC won two. The *AB*:

(1) *upheld* the finding that licensing procedures for tariff quotas were within the scope of the Licensing agreement (*MX* and the co-complainants won);
(2) *reversed* the Panel's finding that Article 1.3 of the Licensing Agreement precluded the imposition of different import licensing systems on like products when imported from different Members (*EC* won);
(3) *reversed* the finding that Article X:3(a) of the GATT precluded the imposition of different import licensing systems on like products when imported from different Members (*EC* won); and
(4) *upheld* the finding that both Article 1.3 of the Licensing Agreement and Article X:3(a) of the GATT apply to the EC import licensing procedures, with the modification that the Panel should have applied the provisions of the Licensing Agreement first because it is the more specific and detailed Agreement (*MX* and the co-complainants won).

(3)   On GATS

There was one finding by the Panel on the GATS; Mexico and the co-complainants won it. The *Panel found* that the Banana Regime violated Articles II and XVII of the GATS (MX and the co-complainants won).

There were eight findings by AB on the GATS: Mexico and the co-complainants won seven of the findings and the EC won one. The *AB:*

(1) *upheld* the conclusions that there was no legal basis for an a priori exclusion of measures within the EC import licensing regime from the scope of the GATS, and that the GATT and the GATS may overlap in applying to a measure (*MX* and the co-complainants won);
(2) *upheld* the findings that 'operators' as defined in the relevant EC regulations were service suppliers within the meaning of Article I:2(c) of the GATS in providing 'wholesale trade services' and that, where such operators formed part of vertically integrated companies, such companies were service suppliers for the purposes of this case (*MX* and the co-complainants won);
(3) *upheld* the conclusion that Article II:1 of the GATS should be interpreted to include de facto, as well as de jure, discrimination (*MX* and the co-complainants won);

(4) *upheld* the conclusion that the scope of its legal examination of the application of II and XVII of the GATS includes only actions that the EC took, or continued to take, or measures that remained in force or continued to be applied by the EC, and thus did not cease to exist after the entry into force of the GATS (*MX* and the co-complainants won);

(5) *upheld* the findings relating to: the companies that were owned or controlled by, or were affiliated with, persons of Complaining Parties' origin, and were providing wholesale trade services in bananas through commercial presence within the EC; the respective market shares of service suppliers of Complaining Parties' origin as compared with service suppliers of EC (or ACP) origin; and the nationality of the majority of operators that 'include or directly represent' EC (or ACP) producers that had suffered damage from hurricanes (*EC* won);

(6) *upheld* the conclusions that the allocation to Category B operators of 30% of the licenses allowing the importation of third-country and non-traditional ACP bananas at in-quota tariff rates was inconsistent with Articles II and XVII of the GATS (*MX* and the co-complainants won);

(7) *upheld* the conclusions that the allocation to ripeners of a certain portion of the Category A and B licenses allowing the importation of third-country and non-traditional ACP bananas at in-quota tariff rates was inconsistent with Article XVII of the GATS (*MX* and the co-complainants won); and

(8) *upheld* the conclusions that the EC practice with respect to hurricane licenses was inconsistent with Articles II and XVII of the GATS (*MX* and the co-complainants won).

(4)   Procedural and Other Findings

There were three findings by the Panel on procedural issues: Mexico and the co-complainants won all three. The *Panel*:

(1) *rejected* the claim that that the case should have been dismissed because the consultations did not perform their function of affording a possibility for arriving at a MAS and a clear setting of the different claims (*MX* and the co-complainants won);

(2) *rejected* the claim that the Panel request was not sufficient to meet the requirements of Article 6.2 of the WTO Understanding on Rules and Procedures Governing the Settlement of Disputes (DSU) (*MX* and the co-complainants won); and

(3) *rejected* the claim that under the DSU the US did not have a right to advance the claims (*MX* and the co-complainants won).

There were four findings by the AB on procedural issues; Mexico and the co-complainants won all four. The *AB*:

(1) *upheld* the conclusion that the US had standing to bring claims under the GATT in this case (*MX* and the co-complainants won);

(2) *upheld* the conclusion that the request for the establishment of the Panel was consistent with Article 6.2 of the DSU (*MX* and the co-complainants won);

(3) *reversed* the conclusions that certain of the claims under Article XVII of the GATS were not to be included within the scope of the case (*MX* and the co-complainants won); and

(4) *upheld* the finding that the EC had not succeeded in rebutting the presumption that its breaches of the GATT had nullified or impaired the benefits of the US, with the modification that that finding should be limited to the US and to the EC's obligations under the GATT (*MX* and the co-complainants won).

The EC won the sole finding by arbitration to define the RPT based on Article 21.3(c) of the DSU. The arbitrator *found* that the RPT was fifteen months and one week (*EC* won, since it sought fifteen months; the co-complainants had sought 9 months).

b.   *Guatemala – Cement I (60)*

This case was the first attempt by Mexico to challenge the AD investigation initiated by Guatemala on cement from Mexico (industrial goods). Guatemala had imposed AD duties. The request for consultations was made on 15 October 1996. After the findings by the AB on Mexico's lack of sufficient identification of the measure at issue, Mexico abandoned the complaint and challenged the final determination of AD on cement in a new case.[37] Guatemala did not implement this case. The provisional AD duty was imposed on 16 August 1996 and the definitive duty on 17 January 1997.

(A)   *Measure Challenged by Mexico*
The AD investigation being carried out by the authorities of Guatemala concerning imports of Portland cement from Mexico.

(B)   *Mexico's Claims*
Articles 2, 3, 5 and 7.1 of the ADA.

(C)   *The Findings of the Adjudicating Bodies*
There were four findings made by the Panel. Mexico won three and Guatemala one. There were three findings made by the AB. Mexico did not win any of them. The AB concluded, based on its findings, that there was no need for recommendations against Guatemala. The *Panel:*

(1) *declined to recommend* that Guatemala (1) revoke the AD measure, and (2) refund the AD duties collected (*Guatemala* won);

(2) *suggested* the revocation of the AD measure – the only appropriate means of implementation (*MX* won);

---

37. We have classified this case as abandoned. Arguably, Mexico would still have been able to identify the provisional measure and restart the case. However, it decided to challenge the final AD measure.

(3) *found* that by failing to notify the government of Mexico before proceeding to initiate, there had been a violation by Guatemala of Article 5.5 of the ADA (*MX* won); and

(4) *found* that because initiation began without sufficient evidence to justify it, there had been a violation by Guatemala of Article 5.3 of the ADA (*Mexico* won).

The *AB*:

(1) *reversed* the finding that Article 17 of the ADA '… replaces the more general approach of the DSU' (*Guatemala* won);

(2) *reversed* the alternative finding relating to the term 'measure' (*Guatemala* won); and

(3) *reversed* the conclusion that 'the matters referred to in Mexico's request for establishment of a Panel' were properly before the Panel. Hence, there were no recommendations (*Guatemala* won).

c.   *Guatemala – Cement II (156)*

This was the second attempt by Mexico to challenge the AD order imposed by Guatemala on cement (industrial goods). The provisional AD duty was imposed on 16 August 1996 and the definitive AD duty on 17 January 1997. The request for consultations was issued on 5 January 1999, and the Panel report was distributed on 24 October 2000. The report was not appealed, and the case did not go any further. Guatemala implemented the measure on 4 October 2000 even before the distribution of the Panel report.

(A)   *Measures Challenged by Mexico*

(1) The definitive AD measure on imports of grey Portland cement from the Mexican firm La Cruz Azul S.C.L.

(2) The actions that preceded it.

(B)   *Mexico's Claims*

(1) Articles 1, 2, 3, 5, 6, 7, 9, 12 and 18 and Annexes I and II of the ADA.

(2) Article VI of the GATT.

(C)   *The Findings of the Adjudicating Bodies*
The Panel report contained nineteen findings. Mexico won eighteen and Guatemala won one. There was neither an appeal nor any subsequent procedural stage.

The *Panel*:

(1) *found* violation on the sufficiency of evidence of dumping and threat of injury to initiate an investigation in accordance with Article 5.3 of the ADA (*MX* won);

(2) *found* violation on the failure to reject the application for AD duties in accordance with Article 5.8 of the ADA (*MX* won);

(3) *found* violation on the failure to notify Mexico in a timely fashion in accordance with Article 5.5 of the ADA (*MX* won);

(4) *found* violation on the failure to meet the requirements for a public notice of initiation of the investigation in accordance with Article 12.1.1 of the ADA (*MX* won);

(5) found violation on the failure to provide in a timely fashion to Mexico and Cruz Azul the full text of the application in accordance with Article 6.1.3 of the ADA (*MX* won);

(6) found violation on the failure to grant Mexico access to the file of the investigation in accordance with Articles 6.1.2 and 6.4 of the ADA (*MX* won);

(7) *found* violation on the failure to make Cementos Progreso's submission dated 19 December 1996 available in a timely fashion (not until 8 January 1997) to Cruz Azul in accordance with Article 6.1.2 of the ADA (*MX* won);

(8) *found* violation on the failure to provide two copies of the file of the investigation as requested by Cruz Azul in accordance with Article 6.1.2 of the ADA(*MX* won);

(9) *found* violation on Guatemala's extension of the period of investigation requested by Cementos Progreso without providing Cruz Azul with a full opportunity of defence in accordance with Article 6.2 of the ADA (*MX* won);

(10) *found* violation on the failure to inform Mexico of the inclusion of non-governmental experts in the verification in accordance with paragraph 2 of Annex I of the ADA (*MX* won);

(11) *found* violation on the failure to require Cementos Progreso to provide a statement of the reasons why summarization of the information submitted during verification was not possible in accordance with Article 6.5.1 of the ADA (*MX* won);

(12) *found* violation of Article 6.5 of the ADA in Guatemala's decision to grant Cementos Progreso's 19 December submission confidential treatment on its own initiative (*MX* won);

(13) *found* violation on the failure to inform 'the essential facts … which form the basis … [of the] definitive measures' in accordance with Article 6.9 of the ADA (*MX* won);

(14) *found* violation on the recourse to 'best information available' for its final dumping determination in accordance with Article 6.8 of the ADA (*MX* won);

(15) *found* violation in Guatemala's failure to take into account imports by the company MATINSA in its determination of injury and causality in accordance with Articles 3.1, 3.2 and 3.5 of the ADA (*MX* won);

(16) *found* violation in Guatemala's failure to evaluate all relevant factors for the examination of the impact of the allegedly dumped imports on the domestic industry in accordance with Article 3.4 of the ADA (*MX* won);

(17) *found* that Guatemala failed to rebut the presumption of nullification or impairment in accordance with Article 3.8 of the DSU (*MX* won);

(18) *suggested* that Guatemala revoke the measure – the only way to properly implement (*MX* won); and

(19) *declined* Mexico's request to suggest that Guatemala refund the AD duties collected – not fully explored in the dispute (*Guatemala* won).

d.   *US – Offset Act (217/234)*

This case was initiated on 21 May 2001 by Mexico, Canada, Australia, Brazil, Chile, EC, India, Indonesia, Japan, Korea and Thailand. They challenged a legislative measure relating to countervailing duties (CVD) and AD imposed by the US whereby the US distributed to the domestic industry the AD/CVD duties collected if it had participated in the investigation and supported the request to investigate in order to impose AD/CVD duties. The challenge was pursued up to the stage of retaliation. But there has been no procedure under Article 21.5 of the DSU because there was no disagreement about the fact that the US did not comply at the time. The products protected by the US were general goods (those subject to AD duties and CVD). According to the co-complainants the measure has not been implemented. Yet, the US claims it has complied with the report of the Panel/AB. The Parties have not gone to an Article 21.5 Panel.

Mexico initiated retaliatory measures through decree (with a validity of twelve months) published on 17 August 2005, notified to the WTO Dispute Settlement Body (DSB) on 31 August 2005 (WT/DSB/M/196). Japan, Canada and the EC had already imposed retaliatory measures at the time. Through a decree published on 13 September 2006, Mexico imposed a second set of retaliatory measures. The second decree expired on 31 October 2006.

(A)   *Measure Challenged by Mexico*
The amendment to the Tariff Act of 1930 entitled the 'Continued Dumping and Subsidy Offset Act of 2000' which disburses the duties collected through AD/CVD duties to the domestic industry.

(B)   *Mexico's Claims*
    (1) Articles 1, 5, 8, 18 of the ADA;
    (2) Articles 1, 5, 6, 10, 11, 18, 32 of the SCM;
    (3) Articles VI, X and XXIII (violation and non-violation cases) of the GATT; and
    (4) Article XVI of the WTO Agreement.

(C)   *The Findings of the Adjudicating Bodies*
The Panel made fourteen findings; Mexico and the co-complainants won ten and the US won the remaining four. The AB made eleven findings; Mexico and the co-complainants won seven and the US four. The arbitrator asked to define the RPT issued one finding: Mexico and the co-complainants won one-half of the finding and the US won the other half. The arbitrator asked to calculate the

nullification or impairment issued one finding; Mexico and the co-complainants won one-half of the finding and the US won the other half.[38]

(1)   Findings on the ADA
There were four findings by the Panel on the ADA. Mexico and the co-complainants won three, and the US won one. The *Panel*:

    (1) *found* violation of Article 5.4 of the ADA (*MX* and the co-complainants won);
    (2) *found* violation of Article 18.1 of the ADA (*MX* and the co-complainants won);
    (3) *found* violation of Article 18.4 of the ADA (*MX* and the co-complainants won); and
    (4) *did not find* violation of Articles 8.3 and 15 of the ADA (*US* won).

There were four findings by the AB on the ADA. Mexico and the co-complainants won two, and the US won two. The *AB*:

    (1) *reversed* the finding on Article 5.4 of the ADA (*US* won);
    (2) *rejected* the conclusion that the US could be regarded as not having acted in good faith (*US* won);
    (3) *upheld* the violation of Article 18.1 of the ADA – the CDSOA was a non-permissible specific action against dumping or a subsidy (*MX* and the co-complainants won); and
    (4) *upheld* the finding on Article 18.4 of the ADA (MX and the co-complainants won).

(2)   Findings on the SCM
There were five findings by the Panel on the SCM Agreement. Mexico and the co-complainants won three, and the US won two. The *Panel:*

    (1) *found* violation of Article 11.4 of the SCM Agreement (*MX* and the co-complainants won);
    (2) *found* violation of Article 32.1 of the SCM Agreement (*MX* and the co-complainants won);
    (3) *found* violation of Article 32.5 of the SCM Agreement (*MX* and the co-complainants won);
    (4) *did not find* violation of Articles 4.10, 7.9 or 18.3 of the SCM Agreement (*US* won); and
    (5) *did not find* violation on Mexico's claim that the CDSOA violated Article 5(b) of the SCM Agreement (*US* won).

---

38. We allocate half of the finding to each disputing Parties on both arbitrations. Arbitrators, both RPT and nullification or impairment, made a Solomonic judgment that cut the arguments of both Parties by half. Hence, we allocate one-half of a unit of account (finding) per disputing Party for both arbitrations.

There were four findings by the AB on the SCM Agreement. Mexico and the co-complainants won two, and the US won the other two. The *AB*:

(1) *reversed* the violation of Article 11.4 of the SCM Agreement (*US* won);

(2) *rejected* the conclusion that the US could be regarded as not having acted in good faith (*US* won);

(3) *upheld* the violation of Article 32.1 of the SCM Agreement – the CDSOA was a non-permissible specific action against dumping or a subsidy (*MX* and the co-complainants won); and

(4) *upheld* the violation of Article 32.5 of the SCM Agreement (*MX* and the co-complainants won).

(3)   Other Issues

There were five findings by the Panel on other issues. Mexico and the co-complainants won four, and the US won one. The *Panel*:

(1) *found* violation of Articles VI:2 and VI:3 of the GATT (*MX* and the co-complainants won);

(2) *found* violation of Article XVI:4 of the WTO Agreement (*MX* and the co-complainants won);

(3) *did not find* violation on the claim based on Article X:3(a) of the GATT (*US* won);

(4) *found* violation of Article 3.8 of the DSU that the CDSOA nullified or impaired benefits (*MX* and the co-complainants won); and

(5) *suggested* that the US repeal the CDSOA – since it found no other more appropriate and/or effective method to implement than eliminating the measure (*MX* and the co-complainants won).

There were three findings by the AB on other issues. Mexico and the co-complainants won all of them. The *AB*:

(1) *upheld* the violation of Article XVI:4 of the WTO Agreement (*MX* and the co-complainants won);

(2) *upheld* the violation of Article 3.8 of the DSU that the CDSOA nullified or impaired benefits (*MX* and the co-complainants won); and

(3) *rejected* the US claim of inconsistency with Article 9.2 of the DSU, by not issuing a separate Panel report for Mexico (*MX* and the co-complainants won).

(4)   Arbitration to Define the RPT (Article 21.3(c)of the DSU)

There was one finding by the arbitrator to define the RPT based on Article 21.3(c) of the DSU. We allocate half of the finding to Mexico and the co-complainants and half to the US. The RPT found by the arbitrator (eleven months) is almost the mid-point between what the co-complainants asked for (six months) and what the US requested (fifteen months).

The *arbitrator found* that the RPT was eleven months. The US sought fifteen months and the co-complainants along with Mexico six months. For our analysis, *MX* and the co-complainants won one-half and the *US* won one-half of this claim.

(5)   Arbitration to Calculate the Nullification or Impairment (Article 22.6 of the DSU)

There is one finding by the arbitrator on the nullification or impairment based on Article 22.6 of the DSU. We are allocating one-half of the finding to Mexico and the co-complainants and one-half to the US. The award says that nullification or impairment was 72% of the CDSOA paid on imports from Mexico. The co-complainants claimed that it was the payments coming from all sources to be divided by the co-complainants. The US, on the other hand, argued that the nullification or impairment was zero. Hence, neither the US nor the co-complainants won entirely.

The *arbitrator found* that the equivalent nullification or impairment was 72% of the CDSOA paid on imports from Mexico, and for each co-complainant accordingly, in the most recent year (calculated yearly):

(1) Mexico argued that the level was the amount of the CDSOA payments in total (including the payment coming from duties collected from exports of non-complainants), to be distributed among all complainants.
(2) US argued that the level was zero. (*MX* and the co-complainants won half and the *US* won half).

e.   *US – OCTG (282)*

This case was initiated by Mexico against some AD measures and other legislative measures imposed by the US. The US had imposed AD duties. The request for consultations was presented on 18 February 2003. It was pursued up to an Article 21.5 Panel. The products protected by the US were industrial goods – oil country tubular goods, or OCTG (steel tubes for oil transportation). The US has not complied with the report.

(A)   *Measures Challenged by Mexico*
  (1) Determinations:
      (a) Oil Country Tubular Goods from Mexico: Final Results of Sunset Review, 66 Fed. Reg. 14131 (9 March 2001) and the Issues and Decision Memorandum ('Sunset Review by the Department');
      (b) Oil Country Tubular Goods from Argentina, Italy, Japan, Korea and Mexico: 66 Fed. Reg. 35997 (10 July 2001) ('Sunset Review by the Commission');
      (c) Oil Country Tubular Goods from Mexico and Other Countries: Final Determination to Continue Applying AD Duties, 66 Fed. Reg. 38630 (25 July 2001); and

(d) Oil Country Tubular Goods from Mexico: Final Results of AD Duty Administrative Review – 1 August 1998–31 July 1999, 66 Fed. Reg. 15832 (21 March 2001) (Final Results of the Fourth Administrative Review).

(2) US laws, regulations and administrative practices:

(a) Sections 751 and 752 of the Tariff Act of 1930, codified in Title 19 of the US Code, sections 1675 and 1675a; and the US Statement of Administrative Action accompanying the Uruguay Round Agreements Act.

(b) The Department of Commerce (DOC) Policies Regarding the Conduct of Sunset Reviews of AD and Countervailing Duties; Policy Bulletin, 63 Federal Register 18871 (16 April 1998) (Department's Sunset Policy Bulletin).

(c) The Department of Commerce (DOC) regulations for sunset reviews of AD duties, codified in Title 19 of the US Code of Federal Regulations, section 351.218.

(d) The US International Trade Commission (USITC) regulations for sunset reviews of AD duties, codified in Title 19 of the US Code of Federal Regulations, section 207.60-69 (Subpart F).

(e) The DOC's regulations for administrative review, including those codified at Title 19 of the US Code of Federal Regulations, Sections 351.213, 351.221 and 351.222.

(B) *Mexico's Claims*
(1) Articles 1, 2, 3, 6, 11 and 18 of the ADA.
(2) Articles VI and X of the GATT.
(3) Article XVI:4 of the WTO Agreement.

(C) *The Findings of the Adjudicating Bodies*
There were ten findings by the Panel. Mexico won two and the US eight. The AB issued eleven findings; the US won them all. The only finding on violation made by the Panel that was not appealed was that the DOC's determination on likelihood of dumping in the sunset review was inconsistent with Article 11.3 of the ADA.[39]

(1) Findings on the measures as such
There was one finding by the Panel on the measures as such. Mexico won it. The *Panel found* that the Sunset Policy Bulletin, in Section II.A.3, establishes an irrefutable presumption that termination of the AD duty would be likely to lead to continuation or recurrence of dumping and therefore is, in this respect, inconsistent, as such, with the obligation set forth in Article 11.3 of the ADA to determine likelihood of continuation or recurrence of dumping (*MX* won)

---

39. The Panel/AB recommendations in this case relate only to this violation. See *US – OCTG* (282), Report of the AB, para. 220.

There were four findings by the AB on the measures as such. The US won all four. Regarding the Sunset Policy Bulletin, the *AB:*

(1) *found* that, in assessing the consistency of the Sunset Policy Bulletin, as such, with Article 11.3 of the ADA, the failed to make an objective assessment of the matter and of the facts of the case, as required by Article 11 of the DSU (*US* won);

(2) *reversed* the Panel's finding that section II.A.3 of the Sunset Policy Bulletin, as such, was inconsistent with Article 11.3 of the ADA (*US* won);

(3) *found* that the Panel's statement that Mexico had established a prima facie case that the Sunset Policy Bulletin, as such, was inconsistent with Article 11.3 of the ADA was moot and of no legal effect (*US* won); and

(4) having reversed the Panel's finding that the Sunset Policy Bulletin was inconsistent with Article 11.3 of the ADA, *found* no merit in the argument that the Tariff Act, the Statement of Administrative Action, and the Sunset Policy Bulletin 'collectively and independently' established a standard that was inconsistent with Article 11.3 of the ADA (*US* won).

(2)   Findings regarding DOC's sunset review

There were two findings by the Panel on the DOC's Sunset Review. Mexico and the US each won one of these findings. The *Panel:*

(1) *found* that the DOC acted inconsistently with Article 11.3 of the ADA in that its determination that dumping was likely to continue or recur was not supported by reasoned and adequate conclusions based on the facts before it (*MX* won);[40]

(2) *made no findings* concerning Mexico's claims under Articles 2 and 6 of the ADA in the context of the DOC sunset review at issue in this dispute; and

(3) *concluded* that claims regarding alleged inconsistency of DOC practice in sunset reviews were not within the Panel's terms of reference (*US* won).

There was one finding by the AB on the DOC's sunset review. The US won it. Regarding dumping margins, the *AB:*

(1) *found* that the Panel did not act inconsistently with Article 11 of the DSU in not addressing Mexico's claim under Article 2 of the ADA (*US* won); and

(2) *found* it unnecessary to rule on Mexico's claim relating to Article 2 of the ADA.

---

40. This finding was not appealed by the US.

(3)   Findings regarding the USITC's Sunset Review
There were four findings by the Panel on the USITC's Sunset Review. The US
won all four. The *Panel*:

(1) *found* that the 'would be likely to lead to continuation or recurrence of
injury' standard applied by the USITC was not inconsistent with Article
11.3 of the ADA as such, or as applied in the sunset review at issue in this
dispute (*US* won);
(2) *found* that the relevant provisions of US law, 19 U.S.C. §§ 1675a(a)(1)
and (5), regarding the temporal aspect of USITC determinations of likelihood of continuation or recurrence of injury were not, as such, or as
applied in the sunset review before it in that dispute, inconsistent with
Articles 3.1, 3.2, 3.4, 3.5, 3.7, 3.8, 11.1, and 11.3 of the ADA
(*US* won);
(3) *found* that the USITC did not act inconsistently with Article 11.3 of the
ADA in making its determination of likelihood of continuation or recurrence of injury in the sunset review at issue in that dispute (*US* won);
(4) *found* that the determination was not inconsistent with Articles 3.3 and
11.3 of the ADA because it involved a cumulative analysis (*US* won);
and
(5) *made no findings* regarding the remaining aspects of Mexico's claims
under 3.1, 3.2, 3.3, 3.4, 3.5, 3.7 and 3.8 of the ADA.

There were four findings by the AB on the USITC's sunset review. The US won
all four.
Regarding the analysis on cumulation, the *AB:*

(1) *upheld* the finding of no inconsistency with Articles 3.3 and 11.3 of the
ADA because it involved a cumulative analysis (*US* won); and
(2) *found* that the Panel did not act inconsistently with Article 11 of the DSU
(*US* won).

Regarding causation, the *AB:*

(1) *found* that there was no requirement to establish the existence of a causal
link between likely dumping and likely injury, as a matter of legal obligation, in a sunset review determination under Article 11.3 of the ADA.
Hence, the USITC was not required to so (*US* won); and
(2) *found* the Panel did not act inconsistently with Article 11 of the DSU (*US*
won).

(4)   Claims regarding the DOC's fourth administrative review
There were two findings by the Panel on the DOC's Fourth Administrative Review;
the US won both. The *Panel:*

(1) *found* that the DOC did not act inconsistently with Article 11.2 of the
ADA in determining not to revoke the AD duty in the fourth administrative review (*US* won);

(2) *found* that it was not necessary for it to address claims under Articles 11.2, 2.4, and 2.4.2 of the ADA with respect to the calculation of dumping margins in the fourth administrative review; and

(3) *found* that the DOC did not act inconsistently with Article X:2 of the GATT in the conduct of the fourth administrative review (*US* won).

(5)   Other issues

The Panel made no further findings on two other issues. The *Panel:*

(1) *made no findings* concerning alleged inconsistency with Article X:3(a) of the GATT in the administration of US AD laws, regulations, decisions and rulings with respect to the DOC's conduct of sunset reviews of AD duty orders; and

(2) *made no findings* concerning asserted subsidiary violations of the provisions of Article VI of the GATT, Articles 1 and 18 of the ADA, and Article XVI:4 of the WTO Agreement.

There was one finding by the AB on other issues. The US, not Mexico, won it. Having reversed the Panel's finding that the Sunset Policy Bulletin was inconsistent with Article 11.3 of the ADA, the *AB found* that it was not in a position to rule on the claim that the DOC did not administer US laws and regulations on sunset reviews in a manner in accordance with Article X:3(a) of the GATT (*US* won).

(6)   Specific suggestion based on Article 19.1 of the DSU

The Panel made one finding on the issue of suggestion. The US won it. The *Panel did not make* a specific suggestion (*US* won)

There was one finding by the AB on the issue of suggestion. Mexico did not win it. The AB *found* that the Panel did not act inconsistently with Article 11 of the DSU in declining to make a specific finding that the US had no legal basis to continue the AD duties on OCTG from Mexico beyond the five-year period established by Article 11.3 of the ADA (*US* won)

2.   **Findings in the Cases of Mexico as Defendant**

a.   *Mexico – Corn Syrup II (132)*

This case was initiated by the US on 8 May 1998 related to trade in agricultural goods (high-fructose corn syrup and other sweeteners). Previously, the US had requested consultations on the provisional AD measure.[41] Mexico had imposed AD duties. After consultations, the case was before the original Panel. It was not appealed, and both Parties agreed on the RPT. Later, the US initiated an Article 21.5

---

41. See *Mexico – Corn Syrup I* (101).

Panel procedure, to be followed by an Article 21.5 appeal. Mexico implemented on 20 May 2002.

(A)   *Measure Challenged by the US*
The Final AD Determination of the Order in High-Fructose Corn Syrup (HFCS) dated 23 January 1998.

(B)   *US Claims*
The *initiation*:

> (1) violation of Articles 2, 4 and 5 of the ADA by determining the initiation and accepting an application without the information required; and
> (2) violation of Article 12 of the ADA by not meeting the requirements of public notice.

The *determination of threat of injury* violation of Articles 3 and 12 of the ADA by failing to evaluate all relevant economic factors and indices and failing to determine that injury would occur without the imposition of AD duty; and by failing to consider the impact of dumped imports on the full range of operations of the domestic industry producing the like product.

The *determination of dumping* violation of Article 2 of the ADA by not calculating correctly the margin of dumping for the US exporter, Archer Daniels Midland Company.

The *provisional AD measure* violation of Article 7.4 of the ADA by exceeding the time frame for provisional AD measures

The *definitive AD measure:*

> (1) violation of Articles 9 and 12 of the ADA by failing to include in the public notice advice of any decision regarding whether the AD duty was the full margin of dumping or less;
> (2) violation of Article 10.2 of the ADA by failing to determine that the effect of the dumped imports would, in the absence of the provisional measures, have led to a determination of injury; and
> (3) violation of Article 10.4 of the ADA by failing to release the bonds posted by US exporters.

The *procedural issues:*

> (1) violation of Article 6 of the ADA by failing to comply with its requirements, including:
>
> > (a) failing to satisfy the accuracy of information provided by the domestic industry;
> > (b) failing to provide exporters with opportunities to review the information and to prepare presentations on the basis of such information;
> > (c) failing to advise the essential facts under consideration which formed the basis for its decision; and

       (d) failing to require all interested Parties to provide non-confidential summaries.

   (2) violation of Article 6.5 of the ADA by authorizing a representative of the domestic industry to inspect the confidential information provided by exporters without providing the exporters with advance notice and without obtaining specific permission to do so.

(C)   *The Findings of the Adjudicating Bodies*

The original Panel issued six findings; Mexico won one of them, and the US won five. The Article 21.5 Panel issued two findings; the US won them both. Finally, the Article 21.5 AB issued five findings, and the US won them all as well.

(1)   The original panel

On the initiation, the *Panel found* that the initiation of the investigation was consistent with the requirements of Articles 5.2, 5.3, 5.8, 12.1 and 12.1.1(iv) of the ADA (*MX* won).

On the imposition of the definitive AD measure, the *Panel*:

   (1) *found* violation of Articles 3.1, 3.2, 3.4, 3.7 and 3.7(i) of the ADA through the inadequate consideration given by Mexico to the impact of dumped imports on the domestic industry, its determination of threat of material injury on the basis of only a part of the domestic industry's production – that part sold in the industrial sector – rather than on the basis of the industry as a whole, and its inadequate consideration of the potential effect of the alleged restraint agreement in its determination of likelihood of substantially increased importation (*US* won);

   (2) *found* violation of Article 7.4 of the ADA by extending the period of application of the provisional measure (*US* won);

   (3) *found* violation of Article 10.2 of the ADA by the retroactive levying of the AD duties for the period of application of the provisional measure (*US* won);

   (4) *found* violation of Article 10.4 of the ADA by failing to expeditiously release bonds and/or cash deposits collected under the provisional measure (*US* won); and

   (5) *found* violation of Articles 12.2 and 12.2.2 of the ADA by failing to set forth findings or conclusions on the issue of the retroactive application of the final AD measure (*US* won).

(2)   The Article 21.5 Panel/AB

The *Article 21.5 Panel*:

   (1) *found* violation of Articles 3.1, 3.4, 3.7 and 3.7(i) of the ADA regarding the final re-determination by Mexico of the impact of dumped imports on

the domestic industry and of the potential effect of the alleged restraint agreement in its determination of likelihood of substantially increased importation (*US* won); and
(2) *found* that Mexico failed to implement the recommendation of the original Panel (*US* won).

The *Article 21.5 AB:*

(1) *upheld* the violation of Article 3.7(i) of the ADA given the *Secretaría de Comercio y Fomento Industrial* (now *Secretaría de Economía,* the Mexican Ministry of Trade) (SECOFI) conclusion, in the re-determination, that there existed a significant likelihood of increased imports (*US* won);
(2) *upheld* the violation of Articles 3.1, 3.4, and 3.7 of the ADA relating to SECOFI's conclusion, in the re-determination, with respect to the likely impact of dumped imports of HFCS from the US on the domestic industry (*US* won);
(3) *found* that the Panel did not err in refraining from addressing in its report the alleged violation of Article 6.2 of the DSU because the US did not indicate whether consultations had been held; and the alleged violation of Article 3.7 of the DSU on whether action under the DSU would be 'fruitful' (*US* won);
(4) *found* that the Panel satisfied its duty under Article 12.7 of the DSU to set out a 'basic rationale behind [its] findings' with respect to Articles 3.1 and 3.4 of the ADA (*US* won); and
(5) *found* that the Panel did not act inconsistently with the standard of review of Article 17.6(ii) of the ADA (*US* won).

b.   *Mexico – Telecoms (204)*

This case was initiated by the US on 17 August 2000. It related to trade in services (telecommunications) and addressed the problem raised by the US of Mexico's failure to open its market to foreign telecoms suppliers as agreed in its schedule. The case has been implemented by Mexico. After consultations, the US took this case to the Panel, and there was no appeal. The case was settled at the end of the RPT by Mexico's compliance with the report. Mexico amended the measure in two steps: 1 August 2004 and 19 August 2005.

(A)   *Measures Challenged by the US*
(1) The Federal Telecommunications Law (*Ley Federal de Telecomunicaciones*) of 18 May 1995.
(2) The Rules for Long Distance Service (*Reglas del Servicio de Larga Distancia*) published by the Secretariat of Communications and Transportation (*Secretaría de Comunicaciones y Transporte*) on 21 June 1996.

(3) The International Long Distance Rules (*Reglas para prestar el servicio de larga distancia internacional*) published by the Secretariat of Communications and Transportation on 11 December 1996.

(4) The Agreement of the Secretariat of Communications and Transportation Establishing the Procedure to Obtain Concessions for the Installation, Operation or Exploitation of Interstate Public Telecommunications Networks, Pursuant to the Federal Telecommunications Law (*Acuerdo de la Secretaría de Comunicaciones y Transporte por el que se establece el procedimiento para obtener concesión para la instalación, operación o explotación de redes públicas de telecomunicaciones interestatales, al amparo de la Ley Federal de Telecomunicaciones*) published on 4 September 1995.

(B)   *US Claims*

(1) Articles VI, XVI, and XVII of the GATS.

(2) Mexico's additional commitments under Article XVIII as set forth in the Reference Paper inscribed in Mexico's Schedule of Specific Commitments, including sections 1, 2, 3 and 5.

(3) the GATS Annex on Telecommunications, including sections 4 and 5.

Mexico's commitments and obligations according to the US:

(1) provide market access and national treatment for basic and value-added telecommunications services (GATS XVI and XVII and Mexico's Schedule of Specific Commitments annexed to the GATS);

(2) maintain appropriate measures for the purpose of preventing a major supplier of basic telecommunications services from engaging in or continuing anti-competitive practices, such as anti-competitive cross-subsidization (section 1 of the Reference Paper on Pro-Competitive Regulatory Principles (the Reference Paper), which Mexico has inscribed in its Schedule of Specific Commitments as 'additional commitments' pursuant to GATS XVIII);

(3) ensure interconnection with a major supplier at any technically feasible point in the network; under non-discriminatory terms, conditions and rates; in a timely fashion; and at cost-oriented rates that are transparent, reasonable, and sufficiently unbundled; and provide recourse to an independent domestic body to resolve interconnection disputes within a reasonable period of time (section 2 of the Reference Paper);

(4) administer any universal service obligation in a transparent, non-discriminatory and competitively neutral manner that is not more burdensome than necessary for the kind of universal service defined by Mexico (section 3 of the Reference Paper);

(5) ensure that its regulatory body is not accountable to any supplier of basic telecommunications services and that the regulator's decisions and

procedures are impartial with respect to all market participants (section 5 of the Reference Paper);

(6) administer in a reasonable, objective, and impartial manner its laws, rules, regulations, and other measures of general application affecting trade in basic and value-added telecommunications services (GATS VI:1); and

(7) ensure access to and use of public telecommunications transport networks and services on reasonable and non-discriminatory terms and conditions for the supply of basic and value-added telecommunications services and ensure that relevant information on conditions affecting access to and use of public telecommunications transport networks and services is publicly available (GATS Annex on Telecommunications, sections 4 and 5).

(C)   *The Findings of the Adjudicating Bodies*
The Panel issued seven findings. Mexico won three of these findings and the US four. The *Panel*:

(1) *found* violation of the undertakings in section 2.2(b) of Mexico's Reference Paper, because Mexico failed to ensure that a major supplier could provide interconnection of the basic telecommunications services at issue at cost-oriented rates to US suppliers for the cross-border supply on a facilities basis in Mexico (*US* won);

(2) *found* violation of the undertaking in section 1.1 of Mexico's Reference Paper to maintain appropriate measures to prevent anti-competitive practices, because it maintained measures that require anti-competitive practices among competing suppliers which, alone or together, were a major supplier of the services at issue (*US* won);

(3) *found* violation of section 5(a) of the GATS Annex on Telecommunications through Mexico's failure to ensure access to and use of public telecommunications transport networks and services on reasonable terms to US service suppliers for the cross-border supply, on a facilities basis in Mexico, of the basic telecommunications services at issue (*US* won);

(4) *found* violation of section 5(b) of the GATS Annex on Telecommunications, because of Mexico's failure to ensure that US commercial agencies, whose commercial presence Mexico it committed to allow, had access to and use of private leased circuits within or across the border of Mexico and were permitted to interconnect those circuits to public telecommunications transport networks and services or with circuits of other service suppliers (*US* won);

(5) *found* no violation of the commitments in section 2.2(b) of Mexico's Reference Paper with respect to cross-border supply on a *non-facilities* basis in Mexico of the basic telecommunications services at issue (*MX* won);

(6) *found* no violation of section 5(a) of the GATS Annex on Telecommunications with respect to the cross-border supply on a *non-facilities* basis in Mexico of the basic telecommunications services at issue (*MX* won);

(7) *found* no violation of section 5(b) of the GATS Annex on Telecommunications with respect to the cross-border supply on a *non-facilities* basis into Mexico of the basic telecommunications services at issue (*MX* won); and
(8) *noted* that it had taken into account the special and differential treatment (S&D) principles based on Article 12.11 of the DSU and that its findings did not prevent Mexico's development.

c.   *Mexico – Beef and Rice (295)*

This case was initiated by the US against Mexico on 16 June 2003. It related to trade in agricultural goods (beef[42] and rice). Mexico had imposed AD duties. The US pursued this case at the consultations, Panel and AB stages. Both Parties agreed on the RPT, and Mexico implemented the case at the RPT stage. It finalized its implementation of the legislative measure on 21 December 2006 (its AD duty on rice was implemented on 11 September 2006).

(A)   *Measures Challenged by the US*
   (1) Definitive AD measures on:
      (a) beef (*Diario Oficial* on 28 April 2000) – but the US did not challenge the measure on beef in its Panel request;
      (b) long grain white rice (*Diario Oficial* on 5 June 2002).
   (2) Mexico's Foreign Trade Act and its Federal Code of Civil Procedure.

(B)   *US Claims*
   (1) Articles 3, 5, 6, 7, 9, 10, 11, 12 and Annex II of the ADA.
   (2) Articles 11, 12, 17, 19, 20 and 21 of the SCM Agreement.
   (3) Article VI of the GATT.

(C)   *The Findings of the Adjudicating Bodies*
The Panel made fifteen findings. Mexico won two and the US thirteen. The AB made seventeen findings, of which Mexico won one and the US sixteen.

(1)   The determination of injury on rice
The Panel issued three findings on the determination of injury on rice. The US won all three. The *Panel*:

   (1) *found* violation of Articles 3.1, 3.2, 3.4 and 3.5 of the ADA through Mexico's use of a period of investigation which ended more than fifteen months before the initiation of the investigation (*US* won);
   (2) *applied judicial economy* on Article VI:2 of the GATT and Article 1 of the ADA;

---

42. After the consultations, the US did not pursue the complaint relating to beef. Hence, the Panel dealt only with the AD on rice and the Mexican Foreign Trade Act.

(3) *found* violation of Articles 3.1 and 3.5 of the ADA through Mexico's limiting its injury analysis to only six months of the years 1997, 1998, and 1999 (*US* won);

(4) *applied judicial economy* on Articles 1 and 6.2 of the ADA;

(5) *found* violation of Articles 3.1 and 3.2 of the ADA through Mexico's failure to conduct an objective examination based on positive evidence of the price effects and volume of dumped imports (*US* won); and

(6) *applied judicial economy* on Article 6.8 and Annex II of the ADA.

The AB issued four findings on the determination of injury on rice. The US won all four. The *AB:*

(1) *found* that the Panel did not exceed its terms of reference in concluding that Economía's use of a period of investigation ending in August 1999 was inconsistent with Articles 3.1, 3.2, 3.4, and 3.5 of the ADA (*US* won);

(2) *upheld* the findings that Economía's use of a period of investigation ending in August 1999 resulted in a failure to make a determination of injury based on 'positive evidence' as required by Articles 3.1, 3.2, 3.4, and 3.5 of the ADA (*US* won);

(3) *upheld* the findings that, in limiting the injury analysis to the March to August periods of 1997, 1998, and 1999, Mexico failed to make an 'objective examination' against Articles 3.1 and 3.5 of the ADA (*US* won); and

(4) *upheld* the findings that Economía's injury analysis with respect to the volume and price effects of dumped imports was inconsistent with Articles 3.1 and 3.2 of the ADA (*US* won).

Having found violation on Articles 3.1, 3.2, 3.4 and 3.5 of the ADA, the Panel applied judicial economy and made no findings on the following:

(1) increase in the volume of dumped imports or a significant effect of dumped imports on prices, violating Articles 3.1 and 3.2 of the ADA;

(2) objective analysis of the relevant economic factors, violating Articles 3.1 and 3.4 of the ADA;

(3) inclusion of non-dumped imports in the evaluation of volume, price effects, and impact of the dumped imports on the domestic industry, violating Articles 3.1, 3.2, and 3.5 of the ADA; and

(4) failure to provide the findings and conclusions reached on all issues of fact and law with the determination of injury, violating Article 12.2 of the ADA.

(2)   The dumping margin determination on rice
The Panel issued three findings on the dumping margin on Rice. The US won all three findings. The *Panel:*

(1) *found* violation of Article 5.8 of the ADA by not terminating the investigation on two US exporters which exported at undumped prices and by not excluding them from the definitive AD measure (*US* won);

(2) *found* violation of Article 6.8 and paragraph 7 of Annex II of the ADA in its application of a facts available-based dumping margin to the non-shipping exporting company Producers Rice (*US* won);

(3) *applied judicial economy* on Articles 6.2, 6.4, and 9.5 of the ADA and paragraphs 3, 5 and 6 of Annex II;

(4) *found* violation of Articles 6.1, 6.8, paragraph 1 of Annex II, 6.10 and 12.1 of the ADA in its application of a facts available-based dumping margin to the US producers and exporters that it did not investigate (*US* won); and

(5) *applied judicial economy* on Articles 6.6, 9.4, 9.5 and paragraph 7 of Annex II of the ADA.

The AB issued four findings on the dumping margin on rice. Mexico won one, and the US won the remaining three. The *AB:*

(1) *upheld* the findings that Mexico did not terminate immediately the investigation regarding Farmers Rice and Riceland because it did not exclude them from the definitive ADD in violation of Article 5.8 of the ADA (*US* won);

(2) *found* that the Panel did not exceed its terms of reference in concluding that Economía calculated a margin of dumping on the basis of the facts available for Producers Rice in a manner inconsistent with Article 6.8 and paragraph 7 of Annex II of the ADA (*US* won);

(3) *reversed* the Panel's findings that, with respect to the exporters that Economía did not investigate, Mexico acted inconsistently with Articles 6.1, 6.10, and 12.1 of the ADA (*MX* won); and

(4) *upheld* the Panel's findings that, by applying the facts available contained in the application submitted by the petitioner in calculating the margin of dumping for those US exporters that Economía did not investigate, Mexico acted inconsistently with Article 6.8 and paragraph 1 of Annex II of the ADA (*US* won).

Having found violations on Articles 5.8, 6.1, 6.8, 6.10 and 12.1 of the ADA, the Panel applied judicial economy, and made no findings, on the following:

(1) failure to provide sufficient information on the findings and conclusions of fact and law and the reasons that led to the imposition of the adverse facts available-based margin to Producers Rice and to unexamined exporters and producers, violating Article 12.2 of the ADA;

(2) application of an adverse facts available-based margin to Producers Rice and to the unexamined exporters and producers, violating Articles 1 and 9.3 of the ADA; and

(3) levying of an AD duty greater than the margin of dumping, violating Article VI:2 of GATT.

(3)   Concerning the challenges against Mexico's Foreign Trade Act
                       as such

The Panel issued eight findings on Mexico's Foreign Trade Act as such. Mexico
won two findings and the US six. The *Panel*:

(1) *found* that Article 53 of Mexico's law was inconsistent as such with
    Articles 6.1.1 of the ADA and 12.1.1 of the SCM Agreement (*US* won);
(2) *found* that Article 64 of Mexico's law was inconsistent as such with
    Article 6.8 and paragraphs 1, 3, 5 and 7 of Annex II of the ADA and
    Article 12.7 of the SCM Agreement (*US* won);
(3) *applied judicial economy* on Articles 9.3, 9.4, and 9.5 of the ADA and
    Article 19.3 of the SCM Agreement;
(4) *found* that Article 68 of Mexico's law was inconsistent as such with
    Articles 5.8, 9.3, and 11.2 of the ADA and Articles 11.9 and 21.2 of the
    SCM Agreement (*US* won);
(5) *found* that Article 89D of Mexico's law was inconsistent as such with
    Article 9.5 of the ADA and Article 19.3 of the SCM Agreement (*US* won);
(6) *found* that Article 93V of Mexico's law was inconsistent as such with
    Article 18.1 of the ADA and Article 32.1 of the SCM Agreement (*US* won);
(7) *found* that Articles 68 and 97 of Mexico's law were inconsistent as such
    with Articles 9.3 and 11.2 of the ADA and Article 21.2 of the SCM
    Agreement (*US* won);
(8) *found* that the US failed to make a prima facie case that Article 366 of the
    Federal Code of Civil Procedures was inconsistent with Articles 9.3, 9.5
    and 11.2 of the ADA and Articles 19.3 and 21.2 of the SCM Agreement
    (*MX* won); and
(9) *found* that the US failed to make a prima facie case that Articles 68 and
    97 of Mexico's law were in violation of Article 9.5 of the ADA and
    Article 19.3 of the SCM (*MX* won).

The AB issued eight findings on Mexico's Foreign Trade Act (FTA) as such.
Mexico did not win any of these findings. The US won all eight. The *AB*:

(1) *found* that the Panel did not err in considering that a prima facie case had
    been made concerning the consistency of the challenged provisions of the
    FTA with Mexico's obligations under the ADA and the SCM Agreement
    (*US* won);
(2) *found* that the Panel did not disregard Article 2 of the FTA, or Mexico's
    argument in relation thereto, in concluding that the measures were of a
    mandatory nature (*US* won);
(3) *upheld* the Panel's findings that Article 53 of the FTA was inconsistent as
    such with Article 6.1.1 of the ADA and Article 12.1.1 of the SCM
    Agreement (*US* won);
(4) *upheld* the Panel's findings that Article 64 of the FTA was inconsistent as
    such with Article 6.8 and paragraphs 1, 3, 5, and 7 of Annex II of the ADA
    and Article 12.7 of the SCM Agreement (*US* won);

(5) *upheld* the Panel's findings that Article 68 of the FTA was inconsistent as such with Articles 5.8, 9.3, and 11.2 of the ADA and Articles 11.9 and 21.2 of the SCM Agreement (*US* won);

(6) *upheld* the Panel's findings that Article 89D of the FTA was inconsistent as such with Article 9.5 of the ADA and Article 19.3 of the SCM Agreement (*US* won);

(7) *found* that, in its interpretation of Article 93V of the FTA, the Panel did not fail to fulfil its obligations under Article 11 of the DSU (*US* won); and

(8) *upheld* the Panel's findings that Articles 68 and 97 of the FTA, read together, were inconsistent as such with Articles 9.3.2 and 11.2 of the ADA and Article 21.2 of the SCM Agreement (*US* won).

(4)   Mexico's procedural defences on Article 6.2 of the DSU

The Panel issued one finding on Article 6.2 of the DSU procedural defences; the US won it. The *Panel found* that the claims in the US' Panel request, which were not indicated in the request for consultations, did not fall outside the Panel's terms of reference (*US* won).

The AB issued one finding on Article 6.2 of the DSU procedural defences, which the US won. The *AB upheld* the finding that the claims in the US Panel request, not indicated in the request for consultations, did not fall outside the terms of reference (*US* won)

d.   *Mexico – Soft Drinks (308)*

This case was initiated by the US on 16 March 2004. The US challenged the Mexican internal tax on agricultural goods (sugar and other sweeteners). The case was implemented by Mexico at the RPT stage on 27 December 2006 through the publication of the Federal Revenue Law for 2007 in the Official Journal.

(A)   *Measures Challenged by the US*

Mexico's tax measures on soft drinks and other beverages that used any sweetener other than cane sugar (*Ley de Impuesto Especial sobre Producción y Servicios*), which included:

(1) a 20% tax on soft drinks and other beverages that used any sweetener other than cane sugar; and

(2) a 20% distribution tax (also applied at other stages of trade) on soft drinks and other beverages that used any sweetener other than cane sugar.

(B)   *US Claims*

(1) Article III of the GATT.

(2) In particular, Article III:2, first sentence.

(3) Article III:2, second sentence.

(4) Article III:4 of the GATT.

(C)   *The Findings of the Adjudicating Bodies*
The Panel made eight findings. The US won them all. The AB made three findings, and the US similarly won them all.

(1)   With respect to Mexico's soft drink tax and distribution tax
The Panel issued four findings on the distribution tax. The US won them all. The
Panel:

  (1) *found* violation of Article III:2, first sentence, of the GATT, because
      imported beet sugar was subject to internal taxes in excess of those
      applied to like domestic sweeteners (*US* won);
  (2) *found* violation of Article III:2, second sentence, of the GATT, because
      imported corn syrup was being taxed dissimilarly to the directly com-
      petitive or substitutable products, so as to afford protection to the Mexican
      domestic production of cane sugar (*US* won);
  (3) *found* violation of Article III:4 of the GATT, because imported beet sugar
      and corn syrup were accorded less favourable treatment than that accorded
      to like products of national origin (*US* won); and
  (4) *found* violation of Article III:2, first sentence, of the GATT, because
      imported soft drinks and syrups sweetened with non-cane sugar
      sweeteners (including corn syrup and beet sugar) were subject to
      internal taxes in excess of those applied to like domestic products
      (*US* won).

(2)   With respect to Mexico's book-keeping requirements
The Panel issued one finding on bookkeeping requirements. The US won it. The
Panel found violation of Article III:4 of the GATT, because imported beet sugar
and corn syrup were accorded less favourable treatment than that accorded to like
products of national origin (*US* won).

(3)   Mexico's defences (decline jurisdiction, Article XX(d)
                        of the GATT, and special recommendations)
The Panel issued three findings on the defences by Mexico. The US won all three.
The *Panel:*

  (1) *found* that under the DSU it had no discretion to decline to exercise
      its jurisdiction in the case that had been brought before it (*US*
      won);
  (2) *found* that the challenged tax measures were not justified as measures that
      were necessary to secure compliance by the US with laws or regulations
      which were not inconsistent with the provisions of the GATT (*US* won);
      and
  (3) *found* that it had no discretion to depart from the procedure stated in
      Article 19.1 of the DSU and could not make the special recommendations
      requested by Mexico (*US* won).

The AB issued three findings on the defences by Mexico. Mexico did not win any of them. The *AB:*

(1) *upheld* the conclusion that the Panel had no discretion to decline to exercise its jurisdiction in the case that had been brought before it (*US* won);

(2) *upheld* the conclusion that the measures were not justified under XX(d) of the GATT (*US* won); and

(3) *rejected* Mexico's claim that the Panel failed to fulfil its obligations under Article 11 of the DSU, in finding that 'Mexico has not established that its measures contribute to securing compliance in the circumstances of this case' (*US* won).

VI.   THE RATE OF IMPLEMENTATION

As mentioned, Mexico has had sixteen cases as complainant and fourteen cases as defendant in the WTO. When it participated as complainant, 43% of its complaints (seven of sixteen cases) were abandoned:

(1) *US – AD on Steel Zeroing I* (325);
(2) *US – CVD on Steel* (280);
(3) *Ecuador – Cement I* (182);
(4) *EC – Bananas III New Request* (158);
(5) *Guatemala – Cement I* (60);
(6) *EC – Bananas III* (27); and
(7) *EC – Bananas III Old Request* (16).

Three of sixteen cases (19%) were pending as of the closing date of this work:

(1) *US – AD on Steel Zeroing II* (344);
(2) *US – OCTG* (282); and
(3) *US – Offset Act* (217/234).

Mexico was able to achieve implementation in 38% (six of sixteen cases) when acting as complainant:

(1) *Panama – Milk* (329);
(2) *US – Cement* (281);
(3) *Ecuador – Cement II* (191);
(4) *Guatemala – Cement II* (156);
(5) *US – Tomatoes* (49); and
(6) *Venezuela – OCTG* (23).

When Mexico was acting as a defendant, a total of 36% of the cases against it (five of fourteen) were abandoned by the complainant:

(1) *Mexico – Olive Oil I* (314);
(2) *Mexico – Transformers* (216);
(3) *Mexico – Swine* (203);

(4) *Mexico – Corn Syrup I* (101); and
(5) *Mexico – Customs Valuation from EC* (53).

Two of the fourteen of the cases (14%) were pending as of the closing date of this work:

(1) *Mexico – Olive Oil II* (341); and
(2) *Mexico – AD on Tubes* (331).

Mexico has implemented 50% (seven of fourteen cases) of the complaints when defending:

(1) *Mexico – Soft Drinks* (308);
(2) *Mexico – Customs Valuation from Guatemala* (298);
(3) *Mexico – Beef and Rice* (295);
(4) *Mexico – Beans* (284);
(5) *Mexico – Matches* (232);
(6) *Mexico – Telecoms* (204); and
(7) *Mexico – Corn Syrup II* (132).

Table 4.35 Percentage of Implemented Cases (Complainant/Defendant)

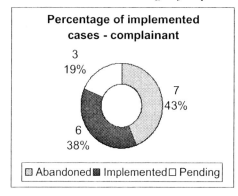

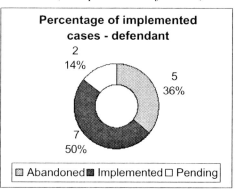

VII.   THE LEGAL REMEDIES USED IN MEXICO'S CASES

As we saw at the introduction of this work, there are three main legal remedies in the DSU – compliance, compensation and suspension of concessions – and one derivative legal remedy – MAS, because it is more like an agreed compliance or compensation. We have made a distinction between *ex ante* compliance or MAS, on one hand, and *ex post* compliance or MAS, on the other. This distinction is explained as follows:

Ex ante compliance or MAS   Compliance or MAS achieved before a Panel/
                                   AB ruling on the legality of a measure; here,
                                   the obligation derives from Article XVI:4 of
                                   the WTO Agreement, which is designed to

	ensure the conformity of its measures with the obligations provided in the WTO covered agreements, regardless of any ruling on the legality of a particular measure.
Ex post compliance or MAS	Compliance or MAS achieved after a Panel/AB has ruled that a measure is WTO-inconsistent; here, there is an obligation to modify or withdraw the measure in light of the Panel/AB analysis and findings. Compensation and suspension of concessions may be triggered after this stage.[43]

When Mexico was the complainant (sixteen cases), it was able to use a legal remedy in 44% of its complaints (seven of sixteen cases) but it was not able to do so in the remaining 56% (nine of sixteen cases). When Mexico has defended its measures (fourteen cases), the complainant was able to use a legal remedy in 50% of the total (seven of fourteen cases), but not able to do so in the other 50% of the cases.[44]

Table 4.36 Availability of Legal Remedy (Complainant/Defendant)

We now disaggregate this information. First, we note that there are cases in which Mexico was involved where no legal remedy was achieved. Where Mexico was the complainant there were nine such cases:

(1) *US – AD on Steel Zeroing II* (344) – pending;
(2) *US – OCTG* (282) – pending;
(3) *US – AD on Steel Zeroing I* (325) – abandoned;
(4) *US – CVD on Steel* (280) – abandoned;
(5) *Ecuador – Cement I* (182) – abandoned;

---

43. See Ch. 1, 'Mexico's Options for Settlement of International Trade Disputes', where we explain the DSU process.
44. With Mexico as complainant, there is one more case with legal remedy than the number of cases implemented. In *US – Offset Act* (217/234), Mexico was authorized and had imposed retaliatory measures even when the case was pending at our cut-off date for WTO cases.

(6) *EC – Bananas III New Request* (158) – abandoned;
(7) *Guatemala – Cement I* (60) – abandoned;
(8) *EC – Bananas III* (27) – abandoned; and
(9) *EC – Bananas III Old Request* (16) – abandoned.

Where Mexico was the defendant there are seven such cases:

(1) *Mexico – Olive Oil II* (341) – pending;
(2) *Mexico – AD on Tubes* (331) – pending;
(3) *Mexico – Olive Oil I* (314) – abandoned;
(4) *Mexico – Transformers* (216) – abandoned;
(5) *Mexico – Swine* (203) – abandoned;
(6) *Mexico – Corn Syrup I* (101) – abandoned; and
(7) *Mexico – Customs Valuation from EC* (53) – abandoned.

We turn now to Mexico's cases that were solved through MAS *ex ante*. With Mexico as complainant, there are four cases with MAS *ex ante*:

(1) *Panama – Milk* (329);
(2) *US – Cement* (281);[45]
(3) *US – Tomatoes* (49); and
(4) *Venezuela – OCTG* (23).

With Mexico as a defendant, there are three cases with MAS *ex ante*:

(1) *Mexico – Customs Valuation from Guatemala* (298);
(2) *Mexico – Beans* (284); and
(3) *Mexico – Matches* (232).

We found no case of Mexico as complainant that was agreed on MAS *ex post*. But there are three where Mexico, as defendant, agreed on MAS *ex post*:

(1) *Mexico – Soft Drinks* (308);
(2) *Mexico – Beef and Rice* (295); and
(3) *Mexico – Telecoms* (204).

One case has been complied *ex ante* when Mexico has been the complainant (there is no case as defendant): *Ecuador – Cement II* (191)
Regarding compliance *ex post*, there is one case with Mexico as a complainant and one case as defendant:

(1) *Guatemala – Cement II* (156); and
(2) *Mexico – Corn Syrup II* (132), respectively.

---

45. The original investigation was held to be illegal by a GATT Panel and the report was not adopted. However, Mexico did not allege that the GATT case created further WTO obligations. Hence, we classify this case as complied *ex ante*. For the GATT case *US – Cement*, see Ch. 2, 'Mexico's GATT and WTO Cases'.

Finally, there is only one pending case with Mexico as the complainant where the remedy of suspension of concessions or other obligation (retaliation) has been used: in *US – Offset Act* (217/234), Mexico imposed retaliation against the US. However, the retaliation had not had induced the US to comply as of the closing date of this work.[46]

Table 4.37 Legal Remedy Used per Case (Complainant/Defendant)

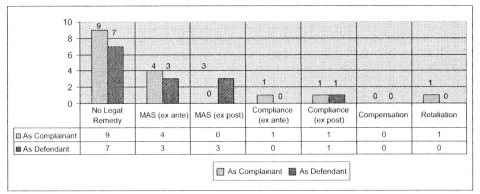

	No Legal Remedy	MAS (ex ante)	MAS (ex post)	Compliance (ex ante)	Compliance (ex post)	Compensation	Retaliation
As Complainant	9	4	0	1	1	0	1
As Defendant	7	3	3	0	1	0	0

From this chart on Mexico's cases by legal remedy, we can distil four clusters into which the cases may be classified:

(1) cases with no legal remedy (all of these would be pending or abandoned);

(2) cases with MAS or compliance *ex ante* (all of these would be implemented);

(3) cases with MAS or compliance *ex post* (all of these would be implemented); and

(4) cases with compensation or retaliation (which could be pending, abandoned or implemented).

We propose to assess the time it has taken to achieve the legal remedy in Mexico's cases by using the period from the request for consultations[47] until the application of the legal remedy or the closing date of this work.[48]

First, we start with the cases with MAS *ex ante* and compliance *ex ante*. We note that the challenged measures in these cases were only allegedly WTO-inconsistent, because there was no Panel/AB examination on the

---

46. This may suggest that retaliation is not an effective legal remedy for Mexico.

47. We use the request for consultations because it is the first official action taken by a complainant and it triggers the whole DSU process. We could have used the date of the challenged measure, but at that time the complainant plays a passive role, at least officially. Also, the request for establishment of a Panel would be the second official action by the complainant.

48. For the information on the dates used for this calculation, see the Appendix, Table 12, 'Months between Consultations and the Application of the Legal Remedy'.

legality of the measure given that they were *ex ante*. There have been five cases as complainant:

(1) *Panama – Milk* (329) (MAS *ex ante*). It took Panama 6.27 months from the request for consultations to implementation through a MAS.

(2) *US – Cement* (281) (MAS *ex ante*). It took the US 36.03 months from the request for consultations to implementation through a MAS.

(3) *US – Tomatoes* (49) (MAS *ex ante*). It took the US 4.10 months from the request for consultations to implementation through a MAS.

(4) *Venezuela – OCTG* (23) (MAS *ex ante*). It took Venezuela 17.27 months from the request for consultations to implementation through a MAS.

(5) *Ecuador – Cement II* (191) (compliance *ex ante*). It took Ecuador 3.03 months from the request for consultations to implementation through compliance.

There are three cases with Mexico as the defendant that were resolved by MAS *ex ante* (none with compliance *ex ante*):

(1) *Mexico – Customs Valuation from Guatemala* (298) (MAS *ex ante*). It took Mexico 25.63 months from the request for consultations to implementation through a MAS.

(2) *Mexico – Beans* (284) (MAS *ex ante*). It took Mexico 11.90 months from the request for consultations to implementation through a MAS.

(3) *Mexico – Matches* (232) (MAS *ex ante*). It took Mexico 33.03 months from the request for consultations to implementation through a MAS.

Table 4.38 Time (Months) from Consultations to Legal Remedy Ex Ante (Complainant/Defendant)

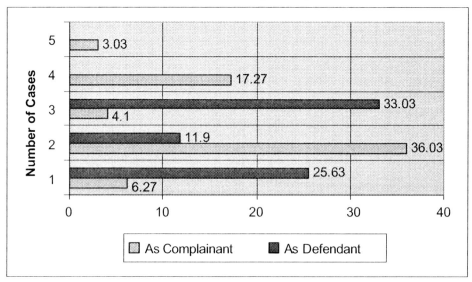

We now turn to the cases with MAS *ex post* or compliance *ex post*. We note that the challenged measures in these cases were WTO-inconsistent – there was a Panel/AB conclusion affirming this as they were *ex post*. There is one case as complainant with compliance *ex post* (none with MAS *ex post*): *Guatemala – Cement II* (156) (compliance *ex post*). It took Guatemala 21.27 months from the request for consultations to implementation through compliance.

With Mexico as defendant there are four cases with MAS *ex post* or compliance *ex post*:

(1) *Mexico – Soft Drinks* (308)(MAS *ex post*). It took Mexico 33.53 months from the request for consultations to implementation through a MAS.

(2) *Mexico – Beef and Rice* (295)(MAS *ex post*). It took Mexico 42.80 months from the request for consultations to implementation through a MAS.

(3) *Mexico – Telecoms* (204)(MAS *ex post*). It took Mexico 60.70 months from the request for consultations to implementation through a MAS.

(4) *Mexico – Corn Syrup II* (132)(compliance *ex post*). It took Mexico 49.10 months from the request for consultations to implementation through compliance.

Finally, we present Mexico's cases with compensation and retaliation. As in cases *ex post*, they were WTO-inconsistent given that the Panel/AB made findings of violation. We found one case as complainant in retaliation that was not implemented as of the closing date of this work:

(1) *US – Offset Act* (217/234)(retaliation). It took the US 68.37 months from the request for consultations to the closing date of this work.

Table 4.39 Time (Months) from Consultations to Legal Remedy Ex Post (Complainant/Defendant)

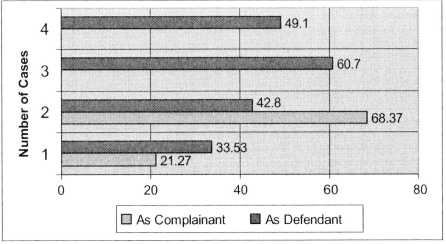

Chapter 5

Interpretations of the Data

It is difficult to distinguish objectives in life. However, one of them would very likely be the constant learning process of becoming skilful at the art of living your own life.

Jorge Alberto Huerta-Goldman

The previous chapters of this work present the options open to Mexico in adjudicating international trade disputes (Chapter 1) and the cases it has litigated over a period of almost twenty years (Chapters 2 to 4). The objective of this final chapter is to present my interpretation of that picture.

I am not trying to establish or clarify Mexico's international trade objectives; they depend on many changing factors such as internal politics, the world economy, the strength of Mexico's industries, consumer trends and the environment, to mention just a few. Here, I am simply trying to make a contribution, albeit small and using my opinions and observations, to Mexico's constant learning process regarding the art of living in the international trade arena.

The following clarification may be useful to understand the terms used in this chapter:[1]

Abandoned case	A case which is not procedurally active due to: (a) inactivity for more than three years (because after three years one cannot reasonably expect a renaissance); or (b) the presentation of a new request for consultation challenging the original measure or its modified version, such as provisional and definitive antidumping

---

1. These definitions refer to both the GATT era and the WTO. Hence those definitions for the cases taken under GATT have to be read without the additional and later WTO elements, and vice versa.

measures;[2] we further classify the abandoned cases by declaration or no declaration of abandonment by the complainant.

AD/CVD orders	The AD/CVD investigations and procedures towards the imposition of duties; they may contain original investigations, yearly reviews and sunset reviews, among others.
Adoption of GATT Panel reports	Under the GATT rules, Panel reports were not automatically adopted. They were adopted only if there was consensus.[3] Hence, any Contracting Party had veto power. The current WTO rules allow for adoption of a Panel/AB report unless there is a consensus not to adopt it – i.e., the negative consensus rule.[4] A report not adopted means no legal obligation with respect to implementation.
Ex ante compliance or MAS	Compliance or MAS achieved before a Panel/AB ruling on the legality of a measure; here, the obligation derives from Article XVI:4 of the WTO Agreement, which is designed to ensure the conformity of its measures with the obligations provided in the WTO covered agreements, regardless of any ruling on the legality of a particular measure.
Ex post compliance or MAS	Compliance or MAS achieved after a Panel/AB has ruled that a measure is WTO inconsistent; here, there is an obligation to modify or withdraw the measure in the light of the Panel/AB analysis and findings. Compensation and suspension of concessions may be triggered after this stage.[5]
Finding won/lost by Mexico	Any successful finding by a GATT Panel, PTA Panel, WTO Panel/AB (original or Article 21.5 of the DSU) or arbitrator (Articles 21.3 or 22.6

---

2. We count these reformulated cases – e.g., provisional and definitive AD measures – as a single case per each request for consultations. This is important for our analysis of legal remedies in Ch. 5, 'Interpretations of the Data'.
3. There is consensus if no Member, present at the meeting when the decision is taken, formally objects to the proposed decision. See n. 1 of the WTO Agreement for the WTO description of consensus.
4. See Arts 16.4 and 17.14 of the DSU.
5. See Ch. 1, 'Mexico's Options for Settlement of International Trade Disputes', where we explain the DSU process.

of the DSU).[6] We use findings as a unit of account. We do not pronounce on overall win/ loss, which is a very difficult issue to tackle.[7] For WTO cases, we distinguish the Panel findings from the AB findings by counting them separately. We do not count findings under Article 3.8 of the DSU – although we do take them into account if the Article was the legal base of a defence. Nor do we count absence of findings through judicial economy.

The findings from the Panel, as amended by the AB, may come from two sources: claims that were the basis of the complaint (Article 6.2 of the DSU) or defences presented by the defendant (such as Article XX of the GATT).

Implementation or measure amended	A measure is deemed to be amended or implemented when: (a) the complainant is satisfied with the amendment; or (b) the measure has been withdrawn no later than one year from the last communication of a disputing Party or an adjudicative body, and the complainant does not oppose the modification or elimination of the measure; or (c) there is a MAS.
	Under WTO law, one finding of violation is sufficient to trigger the obligation to implement, unless the measure is no longer in force when the Panel/ AB issues the finding. Article 19.1 of the DSU obliges Panels to recommend that the measure be brought into conformity, if a violation is found.
Legal remedies	The means to solve a wrongful act; we found three main legal remedies in the DSU: compliance, compensation pending compliance, and suspension of concessions or other obligations. We count a MAS as a secondary legal remedy.
MAS	Mutually agreed solution, including: (a) notified agreements or agreements publicly available;

6. We determine success in findings by the arbitrator under Arts 21.3 or 22.6 of the DSU by comparing them with the position sustained by each party to the arbitration. As an example, assume that a finding on RPT of two months and one party's position was one month and the other party's position was three months. Here we would allocate a one-half finding of success to each Party.
7. For instance, even when the findings were in favour of the US in the *Mexico – Telecoms* (204) case, there were internal interests in Mexico that wanted to amend the domestic regulations and some government officials used the Panel report as a leverage to do so.

(b) a unilateral manifestation of compliance not followed by opposition by the complainant; (c) requests for suspension under Article 12.12 of the DSU; and (d) implemented cases.

Other Party involved

When Mexico is attacking, the other Party involved is the defendant. When Mexico is defending, the other Party involved is the complainant. We further classify the other Party involved – the 153 WTO Members[8] – in accordance with their economic development as (a) US/EC (29 Members),[9] (b) other OECD Members (10 Members including Mexico),[10] (c) non-Members of OECD (80 non-Members)[11] and (d) LDCs or least developed countries (32 Members).[12]

Product

The good, service or intellectual property right subject to the dispute settlement mechanism; we classify them under four clusters: (a) industrial goods; (b) agricultural goods; (c) general goods; and (d) services (Mexico has had no TRIPS cases). There are some cases covering two products at the same time – e.g., *EC – Bananas III* (27), which dealt with agricultural goods and

8. See <www.wto.org/english/thewto_e/whatis_e/tif_e/org6_e.htm>, August 2009.
9. This classification includes the twenty-seven Member States from the EC, the EC itself, and the US. In addition to its Member States, the EC is also a WTO Member. However, as n. 2 of the WTO Agreement indicates with respect to the decision-making process of the WTO, 'the number of votes of the European Communities and their Member States shall in no case exceed the number of the Member States of the European Communities'.
10. Excluding the US and the EC, they are: Australia, Canada, Iceland, Japan, Korea, New Zealand, Norway, Switzerland, and Turkey (and, of course, Mexico).
11. These are the WTO Members that are neither OECD Members nor LDCs: Albania; Antigua and Barbuda; Argentina; Armenia; Kingdom of Bahrain; Barbados; Belize; Bolivia; Botswana; Brazil; Brunei Darussalam; Cameroon; Chile; China; Colombia; Costa Rica; Côte d'Ivoire; Croatia; Cuba; the Democratic Republic of the Congo; Dominica; Dominican Republic; Ecuador; Egypt; El Salvador; Fiji; the Former Yugoslav Republic of Macedonia; Gabon; Georgia; Ghana; Grenada; Guatemala; Guyana; Honduras; Hong Kong, China; India; Indonesia; Israel; Jamaica; Jordan; Kenya; Kuwait; the Kyrgyz Republic; Liechtenstein; Macao; Malaysia; Mauritius; Moldova; Mongolia; Morocco; Namibia; Nicaragua; Nigeria; Oman; Pakistan; Panama; Papua New Guinea; Paraguay; Peru; the Philippines; Qatar; Saint Kitts and Nevis; Saint Lucia; Saint Vincent and the Grenadines; Saudi Arabia; Singapore; South Africa; Sri Lanka; Suriname; Swaziland; Chinese Taipei; Thailand; Tonga; Trinidad and Tobago; Tunisia; United Arab Emirates; Uruguay; Venezuela; Viet Nam; and Zimbabwe.
12. Those that are Members of the WTO are: Angola, Bangladesh, Benin, Burkina Faso, Burundi, Cambodia, the Central African Republic, Chad, the Democratic Republic of the Congo, Djibouti, Gambia, Guinea, Guinea Bissau, Haiti, Lesotho, Madagascar, Malawi, Maldives, Mali, Mauritania, Mozambique, Myanmar, Nepal, Niger, Rwanda, Senegal, Sierra Leone, the Solomon Islands, Tanzania, Togo, Uganda, and Zambia. See <www.wto.org/english/thewto_e/whatis_e/tif_e/org7_e.htm>, August 2007.

services. Those cases have been recorded by half units for each product (i.e., 0.5 for agricultural product and 0.5 for services).[13]

PTAs   Preferential trade agreements, as in Article XXIV of the GATT; they could be customs unions or free trade agreements. Other forms of economic integrations, such as ALADI, are allowed in the WTO through the so-called Enabling Clause.[14]

This chapter is divided into three sections. The first presents general and horizontal observations stemming from this work. The second contains observations with respect to Mexico's experience in the multilateral arena (GATT and WTO). Finally, the third section presents our interpretation of Mexico's experience with the dispute settlement mechanisms in the PTAs.

I.   THE DATA ACROSS THE BOARD

A.   THE RATE OF INITIATIONS PER YEAR (COUNTRY VERSUS COUNTRY CASES)

The table below shows the country versus country cases initiated by and against Mexico from 1986 to 2006. It also presents the value (in USD billions) of Mexico's exports and imports on an annual basis. The cases include those under the GATT, the WTO and the PTAs, but exclude those under Chapter 19 of NAFTA (private party versus country on trade remedies). All the cases before 1995 are GATT cases. The three country versus country PTA cases as complainant were taken in 1995, 1996 and 2002. Mexico's PTA case as defendant is from 2003. The rest of the cases mentioned in the table are under the WTO (sixteen as complainant and fourteen as defendant).

We note that Mexico has never initiated or faced as a defendant more than four cases in a single year. Only in 2003 did Mexico have to defend four cases in the same year (three WTO and one from a FTA). Also, only in 1996, as complainant, did it take four cases in one year (three WTO and one NAFTA Chapter 20). In 1995, 1999 and 2005, it initiated three WTO cases each year, whereas in 2000 three WTO cases were taken against it. In the other years, Mexico did not have more than two cases per year, either as complainant or as defendant. Finally, there were several years when it did not initiate any cases at all.

Trade, as presented by the individual figures on exports and imports[15], increased significantly during the period in our review, 1986 to 2006. The 2006 figures of trade are thirteen times the corresponding figures in 1986. From 1986 to 1990 trade did

---

13. There is one NAFTA case dealing with services and investment at the same time.
14. See WTO decision of 28 Nov. 1979 (L/4903) agreed under the GATT on differential and more favourable treatment reciprocity and fuller participation of developing countries.
15. Exports and imports behaved in similarly way from 1986 to 2006. Hence, we do not need to observe them separately

not grow greatly, but in 1991–1992 there was a higher rate of increase. From 1996 to 2006 it went up sharply, though with a slowdown in 2001–2003.

Notwithstanding this increase in trade, the number of disputes initiated per year does not gradually increase over the same period, nor does it grow in the same proportion as trade. Even in 1995, when trade and the number of disputes per year started going up in at the same time, there seems to be no relationship between the increase in trade and the increased use to dispute settlement mechanisms (country versus country).

From 1986 to 1995, Mexico used the GATT dispute settlement procedures only three times, whereas after 1995 it became a more frequent user of the systems available to it. NAFTA entered into force in 1994 and the WTO in 1995. Mexico has used their mechanisms at least once every year since 1995.

These figures suggest that Mexico uses the dispute settlement mechanisms available to it more often when the systems are stronger[16] and trade is increasing. But the numbers have not been higher than four cases per year, which suggests that there is no link with the rate of growth in trade.

Table 5.1 Relationship between Trade and the Rate of Initiation of Cases (Country versus Country)

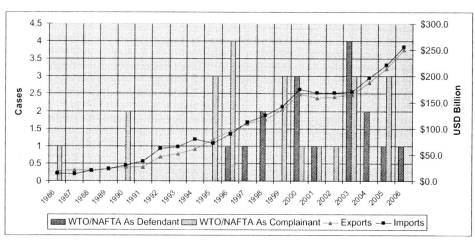

Source for exports and imports: United Nations Comtrade Database (SITC Rev.2 and Rev.3) <http://comtrade.un.org/>, August 2009.

I believe that Mexico is capable of or handling more than the yearly ceiling of four disputes. Certainly, its growth of trade suggests that there is a need for that. Even though Mexico's trade was three times higher in 2006 than ten years before, it did not show any specific offensive trade concern that year, whereas it initiated four

---

16. As explained above, the dispute settlement system under the GATT was significantly weaker than the WTO system, even after it became stronger with time. The NAFTA general dispute settlement mechanism has a stronger nature than the old GATT system, even with NAFTA problems on composition of Panels. See Ch. 1, 'Mexico's Options for Settlement of International Trade Disputes'.

cases as complainant in 1996, a year with fewer exports than 2006. Hence, the number of cases initiated per year may not represent the specific trade concerns faced by Mexican exporters or the domestic industry. The explanation lies elsewhere, perhaps in administrative capacity. Even if an issue is important for the economy, internal politics or the strength of the legal system may influence decisions on whether to initiate or defend a case.

When facing a potential case, either as complainant or as defendant, any country has three main options: (a) to initiate/litigate the case, (b) to negotiate a settlement; and (c) to accommodate the position of the counterpart. The decision regarding which action to take is often highly influenced by resources available.

A country with few resources may be able to get external legal assistance from private law firms or from the Advisory Centre in WTO Law (ACWL) if it is a WTO developing county.[17] However, it still needs the resources to cope with the requirements of the external advisors.

Country versus country systems allow standing to WTO Members and Parties to a PTA. But the team of in-house litigators from a country may not be able to cope with more than a certain number of cases per year because they need to maintain a minimum level of control over each case.

Perhaps one question we could ask ourselves is whether those WTO Members without adequate human and monetary resources find the right incentives to attract the means needed to pursue an objective through the dispute settlement of the WTO (or a PTA).

We could use two measurements: a cost-result analysis (we will partially deal with this idea below when analysing WTO legal remedies) and the level of communication between a government and relevant industries/consumers (see section II, D, 2, 'The Most Frequent Products', below).

Conclusions

Mexico's experience of litigation of country versus country cases demonstrates that trade has increased at a much faster rate than the initiation of cases. After the entry into force of NAFTA and the WTO (the second half of our period of observation), Mexico significantly increased its rate of participation in cases, and trade started a steady increase as well. But the growth in the number of initiations does not road that of trade expansion.

Resources probably play a central role in the rate of utilization of dispute settlement systems, creating a ceiling of 4 cases per year each as complainant and as defendant.

---

17. The ACWL is an intergovernmental organization created to assist developing countries in handling WTO disputes. It has an efficient legal team, and its fees are graduated according to the WTO Member; see <www.acwl.ch/e/index_e.aspx>, August 2009. Mexico is entitled to benefit from the services provided by the ACWL upon payment of legal fees. It would have to pay non-Member fees, which are higher than Member fees. But it does not seem to have used the ACUL, even as a non-Member.

II.   THE GATT AND THE WTO

A.   THE SUBJECT MATTER IN MEXICO'S CASES WITH
             OTHER-OECD MEMBERS

We now compare the subject matter of cases where other-OECD Members[18] were
involved as complainant or defendant. Two sets of information were used for this
comparison: our data for the subject matter of Mexico's cases as presented in
Chapters 2 and 4; and material from the World Bank regarding the subject matter
of cases involving the remaining other-OECD Members.

    With respect to Mexico, there are two valuable observations: first, Mexico is
a high user of the GATT as complainant (thirteen times cited), the second-most-
frequent user within the 'other-OECD' group. Second, in that group it is the most
frequent user of the ADA as complainant, claiming violation of the ADA eleven
times, followed by Canada with six claims of violation.

Table 5.2 Other-OECD Members as Complainant: Subject Matter[19]

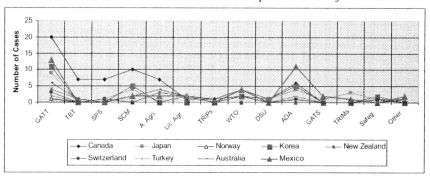

Source for other-OECD Members: The World Bank, WTO Dispute Settlement Database,
<http://go.worldbank.org/X5EZPHXJY0>, August 2009.

Mexico has had to defend claims based on the GATT and on the Agreement on
Agriculture more frequently than any other country in the 'other-OECD' group,
except one – Korea. Korea is the highest defender of GATT cases with eleven,
followed by Mexico with nine. Also, Korea is the country that most frequently has
had to defend cases based on the Agreement on Agriculture, with five cases, followed by Mexico with four.

    Complainants choose the claims they want to pursue. But defendants do not
choose the claims they will face. Perhaps that is why other-OECD Members as
defendants do not display similar patterns with respect to subject matter.

---

18.   The OECD Members excluding the US and the EC; see 'Acronyms and Definitions'.
19.   There is a caveat regarding this table: the data from the WTO Dispute Settlement Database
      covers the period from 1 Jan. 1995 until 21 Jul. 2004. The data we used for Mexico in this chart
      goes up to 1 Jan. 2007.

With respect to the ADA, Mexico has had to defend far more cases (six) than any other other-OECD country, followed by Turkey and Australia (one case each). This makes it the main user of ADA, both as complainant and defendant. In addition, Mexico is the second-most-frequent defender of GATT cases (nine) within the other-OECD group, behind Korea (eleven cases). Mexico is also the second-most-frequent defender of cases on the Agreement on Agriculture (four), again behind Korea (five).

Table 5.3 Other-OECD Members as Defendant: Subject Matter

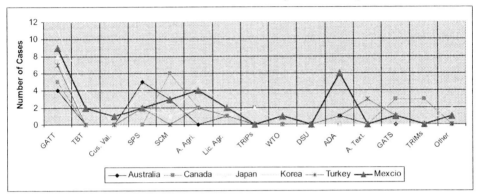

Source for other-OECD Members: The World Bank, WTO Dispute Settlement Database, <http://go.worldbank.org/X5EZPHXJY0>, August 2009.

Conclusions

Within the group of other-OECD Members, Mexico has been more involved than any other country, both as complainant and as defendant, in ADA cases. Mexico is the second-most-involved country as complainant and defendant in GATT cases.

With respect to subject matter, other-OECD Members act consistently as complainants – i.e., the number of times they decide to use each WTO Agreement to challenge others is more or less the same – whereas they act inconsistently as defendants.

B.   THE OTHER PARTY INVOLVED AND THE RESULTS
        OF MEXICO'S WTO CASES

1.   The Other Party Involved and the Procedural Stage

Only with US/EC did Mexico take its cases, both as complainant and defendant, to the final stages. Those cases which went as far as Article 21.5 Panel/AB and RPT were also only against the US/EC. The number of cases which went only to the consultations stage is equal with respect to US/EC and non-Members of OECD.

Table 5.4 Procedural Stage by the Other Party Involved

Stage	As Complainant	As Defendant
Retaliation	US/EC: one case[20]	
Article 21.5	US/EC: 2 cases[21]	US/EC: one case[22]
Panel/AB		
RPT		US/EC: 3 cases[23]
Panel/AB	US/EC: 3 cases Non-OECD: 2 cases[24]	US/EC: one case Non-OECD: one case[25]
Consultations	Non-OECD: 4 cases US/EC: 4 cases[26]	Non-OECD: 4 cases US/EC: 4 cases[27]

Conclusions

Mexico litigated its cases, both as complainant and defendant, to the Retaliation, Article 21.5 Panel/AB and RPT stages only against the US/EC.

The cases which Mexico took, as complainant and defendant, only to the consultations stage are equally divided between US/EC and non-Members of OECD. There are no cases against LDCs or any other – OECD Members.

2.   The Other Party Involved and the Findings Won

The following table shows the range of findings won by Mexico at the Panel stage (including Article 21.5 Panels) classified according to the other Party involved.[28] As complainant, Mexico won more than 60% of the findings at the Panel stage in

---

20. *US – Offset Act* (217/234).
21. *US – OCTG* (282) and *EC – Bananas III* (27).
22. *Mexico – Corn Syrup II* (132) from the US.
23. *Mexico – Soft Drinks* (308) from the US, *Mexico – Beef and Rice* (295) from the US and *Mexico – Telecoms* (204) from the US.
24. *US – AD on Steel Zeroing II* (344); *US – Cement* (281); *US – CVD on Steel* (280); *Guatemala – Cement II* (156); and *Guatemala – Cement I* (60).
25. *Mexico – Olive Oil II* (341) from the EC and *Mexico – AD on Tubes* (331) from Guatemala.
26. *US – AD on Steel Zeroing I* (325); *EC – Bananas III New Request* (158); *US – Tomatoes* (49); *EC – Bananas III Old Request* (16); *Panama – Milk* (329); *Ecuador – Cement II* (191); *Venezuela – OCTG* (23); and *Ecuador – Cement I* (182).
27. Mexico – Olive Oil I (314) from the EC; Mexico – Swine (203) from the US; Mexico – Corn Syrup I (101) from the US; Mexico – Customs Valuation from EC (53); Mexico – Customs Valuation Guatemala (298); Mexico – Beans (284) from Nicaragua; Mexico – Matches (232) from Chile; and Mexico – Transformers (216) from Brazil.
28. This is based on our presentation of Mexico's WTO cases in Ch. 4, 'Mexico's Conduct of Its Cases: An Explanation of the WTO Experience'. For a detailed presentation of the background, measures, claims and findings of the cases, see that chapter.

four cases, two against the US/EC and two against non-Members of OECD. The two cases against non-Members of OECD were interrelated, because both challenged the same AD order imposed by Guatemala (*Guatemala – Cement I* (60) and *Guatemala – Cement II* (156)). The two cases litigated against the US/EC, on the other hand, were challenged by several complainants, including Mexico. The most important complainant in both cases was either the US or the EC (*EC – Bananas III* (27) and *US – Offset Act* (217/234)). Finally, Mexico won 15%–29% of the findings at the Panel stage in one case against the US/EC. It was the sole complainant against the US (*US – OCTG* (282)).

As defendant, Mexico has only litigated cases initiated by the US/EC. Indeed, the US was the complainant in all of the cases. We note that Mexico did not win any findings in two of those cases. It won 1%–14% of the findings in the third case, 15%–29% in the fourth case and 30%–44% in the fifth case. As defendant, the highest rate of findings it won was 43%, followed by a case with 17%.

Table 5.5 Findings Won by the Other Party Involved
(Panel and 21.5 Panel)

Findings Won by Mexico (%)	As Complainant	As Defendant
100	1 US/EC[29]	
99–85	1 non-OECD[30]	
84–60	1 US/EC and 1 Non-OECD[31]	
59–45		
44–30		1 US/EC[32]
29–15	1 US/EC[33]	1 US/EC[34]
14–1		1 US/EC[35]
0		2 US/EC[36]

At the AB stage, when acting as complainant, Mexico won 60%–84% of the AB findings in two cases against the US/EC. It was amongst several complainants in

---

29. In the case *EC – Bananas III* (27), Mexico and the other co-complainants won 100% of the Panel findings.
30. In the case *Guatemala – Cement II* (156), Mexico won 95% of the Panel findings.
31. In *US – Offset Act* (217/234), Mexico and the co-complainants won 71% of the Panel findings, whereas in *Guatemala – Cement I* (60), Mexico won 75%.
32. In *Mexico – Telecoms* (204), Mexico won 43% of the Panel findings.
33. In *US – OCTG* (282), Mexico won 20% of the Panel findings.
34. In *Mexico – Corn Syrup II* (132), Mexico won 17% of the Panel findings.
35. In *Mexico – Beef and Rice* (295), Mexico 13% of the Panel findings.
36. Mexico won no Panel findings in *Mexico – Soft Drinks* (308) and in *Mexico – Corn Syrup II* (132) Art. 21.5 Panel.

both cases and the largest was either the US or the EC (*US – Offset Act* (217/234) and *EC – Bananas III* (27)). As complainant, Mexico did not win any of the AB findings in two cases, one against the US/EC and one against a non-Member of OECD (*US – OCTG* (282) and *Guatemala – Cement I* (60)).

As defendant, Mexico won between 1% and 14% of the AB findings in one case initiated by the US (*Mexico – Beef and Rice* (295)). Finally, there are two cases initiated by the US where Mexico did not win any AB findings, *Mexico – Soft Drinks* (308) and *Mexico – Corn Syrup II* (132) Article 21.5 AB.

Table 5.6 Findings Won by the Other Party Involved
(AB and 21.5 AB)

Findings Won by Mexico (%)	As Complainant	As Defendant
100		
99–85		
84–60	2 US/EC[37]	
59–45		
44–30		
29–15		
14–1		1 US/EC[38]
0	1 US/EC 1 Non-OECD[39]	2 US/EC[39]

The results on findings invite further research, maybe an analysis of developments before and after the initiation of a case (the request for consultations). Further research on the lead-up to the initiation of cases could determine the levels of political pressure to engage in litigation, the clarity of the facts of the case, and the degree of certainty of the legal provisions to be challenged. Downstream, it could be useful to look into the time frames of the litigation and the size and experience of the legal teams. We acknowledge, however, that it could be very difficult to obtain reliable data for such analyses.

Conclusions

As complainant, when Mexico litigates at the Panel stage, it wins the highest number of findings when it cooperates with other complainants; it wins a high number

---

37. In *US – Offset Act* (217/234) Mexico and the co-complainants won 64% of the AB findings. In *EC – Bananas III* (27) Mexico and the co-complainants won 82% of the AB findings.
38. In *Mexico – Beef and Rice* (295) Mexico won 6% of the AB findings.
39. Mexico won no AB findings in both *US – OCTG* (282) and *Guatemala – Cement I* (60).
40. Mexico won no AB findings in *Mexico – Soft Drinks* (308) and *Mexico – Corn Syrup II* (132)(Art. 21.5 AB).

of findings when the defendant is a non-OECD country; and it wins few findings when the defendant is the US/EC.

As defendant, when Mexico litigates at the Panel stage, the cases have only been ones initiated by the US/EC (within our period of observation); and it wins very few findings.

As complainant, when Mexico litigates at the AB stage, it wins more than half of the findings of the AB when attacking the US/EC in cooperation with other complainants; and it has not been able to win any findings of the AB when litigating alone against the US/EC or non-Members of OECD.

As defendant, when Mexico litigates at the AB stage, it wins very few findings when the complainant is the US/EC.

3. The Other Party Involved and Implementation

When Mexico has been the complainant, the defendants have not implemented ten cases but have implemented six.[41] More specifically, the US/EC as defendants have not implemented eight cases initiated by Mexico, but have implemented two. When the defendants against Mexico have been non-Members of OECD, they have not implemented two cases, but have implemented four.

The US

The US has not implemented five cases initiated by Mexico within our period of observation:

(1) *US – AD on Steel Zeroing II* (344);
(2) *US – AD on Steel Zeroing I* (325);
(3) *US – OCTG* (282);
(4) *US – CVD on Steel* (280); and
(5) *US – Offset Act* (217/234).

However, the US has implemented two cases. Both relate to AD and both were implemented through a MAS. The MAS in one case, *US – Cement* (281), was negotiated sixteen years after the imposition of the AD measure, whereas the other, *US – Tomatoes* (49), was negotiated before any AD duty (price undertaking).

The EC

The EC has not implemented three cases initiated by Mexico:[42]

(1) *EC – Bananas III New Request* (158);

---

41. As noted in Ch. 2, 'Mexico's GATT and WTO Cases', the non-implemented cases are either pending or abandoned. For this section we only classify the cases as implemented or non-implemented.
42. As noted above, these three WTO cases are much related since they all focus on the EC banana regime.

(2) *EC – Bananas III* (27); and

(3) *EC – Bananas III Old Request* (16).

Non-Members of OECD

Turning to non-Members of OECD, Guatemala and Ecuador have each not implemented one case:

(1) *Ecuador – Cement I* (182); and

(2) *Guatemala – Cement I* (60);

whereas Venezuela, Panama, Ecuador and Guatemala each have implemented one case:

(1) *Venezuela – OCTG* (23);

(2) *Panama – Milk* (329);

(3) *Ecuador – Cement II* (191); and

(4) *Guatemala – Cement II* (156).

*Table 5.7 Mexico as Complainant: Implementation by
the Other Party Involved*

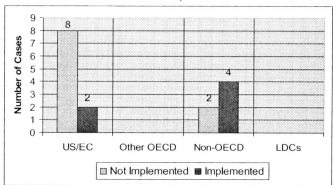

As defendant, Mexico has not implemented seven cases, but it did implement another seven. More specifically, it has not implemented five cases initiated by the US or EC and has implemented four. When the complainants have been non-Members of OECD, Mexico did not implement two cases and implemented three.

The US

Mexico has not implemented two cases initiated by the US:

(1) *Mexico – Swine* (203); and

(2) *Mexico – Corn Syrup I* (101);

but it did implement four others:

   (1) *Mexico – Soft Drinks* (308);
   (2) *Mexico – Beef and Rice* (295);
   (3) *Mexico – Telecoms* (204); and
   (4) *Mexico – Corn Syrup II* (132).

The EC

Mexico has not implemented three cases initiated by the EC:

   (1) *Mexico – Olive Oil II* (341);
   (2) *Mexico – Olive Oil I* (314); and
   (3) *Mexico – Customs Valuation from EC* (53).

Non-Members of OECD

Turning to cases initiated by non-Members of OECD against Mexico: Mexico has not implemented one by Guatemala and one by Brazil:

   (1) *Mexico – AD on Tubes* (331); and
   (2) *Mexico – Transformers* (216).

It did, however, implement one case each from Nicaragua, Chile and Guatemala:

   (1) *Mexico – Beans* (284);
   (2) *Mexico – Matches* (232); and
   (3) *Mexico – Customs Valuation from Guatemala* (298).

Table 5.8 Mexico as Defendant: Implementation by the Other Party Involved

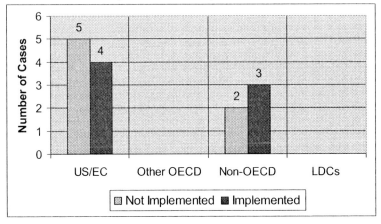

As indicated above in Table 5.1, Mexico as complainant pursued cases at the Article 21.5 Panel/AB and retaliation stages seeking implementation by the defendant only against the US/EC in the following sectors: general goods (*US – Offset Act* (217/234)), industrial goods (*US – OCTG* (282)) and agricultural goods (*EC – Bananas III* (27)). Only the case against the EC was abandoned. The others are pending.

This information, combined with our observations on the bargaining power of Mexico versus non-OECD countries with respect to legal remedies, suggests the following: when Mexico does not have bargaining power to press for legal remedies, mainly *ex ante*, it takes sensitive cases such as those against the US/EC to an advanced level. It has abandoned only one case against the EC. As noted in Chapter 1, NAFTA partners accounted for 70.1% of Mexico's total trade in 2006, whereas the share of trade with the European Union was 7.89%.[43]

As defendant, Mexico took only one case to the stage where the complainant was entitled to request retaliation against it before implementation (*Mexico – Corn Syrup II* (132) from the US). It only took three cases as defendant, initiated by the US, to the RPT stage, and all were implemented: *Mexico – Soft Drinks* (308), *Mexico – Beef and Rice* (295), and *Mexico – Telecoms* (204). The implementation in these three cases required regulatory amendments. With respect to the former case, Mexico decided to move on to the stage of implementation even though it could have appealed. In sum, Mexico has implemented all of its cases as defendant when they have gone beyond the Panel/AB stage.

This suggests that when the US initiates cases against Mexico, it has significant bargaining power with respect to implementation. Also, Mexico decided to implement at the last stage, before retaliation, only once.

Conclusions

As defendant, Mexico has implemented 50% of its cases (seven out of a total of fourteen). As complainant it has been able to achieve implementation in 38% of the cases (six out of sixteen).

As defendant, Mexico implemented more cases initiated by the US/EC (four out of nine) than the US/EC did in cases initiated by Mexico (two out of ten).

For cases with non-Members of OECD, the rate of implementation is similar when Mexico acts as defendant (three out of five) to when it acts as complainant (four out of six).

Mexico, as defendant, has implemented more cases initiated by the US (four of six). The US, as defendant against Mexico, has implemented fewer cases initiated by Mexico (two of six). The two cases implemented by the US were through a MAS. Neither Mexico nor the EC has implemented any of the three cases initiated by each against the other.

---

43.   See Ch. 1, 'Mexico's Options for Settlement of International Trade Disputes'.

Bargaining power seems to have a strong influence in implementation. When Mexico does not have bargaining power to press for legal remedies, it litigates to an advanced stage in sensitive cases, such as those against the US/EC. It has abandoned a case at these advanced procedural stages only against the EC, never against the US. Mexico seems to want to inflict reputation costs against defendants with stronger bargaining power.

When the US initiates cases against Mexico, it has significant bargaining power with respect to implementation. Mexico decided to implement at the last stage before retaliation only once.

C. NEGOTIATED IMPLEMENTATION VERSUS LITIGATED IMPLEMENTATION

For this section we differentiate between negotiated implementation – i.e., a MAS or compliance *ex ante* – and litigated implementation – i.e., a MAS or compliance *ex post*. This allows us to see more clearly the impact of a Panel/AB report with respect to the final outcome on implementation.

When Mexico has been the complainant, only one litigated case was subsequently implemented within our period of observation: Guatemala implemented the Panel report in *Guatemala – Cement II* (156) where Mexico won 95% of the Panel's findings. The other four cases litigated by Mexico as complainant were not implemented within our period of observation. Two were against the US. In one case Mexico was the sole complainant and won 20% of the Panel findings, and none before the AB. In the other case, it was one of several complainants (the EC, Canada, and Japan amount others), that won 71% of the Panel findings and 64% of the AB findings. The third litigated case that was not implemented was against the EC, and the complainants, including the US, won 100% of the Panel findings and 75% of the AB findings. Finally, Guatemala did not implement *Guatemala – Cement I* (60) where Mexico won 75% of the Panel findings but lost all the findings at the AB.[44] This case relates to *Guatemala – Cement II* (156), mentioned above, because both cases challenged the same AD order.

We found five negotiated cases that were implemented when Mexico was the complainant. Two, against the US, were implemented through a MAS *ex ante*. As mentioned above, the MAS in *US – Cement* (281) was agreed sixteen years after the imposition of the AD duties while the one in *US – Tomatoes* (49) was agreed before the imposition of AD duties. The remaining three negotiated cases were implemented at the consultations stage. All were against non-Members of OECD (*Venezuela – OCTG* (23), *Panama – Milk* (329) and *Ecuador – Cement II* (191)).

---

44. The AB concluded that there was lack of jurisdiction due to certain omissions in the request for the establishment of a Panel. See Ch. 4, 'Mexico's Conduct of Its Cases: An Explanation of the WTO Experience'.

Finally, we found six negotiated cases that were not implemented. Five were initiated by Mexico against the US/EC and one was against a non-Member of the OECD. One case was pending (*US – AD on Zeroing II* (344)) , and the rest Mexico abandoned.

Table 5.9 Mexico as Complainant: Litigated Implementation versus Negotiated Implementation

	Not implemented	**Implemented**
Litigated	– *US – OCTG* (282): findings won by Mexico, 20% Panel and 0% AB – *US – Offset Act* (217/234): findings won by Mexico and complainants, 71% Panel and 64% AB – *EC – Bananas III* (27): findings won by Mexico and complainants, 100% Panel and 82% AB – *Guatemala – Cement I* (60): findings won by Mexico, 75% Panel and 0% AB	– *Guatemala – Cement II* (156): findings won by Mexico, 95% Panel
Negotiated	– *US – AD on Steel Zeroing II* (344) – *US – AD on Steel Zeroing I* (325) – *US – CVD on Steel* (280) – *EC – Bananas III New Request* (158) – *EC – Bananas III Old Request* (16) – *Ecuador – Cement I* (182)	– *US – Cement* (281) – *US – Tomatoes* (49) – *Venezuela – OCTG* (23) – *Panama – Milk* (329) – *Ecuador – Cement II* (191)

When Mexico has been the defendant, it has implemented all of the litigated cases. As we have already mentioned, all such cases were initiated by the US. Only in one case did Mexico win more than 17% of the findings at the Panel stage, and there was no case where it won more than 6% at the AB stage.

Mexico implemented three negotiated cases initiated by non-Members of OECD (Nicaragua, Chile and Guatemala). Implementation took place at the consultations stage.

Mexico did not implement seven negotiated cases. Five of them were initiated by the US/EC and the other two cases were initiated by non-Members of OECD. Two of these cases were pending (*Mexico – Olive Oil* (341) and *Mexico – AD on Tubes* (331)). The rest of the cases have been abandoned.

Table 5.10 Mexico as Defendant: Litigated Implementation versus Negotiated Implementation

	Not implemented	**Implemented**
Litigated		– *Mexico – Soft Drinks* (308): findings won by Mexico, 0% Panel and 0% AB – *Mexico – Beef and Rice* (295): findings won by Mexico, 13% Panel, and 6% AB – *Mexico – Telecoms* (204): findings won by Mexico, 43% Panel. – *Mexico – Corn Syrup II* (132): findings won by Mexico, 17% Panel and 0% AB
Negotiated	– *Mexico – Olive Oil II (341)* – *Mexico – Olive Oil I (314)* – *Mexico – Customs Valuation from EC (53)* – *Mexico – Swine (203)* – *Mexico – Corn Syrup I (101)* – *Mexico – AD on Tubes (331)* – *Mexico – Transformers (216)*	– *Mexico – Beans (284)* – *Mexico – Matches (232)* – *Mexico – Customs Valuation from Guatemala (298)*

Conclusions

When Mexico is the complainant, successful litigation has not been followed by implementation in our period of observation.

When Mexico has been the defendant, the cases initiated by the US have been implemented only after successful litigation (*ex post*), and the cases initiated by non-Members of OECD have been implemented before litigation (*ex ante*).

Some observations based on bargaining power of the disputing Parties:

When the US, a more powerful WTO Member, has been the defendant against Mexico, the influence of successful litigation with respect to implementation matters significantly less. When the complainant in a case is more powerful than the defendant – e.g., the US/EC versus Mexico, or Mexico versus a non-OECD country – successful litigation is always followed by implementation.

With Mexico as complainant, both US/EC and non-OECD defendants have agreed to negotiated implementation (*ex ante*). But when Mexico was the defendant, it has only agreed to negotiated implementation (*ex ante*) when the complainant was a non-Member of OECD.

D.   THE POWER OF LOBBIES IN MEXICO'S CASES

1.   The Most Frequent Opponent: The US

The most frequent opponent of Mexico with respect to dispute settlement is the US. A total of 47% of the cases (seven out of sixteen) initiated by Mexico targeted US measures. All challenged AD/CVD determinations imposed by the US. Five of those cases related to trade in industrial goods, one to agricultural goods and one to general goods. Two were abandoned, and Mexico did not get any legal remedy for them. Two were implemented (both with a MAS *ex ante*). There are three cases pending. Two of them did not get any legal remedy, and Mexico was retaliating in the third.[45]

Of the cases with Mexico as defendant, 43% of the cases (six out of fourteen) were initiated by the US. One related to trade in services and the remaining five to trade in agricultural goods. Mexico implemented four of the cases, three of them with a MAS *ex post* and one with compliance *ex post*. The US abandoned the other two cases without getting any legal remedy.[46]

2.   The Most Frequent Products

a.   Cement

No country except Mexico has launched a WTO case on cement. Mexico has taken one GATT and five WTO cases on trade in this product.[47] The six cases relate to AD orders imposed by the US, Guatemala and Ecuador. There are no cases with Mexico as a defendant relating to trade in cement.

The following table shows three sets of data from 1989 to 2006: the years of the requests for consultations; the annual value of Mexican exports of cement (in

45.   *US – AD on Steel Zeroing II* (344); *US – AD on Steel Zeroing I* (325); *US – OCTG* (282); *US – Cement* (281); *US – CVD on Steel* (280); *US – Tomatoes* (49) and *US – Offset Act* (217/234). The latter case was pending even though Mexico imposed retaliatory measures.
46.   *Mexico – Soft Drinks* (308); *Mexico – Beef and Rice* (295); *Mexico – Telecoms* (204); *Mexico – Corn Syrup II* (132); *Mexico – Corn Syrup I* (101) and *Mexico – Swine* (203).
47.   As noted in Ch. 3, the Mexican cement industry initiated several NAFTA Panels under Art. 1904.

USD millions); and, on an annual basis, the percentage of Mexico's total exports represented by cement.

We note that the value of exports of cement has fluctuated. Its lowest level was in 1991 (USD 59.5 million). That was followed by an increase to USD 230.6 million in 1996. This peak was followed by a gradual decrease down to USD 122.7 million in 2002, but after that it went up to its survey-period peak of USD 277 million in 2006.

Furthermore, we note that the percentage of Mexico's total exports represented by cement was at its survey-period peak in 1989 (0.59% in that year) but decreased in 1990 – the year of imposition by the US of AD duties on cement from Mexico – to 0.30%. After further reduction, the percentage then increased again to 0.24% of Mexico's total exports in 1996, followed by a gradual decrease until 2002. Later, there was a small, gradual increase to 0.11% in 2006.

Mexico initiated its first case on cement in 1990, *US – Cement* (GATT). Even though the value of cement exports was not at its peak, the percentage it represented of Mexico's exports that year was the second highest in the period observed (0.59% of total exports). In 1996, after the creation of the WTO, Mexico initiated its second case on cement, *Guatemala – Cement I* (60). That year represented cement's second peak in terms of both value and percentage of total exports. Two cases on cement were initiated in 1999 (*Guatemala – Cement II* (156) and *Ecuador – Cement I* (182)), the year which marked the beginning of the second decrease in cement exports, both in terms of their value and the percentage of total exports. The fifth case, *Ecuador – Cement II* (191), was initiated in 2000, when exports of cement had not changed much from 1999. Finally, Mexico launched its sixth case on cement in 2003. That was the first year of the second increase in the value of exports, but in terms of percentage of total exports cement represented only 0.08%.

Since 1990, cement has not represented more than 0.24% of Mexico's annual exports, and indeed after 1999 it dropped further to no more than 0.14%. The value in USD, however, almost doubled between 1989 and 2006.[48]

Certainly, the significance of exports of a given product is not the sole factor in deciding whether to initiate cases designed to open up foreign markets. For instance, transportation of cement is costly, and this could have influenced Cemex in its decision to focus on foreign direct investment as a means of growth in recent years.[49] Exports, accordingly, do not necessarily reflect the importance of an industry. Nonetheless, the facts are clear: one out of three cases (33%) initiated by Mexico under the GATT was aimed at further opening up the US cement market, and five out of sixteen cases (31%) under the WTO were aimed at further opening the cement markets in the US, Guatemala and Ecuador.

---

48. Data from United Nations Comtrade Database, SITC Rev3 and Rev2. <http://comtrade.un.org/>, August 2009.
49. Cemex 2006 annual report shows at least twenty-seven principal subsidiaries producing that year; see <www.cemex.com/mc/mc_ar.asp>, August 2009.

This suggests that the cement industry has a very powerful lobby in Mexico, and it has used that lobby to pursue its offensive interests.

Table 5.11 The Six Cases on Cement as Complainant by Trade Data

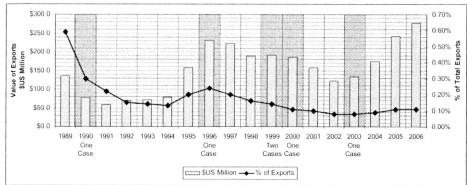

Source: United Nations Comtrade Database SITC rev3 and rev2. <http://comtrade.un.org/>, August 2009.

b.   *Steel*

The same analysis is relevant with respect to cases initiated by Mexico regarding its exports of steel. We have assembled material on all its cases as complainant involving steel: stainless steel, oil country tubular goods (OCTG), and steel plate (the steel products).[50] Mexico initiated five cases in the WTO relating to trade in steel products.[51] In contrast to the case history regarding cement, Mexico has been a defendant in a case related to steel, *Mexico – Tubes from Guatemala* (331), which relates to steel pipe and tubes. We do not further develop this case.

The first case Mexico pursued was in 1995, *Venezuela – OCTG* (23). Steel products represented 1.49% of its total exports for that year (the highest in our period of observation), and the value was USD 1.19 billion. After 1995, both value and percentage of exports decreased, reaching their lowest levels in 2001: USD 0.49 billion and 0.31% of that year's exports. They were slightly higher in 2003 (USD 0.73 billion and 0.45% of the total), a year when Mexico initiated two more cases: *US – OCTG* (282) and *US – CVD on Steel* (280). Finally, it initiated its last two cases in 2005 (*US – AD on Steel Zeroing II* (344) and *US – AD on Steel Zeroing I* (325)), when exports increased further to USD 1.65 billion and 0.77% of the total.

This information suggests that industries producing steel products have a strong lobby power, and they have used it to pursue their offensive interests.

---

50. See the list of products for the HS classification of these goods.
51. As noted in Ch. 3, the Mexican steel products industry initiated several NAFTA Panels under Art. 1904.

Table 5.12 The Five Cases as Complainant: by Trade Data

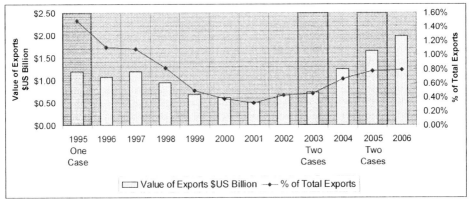

Source: United Nations Comtrade Database HS 1996, <http://comtrade.un.org/>, August 2009.[52]

c. *Sugar*

We take three factors into account in assessing the power of the lobby in protecting the Mexican sugar industry: the defensive measures imposed by Mexico, the domestic impact of the industry and some trade data.

i.   The Defensive Measures

Mexico argued that it had negotiated with the US under NAFTA an agreement on sugar and corn syrup that involved sweeteners. The products compete with each other in certain market segments in both countries. According to this agreement, Mexico was entitled to further NAFTA market access in sugar.[53] The US rejected that it had breached its NAFTA market access commitments regarding trade in sugar in detriment of Mexico. To resolve the matter, Mexico tried to submit the issue to NAFTA dispute settlement, but the US refused to constitute the Panel under Chapter 20 of NAFTA.[54]

Mexico had imposed two measures directly affecting US exports of corn syrup to Mexico, one by the executive branch and the other by the legislative branch. Both measures were challenged by the US and its exporters in different forums:

(1) *AD order on corn syrup from the US.* On 23 January 1998, Mexico imposed final AD duties on high-fructose corn syrup from the US (USD 55.37 to USD 175.85 per metric ton). The order was challenged in the WTO twice and through Chapter 19 of NAFTA once. The order was revoked on 21 May 2002 through the resolution to comply with the bi-national NAFTA Panel. At the WTO, Mexico defended the AD measure up to the AB based under Article 21.5 of the DSU.

---

52. The products included in this data on steel are: steel stainless (7218 to 7229), oil country tubular goods (730520, 730420, 740431 and 730620) and steel plate (7208 to 7212).
53. Corn syrup may substitute sugar for many uses – for instance, in the production of soft drinks.
54. See the report of the Panel in *Mexico – Soft Drinks* (308), para. 4.72.

(2) *Mexico's tax measures on soft drinks and other beverages that use any sweetener other than cane sugar.*[55] On 16 March 2004, the US initiated a WTO case. The Panel, as modified by the AB, found violation of national treatment. The same measure (the tax law) was the basis for a case resting on investor-State procedures. Mexico implemented the measure on 27 December 2006, but it litigated the case up to the AB.

The enactment of these two measures shows the influence of the sugar industry on Mexico's trade policy. The first was imposed by the executive branch through the AD investigating authority, and the second was directly imposed by the Mexican Congress. These facts suggest that the sugar industry matters in both the executive and legislative branches.

ii.   The Domestic Impact of the Sugar Industry
Sugar is one of the largest agricultural industries in Mexico and is highly sensitive. Production of sugar cane generates 440,000 direct jobs and 2.5 million indirect jobs.[56]

We note that the percentage of Mexico's GDP represented by agriculture, forestry and fisheries fluctuated between 4% and 6% in the period 1995 to 2007. For purposes of comparison, we include here the percentage represented by services. The contribution of the sugar industry to the GDP would be included within these figures, but it is not clear what the exact percentage is. As reported in 2008, the Mexican Ministry of Agriculture indicated that sugar represented 0.4% of the national GDP.[57]

Table 5.13 Mexico's GDP – Percentage Represented by Agriculture, Forestry and Fisheries with a Comparison with Services

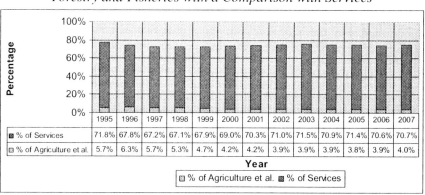

	1995	1996	1997	1998	1999	2000	2001	2002	2003	2004	2005	2006	2007
% of Services	71.8%	67.8%	67.2%	67.1%	67.9%	69.0%	70.3%	71.0%	71.5%	70.9%	71.4%	70.6%	70.7%
% of Agriculture et al.	5.7%	6.3%	5.7%	5.3%	4.7%	4.2%	4.2%	3.9%	3.9%	3.9%	3.8%	3.9%	4.0%

Source: Instituto Nacional de Estadística y Geografía (the National Institute of Statistics and Geography, or INEGI), <http://dgcnesyp.inegi.gob.mx/cgi-win/bdieintsi.exe>, August 2009.

---

55. *Ley de Impuesto Especial sobre Producción y Servicios,* which includes: a 20% tax on soft drinks and other beverages that use any sweetener other than cane sugar; and 20% distribution tax (applied at other stages of trade) on soft drinks and other beverages that use any sweetener other than cane sugar .
56. <www.caneros.org.mx/>, August 2009.
57. <www.sagarpa.gob.mx/cmdrs/sesiones/2008/2a_sesion/4_cana.pdf>, August 2009. However, the Ministry of Agriculture did not specify any period for this figure.

As a further indication of the domestic importance of sugar in Mexico, the Senate created the Special Commission on the Sugar Agro-industry.[58] Some of its main tasks are to participate in the National Sugar Programme; to draft the regulations covering the different players in the production of sugar; to open up foreign markets for Mexican exports of sugar; and to observe and protect Mexico's rights under NAFTA with respect to market access for sugar into the US.

iii.   Some Trade Figures

The following table provides data on production and trade in sugar/corn syrup. The volume of sugar exports decreased after 1997 and increased only in 2005. Similarly, imports of corn syrup decreased significantly from 2002 to 2004. Imports of sugar, on the other hand, gradually increased after 2000. Production of sugar in Mexico did not fluctuate significantly in the period under review. Also, there were imports of both sugar and corn syrup in most of the years reviewed, but imports were very low for corn syrup in 2003 and 2004. This suggests that greater quantities of sweeteners were placed on the Mexican market between 1999 and 2006. However, it is difficult to assess the impact of this in more detail because we do not have reliable information on the consumption of sweeteners.

Table 5.14 Sugar: Production and Trade of Sugar/Corn Syrup

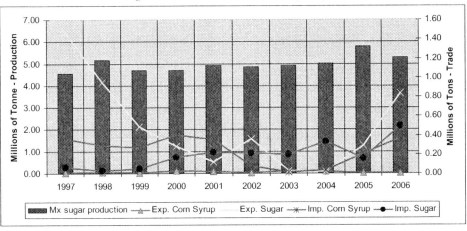

Source: UN Comtrade Database <http://comtrade.un.org/>, August 2009; and National Sugar Union. <http://www.caneros.org.mx/>, August 2009.

Conclusions

Other economically important industries have not demonstrated lobbying power in the same way as the two industries observed. Regarding offensive lobbying, the

58.   The Mexican Senate has only seven special commissions, and one of them is exclusively devoted to sugar. The *Comisión Especial de la Agroindustria Azucarera* is made up of nine Senators from different political Parties and regions. See <www.senado.gob.mx/comisiones/LX/agroindustriaazucarera/>, August 2009.

cement and steel industries have powerful lobbies. When these exports face AD measures, they have used this power. However, even though sugar has offensive interests, the industry has not achieved the same substantive results for its exporters. It's lobbying did not work when the target was the US.

Regarding defensive lobbying, the sugar industry has a powerful lobby. It has used this power for defensive interests.

The power of the sugar lobby can be seen in the defensive measures (AD measure and domestic tax) and the domestic impact (highly labour intensive, very sensitive for politicians) of the sugar industry.

The documented increase in the quantity of sweeteners on the domestic market – due to local production combined with imports and low market access to the US – could have worsened the situation.

3.   The Most Frequent Subject Matter: AD/CVD Cases

As complainant:

When Mexico has been the complainant, 75% of its cases (twelve out of sixteen) relate to AD/CVD: ten cases deal with the ADA, one deals with the ADA and SCM Agreement and one with the SCM Agreement alone. Seven of these cases were initiated against the US, two against Guatemala, two against Ecuador and one against Venezuela. There are ten cases dealing with trade in industrial goods, one in general goods and the other in agricultural goods. Three cases are pending. One of them obtained a legal remedy (retaliation) but is still pending. Defendants against Mexico have implemented five cases: three with a MAS *ex ante*, one with compliance *ex ante*, and one with compliance *ex post*. The remaining four cases were abandoned without any legal remedy.[59]

Mexico has only stopped pursuing ADA cases as complainant when either the AD order is eliminated or both Parties achieve a MAS. This may be because AD duties are imposed on private concerns and it is just such private Mexican actors that drive the litigation. We reached similar conclusions with respect to the most important products in Mexico's cases as complainant: steel and cement, which faced AD duties.

Picking out some data where Mexico is the complainant, three cases against non-Members of OECD have been implemented. On two occasions Mexico had to reinitiate cases from consultations to achieve implementation – *Ecuador – Cement II* (191) and *Guatemala – Cement II* (156). The third implemented case is *Venezuela – OCTG* (23). But Mexico has been able to benefit from implementation in only two out of seven cases against the US within our period of observation – *US – Cement* (281) and *US – Tomatoes* (49).

---

59.   *US – AD on Steel Zeroing II* (344); *US – AD on Steel Zeroing I* (325); *US – OCTG* (282); *US – Cement* (281); *US – CVD on Steel* (280); *US – Offset Act* (217/234); *Ecuador– Cement II* (191); *Ecuador – Cement I* (182); *Guatemala – Cement II* (156); *Guatemala – Cement I* (60); *US – Tomatoes* (49) and *Venezuela – OCTG* (23).

As defendant:

When Mexico has been the defendant, 57% of the cases (eight out of fourteen) related to AD/CVD. Five deal with the ADA, two with the SCM Agreement, and one with the ADA/SCM Agreement. Four of these cases were initiated by the US, two by the EC, and one each by Guatemala and Brazil. Six relate to trade in agricultural goods and two to trade in industrial goods. Finally, within our period of observation, four of those cases were abandoned without any legal remedy and two were pending, similarly without any legal remedy. Mexico implemented two cases: one with a MAS *ex post* and the other with compliance *ex post*.[60]

Picking out some data on AD/CVD cases with Mexico as defendant: Mexico implemented two cases, both initiated by the US: *Mexico – Corn Syrup II* (132) and *Mexico – Beef and Rice* (295). Two were pending: *Mexico – Olive Oil II* (341) and *Mexico – AD on Tubes* (331). Finally, only two cases went beyond the Panel/AB stage. Mexico went to an Article 21.5 appeal in *Mexico – Corn Syrup II* (132) and to the RPT stage in *Mexico – Beef and Rice* (295) where it even had to amend its legislation in order to implement. These figures suggest that Mexico has not been prepared to face retaliation in cases where it is the defendant, even in AD cases.

The following table presents the number of final AD determinations imposed by Mexico from 1995 to 2006. A total of eighty-one final AD determinations were imposed during that period. The US and China were the two largest targets of Mexico's AD determinations. These figures confirm the importance of AD for Mexico's defensive positions.

Table 5.15 Number of AD Orders Imposed by Mexico from 1995 to 2006

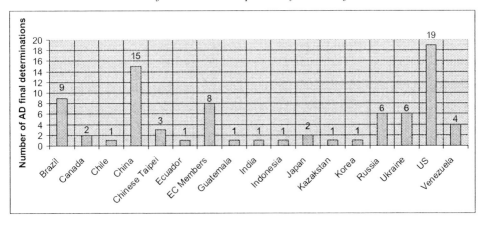

Source: Mexico's notifications to the WTO

---

60. *Mexico – Olive Oil II* (341); *Mexico – AD on Tubes* (331); *Mexico – Olive Oil I* (314); *Mexico – Beef and Rice* (295); *Mexico – Transformers* (216); *Mexico – Swine* (203); *Mexico – Corn Syrup II* (132); and *Mexico – Corn Syrup I* (101).

Conclusions

Most of the cases where Mexico is a complainant are AD/CVD. AD/CVD cases with Mexico as complainant are industry driven. Mexico only stops pursuing those cases when the order is revoked or there is a MAS. Our data suggests that Mexico has been facing problems in achieving implementation in AD/CVD cases.

Similarly, a large part of Mexico's cases as a defendant are AD/CVD. These figures suggest that Mexico has not been prepared to face retaliation in cases as defendant, even AD cases, regardless of the economic development of the complainant.

E.   THE ABANDONED CASES

The most common reason for abandoning cases, both as complainant and as defendant, is the presentation of new cases – e.g., where the first case challenges a provisional AD measure and the second the definitive AD measure. With Mexico as complainant, we found the following three cases in this situation: *US – AD on Steel Zeroing I* (325), *Ecuador – Cement I* (182) and *EC – Bananas III Old Request* (16); and with Mexico as defendant, *Mexico – Olive Oil I* (314) and *Mexico – Corn Syrup I* (101).

The AB in *Guatemala – Cement I* (60) ruled that the request for a Panel presented by Mexico did not identify the challenged measure (provisional/final determination, or price undertaking). It further explained that its finding 'in no way preclude[d] Mexico from seeking consultations ... regarding the ... definitive AD duties ...'[61] The wording used by the AB suggests that Mexico should not challenge the provisional measure. Hence, there may be a tacit acceptance that provisional AD/CVD determinations should not be challenged further than consultations – even if there is no express prohibition against doing so – and that the complainant should challenge the definitive determination. This would be equivalent to saying that the provisional measure is extinguished when the definitive measure is imposed. Certainly, this is what the AB in *Guatemala – Cement I* (60) and other cases we have noted involving Mexico seem to suggest.

Having such an interpretation in all AD/CVD cases would have the following complications:

(1) The interpretation – i.e., provisional and definitive AD measures as distinct and independent measures – would not necessarily apply to provisional and definitive CVD determinations, because the wording in Article 17.4 of

---

61. See Report of the AB, at para. 89. This interpretation by the AB is based on Art. 17.4 of the ADA. The other covered agreements do not have similar wording. We could, accordingly, assume that this interpretation is only relevant to the ADA. But, as we mentioned, the EC decided to present a new request for consultations challenging the final CVD determination imposed by Mexico rather than continue the challenge on the provisional CVD determination.

the ADA is exclusive for AD determinations. Measures in CVD determinations may accordingly not be limited by this interpretation.

(2) The interpretation also leaves 'hit and run measures' applied as a provisional measure without any legal review or any remedy in the WTO.

(3) The relationship between a first assessment review and second assessment review, for instance, in an AD or CVD order, should not be interpreted in the same way as that between a provisional and definitive determination. The time between one review and the other is close to one year, which is shorter than the Panel/AB time frames. An interpretation that the first review is extinguished by the imposition of the second review would just leave them out of the scope of review by the Panel/AB and certainly would have an enormous impact at the implementation stage.

In cases with Mexico as complainant, we note that one request for consultations, in *EC – Bananas III New Request* (158), had a very limited aim: to discuss implementation in *EC – Bananas III* (27). We also note that Mexico as complainant appears to have lost trade interest in one case, *EC – Bananas III* (27). Finally, Mexico abandoned a CVD case against the US, *US – CVD on Steel* (280), without any clear signal why.

In the remaining cases where Mexico is the defendant, one, *Mexico – Transformers* (216), was abandoned by Brazil. It challenged the provisional AD determination of an order initiated by Mexico that did not impose final AD measures. Brazil's export was a single, large-scale electric transformer which by nature does not constitute ongoing trade but rather one-off specific purchase or orders. We have classified this as a hit-and-run measure.

Another case, *Mexico – Customs Valuation from EC* (53), was abandoned by the EC. Since it related to alleged discrimination on customs valuation between NAFTA and EC trade, the discrimination would disappear when NAFTA trade reached zero tariff. Finally, the US abandoned one case without providing any clear signal why – *Mexico – Swine* (203).

Table 5.16 Abandoned Cases

	Mexico as complainant	**Mexico as defendant**
New case (such as provisional AD versus final)	– *US – AD on Steel Zeroing I* (325) – *Ecuador – Cement I* (182) – *EC – Bananas III Old Request* (16)	– *Mexico – Olive Oil I* (314) – *Mexico – Corn Syrup I* (101)
Limited aim for consulting (discuss the implementation)	– *EC – Bananas III New Request* (158)	
Lost trade interest	– *EC – Bananas III* (27)	

Table 5.16 (contd)

	Mexico as complainant	Mexico as defendant
Lost all of the findings	*– Guatemala – Cement I* (60)	
'Hit and run' measures[62]		*– Mexico – Transformers* (216)
PTA solutions		*– Mexico – Customs Valuation from EC* (53)[63]
No clear reason	*– US – CVD on Steel* (280)	*– Mexico – Swine* (203)

Conclusions

Our data suggests that the most common reason for a complainant or defendant to abandon a dispute is the presentation of a new case challenging a reformulated measure. Individual cases show other reasons for abandonment as well.

F.   WTO LEGAL REMEDIES: WHAT THEY DID NOT SOLVE

As noted in Chapters 1 and 4, there are three main legal remedies in the WTO (compliance, compensation and retaliation) and one derivative legal remedy (MAS). We have further distinguished between *ex ante* compliance or MAS[64] and *ex post* compliance or MAS.[65] This section focuses on determining what these legal remedies did not solve in Mexico's cases.

As complainant, Mexico benefited from legal remedies in seven out of sixteen cases (44%).[66] As defendant, legal remedies were applied in seven out of fourteen

---

62. Measures that affect concessions or other obligations for a short period.
63. The request for consultations was made on 27 Aug. 1996. The EC did not withdraw the complaint, and Mexico did not present any information on implementation. Since the case related to alleged discrimination on customs valuation between NAFTA and EC trade, the discrimination would have disappeared when NAFTA trade reached zero tariff.
64. As mentioned in 'Acronyms and Definitions', these refer to compliance or a MAS achieved before a Panel/AB ruling on the legality of the measure. Here, the obligation derives from Art. XVI:4 of the WTO Agreement, which was designed to ensure the conformity of its measures with the obligations provided in the WTO covered agreements, independently of any ruling on the legality of a particular measure.
65. Compliance or a MAS achieved after a Panel/AB has ruled that the measure has been found WTO inconsistent; here, there is an obligation to modify or withdrew the measure in light of the Panel/AB analysis and findings. Compensation and suspension of concessions may be triggered after this stage.
66. Note that the number of cases of Mexico as complainant that were implemented is not the same as the number that benefited from legal remedies. *US – Offset Act* (217/234) was not implemented, but Mexico nonetheless benefited from retaliation.

cases (50%). The status of Mexico's cases with respect to legal remedies is set out in Figure 5.11.[67]

Table 5.17 Legal Remedy Used per Case (Complainant/Defendant)

	No Legal Remedy	MAS (ex ante)	MAS (ex post)	Compliance (ex ante)	Compliance (ex post)	Compensation	Retaliation
As Complainant	9	4	0	1	1	0	1
As Defendant	7	3	3	0	1	0	0

☐ As Complainant ■ As Defendant

The following tables present the period of time (in months)[68] from the date of the request for consultations to the date when the legal remedy appeared – MAS *ex ante* or *ex post*,[69] compliance *ex ante* or *ex post*, or retaliation. For pending cases without a legal remedy, the tables show the period of time from consultations request to 1 January 2007, the cut-off date for this work. This gives us the point at which the legal remedies appeared – the timeliness of each in Mexico's cases. We do not include abandoned cases in this section.

With Mexico as complainant, the longest period of time without a legal remedy was in a pending case with 68.37 months from consultations to the closing date of this work, *US – Offset Act* (217/234).[70] The two cases implemented by the US, both through a MAS *ex ante*, have periods of 36.03 months (*US – Cement* (281)) and 4.10 months (*US – Tomatoes* (49)). Only two cases allowed Mexico to find legal remedies after the Panel/AB report. One was complied in 21.27 months (*Guatemala – Cement II* (156)) and the other was pending but with retaliatory measures imposed by Mexico and with 68.37 months from consultations to 1 January 2007 (*US – Offset Act* (217/234)).

When it is the complainant, Mexico seems to benefit more from *ex ante* remedies than *ex post* remedies.

---

67. We distilled four clusters to classify the cases:

  (1) cases with no legal remedy (all of these would be pending or abandoned);
  (2) cases with a MAS or compliance *ex ante* (all of these would be implemented);
  (3) cases with a MAS or compliance *ex post* (all of these would be implemented); and
  (4) cases with compensation or retaliation (which could be pending, abandoned or implemented).

68. For our calculations, a month has thirty days.
69. For the cases with a MAS, we refer to the date of the MAS except for the MAS *ex post* if it includes the RPT for implementation.
70. Note that the retaliation took place before the cut-off date of this work. The case was still pending at that time.

*Table 5.18 Mexico as Complainant: Time per Case from Consultations
to Legal Remedy or Cut-off Date for WTO Cases*

	Ex ante	**Ex post**
Compliance	– 3.03 months (*Ecuador – Cement II* (191))	– 21.27 months (*Guatemala – Cement II* (156))
MAS	– 6.27 months (*Panama – Milk* (329)) – 36.03 months (*US – Cement* (281)) – 4.10 months (*US – Tomatoes* (49)) – 17.27 months (*Venezuela – OCTG* (23))	
Retaliation		– 68.37 months (*US – Offset Act* (217/234))
Pending	– 19.50 months (*US – AD on Steel Zeroing II* (344))	– 47.10 months (*US – OCTG* (282)) – 68.37 months (*US – Offset Act* (217/234))[71]

The case with the longest period of time without a legal remedy with Mexico as
the defendant was one implemented through a MAS *ex post,* with 60.70 months
from consultations to the MAS (Mexico – Telecoms (204)). It was initiated by the
US. The period of time for cases implemented though compliance and a MAS *ex
post* is longer than for those implemented through a MAS *ex ante* (there is no case
of compliance *ex ante*). The two periods relating to pending cases are shorter,
except for one MAS *ex ante.*

*Table 5.19 Mexico as Defendant: Time per Case from Consultations
to Legal Remedy or to Cut-off Date for WTO cases*

	Ex ante	**Ex post**
Compliance		– 49.10 months (*Mexico – Corn Syrup II* (132), initiated by the US)
MAS	– 25.63 months (*Mexico – Customs Valuation from Guatemala* (298)) – 11.90 months (*Mexico – Beans* (284), initiated by Nicaragua) – 33.03 months (*Mexico – Matches* (232), initiated by Chile)	– 33.53 months (*Mexico – Soft Drinks* (308), initiated by the US) – 42.80 months from consultations to MAS (*Mexico – Beef and Rice* (295), initiated by the US) – 60.70 months (*Mexico – Telecoms* (204), initiated by the US)

---

71.   We have included this case twice in this chart, once for retaliation and once for pending cases.

Table 5.19 (contd)

	Ex ante	**Ex post**
Pending	– 9.20 months (*Mexico – Olive Oil II* (341), initiated by the EC) – 18.77 months (*Mexico – Tubes from Guatemala* (331))	

We note that the periods of time vary significantly. Even when we can see some patterns in Mexico's cases as defendant, they are not the same as when it is the complainant. They are not even the same with the same counterpart, such as Mexico's cases against the US, where two have very long periods of time and one a very short period.

However, if we observe these cases from the point of view of the product involved, we can distil some patterns. With Mexico as complainant, the two dealing with agricultural goods (*Panama – Milk* (329) and *US – Tomatoes* (49)) have the second and third shortest periods of time amongst agricultural goods cases. Those with industrial goods tend to have much longer periods of time, except for *Ecuador – Cement II* (191), which had the shortest period in the industrial goods sector.

As defendant, the case dealing with trade in services (*Mexico – Telecoms* (204)) has the longest period of time, although there was a MAS *ex post* and Mexico did not appeal the Panel report, turning rather to the RPT for implementation. The other cases do not seem to present any pattern.

1.   The Power of a Defendant to Postpone Legal Remedies

With Mexico as the complainant, the shortest timing for legal remedies relates to cases against Ecuador, Panama and the US, with less than 6.3 months on each case (*Ecuador – Cement II* (191), *Panama – Milk* (329), and *US – Tomatoes* (49)). But in another case, the US agreed to a MAS *ex ante* in 36.03 months (*US – Cement* (281)). This may suggest the following:

(1) Panama and Ecuador showed flexibility in allowing for legal remedies earlier when Mexico was the complainant. Perhaps they were not so able to bear the political and financial cost of litigating and hence of postponing the legal remedy. Perhaps milk or cement, or having Mexico as complainant, did not justify those costs.

We note that Mexico is an 'other-OECD Member', whereas Panama and Ecuador are non-Members of OECD. This suggests that Mexico has greater bargaining power when dealing with legal remedies in cases where the defendant is a non-OECD country. Perhaps Mexico is stronger in these cases.

(2) The US also has allowed early legal remedies, depending on the case. In the two US cases just mentioned, the Parties and the subject matter were

the same, but the products were different (agricultural goods compared to industrial goods). It is not the same thing for the US to cooperate with legal remedies on exports of tomatoes as, for example, to cooperate on cement – the two products have different constituencies, consumer behaviour, and domestic production, among other things. This US conduct invites further research on the following:

(a) Why did the US comply with these two cases and not with respect to the other five AD/CVD cases?
(b) What made the US act so differently with respect to the time period from consultations to the MAS in these two cases?

Furthermore, the US was able to postpone the appearance of legal remedies in the *US – Offset Act* (217/234) case even when there was a coalition of complainants.

With Mexico as the defendant, the shortest timing for legal remedies is 11.9 months for a MAS *ex ante* in a case initiated by Nicaragua (*Mexico – Beans* (284)). The rest of the periods were longer. Also, we note that Mexico agreed to a MAS *ex ante* only when the cases were initiated by Chile, Nicaragua and Guatemala (non-Members of OECD). With respect to those cases initiated by the US, Mexico only agreed to compliance *ex post* or a MAS *ex post*. Those cases related to sugar, rice and telecommunications.

This data suggests that the defendant has a certain degree of control over the timing of the legal remedies. Even if the cost of litigation, cost of personnel familiar with dispute settlement, and political costs, among other things, mean that it may be costly to postpone them.

2.   The Timeliness of Legal Remedies as they Affect Negotiation Between the Disputing Parties

The more a defendant is able to postpone the appearance of a legal remedy, the less favourable the deal will be for the complainant. In other words, the bargaining position of a complainant is markedly diminished if the defendant is able to postpone the appearance of legal remedies.

The defendant's ability to postpone may, moreover, work as an incentive for the complainant simply to accommodate, or at least partially accommodate, the defendant's position.

Let us study the MAS on cement between the US and Mexico (*US – Cement* (281)):

(1) The AD duty was imposed in 1990 and was litigated under the GATT (Mexico won, but the report was not adopted) and NAFTA Chapter 19. Mexico had already initiated a WTO case challenging the AD order. Hurricane Katrina strongly influenced consumption of cement in the US.
(2) The Parties negotiated the MAS before the WTO Panel issued its report. The agreement was signed with the following conditions: 'DOC shall revoke the Mexican Cement Order on 1 April 2009, for all Mexican Cement Producers that have not exported any Mexican Cement since 30

August 1990, or that have not exported over the quota agreed. This will happen if the agreement is not terminated (any Party can terminate it with a 90 day notice).[72]

Under the terms of the MAS, it is not certain that the order will be revoked because any Party may terminate the agreement. In the best of all worlds, it would disappear three years down the road.

Mexico had two options: (a) accept these terms, or (b) maintain litigation. Both the government of Mexico and the Mexican cement industry chose option (a).

What would the terms of the MAS have been if the US had had no control over the timing of the other legal remedies? A very difficult question. We do not have the answer or the means of getting it.

Mexico and the cement industry were, in any case, better off with the MAS than with the status *ex ante*.

3.	**The Length of Time a Complainant Will Wait for a Legal Remedy**

It is very difficult to know how long a complainant will be willing to pursue a case without achieving a legal remedy. We assume that this depends on the case.

We found two practical examples:

(1) *EC – Bananas III* (27): Mexico requested consultations on 5 February 1996, and its last procedural appearance was 18 August 1998, when it requested the establishment of an Article 21.5 Panel. We classify this case as abandoned.[73] It took it 30.83 months to reach the decision to abandon the case. In this time Mexico engaged in consultations and litigation before a Panel, the AB, and the arbitrator to delimit the RPT.

(2) *Mexico – Transformers* (216): As explained above when discussing the abandoned cases, Brazil initiated this case against an AD provisional determination imposed by Mexico on large-scale transformers. Apparently, a Brazilian exporter wanted to ship one unit to Mexico to be used for a construction project. Mexico suspended the provisional measure and did not impose any final AD duty. Brazil abandoned the case: it did not go further than presenting the request for consultations.

In *EC – Bananas III* (27), Mexico pursued the case for a longer time than Brazil in *Mexico – Transformers* (216). Nonetheless, we did not find any way of measuring the maximum time a complainant is willing to pursue a case in the absence of a legal remedy.

---

72. S. XI of the Agreement between the US Trade Representative and the Department of Commerce of the US and the Ministry of Economy of Mexico (*Secretaría de Economía*) on Trade in Cement, <http://ia.ita.doc.gov/cement-agreement/cement-final-agreement.pdf>, August 2009.

73. Mexico had already initiated an earlier case on the banana import regime from the EC on 28 Sept. 1995, *EC – Bananas III Old Request* (16).

Conclusions

We found that the time from the request for consultations to the appearance of any legal remedy, whatever the type, varies from case to case. For instance, in *Ecuador – Cement II* (191), compliance *ex ante* occurred 3.03 months after the consultations request. However, in *Mexico – Telecoms* (204) the MAS *ex post* was agreed 60.70 months fter the request for consultations.

The defendant is to a certain extent able to postpone the appearance of WTO legal remedies. This ability affects the strength of each Parties' negotiation position. The complainant's bargaining power is markedly diminished.

The only case where Mexico reached retaliation stage suggests that retaliation is not an effective legal remedy for Mexico against the US. But Mexico does not have enough cases at this procedural stage to draw stronger conclusions.

In sum, the defendant seems to have the ability to decide to a certain extent (a) whether implementation will occur; (b) the time when implementation will occur; and the conditions of the implementation.

G.   THE LEGAL, ECONOMIC AND POLITICAL RESULTS
            (GATT AND WTO)

1.   **The GATT Dispute Settlement**

Mexico has initiated three GATT cases, all against the US. Two were taken by Mexico alone and were neither adopted nor implemented, *US – Tuna (Mexico)* and *US – Cement*). The third case, *US – Superfund*, was initiated by Mexico and two other complainants (EEC and Canada). It was adopted and implemented on an MFN basis by the US.[74]

Table 5.9 presents some of the legal, economic and political gains that Mexico achieved during its experience in litigating under the GATT.

Table 5.20   Mexico's GATT Cases: Legal, Economic and Political Test

Case	Legal	Economic	Political
Overall	– Experience for the legal team – Some findings in favour of Mexico		– Utilization of the system – Spillover effect of having won many findings in all of the cases

---

74. For a full discussion of these cases, see Ch. 2, 'Mexico's GATT and WTO Cases'.

Table 5.20 (contd)

Case	Legal	Economic	Political
US – Superfund	– MFN implemented, Mexico with the same benefits as other non-litigating contracting Parties	– Discriminatory tax eliminated on an MFN basis (Mexico could have been a free rider in this case by not participating as a complainant)	– Potential to use cases as leverage to put the house in order – Internally: response to constituencies – Externally: better bargaining position
US – Tuna	– Nothing (not adopted/implemented)	– De facto confirmation of the embargo in force for a longer time	– Internally: response to constituencies by winning the findings – Externally: blame for weak system
US – Cement	– Nothing (not adopted/implemented)	– De facto confirmation of the AD measure in force for a longer time	– Internally: response to constituencies by winning the findings – Externally: blame for the weak system

2. The WTO Dispute Settlement

Table 5.10 presents, in general terms, some of the legal, economic, and political gains Mexico achieved from its experience as a WTO litigator.

Table 5.21 Mexico's WTO Cases: Legal, Economic and Political Test

Case	Legal	Economic	Political
Overall	– Development of legal experts (three generations of lawyers)	– Elimination of some trade barriers as complainant – Consequences of timeliness of legal remedies (as complainant and as defendant)	– Better standing to negotiate *ex ante* implementation with smaller Members – Leverage to eliminate WTO inconsistencies imposed by different internal players

Table 5.21 (contd)

Case	Legal	Economic	Political
Abandoned cases	– Nothing	– De facto acceptance of the economic effects of the challenged measure	– Externally: less credibility with respect to new legal claims; – less aggression by accommodating its position
Litigated cases	– Adverse legal results from cases with low findings won	– Elimination of AD orders against Mexico – Suspension of concessions in one case (but not for the full length of time allowed)	
Implemented cases	– More legal certainty with respect to WTO obligations and rights	– Elimination of trade barriers, benefiting consumers and/or industry – Utilization of the period of non-application of legal remedies (although this cuts both ways)	– Externally: better standing position – Internally: response to constituencies – Internally: using WTO as a leverage for internal reforms

III.   THE PREFERENTIAL TRADE AGREEMENTS

A.   SOME OBSERVATIONS ON DOUBLE FORUMS: WTO AND PTAS

This section compares WTO jurisdiction with the jurisdictions of Chapter 20 of NAFTA[75] and Chapter 19 of NAFTA (private party versus country in trade remedies). First, we make a brief comparison of NAFTA and WTO substantive law, and then we compare part of the procedural law of these systems.[76]

To better understand the interaction between NAFTA law and WTO law, we need to bear in mind that NAFTA entered into force one year before the WTO.

75. We also cover the general dispute settlement mechanisms of other PTAs, since, as mentioned in Ch. 1, they are very similar to Ch. 20 of NAFTA.
76. For an explanation of these three jurisdictions, see Ch. 1, 'Mexico's Options for Settlement of International Trade Disputes'. For the presentation of the cases adjudicated under PTAs, see Ch. 3, 'Mexico's Cases under Preferential Trade Agreements'. For those cases adjudicated under GATT and WTO, see Ch. 2, 'Mexico's GATT and WTO Cases' and Ch. 4, 'Mexico's Conduct of Its Cases: An Explanation of the WTO Experience'.

So it had to be designed to work even in the case of a failure of the Uruguay Round. We believe that NAFTA Parties were heavily influenced by the Uruguay Round negotiations in designing the NAFTA dispute settlement mechanisms.

1.   The DSU Process, NAFTA Chapter 20 and NAFTA 1904 Panels: Who Has Standing?

As noted in Chapter 1, 'Mexico's Options for Settlement of International Trade Disputes' NAFTA Chapter 20 and WTO procedures are exclusive to WTO Members and NAFTA Parties. Only countries have standing to initiate these procedures against other countries (country versus country).[77] On the other hand, a 1904 Panel may be initiated by either a government Party to NAFTA or any private party with standing to trigger an internal judicial review.[78] As mentioned, 1904 Panels substitute the appeal process (judicial review) under domestic procedures of the NAFTA Party imposing the AD/CVD order.[79]

2.   The Substantive WTO Law and the Substantive NAFTA Law

The substantive law of Panels under Article 1904 of NAFTA is the domestic law of the importing Party (the one imposing the AD/CVD measure).[80] WTO law (ADA and SCM Agreement) is accordingly not inserted in these Panel procedures because of NAFTA rules. However, as we noted in Chapter 3, in practice Mexico applies the WTO Agreements on trade remedies as its domestic law. It uses a monistic system with respect to international agreements. One can argue that, by Constitution, the US should also apply the same monistic system. But because of executive agreements, it does not apply directly international agreements like WTO Agreements. That is why 1904 Panels analysing US AD/CVD orders apply only domestic legislation. Hence, for Mexico the substantive law for these Panels will be its domestic laws, which include WTO law. But the US will only use domestic laws without WTO law.

We now turn to the substantive law applicable to dispute settlement in the WTO and Chapter 20 of NAFTA. The substantive law for a DSU process is WTO law.[81] That applicable to Panels under Chapter 20 of NAFTA would, however, be NAFTA contact law with the exception of Chapter 19 and to some extent Chapter 11.[82]

The interaction between the substantive law of the WTO and NAFTA generates some observations. The WTO Agreements are silent with respect to interaction with FTA substantive laws. However, NAFTA contains a general rule for conflicts of substantive law. Article 103 of NAFTA affirms the existing rights and obligations

---

77.   We note that some WTO Members are not countries but economic territories.
78.   See Art. 1904.5 of NAFTA.
79.   See Art. 1904.1 of NAFTA.
80.   See Art. 1904.2 of NAFTA.
81.   See Art. 1 and Appendix 1 of the DSU.
82.   See Art. 2004 of NAFTA. For investment, see Art. 1115 of NAFTA.

under the GATT. In the event of inconsistency between NAFTA law and GATT law, NAFTA would prevail to the extent of the inconsistency, except as otherwise provided in NAFTA. One example of a NAFTA provision 'providing otherwise' is national treatment with respect to NAFTA goods. Article 301 of NAFTA not only states that NAFTA national treatment should be interpreted in the light of Article III of GATT, but also incorporates Article III of GATT (and any evolution of it) into NAFTA substantive law.[83]

Table 5.11 presents a bird's-eye view of some issues of substantive law that are incorporated in both NAFTA and WTO. We note that in some cases the substantive law of NAFTA is much more complete than WTO law (such as regarding investment), but sometimes the WTO provisions are significantly more complete (such as regarding national treatment for goods).

Table 5.22 NAFTA Substantive Law and WTO Substantive Law:
A Bird's Eye View

	NAFTA substantive law	**WTO substantive law**
Investment	– Whole Chapter 11	– Only TRIMS and some services (mode 3 on commercial presence)
Services	– Chapter XII: NAFTA uses a negative list (everything is open to market access unless mentioned in the list)	– GATS: The WTO uses a positive list (nothing is open to market access unless mentioned in the list)
Trade remedies	– Referral to domestic laws	– ADA and SCM Agreement: Those Agreements contain substantive law.
National treatment in goods	– Article 301 (chapter on market access for goods) in conformity with Article III of GATT	– Article III of GATT
Safeguards	– Chapter 8: It contains similar provisions to the WTO Agreement on Safeguards,[84] but the affected Party may suspend concessions at any time	– Agreement on Safeguards: The affected Party, in practice may not suspend concessions before three years.
Government procurement	– Chapter 4	– Plurilateral Trade Agreement (Mexico is not a Member to this Agreement

---

83. Other examples of provisions providing otherwise are NAFTA Art. 318 on Goods, Annex 702.1 on Agriculture, and Art. 903 on the Agreement on Technical Barriers to Trade.
84. The Panel in US – Safeguard on Broom Corn Brooms (NAFTA 20) concluded that the provisions of NAFTA and the WTO on safeguards are very similar.

3. Procedural Law

We analyse in this section the interrelationship among three different forums: the DSU procedure, the Article 1904 Panel procedure, and the Chapter 20 Panel procedure.

a.   The Relationship between the Article 1904 NAFTA Panels and the Chapter 20 NAFTA Panels

The relationship between Article 1904 Panels and Chapter 20 Panels is defined within NAFTA. The matters covered in Chapter 19 (Review and Dispute Settlement in Anti-dumping and Countervailing Duty Matters) are not covered by the dispute settlement of Chapter 20 of NAFTA.

Hence, we only need to address the relationship between Article 1904 Panels and the DSU, on one hand, and the relationship between Chapter 20 of NAFTA Panels and the DSU, on the other hand.

b.   The Relationship between the Chapter 20 of NAFTA Panel and the DSU

The WTO is silent on the issue of double forums with NAFTA Chapter 20. Indeed, Mexico asked the Panel and the AB in *Mexico – Soft Drinks* (308) to decline jurisdiction over a NAFTA Panel in order to solve the broader matter of the sweetener dispute between Mexico and US. The AB upheld the Panel's finding that 'under the DSU, it ha[d] no discretion to decline to exercise its jurisdiction in the case that ha[d] been brought before it'.[85] This suggests that from the WTO perspective, rules of double jurisdiction under the FTA do not easily amend the DSU process when it has been triggered.

Nonetheless, as noted in Chapter 1, there are some rules on overlapping jurisdictions in Chapter 20 of NAFTA with respect to the DSU jurisdiction (Article 2005 of NAFTA). The general rule is that disputes regarding any matter[86] arising under both NAFTA and the WTO[87] may be settled in either forum at the choice of the complainant. There are three exceptions to this general rule where Chapter 20 of NAFTA prevails over the WTO:

(1) Before initiating a WTO case, a complainant must notify the NAFTA Parties if the matter may also be covered by NAFTA. If there is a third Party wishing to have recourse to dispute settlement under NAFTA regarding the same matter, the Parties must try to agree on a single forum. If there

---

85. AB Report, *US – Soft Drinks* (308), para. 85.
86. Under WTO law, the matter means the measure – i.e., the act or omission of a Member – and the legal claims. See the report of the AB, *Guatemala – Cement* (60), paras 70 to 73. Even though this definition is WTO law, it may help us to understand NAFTA law.
87. The text of NAFTA refers to the GATT or any subsequent agreement.

is no agreement on the forum, NAFTA will normally be the proper forum.

(2) If a respondent Party claims that an action is subject to Article 104 of NAFTA (Relation to Environmental and Conservation Agreements) and requests that the matter be solved under NAFTA, the complaining Party may only use NAFTA for that matter.

(3) If any dispute arises under Section B of Chapter 7 (Sanitary or Phytosanitary Measures) or Chapter 9 (Standards-Related Measures) of NAFTA and the responding Party requests that the matter be solved under NAFTA, the complaining Party may only use NAFTA for that matter.[88]

As Gantz (1999) notes, the issues of double forums between the DSU and Chapter 20 of NAFTA depends on whether the substantive law of both WTO and NAFTA or just one of them regulates the measure at issue. For instance, if only the substantive law of the WTO regulates the measure to be challenged, the complainant does not have a NAFTA option, and vice versa. However, if the measure at issue is covered by both Agreements, NAFTA and the WTO, the rules of jurisdiction under NAFTA would apply – the choice of the complainant with the three exceptions mentioned.[89]

However, the NAFTA rules on double jurisdiction are not clear with respect to two situations.

i.   A Subsequent Initiation of a New Case in the Other Forum

This situation could occur if the case is not solved in the first forum or if the complainant does not like the ruling from it. If the second forum is NAFTA Chapter 20, the Panel is bound to interpret the NAFTA rules on double jurisdiction. But if the second forum is the WTO, the Panel would have no obligation to do so. That, at least, is what was suggested by *Mexico – Soft Drinks* (308), because the WTO Panel had an obligation to issue its report.

Pauwelyn (2006) suggests res judicata – i.e., the same Parties, the same subject matter, and the same legal claims – as a tool to solve possible cases of double jurisdiction between NAFTA and the WTO.[90] But this is more complicated than what it appears.[91]

The test of the same Parties seems easily resolved. We do not expand on it.

The test for same claims may pose more difficulties. The NAFTA provisions 'providing otherwise' may fall under similar claims with respect to this test, as mentioned above: same law. One example we mentioned was national treatment

---

88. See Art. 2005 of NAFTA.
89. Busch (2007) presents an assessment of the decision-making process by complainants with respect to the strength of precedents in each forum.
90. For a more comprehensive discussion on conflicts of norms, see Pauwelyn (2003).
91. It seems that *res judicata* does not cover situations where the three elements are the same but the forums are different. This could happen with cases where WTO law has been inserted into PTAs by direct reference to the WTO provisions. There, the only guidance would be the PTA rules on double jurisdiction with WTO law. We deal with these situations below.

for NAFTA goods (Article 301), which incorporates Article III of GATT into NAFTA. There may be many situations with cases having the same legal claim. But if the legal claims are not the same, a NAFTA Party may trigger the second procedure in the other forum.

We have another question on the issue of legal claims. We do not know whether there is a need to distinguish market access concessions from the more rule-oriented law. For instance, in the *US – Cross-Border Trucking* (NAFTA 20) case, a NAFTA Panel ruled that the US does not provide NAFTA market access for services on cross-border trucking. The US has not implemented the report. We note that the US has some WTO commitments on market access on freight transport. Would Mexico be banned from initiating a new case under the WTO because market access commitments under NAFTA and the WTO could be considered to be the same legal claims? This is a difficult question, because we are not talking about a rule-oriented provision but concessions negotiated under two different but related contract laws.

The issue of subject matter seems to be the most complicated of all, if it refers to the measure. Under WTO law, the measure normally refers to the act or omission of a Member. However, neither NAFTA law nor WTO law helps us to define the size, shape, or limits of a measure – i.e., act or omission of a Member. We have many questions with respect to whether two measures are the same: When does a measure stop being that measure and turn into a new measure? Would a measure be a law or one of its articles? What about non-continuous acts? Are they different measures or the same measure? The boundaries of a measure are not very clear. It seems to us that the measure is shaped in a certain way by the complainant, based on the acts or omissions by the defendant.

ii.   Triggering the Other Forum by a Third NAFTA Party

The rules on jurisdiction under NAFTA deal with the issue of a third NAFTA Party wanting to initiate a new case with the same matter. In that case, the Parties are required to try to agree on a single forum. But what if the third NAFTA Party decides to challenge the same measure (assuming we know what 'the same measure' means), but after the Panel report has been issued by the first forum. Would the new complainant be able to use a different forum than the one used by the previous complainant? In this case, res judicata may not offer a solution because the Parties are not the same.

iii.   The Problems Down the Road

The rules on double forums aim to solve the issues when the procedures, or at least one, are about to be started. Assume a Party was able to circumvent these rules. What would be the problem if the two Panels issued opposing resolutions? We think none. It would only mean that the same measure, if it is the same, was found to be not in violation of NAFTA law and in violation of WTO law (or vice versa). One case would continue to the implementation stage and the other not. But this could be more complicated if NAFTA law and the WTO law were the same, such as the provisions on national treatment of goods.

Further down the road, let us assume that both Panels find violation (one a NAFTA violation and the other a WTO violation). Should the complainant be entitled to double reparation[92] for the same measure, assuming it is the same measure? If the substantive law of NAFTA and WTO refer to the same legal claims, national treatment for instance, res judicata may suggest not. Would this interpretation mean that if the legal claims are not the same, the complainant would be entitled to double reparation?

Unfortunately, we seem to have found more questions than answers.

Finally, we will briefly deal with the issue of whether the four PTA cases could have been taken to the WTO. The *US – Safeguard on Broom Corn Brooms* (NAFTA 20) case could have been taken to the WTO by challenging the Safeguard Agreement.[93] The *US – Cross-Border Trucking* (NAFTA 20) case could not have been taken to the WTO with respect to investment but might have been with respect to services. The *Peru – Origin of Computers from Mexico* (ALADI) case could not have been taken to the WTO because it dealt with preferential tariffs for Mexican computers and ALADI's preferential rules of origin. Finally, the *Mexico – Sanitarian Registry and Access on Medicines* (FTA among Mexico, El Salvador, Guatemala and Honduras) case could have been brought to the WTO under the SPS Agreement.[94]

c.   *The Relationship between the Article 1904 Panel and the DSU*

An Article 1904 Panel and a WTO Panel may not overlap. There are no issues of double forums.

As mentioned above, Article 1904 Panels substitute the appeal process (judicial review) under the domestic procedures of the NAFTA Party imposing the AD/CVD order.[95] An Article 1904 Panel may be initiated by either a government Party to NAFTA or any private party with standing to trigger the internal judicial review.[96] The main users are private parties challenging AD/CVD orders imposed by a NAFTA Party, because they decide to use Article 1904 Panels rather than domestic tribunals. We did not, however, seek to analyse utilization of the procedures by disputing party (government or private party).

Moreover, the applicable law is domestic law, as mentioned above. Mexico applies the ADA and the SCM Agreement as part of its domestic law[97] by using a

---

92. This would be an issue in determining the level of nullification or impairment in both forums.
93. Indeed, on 28 Apr. 1997, Colombia challenged the same safeguard measure – in Presidential Proclamation 6961 – under the WTO dispute settlement mechanism. It claimed violation of Arts 2, 4, 5, 9 and 12 of the Safeguards and Arts II, XI, XIII and XIX of the GATT 92.
94. Certainly, this is a very superficial analysis. Serious analysis is needed to assess whether a measure could be in violation of the WTO.
95. See Art. 1904.1 of NAFTA.
96. See Art. 1904.5 of NAFTA.
97. For an example of this, see the Appendix, Table 14, 'NAFTA Chapter 19 cases (private party versus country on trade remedies)'.

monistic approach. The US has this approach in its Constitution, but in practice it uses executive agreements and hence, domestic laws.

There would be no res judicata between the two forums. The legal claims are not the same, nor the Parties. The measure may be the same, but the other two requirements have not been met.

Arguing that the two forums overlap would be like saying that domestic judicial procedures overlap with WTO Panels or that the procedures at the European Court of First Instance overlap with WTO law.

We note that some authors argue in favour of 'exhaustion of local remedies' in WTO law with respect to NAFTA Chapter 19.[98] We strongly disagree with this suggestion.[99] WTO law has more of a contractual nature. Besides, from the practical point of view, postponing the initiation of a WTO case until the termination of an Article 1904 Panel would just defer the resolution of the dispute. Time frames for Article 1904 Panels can be enormously long.

As to the question of whether the measures reviewed by Article 1904 Panels could be reviewed in the WTO, the answer would be yes to all of them.

Finally, we will briefly discuss Article 1904 Panels reviewing AD/CVD determinations that were also challenged through the WTO. We found four AD orders reviewed by an Article 1904 Panel which where subsequently reviewed under WTO jurisdiction.[100] We start with the orders imposed by the US against Mexico's exports:

(1) *AD – Order of Cement from Mexico*: on 30 August 1990, the DOC imposed a definitive AD duty of 58.38% for Cemex, 53.26% for Apasco, 3.69% for Hidalgo, and 58.05% for all others. At the cut-off date of our work, the measure was still in effect, but with a MAS. A GATT Panel found in favour of Mexico, but the report was not adopted. Later, under the WTO, Mexico initiated *US – Cement* (281). The exporters requested review by an Article 1904 Panel sixteen times to review different stages of the AD order. Since the WTO Panel was suspended, there were no opposing findings from the Article 1904 Panels or the WTO. However, an Article 1904 Panel affirmed the finding, based on US law, by the investigating authority stating that the order should not be revoked because of

---

98. See Kennedy (2007).

99. We note that the US has also disagreed with this theory by saying that 'even though governments often brought an issue before the WTO on behalf of private citizens, disputes were fundamentally between Countries ...' Panel Report, *Argentina – Measures Affecting Imports of Footwear, Textiles, Apparel and Other Items*, para. 3.246. Moreover, the EC argued against this theory in the WTO while distinguishing it from the obligation to provide independent domestic tribunals as a WTO obligation; Panel Report, *US – Section 211 Omnibus Appropriations Act of 1998*, para. 8.95. Finally, the EC argued more clearly against the theory of exhaustion of local remedies in the WTO. See Panel Report, *Argentina – Measures Affecting the Export of Bovine Hides and the Import of Finished Leather*, para. 11.249.

100. For more detail on the presentation of the Art. 1904 Panel procedures relating to Mexico, see Ch. 3, 'Mexico's Cases under Preferential Trade Agreements'.

violations on the initiation, whereas the GATT Panel found GATT violations in the initiation of the investigation.

(2) *AD – Order on OCTG from Mexico*: On 11 August 1995, DOC imposed a final AD duty (23.79%). The measure expired on 25 July 2006 by a resolution published on 22 June 2007 (Second Five-Year Sunset Review). Mexico initiated *US – OCTG* (282).[101] With respect to the Sunset Reviews, regarding likelihood of dumping. The WTO Panel found (finding not appealed) that the likelihood-of-dumping determination in the first Sunset Review was inconsistent with WTO law. The Article 1904 Panel remanded the file to the investigating authority to make a determination to the effect that, under US law, the evidence did not support a finding of likelihood of recurrence or continuation of dumping upon revocation of the AD duty order with respect to the same Sunset Review. The US revoked the order through the Second Sunset Review, as it did not find likelihood of injury.

We now present the two cases with parallel procedures reviewing Mexico's AD orders on US exports:

(1) *AD – Investigation on Bovine Carcasses and Half Carcasses, Fresh or Chilled from the US*: On 28 April 2000 Mexico imposed definitive AD duties from USD 0.03 per kg to USD 0.80 per kg on US exports. At the cut-off date, the order was still in effect (five years from 28 April 2005). The US initiated a WTO case challenging this AD order (*Mexico – Beef and Rice* (295)), but the US did not challenge the AD measure on beef beyond the consultations stage.

(2) *AD – Investigation on Fructose Corn Syrup from the US*: On 23 January 1998, Mexico imposed a final AD duty from USD 55.37 to USD 175.85 per metric ton. The order was revoked on 21 May 2002 through the resolution published on 20 May 2002. The US initiated two cases in the WTO challenging this AD order: *Mexico – Corn Syrup II* (132); and *Mexico –Corn Syrup I* (101). The two Panels, WTO and Article 1904 of NAFTA, found violation in the same line on violation of threat of injury provisions.

B.　　　　　The Article 1904 Panel Procedures: The Legal, Economic and Political Results

This section presents the legal, economic and political results of Mexico's experience in Article 1904 Panels. Because cases from the Canadian investigating authority are few, we do not include them in Table 5.12.

---

101. Argentina initiated US – Anti-Dumping Administrative Review on Oil Country Tubular Goods from Argentina (346) and US – Sunset Reviews of Anti-Dumping Measures on Oil Country Tubular Goods from Argentina (268) challenging the same AD order but with respect to Argentina.

Table 5.23 The 1904 Panels: Legal, Economic and Political Test

Case	Legal	Economic	Political
Overall	– Legal remedies not designed to declare violation but to remand or affirm the determination – Limited legal remedy from remand; some Panels remedied more by requesting the elimination of the order – Article 1904 Panel sometimes not efficient in cases of injunctions		– Difficult to find panellists, because they may be litigants of AD/CVD and plead in front of investigating authorities they have to review
Cases against Mexican AD/ CVD orders	– WTO law included in Mexican law for purpose of reviewing AD/CVD orders		– Many cases suspended without further information
Cases against US AD/CVD orders	– System of remand/ affirmed similar to the US internal system		– US failure to reflect that revocation of OCTG was in compliance with Article 1904 or WTO Panels

C.   THE PTAs (COUNTRY VERSUS COUNTRY): THE LEGAL, ECONOMIC AND POLITICAL RESULTS

Mexico participated in four country versus country cases. Out of the three cases as complainant, one was implemented by the US (*US – Safeguard on Broom Corn Brooms* (NAFTA 20)), one was not implemented by the US (*US – Cross-Border Trucking* (NAFTA 20)), and in the third case the preferential tariff was eroded when Peru applied MFN liberalization for the product subject to the dispute (*Peru – Origin of Computers from Mexico* (ALADI)). Mexico won a significant number of findings in all cases.

The sole case as defendant was implemented by Mexico with respect to the complainant, El Salvador. It covered sanitarian issues in relation to medicines

(*Mexico – Sanitarian Registry and Access on Medicines* (FTA among Mexico, El Salvador, Guatemala and Honduras)).[102]

Table 5.24 PTA Cases (Country versus Country):
Legal, Economic and Political Test

Case	Legal	Economic	Political
As complainant	– Lack of constitution of a Panel to rule on legitimization of parallel letters to amend market access quotas – Recognition of a legal right to preferential tariff for computers.	– Elimination of a safeguard and suspension of concessions – Bearing of consequences of not having an integrated market with respect to trucking services – No benefit from a tariff preference	– US exclusion of Mexico from subsequent global safeguards (after *US – Safeguard on Broom Corn Brooms*)[103]
As defendant	– Legitimization of parallel letters signed to amend the FTA[104]	– One less trade barrier for trade in medicines with El Salvador	– Questioning by other trade partners of a non-MFN implementation of a case

102. For a full presentation of these cases, see Ch. 3, 'Mexico's Cases under Preferential Trade Agreements'.
103. See report of the panel in *US – Steel Safeguards* (248, 249, 251, 252, 253, 254, 258 and 259), 8.17 et seq.
104. What would be the equivalent instrument at the WTO to parallel letters in PTAs? Perhaps the answer would be a waiver under Art. IX of the WTO Agreement. There WTO Members may waive a WTO-rule-based obligation by agreement. But, what would be the equivalent in WTO of legitimization of PTA parallel letters? Perhaps legitimization of waivers in dispute settlement. See Nottage and Sebastian (2006) for a discussion of WTO legal instruments to reform WTO law.

Appendix

Charts

1. GATT cases at a glance

Source: GATT Panel reports.

Mexico only participated as complainant in GATT cases.

Case	Won / Lost		Adoption / Implementation
US – Superfund **Defendant:** US **Other Complainant:** Canada and EEC **Product:** industrial goods (petroleum and feedstock chemicals) **Consultations:** 10 November 1986 **Panel Report:** 5 June 1987 **Adoption:** 17 June 1987	Total Findings The US won Mexico won	2 1 (50%) 1 (50%)	Adopted / Implemented
US – Tuna (Mexico) **Defendant:** US **Product:** industrial goods (Tuna) **Consultations:** 5 November 1990	Total Findings The US won Mexico won	4 2 (50%) 2 (50%)	Not adopted / Not implemented
Panel Report: 3 September 1991 **Adoption:** N/A			

Case	Won / Lost		Adoption / Implementation
US – Cement **Defendant:** US **Product:** industrial goods (Cement) **Consultations:** 24 October 1990 **Panel Report:** 7 September 1992 **Adoption:** N/A	**Total Findings** **The US won** **Mexico and other complainants won**	**2** **0 (0%)** **2 (100%)**	Not adopted / Not implemented

2. GATT Cases Where Mexico Participated as Third Party

Source: GATT Panel reports.

Case	Product	Statements by Mexico	Subject Matter of the Complaint	Conclusion of the Panel
EEC – Bananas I (DS32/R) Not Adopted *Colombia, Costa Rica, Guatemala, Nicaragua, and Venezuela vs EEC*	agricultural goods (Banana)	Import restrictions for bananas violated • Art. XI:1 on elimination of quantitative restrictions (not justifiable under Art. XI:2) of the GATT. • Art. XIII:1 (discrimination), XIII:2 (lack of proper allocation) • Art. XXXVII:1(a) and (b) on trade obstacles and non-tariff import barriers.	I, II, III, VIII, XI and XIII, XXIII:1(b) (non violation), XXIV, XXXVI, XXXVII, and Part IV of the GATT	Violation of: • Art. XI:1 of the GATT (not justified by Art. XI:2(c)(i) of the GATT, Art. XXIV, of the GATT or protocols of accession) • Art. I (not justified by Art. XXIV of the GATT unless exempted by a waiver under XXV of the GATT)

Case	Product	Statements by Mexico	Subject Matter of the Complaint	Conclusion of the Panel
		• Art. VIII: 1(a) and (c) by being an indirect protection and by not minimizing the effects and complexity of the formalities		
EEC – Parts and Components (BISD 37S/132 L/6657) Adopted *Japan vs EEC*	general goods (Goods circumventing ADD)	Mexico made no statement	VI and I, II, III, X and XX(d) of the GATT	• The EEC Council Regulation on parts and components of products subject to ADD violates Art. III.2 first sentence of the GATT (not justified by XX(d)); • The decision to suspend the procedures violates III.4 of the GATT (not justified by XX(d)).
US – Customs User Fee (BISD 35S/245 L/6264) Adopted *Canada and EEC vs US*	general goods (an *ad valorem* charge imposed for the processing of commercial merchandise entering the US)	Mexico made no statement	II and VIII of the GATT	• The US merchandise processing fee violated Art. II.2(c) and VIII.1(a) of the GATT as it levies in excess of approximate costs.

Case	Product	Statements by Mexico	Subject Matter of the Complaint	Conclusion of the Panel
Japan – Semi-Conductors (35S/116 L/6309) Adopted *EEC vs Japan*	industrial goods (semi-conductors)	Mexico made no statement	I, VI, X, XI, and XVII:1(c) of the GATT	• The measures restricting the sale for export of semi-conductors at prices below company-specific costs to markets other than the US is inconsistent with Art. XI:1.

3.   Mexico's Abandoned Cases in WTO

Source: WT/DS series.

i. Abandoned Cases as Complainant

Case	Declaration of Abandonment	Subject Matter	The Other Party Involved	Product Involved	Procedural Stage
US – AD on Steel Zeroing I (325)	Yes	• 1, 2, 5, 9, 11 and 18 of the ADA; • VI and X of the GATT; • XVI of the WTO Agreement.	US	industrial goods (Steel)	Consultations
US – CVD on Steel (280)	No	• 1, 10, 14, 19 and 21 of the SCM;	US	industrial goods (Steel)	Panel/AB (Panel requested)
Ecu. – Cement I (182)	Yes	• 1, 2, 3, 4, 5, 6, 7, 9, 12 and 18 and Annex II of the ADA • VI of the GATT '94.	Ecuador	industrial goods (Cement)	Consultations

Case	Declaration of Abandonment	Subject Matter	The Other Party Involved	Product Involved	Procedural Stage
EC – Bananas III New Request (158)	No	• There is no claim of violation. The complainants wanted to consult on EC's implementation of EC – Bananas III (27)	EC	agricultural goods and Services (Banana and distributions)	Consultations
Guat. – Cement I (60)	Yes	• 2, 3, 5 and 7 of the ADA.	Guatemala	industrial goods (Cement)	Panel/ AB
EC – Bananas III (27)	No	• I, II, III, X, XI and XIII of the GATT; • 1 and 3 of the Import Licensing Agreement; • Agreement on Agriculture; • II, IV, XVI and XVII of the GATS; • 2 and 5 of the TRIMS.	EC	agricultural goods and Services (Bananas and distributions)	21.5 Panel/ AB – Mexico requested consultations under Art. 21.5 but abandoned the case later. (WT/DS27/18 and WT/DS27/33). The US and Ecuador went further and got authorization to retaliate.
EC – Bananas III Old Request (16)	Yes	• I, II, III, X and XIII of the GATT; • 1 and 3 of the Import Licensing Agreement; • II, XVI and XVII of the GATS.	EC	agricultural goods and Services (Bananas)	Consultations

ii. Abandoned Cases as Defendant

Case	Declaration of Abandonment	Subject Matter	The Other Party Involved	Product Involved	Procedural Stage
Mx – Olive Oil I (314)	Yes	• 10, 11, 15, 16 and 17 of the SCM; and • 13 and 21 of the A on Agriculture.	EC	agricultural goods (olive oil)	Consultations
Mx – Transformers (216)	No	• 2, 3, 5, 6, 7, and Annex II of the ADA.	Brazil	industrial goods (electric transformer)	Consultations
Mx – Swine (203)	No	• 3, 6 and 12 of the ADA; • 2, 3, 5, 7 and 8 of the SPS; • 4 of the A on Agriculture; • 2 and 5 of the TBT; and • III and XI of the GATT.	US	agricultural goods (Live swine)	Consultations
Mx – Corn Syrup I (101)	Yes	• 2, 4, 5 and 6 of the ADA.	US	agricultural goods (Corn syrup sweetener and sugar)	Consultations
Mx – Customs Valuation from EC (53)	No	• XXIV of GATT	EC	general goods (it challenges a regulation, without specifying any good).	Consultations

4. Mexico's Implemented Cases in WTO

Source: WT/DS series.

i. Implemented Cases as Complainant

Case	Subject Matter (based on request for consultations)	The Other Party Involved	The Product Involved	Procedural Stage
Panama – Milk (329)	• I, II, XXIII (non-violation) and XXVIII of the GATT; and • 4 of the A on Agriculture.	Panama	agricultural goods (Milk)	Consultations
US – Cement (281)	• 1, 2, 3, 4, 6, 8, 9, 10, 11, 12 and 18 of the ADA; • III, VI and X of the GATT; and • XVI of the WTO Agreement.	US	industrial goods (Cement)	Panel/AB
Ecu. – Cement II (191)	• 1, 2, 3, 4, 5, 6, 7, 9, 12 and 18 and Annex II of the ADA. • VI of the GATT '94;	Ecuador	industrial goods (Cement)	Consultations
Guat. – Cem. II (156)	• 1, 2, 3, 5, 6, 7, 9, 12 and 18 and Annexes I and II of the ADA, and • VI of the GATT.	Guatemala	industrial goods (Cement)	Panel/AB
US – Toma-toes (49)	• The principle of non-discriminatory treatment in international trade, • VI and X of GATT, and • 2, 3, 5, 6 and 7 of the ADA.	US	agricultural goods (Tomatoes)	Consultations
Venezuela – OCTG (23)	• 1, 3, 4, 5, 6, 12 and 16 of the ADA; and • VI of the GATT.	Venezuela	industrial goods (Steel)	Consultations

ii. Implemented Cases as Defendant

Case	Subject Matter (based on request for consultations)	The Other Party Involved	The Product Involved	Procedural Stage
Mx – Soft Drinks (308)	• III of the GATT	US	agricultural goods (sweeteners, mainly sugar)	RPT
Mx – Customs Valuation from Guatemala (298)	• I, II, VII and X of the GATT; • 1, 2, 3, 4, 5, 6, 7, 8, 12, 13, 15, 16, 22 and Annex I of the Customs Valuation; • the Ministerial Decision Regarding Cases Where Customs Administrations Have Reasons to Doubt the Truth or Accuracy of the Declared Value. • 4 of the A on Agriculture, • XVI of the WTO Agreement. • XXIII of the GATT, claiming a violation and non-violation case.	Guatemala	general goods (300 different products, but Guatemala settled with footwear and brushes)	Consultations
Mx – Beef and Rice (295)	• 3, 5, 6, 7, 9, 10, 11, 12, Annex II of the ADA; • VI of GATT; and • 11, 12, 17, 19, 20, 21 of SCM.	US	agricultural goods (beef and rice)	RPT
Mx – Beans (284)	• I, X, XI and XIII of the GATT, • 1 and 2 of the Licensing Agreement. • 2, 5, 7 and Annex B of the SPS Agreement.	Nicaragua	agricultural goods (Black Beans)	Consultations

Case	Subject Matter (based on request for consultations)	The Other Party Involved	The Product Involved	Procedural Stage
Mx – Matches (232)	• 1, 2 and 5 of the TBT • 1, 3 and 5 of the Licensing Procedures, and • III of the GATT.	Chile	industrial goods (Matches)	Consultations
Mx – Telecoms (204)	• VI, XVI, XVII, XVIII of the GATS; • Mexico's Reference Paper inscribed in Mexico's Schedule of Specific Commitments; and • GATS Annex on Telecommunications.	US	Services (Telecommunication Services)	RPT
Mx – Corn Syrup II (132)	• 2, 3, 4, 5, 6, 7, 9, 10, 12 of the ADA	US	agricultural goods (Corn syrup sweetener and sugar)	21.5 Panel/AB

5. Mexico's Pending Cases in WTO

Source: WT/DS series.

i. Pending Cases as Complainant

Case	Subject Matter (based on request for consultations)	The Other Party Involved	The Product Involved	Stage
US – AD on Steel Zeroing II (344)	• VI of GATT; • 1, 2, 5, 6, 9, 11 and 18 of the ADA; and • XVI of the WTO Agreement.	US	industrial goods (Steel)	Panel/AB
US – OCTG (282)	• 1, 2, 3, 6, 11 and 18 of the ADA; • VI and X of the GATT; • XVI of the WTO Agreement.	US	industrial goods (Steel)	21.5 Panel/AB

Case	Subject Matter (based on request for consultations)	The Other Party Involved	The Product Involved	Stage
US – Offset Act (217/234) Not amended to the satisfaction of Mx	• 1, 5, 8, 18 of the ADA; • 1, 5, 6, 10, 11, 18, 32 of the SCM; • XVI of the WTO Agreement, • VI, X, and XXIII (on violation and non-violation) of GATT	US	general goods (goods subject to AD duties)	Retaliation

ii. Pending Cases as Defendant

Case	Subject Matter (based on request for consultations)	The Other Party Involved	The Product Involved	Procedural Stage
Mx – Olive Oil II (341)	• VI of the GATT; • 1, 10, 11, 12, 13, 14, 15, 16, 19, 22 and 32 of the SCM ; and • 13 and 21 of the A on Agriculture.	EC	agricultural goods (Olive oil)	Panel/AB
Mx – Tubes from Guatemala (331)	• 1, 2, 3, 4, 5, 6, 9, 12, 18 and Annex II of the ADA; and • VI of the GATT	Guatemala	industrial goods (steel)	Panel/AB

6. WTO Cases Where Mexico Participated as Third Party

Source: WT/DS series.

Case[1]	Complainant[2]	Defendant	Stage	Product	Statements by Mexico Reflected in the Report
Japan – Measures Affecting Consumer Photographic Film and Paper (44) *US vs Japan*	US/EC	Other-OECD	Panel/AB (Panel issued a report)	industrial goods (photographic film and paper)	No intervention. There is nothing relevant from Mexico.

1. We are merging cases that were consolidated in one single Panel.
2. When there are several WTO members involved, complainants or defendants, we classify all them in the category of the most developed Member. For instance, if the complainants are Brazil and the US, we classify them as US/EC since, in practice, the US would be leading the team.

Case[1]	Com-plain-ant[2]	Defen-dant	Stage	Product	Statements by Mexico Reflected in the Report
US – Import Prohibition of Certain Shrimp and Shrimp Products (58) *India, Malaysia, Pakistan, Thailand vs US*	Non-OECD	US/EC	21.5 Panel/AB	industrial goods (Shrimp)	**Panel:** There is nothing relevant from Mexico. **AB** In response to briefs from NGOs attached in US submissions: • They are outside of the terms of reference. (Para 87) **21.5 Panel** • Panel's terms of reference are to determine whether the new measure is WTO consistent; and • XX of GATT exception has not been proved; • Communications from NGOs attached to US statements should not be taken into account. (Para 7.43 *et seq.*) **21.5 AB** • Same as the Panel. (Para 69 and 70)
Korea – Taxes on Alcoholic Beverages (75 and 84) *EC and US vs Korea*	US/EC	Other-OECD		industrial goods (alcoholic Beverages)	**Panel:** • III:2, first and second sentence, of GATT (Para 8.23) **AB:** • It developed the legal interpretation of its position. (Para 92 *et seq.*)

Case[1]	Com-plain-ant[2]	Defen-dant	Stage	Product	Statements by Mexico Reflected in the Report
Chile – Taxes on Alcoholic Beverages (87) *EC vs Chile*	US/EC	Non-OECD	RPT	industrial goods (alcoholic Beverages)	**Panel:** • III.2, second sentence of the GATT (Para 5.47) **Panel:** • III.2, second sentence of the GATT (Para 21 *et seq.*)
Canada – Measures Affecting the Importation of Milk and the Exporta-tion of Dairy Products (103, 113) *US, New Zealand vs Canada*	US/EC	Other-OECD	21.5 Panel/AB	agricultural goods (Dairy products)	Mexico only partici-pated in the **21.5 Panel** • Even in accelerated Panel procedures, 10.3 DSU says that Third Parties shall receive the submis-sions to the first meeting of the Panel. (Para. 2.31)
Australia – Subsidies Provided to Producers and Export-ers of Auto-motive Leather (126) *US vs Australia*	US/EC	Other-OECD	21.5 Panel/AB	industrial goods (Automotive Leather)	No intervention. Mexico only partici-pated in the **21.5 Panel:** • The lack of trans-lation into Spanish of the submissions made it impossible for Mexico to react in a prompt manner (Para 4.2).
US – AD Act of 1916 (136) *EC vs US*	US/EC	US/EC	Retalia-tion	general goods	**The Panel:** • Art. III, and VI of the GATT • Art. 1, 2, 3, of the AD Agreement • Art. XVI:4 of the WTO (para. 4.26–4.28)

Case[1]	Com-plain-ant[2]	Defen-dant	Stage	Product	Statements by Mexico Reflected in the Report
					The AB: • The 1916 Act objectively addresses "dump-ing" within the meaning of Art. VI of GATT • that AD duties are the sole remedy authorized under Art. VI of the GATT (para. 49).
US – Imposi-tion of Coun-tervailing Duties on Certain Hot-Rolled Lead and Bismuth Carbon Steel Products Originating in the United Kingdom (138) *EC vs US*	US/EC	US/EC	Panel/AB	industrial goods (Steel products)	**Panel:** Subsidy not estab-lished, violates: • 10 with 19.1 and 14 of the SCM; • VI of the GATT, *Arguendo* subsidy would be zero: • 19.4 of the ASCM. (Para 4.109 and 4.110) **AB:** • 11 of the DSU is applicable in this case Violation of: • 10 of the SCM, and • VI:3 of the GATT. (Para 34 *et seq.*)
EC – Protec-tion of Trade-marks and Geographical Indications for Agricul-tural Prod-ucts and Foodstuffs (174) *US vs EC*	US/EC	US/EC	Panel/AB	agricultural goods (Agricultural products and foodstuffs)	**Panel:** • 3.1 of TRIPS on national treatment; • 4 of TRIPS on MFN; • 24.5 and 16.1 of TRIPS on geo-graphical indica-tions and trademarks.

Case[1]	Complainant[2]	Defendant	Stage	Product	Statements by Mexico Reflected in the Report
					• Removal of "cochineal" (Coccus Cacti) from EC's regulation. (Annex C-27)
US – Definitive Safeguard Measures on Imports of Circular Welded Carbon Quality Line Pipe from Korea (202) *Korea vs US*	Other-OECD	US/EC	RPT	industrial goods (Carbon line pipe)	**Panel:** • Exclusion of Mexico from the safeguard by virtue of 802 of NAFTA; (annex A7 and B6) **AB:** • Same as in Panel; (Para 73–75)
US – Countervailing Measures Concerning Certain Products from the European Communities (212) *EC vs US*	US/EC	US/EC	21.5 Panel/AB	general goods	**Panel:** • The same person methodology violates VI of the GATT and 14, 19 and 21 of the SCM; • Section 1677(5)(F) violates 1, 10, 19, 21 and 32 of the SCM (Para 5.9 *et seq*) **AB:** • Intervention not reflected. **21.5 Panel/AB:** • Mexico did not become a Third Party in the 21.5 procedures.
EC – AD Duties on Malleable Cast Iron Tube or Pipe Fittings from Brazil (219) *Brazil vs EC*	Non-OECD	US/EC	Panel/AB	industrial goods (Pipe fittings)	No intervention.

Case[1]	Com-plain-ant[2]	Defen-dant	Stage	Product	Statements by Mexico Reflected in the Report
US – Defini-tive Safe-guard Mea-sures on Imports of Certain Steel Products (248, 249, 251, 252, 253, 254, 258 and, 259) *EC, Japan, Korea, China, Switzerland, Norway, New Zealand, and Brazil vs US*	US/EC	US/EC	Panel/AB	industrial goods (Steel products)	**Panel:** • Exclusion of Mex-ico from the safe-guard by virtue of 802 of NAFTA; (Para 8.17 *et seq.*) **AB:** Mexico did not pres-ent a written submis-sion; it only appeared at the AB hearing. • Mexico opposed the *amicus curiae* brief at the AB hearing (Para 268);
US – Sunset Reviews of AD Measures on Oil Coun-try Tubular Goods from Argentina (268) *Argentina vs US*	Non-OECD	US/EC	21.5 Panel/AB	industrial goods (Oil Country Tubular Goods)	**Panel:** • Violation of 11.3 of ADA (Annex D-5) **AB:** • Mexico commented on all the measures argued to be in vio-lation of 11.3 of the ADA (143 *et seq.*) **21.5 Panel:** • 11.3 of the ADA would not allow the US to gather de novo all the infor-mation. (Para 7.46) **21.5 AB:** (This procedure is out of our period of observation) • Suggestion to termi-nate the ADD by 19.1 of the DSU; • 11.3 of the ADA mandates the termi-nation of the ADD. (Para 85)

Case[1]	Com-plain-ant[2]	Defen-dant	Stage	Product	Statements by Mexico Reflected in the Report
Korea – Measures Affecting Trade in Commercial Vessels (273) *EC vs Korea*	US/EC	Other-OECD	Panel/AB	industrial goods (Vessels)	No intervention. (para. 5.1 of the Panel report)
Canada – Measures Relating to Exports of Wheat and Treatment of Imported Grain (276) *US vs Canada*	US/EC	Other-OECD	Panel/AB	agricultural goods (Wheat and grain)	No intervention. **Panel:** There is nothing relevant from Mexico. **AB:** There is nothing relevant from Mexico.
US – Measures Affecting the Cross-Border Supply of Gambling and Betting Services (285) *Antigua and Barbuda vs US*	Non-OECD	US/EC	Retalia-tion	Services (Gambling and Betting)	**Panel:** • The CPC[3] and W/120[4] help to interpret US Schedules. (Para 4.47) **AB:** There is nothing relevant from Mexico. **21.5 Panel** (This procedure is out of our period of observation) Mexico did not participate in this Panel.
EC – Protection of Trademarks and Geographical Indications for Agricultural Products and Foodstuffs (290) *Australia vs EC*	Other-OECD	US/EC	Panel/AB	agricultural goods (Agricultural products and foodstuffs)	**Panel:** • 3.1 of TRIPS on national treatment; • 4 of TRIPS on MFN; • 24.5 and 16.1 of TRIPS on geographical indications and trademarks. • Removal of "cochineal" (Coccus Cacti) from EC's regulation. (Annex C-27)

3. United Nations, Statistical Papers, Series M, No. 77, Provisional Central Product Classification, 1991.
4. Services Sectoral Classification List: Note by the Secretariat, MTN.GNS/W/120, 10 July 1991.

Case[1]	Complainant[2]	Defendant	Stage	Product	Statements by Mexico Reflected in the Report
EC – Measures Affecting the Approval and Marketing of Biotech Products (291, 292, 293) *US, Canada, and Argentina vs EC*	US/EC	US/EC	Panel/AB	agricultural goods (Biotech products)	No intervention. **Panel:** There is nothing relevant from Mexico.
US – Laws, Regulations and Methodology for Calculating Dumping Margins (Zeroing) (294) *EC vs US*	US/EC	US/EC	Panel/AB	general goods (Zeroing)	**Panel:** • Zeroing is prohibited by 2.4.2 of the ADA; • 2.4.2 of the ADA applies to duty assessment proceedings; • Average compared to transaction is permitted only in certain circumstances; and • "Standard Zeroing Procedures" can be challenged *as such.* (Para 5.71 *et seq.*) **AB:** • The AB held that dumping can be found only for the product "as a whole." Intermediate comparisons are not "margins of dumping". • Art. 2.4.2 of the ADA applies to all types of AD proceedings. Prohibition to "to zeroing" is VI of the GATT. (Para 95 *et seq.*)

Case[1]	Complainant[2]	Defendant	Stage	Product	Statements by Mexico Reflected in the Report
US – Continued Suspension of Obligations in the EC – Hormones Dispute (320, and 321) *EC and Canada vs US*	US/EC	US/EC	Panel/AB (no report issued)	agricultural goods (hormones)	There is no report.
US – Measures Relating to Zeroing and Sunset Reviews (322) *Japan vs US*	Other-OECD	US/EC	Panel/AB	general goods (Zeroing)	**Panel:** • Zeroing Procedures are measures with potential as such violations; • As such violations of 2 of ADA; • As such violations of 9 of ADA; (Para 5.70 *et seq.*) **AB:** (This procedure is out of our period of observation) • Zeroing in transaction to transaction in original investigations is as such inconsistent with 2 of the ADA and VI of the GATT. • There is no mathematical equivalence in different methods of comparing. • Calculation of the margins of dumping for the product as a whole applies to periodic reviews under 9.3 of ADA.

Case[1]	Com-plain-ant[2]	Defen-dant	Stage	Product	Statements by Mexico Reflected in the Report
					• Zeroing in New Shipper Reviews and Sunset Reviews is inconsistent with 9.5 and 11.3 of the ADA (Para 58 *et seq.*)
Brazil – Measures Affecting Imports of Retreaded Tyres (332) *EC vs Brazil*	US/EC	Non-OECD	Panel/AB (no report issued)	industrial goods (Retreaded Tyres)	There is no report. The Panel and AB procedures are out of our period of observation.
US – The Cuban Liberty and Democratic Solidarity Act (38) *EC vs US*	US/EC	US/EC	Panel/AB (no report issued)	general goods (Embargo to Cuba)	There is no report.
US – Definitive Safeguard Measures on Imports of Steel Wire Rod and Circular Welded Quality Line Pipe (214) *EC vs US*	US/EC	US/EC	Panel/AB (no report issued)	industrial goods (Steel line pipe)	There is no report.
US – Equalizing Excise Tax Imposed by Florida on Processed Orange and Grapefruit Products (250) *Brazil vs US*	Non-OECD	US/EC	Panel/AB (no report issued)	agricultural goods (Orange and grapefruit)	There is no report.

Case[1]	Com-plain-ant[2]	Defen-dant	Stage	Product	Statements by Mexico Reflected in the Report
Uruguay – Tax Treat-ment on Cer-tain Products (261) *Chile vs Uruguay*	Non-OECD	Non-OECD	Panel/AB (no report issued)	general goods (tax on certain products)	There is no report.
China – Mea-sures Affect-ing Imports of Automo-bile Parts (339, 340 and 342) *EC vs China*	US/EC	Non-OECD	Panel/AB (no report issued)	industrial goods (Auto-mobile parts)	There is no report.
US – Mea-sures Relat-ing to Shrimp from Thailand (343) *Thailand vs US*	Non-OECD	US/EC	Panel/AB	industrial goods (Shrimp)	There is no report.
US – Contin-ued Existence and Applica-tion of Zero-ing Method-ology (350) *EC vs US*	US/EC	US/EC	Panel/AB	general goods (Zeroing)	There is no report.

7. Mexico's Cases by Subject Matter

Source: WT/DS series.

Mexico as complainant				Mexico as defendant		
Agreement	Provision	Utilization		Agreement	Provision	Utilization
GATT 13 times cited	I	3 times		GATT 9 times cited	I	2 times
	II	3 times			II	1 time
	III	3 times			III	3 times
	VI	10 times			VI	3 times

Mexico as complainant			Mexico as defendant		
Agreement	**Provision**	**Utilization**	**Agreement**	**Provision**	**Utilization**
	X	7 times		VII	1 time
	XI	1 time		X	2 times
	XIII	2 times		XI	2 times
	XVI	1 time		XIII	1 time
	XXIII	2 times		XXIII	1 time
	XXVIII	1 time		XXIV	1 time
WTO Agreement 4 times cited	XVI	4 times	**WTO Agreement** 1 time cited	XVI	1 time
ADA 11 times cited	1	9 times	**ADA** 6 times cited	1	1 time
	2	9 times		2	4 times
	3	8 times		3	5 times
	4	4 times		4	3 times
	5	9 times		5	5 times
	6	8 times		6	6 times
	7	5 times		7	3 times
	8	2 times		9	3 times
	9	6 times		10	2 times
	10	1 time		11	1 time
	11	4 times		12	4 times
	12	5 times		18	1 time
	16	1 time		Annex II	3 times
	18	8 times			
	Annex I	1 time			
	Annex II	3 times			
A. Agriculture 2 times cited	4	1 time	**A. Agriculture** 4 times cited	4	2 times
				13	2 times
				21	2 times
SCM Agreement 2 times cited	1	2 times	**SCM Agreement** 3 times cited	1	1 time
	5	1 time		10	2 times
	6	1 time		11	3 times
	10	2 times		12	2 times
	11	1 time		13	1 time
	14	1 time		14	1 time
	18	1 time		15	2 times
	19	1 time		16	2 times
	21	1 time		17	2 times
	32	1 time		19	2 times

Mexico as complainant			Mexico as defendant		
Agreement	**Provision**	**Utilization**	**Agreement**	**Provision**	**Utilization**
				20	1 time
				21	1 time
				22	1 time
				32	1 time
GATS 2 times cited	II IV XVI XVII	2 times 1 time 2 times 2 times	**GATS** 1 time cited	VI XVI XVII Mx Reference Paper Annex on Telecoms	1 time 1 time 1 time 1 time 1 time
Licensing Agreement 2 times cited	1 3	2 Times 2 Times	**Licensing Agreement** 2 times cited	1 2 3 5	2 times 1 time 1 time 1 time
TRIMS 1 time cited	2 5	1 time 1 time	**Customs Valuation** 1 time cited	1 2 3 4 5 6 7 8 12 13 15 16 22 Annex I	1 time 1 time 1 time 1 time 1 time 1 time 1 time 1 time 1 time 1 time 1 time 1 time 1 time 1 time
The principle of non discrimination 1 time cited	n/a	n/a	**SPS Agreement** 2 times cited	2 3 5 7 8 Annex B	2 times 1 time 2 times 2 times 1 time 1 time
No claim of violation 1 time cited	n/a	n/a	**TBT Agreement** 2 times cited	1 2 5	1 time 2 times 2 times

Mexico as complainant			Mexico as defendant		
Agreement	Provision	Utilization	Agreement	Provision	Utilization
			The Minis-terial Deci-sion regarding cases where Customs Adminis-trations have rea-sons to doubt the truth or accuracy of the Declared Value 1 time cited	n/a	n/a

8. Nationality of decision makers In WTO cases

Source: WT/DS series. The nationality of the Panellists comes from www. worldtradelaw.net (consulted on December 2007).

Unless specified otherwise in the Table, the Panellists were selected by the Director General.

	Mexico as Complainant	Mexico as Defendant
Panellist (composed but with-out a rul-ing at the closing date of this work)	Peter Palecka (Chair) – Czech Republic **US – Cement (281)** Martin Garcia – New Zealand **US – Cement (281)** David Unterhalter – South Africa **US – Cement (281)**	Julio Lacarte-Muro (Chair) – Uruguay **Mexico – AD on Tubes (331) (agreement by Parties)** Cristian Espinosa Cañizares – Ecuador **Mexico – AD on Tubes (331) (agreement by Parties)** Alvaro Espinoza – Chile **Mexico – AD on Tubes (331) (agreement by Parties)** Debra Steger (Chair) – Canada **Mx – Olive oil II (341)** Gloria Peña – Chile **Mx – Olive oil II (341)** Jan Heukelman – South Africa **Mx – Olive oil II (341)**

	Mexico as Complainant	Mexico as Defendant
Panellists	Alberto Juan Dumont (Chair) – Argentina **US – AD on Steel Zeroing II (344)**	Ronald Saborío Soto (Chair) – Costa Rica **Mx – Soft Drinks (308) (agreement by Parties)**
	Bruce Cullen – New Zealand **US – AD on Steel Zeroing II (344)**	Edmond McGovern – United Kingdom **Mx – Soft Drinks (308) (agreement by Parties)**
	Leora Blumberg – South Africa **US – AD on Steel Zeroing II (344)**	David Walker – New Zealand **Mx – Soft Drinks (308) (agreement by Parties)**
	Christer Manhusen (Chair) – Sweden **US – OCTG (282) (agreement by Parties)**	Crawford Falconer (Chair) – New Zealand **Mx – Beef and Rice (295)**
	Alistair James Stewart – United Kingdom **US – OCTG (282) (agreement by Parties)**	Marta Calmon Lemme – Brazil **Mx – Beef and Rice (295)**
	Stephanie Sin Far Man – Australia **US – OCTG (282) (agreement by Parties)**	Enie Neri de Ross – Venezuela **Mx – Beef and Rice (295)**
	Luzius Wasescha (Chair) – Switzerland **US – Offset Act (217/234)**	Christer Manhusen (Chair) – Sweden **Mx – Corn Syrup II (132) (agreement by Parties)**
	Maamoun Abdel-Fattah – Egypt **US – Offset Act (217/234)**	Gerald Salembier – Canada **Mx – Corn Syrup II (132) (agreement by Parties)**
	William Falconer – New Zealand **US – Offset Act (217/234)**	Edwin Vermulst – Netherlands **Mx – Corn Syrup II (132) (agreement by Parties)**
	Johannes Human (Chair) – South Africa **Guat. – Cement II (156)**	Ernst-Ulrich Petersmann (Chair) – Germany **Mx – Telecoms (204)**
	Antonio Buencamino – Philippines **Guat. – Cement II (156)**	Raymond Tam – Hong Kong **Mx – Telecoms (204)**
	Oscar Hernández – Venezuela **Guat. – Cement II (156)**	Björn Wellenius – Chile **Mx – Telecoms (204)**
	Klaus Kautzor-Schröder (Chair) – Germany **Guat. – Cement I (60)**	
	Antonio S. Buencamino – Philippines **Guat. – Cement I (60)**	
	Gerardo Teodoro Thielen Graterol – Venezuela **Guat. – Cement I (60)**	
	Stuart Harbinson (Chair) – Hong Kong **EC – Bananas III (27)**	
	Kym Anderson – Australia **EC – Bananas III (27)**	
	Christian Haberli – Switzerland **EC – Bananas III (27)**	

	Mexico as Complainant	Mexico as Defendant
Division of the AB	A.V. Ganesan (Chair) – India **US – OCTG (282)**	Yasuhei Taniguchi (Chair) – Japan **Mx – Soft Drinks (308)**
	John Lockhart – Australia **US – OCTG (282)**	Merit E. Janow – US **Mx – Soft Drinks (308)**
	Yasuhei Taniguchi – Japan **US – OCTG (282)**	Giorgio Sacerdoti – Italy **Mx – Soft Drinks (308)**
	Giorgio Sacerdoti (Chair) – Italy **US – Offset Act (217/234)**	John Lockhart (Chair) – Australia **Mx – Beef and Rice (295)**
	John Lockhart – Australia **US – Offset Act (217/234)**	Georges Abi-Saab – Egypt **Mx – Beef and Rice (295)**
	Luiz Olavo Baptista – Brazil **US – Offset Act (217/234)**	Yasuhei Taniguchi – Japan **Mx – Beef and Rice (295)**
	Julio Lacarte-Muro (Chair) – Uruguay **Guat. – Cement I (60)**	
	Christopher Beeby – New Zealand – **Guat. – Cement I (60)**	
	Said El-Naggar – Egypt **Guat. – Cement I (60)**	
	James Bacchus (Chair) – US **EC – Bananas III (27)**	
	Christopher Beeby – New Zealand **EC – Bananas III (27)**	
	Said El-Naggar – Egypt **EC – Bananas III (27)**	
21.5 Panel	N/A	Christer Manhusen (Chair) – Sweden **Mx – Corn Syrup II (132) (agreement by Parties)**
		Gerald Salembier – Canada **Mx – Corn Syrup II (132) (agreement by Parties)**
		Paul O'Connor – Australia **Mx – Corn Syrup II (132) (agreement by Parties)**
Division of the 21.5 AB	N/A	(Chair) Florentino P. Feliciano – Philippines **Mx – Corn Syrup II (132)**
		Georges Abi-Saab – Egypt **Mx – Corn Syrup II (132)**
		Claus-Dieter Ehlermann – Germany **Mx – Corn Syrup II (132)**

	Mexico as Complainant	Mexico as Defendant
Arbitrator for RPT	Yasuhei Taniguchi – Japan **US – Offset Act (217/234)** Said El-Naggar – Egypt **EC – Bananas III (27)**	N/A
Arbitrator for Level of Nullification or Impairment (Retaliation)	Luzius Wasescha (Chair) – Switzerland **US – Offset Act (217/234)** Maamoun Abdel-Fattah – Egypt **US – Offset Act (217/234)** William Falconer – New Zealand **US – Offset Act (217/234)**	N/A

9. All Mexico's WTO Cases

Source: WT/DS series.

i. Mexico's Cases as Complainant

Case	The Other Party	Product	Stage	Status	Legal Remedy
US – AD on Steel Zeroing II (344)	US	industrial goods (Steel)	Panel/AB	Pending	None
Panama – Milk (329)	Panama	agricultural goods (Milk)	Consultations	Implemented	MAS (*ex ante*)
US – AD on Steel Zeroing I (325)	US	industrial goods (Steel)	Consultations	Abandoned	None
US – OCTG (282)	US	industrial goods (Steel)	21.5 Panel/AB	Pending	None
US – Cement (281)	US	industrial goods (Cement)	Panel/AB	Implemented	MAS (*ex ante*)
US – CVD on Steel (280)	US	industrial goods (Steel)	Panel/AB (Panel requested)	Abandoned	None

Case	The Other Party	Product	Stage	Status	Legal Remedy
US – Offset Act (217/234)	US	general goods (Goods subject to AD duties)	Retaliation	Pending	Retaliation
Ecu. – Cement II (191)	Ecuador	industrial goods (Cement)	Consultations	Implemented	Compliance (*ex ante*)
Ecu. – Cement I (182)	Ecuador	industrial goods (Cement)	Consultations	Abandoned	None
EC – Bananas III New Request (158)	EC	agricultural goods and services (Banana and distributions)	Consultations	Abandoned	None
Guat. – Cement II (156)	Guatemala	industrial goods (Cement)	Panel/AB	Implemented	Compliance (*ex post*)
Guat. – Cement I (60)	Guatemala	industrial goods (Cement)	Panel/ AB	Abandoned	None
US – Tomatoes (49)	US	agricultural goods (Tomatoes)	Consultations	Implemented	MAS (*ex ante*)
EC – Bananas III (27)	EC	agricultural goods and services (Bananas and distributions)	21.5 Panel/ AB (however, US and Ecuador got authorization to retaliate)	Abandoned (though the cases is active for the Ecuador and others)	None
Venezuela – OCTG (23)	Venezuela	industrial goods (Steel)	Consultations	Implemented	MAS (*ex ante*)
EC – Bananas III Old Request (16)	EC	agricultural goods and services (Bananas)	Consultations	Abandoned	None

ii. Mexico's Cases as Defendant

Case	The Other Party	Product	Stage	Status	Legal Remedy
Mx – Olive Oil II (341)	EC	agricultural goods (Olive oil)	Panel/AB	Pending	None
Mx – AD on Tubes (331)	Guate-mala	industrial goods (Steel)	Panel/AB	Pending	None
Mx – Olive Oil I (314)	EC	agricultural goods (Olive oil)	Consultation	Abandoned	None
Mx – Soft Drinks (308)	US	agricultural goods (Sweeten-ers, mainly sugar)	RPT	Implemented	MAS (*ex post*)
Mx – Customs Valuation Guatemala (298)	Guate-mala	general goods (300 different products, but Guatemala set-tled with Foot-wear and Brushes)	Consultations	Implemented	MAS (*ex ante*)
Mx – Beef and Rice (295)	US	agricultural goods (Beef and Rice)	RPT	Implemented	MAS (*ex post*)
Mx – Beans (284)	Nica-ragua	agricultural goods (Black Beans)	Consultations	Implemented	MAS (*ex ante*)
Mx – Matches (232)	Chile	industrial goods (Matches)	Consultations	Implemented	MAS (*ex ante*)
Mx – Transform-ers (216)	Brazil	industrial goods (electric Trans-former)	Consultations	Abandoned	None
Mx – Tel-ecoms (204)	US	Services (Tel-ecommunication Services)	RPT	Implemented	MAS (*ex post*)

Case	The Other Party	Product	Stage	Status	Legal Remedy
Mx – Swine (203)	US	agricultural goods (Live Swine)	Consultations	Abandoned	None
Mx – Corn Syrup II (132)	US	agricultural goods (Corn Syrup sweetener and Sugar)	21.5 Panel/ AB	Imple- mented	Compliance (*ex post*)
Mx – Corn Syrup I (101)	US	agricultural goods (Corn Syrup sweetener and Sugar)	Consultations	Abandoned	None
Mx – Cus- toms Valu- ation from EC (53)	EC	general goods (it challenges a reg- ulation, without specifying any good).	Consultations	Abandoned	None

10. Findings/Implementation of WTO Cases at a Glance

Source: WT/DS series. The information on implementation is based on "Table 11. WTO Cases: Measures, Claims, and Implementation."

i. Mexico's Cases as Complainant

Case	Won / Lost		Implementation
Guat. – Cement II (156)	Total Findings	19	Implemented
Defendant: Guatemala	Guatemala won	1 (5%)	
Product: industrial Goods (Cement)	Mexico won	18 (95%)	
US – OCTG (282)	Total Findings by the Panel	10	Not implemented
Defendant: US	The US won	8 (80%)	
Product: industrial Goods (Steel)	Mexico won	2 (20%)	
	Total Findings by the AB	11	
	The US won	11 (100%)	
	Mexico won	0 (0%)	

Case	Won / Lost		Implementation
US – Offset Act (217/234) **Defendant:** US **Product:** general Goods (Goods subject to AD duties)	Total Findings by the Panel	14	Not implemented
	The US won	4 (29%)	
	Mexico and other complainants won	10 (71%)	
	Total Findings by the AB	11	
	The US won	4 (36%)	
	Mexico and other complainants won	7 (64%)	
	Total Findings by the Arb. on RPT	1	
	The US won	0.5 (50%)	
	Mexico and other complainants won	0.5 (50%)	
	Total Findings (22.6 Arb.)	1	
	The US won	0.5 (50%)	
	Mexico and other complainants won	0.5 (50%)	
Guat. – Cement I (60) **Defendant:** Guatemala **Product:** industrial Goods (Cement)	Total Findings by the Panel	4	Not implemented
	Guatemala won	1 (25%)	
	Mexico won	3 (75%)	
	Total Findings by the AB	3	
	Guatemala won	3 (100%)[5]	
	Mexico won	0 (0%)	
EC – Bananas III (27) **Defendant:** The EC **Product:** agricultural Goods and Services (Bananas and distributions)	Total Findings by the Panel	6	Not Implemented
	The EC won	0 (0%)	
	Mexico and other complainants won	6 (100%)	
	Total Findings by the AB	28	
	The EC won	5 (18%)	
	Mexico and other complainants won	23 (82%)	

---

5. Based on its findings, the AB concluded that there were no recommendations to Guatemala. Mexico lost all the claims presented to the Panel.

Case	Won / Lost		Implementation
	Total Findings by the Arb. on RPT	1	
	The EC won	1 (100%)	
	Mexico and other complainants won	0 (0%)	

ii. Mexico's Cases as Defendant

Case	Won / Lost		Implementation
Mx – Soft Drinks (308) **Complaint:** US **Product:** agricultural Goods (sweeteners, mainly Sugar)	Total Findings by the Panel	8	Implemented
	The US won	8 (100%)	
	Mexico won	0 (0%)	
	Total Findings by the AB	3	
	The US won	3 (100%)	
	Mexico won	0 (0%)	
Mx – Beef and Rice (295) **Complaint:** US **Product:** agricultural Goods (beef and rice)	Total Findings by the Panel	15	Implemented
	The US won	13 (87%)	
	Mexico won	2 (13%)	
	Total Findings by the AB	17	
	The US won	16 (94%)	
	Mexico won	1 (6%)	
Mx – Telecoms (204) **Complaint:** US **Product:** Services (Telecommunication Services)	Total Findings by the Panel	7	Implemented
	The US won	4 (57%)	
	Mexico won	3 (43%)	
Mx – Corn Syrup II (132) **Complaint:** US **Product:** agricultural Goods (Corn Syrup sweetener and Sugar)	Total Findings by the Panel	6	Implemented
	The US won	5 (83%)	
	Mexico won	1 (17%)	
	Total Findings by the 21.5 Panel	2	
	The US won		
	Mexico won	2 (100%) 0 (0%)	
	Total Findings by the 21.5 AB	5	
	The US won	5 (100%)	
	Mexico won	0 (0%)	

11. WTO Cases: Measures, Claims and Implementation

Source: WT/DS series. Other sources are specified in footnotes.

i. Mexico's Cases as Complainant

Case	Subject Matter (based on request for consultations)	Implementation
US – AD on Steel Zeroing II (344) **Req. Cons:** 26 May 2005	**Measures:** 1. The following determinations of the USDOC concerning the imports of stainless steel sheet and strip in coils from Mexico, Case No. A-201-822: • "Final Determination of Sales At Less Than Fair Value: Stainless Steel Sheet and Strip in Coils from Mexico, published on 8 June 1999 (64 FR 30790), and its amendments; • Final Results of AD Duty Administrative Review: Stainless Steel Sheet and Strip in Coils from Mexico, from January 1999 to June 2000, published on 12 February 2002 (67 FR 6490) and its amendments; • Final Results of AD Duty Administrative Review: Stainless Steel Sheet and Strip in Coils from Mexico, from July 2000 to June 2001, published on 11 February 2003 (68 FR 6889) and its amendments; • Final Results of AD Duty Administrative Review: Stainless Steel Sheet and Strip in Coils from Mexico from July 2001 to June 2002, published on 10 February 2004 (69 FR 6259); • Final Results of AD Duty Administrative Review: Stainless Steel Sheet and Strip in Coils from Mexico, from July 2002 to June 2003, published on 26 January 2005 (69 FR 3677); • Final Results of AD Duty Administrative Review: Stainless Steel Sheet and Strip in Coils from Mexico, from July 2003 to June 2004, published on 12 December 2005 (70 FR 734444). 2. The following US legal instruments: • Sections 736, 751, 771(35)(A) and (B), and section 777A(c) and (d) of the Tariff Act of 1930, as amended;	**Not implemented.** **The measure was not amended.** The Panel was composed on 22 December 2006 of by the DG (WT/DS344/5).

Case	Subject Matter (based on request for consultations)	Implementation
	• The US Statement of Administrative Action that accompanied the Uruguay Round Agreements Act, H.R. Doc. No. 103-316, vol. I; • USDOC regulations codified at Title 19 of the US Code of Federal Regulations, sections 351.212(b), 351.414(c), (d) and (e); • The Import Administration AD Manual (1997 edition), including the computer program(s) to which it refers; • The methodology employed by the DOC to determine the margin of dumping in the original investigation, where it disregarded (treated as zero or "zeroed") negative dumping margins (i.e., dumping margins where the weighted-average export price for the model exceeded the weighted-average normal value); and • The methodology employed by the DOC to determine the margin of dumping in the listed Administrative Reviews where the DOC disregarded (treated as zero or "zeroed") negative dumping margins (i.e. dumping margins where the individual export price for the model exceeded the weighted-average normal value).	
	Claims: • VI:1 and VI:2 of GATT; • 1, 2.1, 2.4, 2.4.2, 5, 6.10, 9 (including but not limited to 9.3), 11 and 18 of the ADA; • XVI: 4 of the WTO Agreement.	
Panama – Milk (329) **Req. Cons:** 16 March 2005	**Measures:** • Decree (17 July 2002) creating a new tariff of 65% for certain milk. Panama's bound tariff is 5%.	**Implemented.** **The measure was amended.** Panama withdrew the measure. • The Parties reached a MAS (20 September 2005) WT/DS329/2.
	Claims: • II of the GATT '94 and 4 of the Agreement on Agriculture (by applying an import tariff higher than the bound tariff);	

Case	Subject Matter (based on request for consultations)	Implementation
	• XXVIII of the GATT '94 (by unilaterally modifying the Schedule of Concessions without following the procedure of that article); and • I of the GATT (by granting a tariff advantage to infant milk formula and not according it immediately and unconditionally to modified milk from Mexico). • Case of nullification or impairment under XXIII(1)(b) of the GATT '94 (non-violation).	• Panama amended its tariff schedule for milk (1901.10.19). It set a new tariff or 5%, in the light of its bound tariff.
US – AD on Steel Zeroing I (325) **Req. cons.** 5 January 2005	**Measures:** The use of Zeroing by the US Department of Commerce in the following: • Final Determination of Sales at Less than Fair Value: Stainless Steel Sheet and Strip in Coils from Mexico, of 8 June 1999; • The Final Results of the Administrative Review (1999–2000), of 12 February 2002; • The Final Results of the Administrative Review (2000–2001), of 11 February 2003; and • The Final Results of the Administrative Review (2001–2002) of 10 February 2004. The following US regulations and administrative practices: • Sections 736, 751, 771(35)(A) and (B), and 777A(c) and (d) of the Tariff Act of 1930; • USDOC regulations codified at Title 19 of the US Code of Federal Regulations, sections 351.212(b), 351.414(c), (d) and (e). **Claims:** • 1, 2 (in particular 2.1, 2.4 and 2.4.2), 5 (in particular 5.8), 9 (in particular 9.3), 11 (in particular 11.2) and 18.4 of the ADA; • VI:1 and VI:2, as well as X:3(a) of the GATT '94; and • XVI:4 of the WTO Agreement.	**Not Implemented.** **The measure was not amended.** Mexico presented a new request for consultations . (DS344).

Case	Subject Matter (based on request for consultations)	Implementation
US – OCTG (282) **Req. cons.** 18 February 2003	**Measures:** The following determinations: • Oil country tubular Goods from Mexico: Final results of Sunset Review, 66 Fed. Reg. 14131 (9 March 2001) and the Issues and Decision Memorandum ("Sunset Review by the Department"); • Oil country tubular Goods from Argentina, Italy, Japan, Korea and Mexico: 66 Fed. Reg. 35997 (10 July 2001) ("Sunset Review by the Commission"); • Oil country tubular Goods from Mexico and other countries: Final determination to continue applying AD duties, 66 Fed. Reg. 38630 (25 July 2001); and • Oil country tubular Goods from Mexico: Final results of AD duty Administrative Review – 1 August 1998 – 31 July 1999, 66 Fed. Reg. 15832 (21 March 2001) (Final results of the Fourth Administrative Review). The following US laws, regulations and administrative practices: • Sections 751 and 752 of the Tariff Act of 1930, codified at Title 19 of the US Code, sections 1675 and 1675a; and the US Statement of Administrative Action accompanying the Uruguay Round Agreements Act; • The Department's Policies regarding the conduct of Sunset Reviews of AD and countervailing duties; Policy Bulletin, 63 Federal Register 18871 (16 April 1998) (Department's Sunset Policy Bulletin); • The Department's regulations for Sunset Reviews of AD duties, codified at Title 19 of the US Code of Federal Regulations, Section 351.218; • The Commission's regulations for Sunset Reviews of AD duties, codified at Title 19 of the US Code of Federal Regulations, Section 207.60–69 (Subpart F); and	**Not Implemented.** **The measure was amended but not to the satisfaction of Mexico.** • Mexico requested consultations under Art. 21.5 of the DSU on 21 August 2006 (WT/DS282/13) • The RPT expired on 28 of May 2006 (21.3b). • On 9 June 2006, the US issued the Final Results of Sunset Review, Oil Country Tubular Goods from Mexico (Case No.: A-201-817). • Mexico's next step would be a 21.5 Panel, in the light of the sequencing agreement (WT/DS282/12).

Case	Subject Matter (based on request for consultations)	Implementation
	• The Department's regulations for Administrative Review, including those codified at Title 19 of the US Code of Federal Regulations, Sections 351.213, 351.221 and 351.222.	
	Claims: Mexico considered that the following Art. were violated: • 1, 2, 3, 6, 11 and 18 of the ADA; • VI and X of the GATT; • XVI:4 of the WTO Agreement.	
US – Cement (281) Req. cons. 31 January 2003	**Measures:** • Final Results of the Fifth Administrative Review – 1 August 1994 – 31 July 1995, Federal Register Vol. 62, p.17148 (9 April 1997); • Final Results of the Sixth Administrative Review – 1 August 1995 – 31 July 1996, Federal Register Vol. 63, p.12764 (16 March 1998); • Final Results of the Seventh Administrative Review – 1 August 1996 – 31 July 1997, Federal Register Vol. 64, p.13148 (17 March 1999); • Final Results of the Eighth Administrative Review – 1 August 1997 – 31 July 1998, Federal Register Vol. 65, p.13943 (15 March 2000) and the accompanying Issues and Decision Memorandum; • Final Results of the Ninth Administrative Review – 1 August 1998 – 31 July 1999, Federal Register Vol. 66, p.14889 (14 March 2001) and the accompanying Issues and Decision Memorandum; • Final Results of the Tenth Administrative Review – 1 August 1999 – 31 July 2000, Federal Register Vol. 67, p.12518 (19 March 2002) and the accompanying Issues and Decision Memorandum;	**Implemented.** **The measure was amended.** Mexico and the US signed a MAS (6 March 2006) not formally notified to the WTO.[6] • The Panel procedure was suspended following the communication dated 16 January 2006 (12.12 of the DSU). • Termination of the AD duty imposed in 1990. The agreement contains the following: – resolution of litigation before U.S. courts and international tribunals;

6. For the text of the MAS relating to the US AD order on Cement, see http://ia.ita.doc.gov/cement-agreement/cement-final-agreement.pdf.

Case	Subject Matter (based on request for consultations)	Implementation
	• Final Results of the Eleventh Administrative Review – 1 August 2000 – 31 July 2001, Federal Register Vol. 67, p.12518 (14 January 2003) and the accompanying Issues and Decision Memorandum; • Department Sunset Review, Federal Register Vol. 65, p.41049 (3 July 2000) and the accompanying Issues and Decision Memorandum; • Commission Sunset Review Nos. 303-TA-21, 731-TA-451, 461 and 519, USITC Publication No. 3361 (October 2000) and Federal Register Vol. 65, p.65327 (1 November 2000); • Gray Portland Cement and Cement Clinker from Japan and Mexico: Continuation of AD Duty Orders, Federal Register Vol. 65, p.68979 (15 November 2000); and • Commission Determination rejecting the request for a review based on changed circumstances, Federal Register Vol. 66, p.65740 (20 December 2001); • Sections 736, 737, 751, 752 and 778 of the Tariff Act of 1930, as amended, codified at Title 19 of the US Code §§ 1673e, 1673f, 1675, 1675a and 1677g (Tariff Act) and the US Statement of Administrative Action accompanying the Uruguay Round Agreements Act (the SAA), H.R. Doc., No. 103-316, Vol.1; • The Department's Policies Regarding the Conduct of Five-Year "Sunset" Reviews of AD and Countervailing Duty Orders; Policy Bulletin, Federal Register Vol. 63, p.18871 (16 April 1998) (Sunset Policy Bulletin); • The Department's Sunset Review regulations, codified at Title 19 of the US Code of Federal Regulations § 351.218; and the Commission's Sunset Review regulations, codified at Title 19 of the US Code of Federal Regulations §§ 207.60–69, Federal Register Vol. 63, p.30599 (5 June 1998); and	– a mechanism permitting imports of 3 million metric tonnes of Mexican cement to the southern tier of the US, with an AD duty of $3 per metric tonne; – a provision permitting additional imports of up to 200,000 metric tonnes at the lower AD duty rate, in responding to a disaster; – elements for mutual trade liberalization, including access for U.S. producers to the Mexican market; – a three-year duration; and – provisions that address the revocation of the AD duty at the end.[7]

---

7. See the Press Release of the US Department of Commerce at http://www.trade.gov/press/press_releases/2006/cement_030606.asp, consulted on 21t of July 2006.

Case	Subject Matter (based on request for consultations)	Implementation
	• The Department's rules governing the calculation of dumping margins, codified at Title 19 of the US Code of Federal Regulations §§ 351.102; 351.212(f); 351.213(j); 351.403 and 351.414(c)(2).	
	Claims: Mexico considered that the following provisions were in violation: • 1, 2, 3, 4, 6, 8, 9, 10, 11, 12 and 18 of the ADA; • III, VI and X of the GATT; and • XVI:4 of the WTO Agreement.	
US – CVD on Steel (280) **Req. cons.** 21 January 2003	**Measures:** • Final Results of Countervailing Duty Administrative Review of 1998 (C-201-810)(66 FR 14549, 13 March 2001), and • the actions that preceded it and led to the imposition of countervailing duties on imports of carbon steel plate in sheets from Mexico.	**Not implemented.** **The measure was not amended.** The Panel has been requested and established but not composed. • The measure was revoked on 12 February 2007 on the second Sunset Review (F.R. Vol. 72, No. 28,659). • The Panel was established by the DSB on 29 August 2003 (WT/DSB/M/155).
	Claims: Mexico considered that the US was in violation of the following provisions: • the Administrative Review by the DOC following the so called "change-in-ownership" methodology (more specifically, proof of "same person") to be inconsistent with 10, 14, 19 and 21 of the SCM Agreement. • the DOC failed to conduct a determination of the existence of a benefit as required under paragraph 1:1(b) of the SCM Agreement.	
US – Offset Act (217/234) **Other co-complainants:** Australia, Brazil, Canada, Chile, EC, India, Indonesia, Japan, Korea, and Thailand **Req. cons.** 21 May 2001	**Measures:** • The amendment to the Tariff Act of 1930 entitled the "Continued Dumping and Subsidy Offset Act of 2000." *Statement of available evidence provided for in 7.2 of the SCMA* • The text of the "Continued Dumping and Subsidy Offset Act of 2000" • The schedule of tariff concessions bound by the US under II of GATT.	**Not implemented.** **The measure was not amended.** • The Byrd amendment *had not been repealed* by the closing date of this work.

Case	Subject Matter (based on request for consultations)	Implementation
	Claims: • 18.1 of the ADA in conjunction with VI:2 of the GATT and 1 of the ADA; • 32.1 of the SCM, in conjunction with VI:3 of the GATT and 10 of the SCM; • X(3)(a) of the GATT; • 5.4 of the ADA and 11.4 of the SCM; • 8 of the ADA and 18 of the SCM; • 5 of the SCM; and • XVI:4 of the WTO Agreement, 18.4 of the ADA and 32.5 of the SCM; • The measure appears to nullify or impair the benefits in the manner described in XXIII:1(a) of GATT. • The measure may nullify or impair benefits in the manner described in XXIII:1(b) of GATT (Non-violation). • The "offset" paid under the measure constitutes specific subsidies (1 of the SCM), which may cause "adverse effects" to their interests (5 of the SCM) and serious prejudice (6 of the SCM).	• On 17 February 2006 (WT/DSB/M/205), *the US notified that it had taken steps to repeal the Byrd Amendment*. The Deficit Reduction Act repealing the CDSOA provides that duties imposed on Goods imported into the US up to 30 September 2007 will still be distributed after their collection.[8] • *Mexico initiated retaliatory measures* through decree published on 17 August 2005 (with a validity of 12 months). Japan and the EC had already imposed retaliatory measures at the time. • Through a decree published on 13 September 2006, Mexico imposed a second set of retaliatory measures. The second decree expired on 31 October 2006.

---

8. See The Library of Congress at http://thomas.loc.gov/cgi-bin/query/F?c109:5:./temp/~c109HaVd10:e475264 Consulted on July 2006.

Case	Subject Matter (based on request for consultations)	Implementation
		• Mexico notified that it had imposed retaliatory measures on 31 August 2005 at the DSB meeting (WT/DSB/M/196). In the same meeting, Japan indicated that also the EC, Canada and Japan have imposed retaliatory measures.
		• On 31 August 2004, an arbitrator under 22.6 *allowed those Members to suspend concessions or other obligations up to a maximum value of trade*. This is calculated, on a yearly basis, by multiplying the published amount of disbursements under the CDSOA paid (for exports coming from each authorized Member) for a given year by 0.72.
		• On 13 June 2003, an arbitration under 21.3 (c) found that *the RPT would expire on 27 December 2003*.

Case	Subject Matter (based on request for consultations)	Implementation
Ecu. – Cement II (191) **Req. cons.** 15 March 2000	**Measures:** • Definitive AD measure of 20 per cent on cement imports from Mexico (published on 14 January 2000), as well as the actions that preceded it, including the provisional AD measure and the initiation of the investigation. **Claims:** • 1, 2, 3, 4, 5, 6, 7, 9, 12 and 18 and Annex II of the ADA. • VI of the GATT '94;	**Implemented.** **The measure was amended.** • The measure was revoked on 14 June 2000 (*Registro Oficial de Ecuador N 89*) • The AD definitive measure expired after six months of its publication, as mentioned in the public notice of the final determination.
Ecu. – Cement I (182) **Req. cons.** 5 October 1999	**Measures:** • The provisional AD measure on imports of cement from Mexico (published on 14 July 99) as well as the actions that preceded it. **Claims:** • 1, 2, 3, 4, 5, 6, 7, 9, 12 and 18 and Annex II of the ADA • VI of the GATT '94.	**Not implemented.** **The provisional measure was not modified.** • Mexico presented a new request for consultations challenging the definitive AD measure – i.e., DS191.
EC – Bananas III New Request (158) **Other complainants:** Guatemala, Honduras, Panama and the US vs EC **Req. cons.** 20 January 1999	**Measures:** • The EC banana regime established by EC Regulation 404/93, as amended and implemented by Council Regulation 1637/98 of 20 July 1998 and EC Commission Regulation 2362/98 of 28 October 1998	**Not implemented.** **The measure was not amended.** • DS27 is still pending. • There is no further DS document after the requests by Belize and Ecuador to be joined in consultations.

Case	Subject Matter (based on request for consultations)	Implementation

	Claims:
	• There is no claim of violation.
	• The objective is to discuss with the EC the various aspects of the EC's modified banana regime (since the RPT of DS/27 Panel/AB report expired some days before this request – 1 of January 1999) including:
	  – their effect on the market,
	  – concerns about their WTO-inconsistency, and
	  – search for a MAS.	

Guat. – Cement II (156) Req. cons. 5 January 1999	**Measures:** • The definitive AD measure on imports of grey portland cement from the Mexican firm La Cruz Azul S.C.L., • As well as the actions that preceded it.	**Implemented.** **The measure was eliminated.** • Guatemala withdrew the measure on 4 October 2000 (see *Diario de Centroamérica* of 3 October 2000)
	Claims: • 1, 2, 3, 5, 6, 7, 9, 12 and 18 and Annexes I and II of the ADA, and • VI of the GATT '94).	
Guat. – Cement I (60) Req. cons. 15 October 1996	**Measures:** • The AD investigation being carried out by the authorities of Guatemala concerning imports of portland cement from Mexico.	**Not implemented.** **The measure was not amended.** • Mexico lost – the AB concluded that the matter was not properly before the Panel – and took no further action in this case. • Mexico challenged the definitive AD measure on a new case: DS156.
	Claims: • 2, 3, 5 and 7.1 of the ADA.	

Case	Subject Matter (based on request for consultations)	Implementation
US – Tomatoes (49) **Req. cons.** 1 July 1996	**Measures:** • The AD investigation on US imports of fresh or chilled tomatoes of any kind from Mexico. **Claims:** • The principle of non-discriminatory treatment in international trade, • VI and X of GATT '94, and • 2, 3, 5, 6 and 7.1 of the ADA.	**Implemented.** **The measure was amended.** • The Department of Commerce of the US published the suspension of the AD investigation through a price undertaking (61 FR 56617) on 1 November 1996 • The Mexican exporter of tomatoes signed a price undertaking with the US investigating authority.[9] • There are no further DS documents after the request for consultations. • The price undertaking was extended in January 2008.[10]
EC – Bananas III (27) **Other Complainants:** Ecuador, Guatemala, Honduras, and the US	**Measures:** • EC regime for the importation, sale and distribution of bananas established by Regulation 404/93 (OJ L 47 of 25 February 1993, p. 1), and • the subsequent instruments, including the Framework Agreement on bananas, which implement, supplement and amend that regime.	**Not implemented.** **The measure was not amended.**

---

9. See http://ia.ita.doc.gov/tomato/1996-agreement/1996-agreement.html (Consulted on November 2007).

10. "See US and Mexico agree on a new suspension agreement for tomato AD case." Published by INSIDE U.S. TRADE (www.InsideTrade.com) on 1 February 2008, Vol. 26, No. 5.

Case	Subject Matter (based on request for consultations)	Implementation

Req. cons. 5 February 1996	**Claims:**
	• I, II, III, X, XI and XIII of the GATT '94;
	• 1 and 3 of the Agreement on Import Licensing Procedures;
	• The Agreement on Agriculture;
	• II, IV, XVI and XVII of the GATS; and,
	• 2 and 5 of the Agreement on Trade-Related Investment Measures.
		• Mexico's last DS document was the request for the establishment of a 21.5 Panel which it presented on 18 August 1998. Its role after that was passive.
		• The case is still active for other members.
		• Mexico participated in the following stages:
		  – Consultations (WT/DS27/1)
		  – Request for the establishment of a Panel (WT/DS27/6)
		  – Panel procedure (WT/DS27/R/MEX)
		  – AB procedure (WT/DS27/AB/R)
		  – RPT arbitration (WT/DS27/15)
		  – Request for 21.5 consultations (WT/DS27/18)
		  – Request for the establishment of a 21.5 Panel (WT/DS27/30)
		  – Reactivation of the request for 21.5 consultations (WT/DS27/33)

Case	Subject Matter (based on request for consultations)	Implementation
Venezuela – OCTG (23) **Req. cons.** 05 December 95	**Measures:** • The AD investigation on imports from Mexico of oil country tubular Goods (OCTG). **Claims:** • 1, 3 (paragraphs 1, 2, 3, 4 and 5), 4 (paragraph 1), 5 (paragraphs 1, 2, 4, 6 and 8), 6 (paragraph 5.1), 12 (paragraph 1) and 16 (paragraph 5) of the ADA; and • VI of the GATT '94.	**Implemented.** **The measure was amended.** • Mexico notified its intention to stop the procedure on 6 May 1997 (WT/DS23/3), even when Venezuela closed the investigation on 12 December 1995. • Venezuela closed the investigation by Decision 007/95 of 12 December 1995 (WT/DS23/2) without imposing AD duties.
EC – Bananas III Old Request (16) **Other co-complainants:** Guatemala, Honduras, and the US **Req. cons.** 28 September 1995	**Measures:** • The EC regime for the importation, sale and distribution of bananas Regulation 404/93 (OJ L 47 of 25 February 1993, p.1) and • And other instruments which implement supplement and amend that regime. **Claims:** • I, II, III, X and XIII of the GATT '94; • 1 and 3 of the Agreement on Import Licensing Procedures; and • II, XVI and XVII of the GATS.	**Not implemented.** **The measure was not implemented.** • There is no further DS document beyond the requests to be joined in the consultations by the following Members: Costa Rica, Venezuela, Dominican Republic, Colombia, Nicaragua, and Santa Lucia. • As of today, there are still problems on implementation of DS27.

ii. Mexico's Cases as Defendant

Case	Subject Matter (measures / claims)	Implementation
Mx – Olive Oil II (341) **Req. cons:** 31 March 2006	**Measures:** • Definitive countervailing measures on imports of olive oil originating in the EC published in the *Diario Oficial de la Federación* of 1 August 2005.	**Not implemented.** **Mexico has not modified the measure.**
	Claims: • VI (in particular VI:3 and VI:6) of the GATT, • 1, 10, 11 (in particular paragraphs 2, 3, 4, 6, 9 and 11), 12 (in particular paragraphs 3 and 4), 13, 14, 15, 16, 19, 22 and 32 of the SCM Agreement, and • 13(b)(i) and 21.1 of the Agreement on Agriculture. The EC explained some of its claims: • a failure to respect 21.1 of the Agreement on Agriculture; • the initiation of an investigation based on an application without sufficient evidence and the failure to review the accuracy and adequacy of the evidence to determine sufficiency for the initiation, in violation of 11.2 and 11.3 of the SCM; • the absence of a determination that the initiation was requested by or on behalf of the domestic industry, in violation of 11.4 and 16 of the SCM; • the decision to initiate on a broader injury basis than that established in the application and without having sufficient evidence to justify the initiation, in violation of 11.6 of the SCM; • the failure to reject the application and to terminate promptly the investigation as there was not sufficient evidence of either subsidization or injury to justify the case, in violation of 11.9 of the SCM; • the failure to conclude the investigation within one year, and in no case more than 18 months, after its initiation, in violation of 11.11 of the SCM Agreement;	• The EC requested a Panel on 7 December 2006 (WT/DS341/2).

Case	Subject Matter (measures / claims)	Implementation
	• the failure by the Mexican authorities to include adequate information on the factors on which the allegation of injury was based in its public notice of the initiation of an investigation in violation of 12.4.1, 12.4.2 and 22.2 (iv) of the SCM Agreement;	
	• the failure to grant the opportunity for consultations before the initiation of the investigation with the aim of clarifying the situation as to matters referred to in paragraph 2 of 11 of the SCM Agreement and arriving at a Mutually Agreed Solution, in violation of 13.1 of the SCM Agreement;	
	• the initiation of a countervailing duty investigation on imports of an Agricultural product (olive oil) outside the circumstances contemplated in 13(b)(i) of the Agreement on Agriculture;	
	• the imposition of countervailing duties following an investigation that was not initiated and conducted in accordance with the provisions of VI of the GATT, the SCM Agreement and the Agreement on Agriculture, in violation of 10 of the SCM Agreement;	
	• the failure of the Mexican authorities to determine properly the existence of subsidisation, *inter alia*, by failing to evaluate the existence of any "pass-through" of any benefit, in violation of 1.1(b), 10 and 32.1 of the SCM Agreement;	
	• the failure to provide all relevant information on the matters of fact and law and reasons which have led to the imposition of final measures, in violation of 12.3, 12.4.1, 12.4.2 and 22 (inter alia paragraph 5) of the SCM Agreement;	
	• the failure to calculate the benefit to the recipient conferred pursuant to paragraph 1 of 1 of the SCM Agreement, in violation of 14 of the SCM Agreement;	

Case	Subject Matter (measures / claims)	Implementation
	• the failure to explain the method of calculation and its application to each particular case in a transparent and adequate way, in violation of 14 of the SCM Agreement;	
	• the imposition of countervailing measures despite the failure to define correctly the domestic industry, in violation of VI:6 of the GATT and 15.4, 15.5 and 16 of the SCM Agreement;	
	• the imposition of countervailing measures despite the failure to examine any known factors other than the alleged subsidized imports which were causing injury to the domestic industry , in violation of 15.5 of the SCM Agreement;	
	• the imposition of countervailing measures despite the failure to determine that the effect of the alleged subsidization was such as to cause material injury to an established domestic industry, in violation of VI:6 of the GATT and 15 of the SCM Agreement, notably 15.1 and 15.4;	
	• the imposition of countervailing duties which are levied in excess of the amount of the alleged subsidy found to exist, in violation of VI:3 of GATT, 19.4 and footnote 36 of the SCM Agreement;	
Mexico – AD on Tubes (331) **Req. cons:** 17 June 2005	**Measures:** • The definitive AD duties imposed by Mexico on imports of certain steel pipes and tubes originating in Guatemala and the investigation leading thereto.	**Not implemented.** **Mexico did not modified its measure.**
	Claims: • Mexico failed to define properly the product under consideration and the like product. This appears to be inconsistent with 2.1, 2,4, 2.6, 3.1, 3.2, 3.4, 3.5, 3.6, 3.7, 4.1, 5.4, 6.4 and 6.9 of the AD Agreement.	• On 8 January 2007 the Chairman of the Panel advised that it hoped to complete the report by the end of March 2007 (WT/ DS331/4).

Case	Subject Matter (measures / claims)	Implementation
	• Mexico initiated the investigation without properly determining whether the application for the investigation contained a complete description of the allegedly dumped product, sufficient evidence of dumping, injury and a causal link, and without properly examining the accuracy and adequacy of the evidence provided in the application. This failure appears to be contrary to 5.2, 5.3, and 5.8 of the AD Agreement.	• The Panel was composed on 11 May 2006. • The Panel procedure is still under the way.
	• Mexico failed to provide in its notice of initiation of the investigation adequate information on the product involved, the basis on which dumping was alleged in the application, and a summary of the factors on which the allegation of injury was based. This failure appears to be contrary to 12.1 of the AD Agreement.	
	• Mexico failed to define properly the relevant domestic industry and to use that definition consistently for the purposes of its analysis of injury and causation. This failure appears to be contrary to 3.1, 3.2, 3.4, 3.5, 3.6, 3.7, 4.1, and 5.4 of the AD Agreement.	
	• Mexico relied on facts available to determine the margin of dumping for the largest Guatemalan exporter of the subject products without properly following the procedures laid out in 6.8 and Annex II to the AD Agreement. This failure appears to be contrary to 6.8, 6.13, and Annex II, as well as to the requirements of 2.1, 2.2, and 2.4 to conduct a fair comparison between the export price and the normal value.	
	• Mexico failed to disclose to the Guatemalan exporters that it had encountered problems in the on-the-spot investigation that warranted the use of facts available. This failure appears to be contrary to 6.2, 6.4, 6.7, 6.8 and 6.9 of the AD Agreement.	

Case	Subject Matter (measures / claims)	Implementation
	• Mexico made adjustments to the export price for certain categories of expenses without making the symmetrical adjustments to the normal value for the same categories of expenses that were necessary to achieve a fair comparison between the normal value and the export price. This failure appears to be contrary to 2.1, 2.2 and 2.4 of the AD Agreement.	
	• In its determination of injury and causal link, Mexico relied on dumping margins determined inconsistently with 2.1, 2.2 and 2.4 of the AD Agreement. This, in turn, appears to render Mexico's determination of injury and causal link inconsistent with 3.1, 3.2, 3.4, 3.5, 3.6 and 3.7 of the AD Agreement.	
	• In its determination of injury and a causal link, Mexico failed to take into account relevant data relating to the period preceding its investigation, resulting in a determination of injury and a causal link that was not based on an objective examination or positive evidence. This failure appears to be inconsistent with 3.1, 3.2, 3.4, 3.5, and 3.7 of the AD Agreement.	
	• Mexico's analysis of both the volume of the allegedly dumped imports and the effect of those imports on prices in the domestic market for like products, and the consequent impact of those imports on the domestic producers of such products, was not based on an objective examination or positive evidence. This failure appears to be contrary to 3.1 and 3.2 of the AD Agreement.	
	• Mexico failed to evaluate properly all relevant economic factors and indices having a bearing on the state of the domestic industry. This failure appears to be inconsistent with 3.1, 3.4 and 3.7 of the AD Agreement.	

Case	Subject Matter (measures / claims)	Implementation
	• Mexico's analysis of the condition of the domestic industry for the purpose of its injury and causation determinations failed to take into account data relating to all of the companies within the defined domestic industry. This failure appears to be inconsistent with 3.1, 3.2, 3.4, 3.5, 3.6, 3.7 and 4.1 of the AD Agreement.	
	• Mexico's analysis of the causal link between dumping and injury failed to analyse properly other known factors, including, inter alia, changes in consumption, cost increases, differences in production methods, technology, productivity, decline in exports, and imports from other countries, that were at the same time causing injury to the domestic industry, and failed to ensure that injury caused by those known factors was not attributed to the imports under investigation. This failure appears to be contrary to 3.1, 3.2, 3.4 and 3.5 of the AD Agreement.	
	• Mexico failed, before issuing its final resolution, to inform the Guatemalan exporters of the essential facts under consideration that formed the basis for Mexico's decision to apply definitive measures, including, *inter alia*, the reasons for its decision to resort to facts available and the basis for Mexico's definition of the like product. These failures appear to be contrary to 6.9 of the AD Agreement.	
	• Mexico failed to disclose in its preliminary and final resolutions in sufficient detail the findings and conclusions reached on all issues of fact and law that were considered material by the Mexican authorities, including, *inter alia*, the reasons for Mexico's definition of the like product and its resort to facts available to calculate dumping margins for the largest Guatemalan exporter. These failures appear to be contrary to 12.2 of the AD Agreement.	

Case	Subject Matter (measures / claims)	Implementation
	• Mexico failed to complete its investigation within 12 months of the initiation without making any finding of special circumstances that warranted extending the period of time to complete the investigation. This failure appears to be contrary to 5.10 of the AD Agreement. • Mexico failed to require the applicants to provide non-confidential summaries and to disclose properly information that was not shown upon good cause to be confidential or to disclose non-confidential summaries of confidential information. This failure appears to be contrary to 6.5 of the AD Agreement. • Mexico has applied the measure to products that were not covered by its investigation and for which Mexico has not made determinations of dumping, injury, and a causal link. This appears to be inconsistent with 2.1, 2.6, 3.1, 3.2, 3.4, 3.5, 9.1, 9.3 and 18.1 of the AD Agreement. • The measure cannot be reconciled with VI of the GATT, 1 and 18.1 of the AD Agreement, and the specific provisions of the AD Agreement cited above.	
Mx – Olive Oil I (314) **Req. cons:** 18 August 2004	**Measures:** • The imposition of provisional CVD measures on imports of olive oil originating in the EC by Resolution of 18 May 2004 published in *Diario Oficial de la Federación* of 10 June 2004. **Claims:** • 10, 11 (in particular paragraphs 2, 3, 4, and 9) 15, 16 and 17 (in particular 17.1(a) and (b)) of the SCM, and • 13 and/or 21.1 of the Agreement on Agriculture. The inconsistencies include: • The initiation of an investigation in the absence of sufficient evidence that a domestic industry is suffering injury as a result of subsidized imports, in violation of 11.2 of the SCM Agreement;	**Not implemented. Mexico did not amend the measure.** • The EC challenged the definitive CVD measure (WT/DS341).

Case	Subject Matter (measures / claims)	Implementation
	• the failure by the Mexican authorities to review the accuracy and adequacy of the evidence provided in the application to determine whether there was sufficient evidence to initiate an investigation, in violation of 11.3 of the SCM Agreement;	
	• the failure to establish whether the application was made by or on behalf of the domestic industry of the like product, in violation of 11.4 of the SCM Agreement;	
	• the imposition of provisional countervailing measures despite the failure to define correctly the domestic industry, in violation of 16 and 17.1 of the SCM Agreement;	
	• the failure to reject the application and to terminate promptly the investigation as soon as the Mexican authorities were satisfied that there was insufficient evidence to initiate and/or proceed with the investigation, in violation of 11.9 of the SCM Agreement;	
	• the imposition of provisional countervailing measures following the conduct of an investigation that was not initiated in accordance with the provisions of 11 of the SCM Agreement, in violation of 17.1(a) of the SCM Agreement;	
	• the imposition of provisional countervailing measures following the conduct of an investigation that was not initiated in accordance with the provisions of the SCM Agreement and the Agreement on Agriculture, in violation of 10 of the SCM Agreement;	
	• the imposition of provisional countervailing measures despite the non-existence of material injury or material retardation, in violation of 15 and 17.1(b) of the SCM Agreement, notably 15.4;	
	• the imposition of provisional countervailing measures despite the failure to establish a causal link between the allegedly subsidized imports and the alleged injury, in violation of 15.5 and 17.1(b) of the SCM Agreement;	

Case	Subject Matter (measures / claims)	Implementation
	• the initiation of a countervailing duty investigation on imports of an Agricultural product (olive oil) outside the circumstances contemplated in 13(b)(i) of the Agreement on Agriculture and/or in violation of 21.1 of the Agreement on Agriculture; and • the imposition of provisional countervailing measures on imports of an Agricultural product (olive oil) outside the circumstances contemplated in 13(b)(i) of the Agreement on Agriculture and/or in violation of 21.1 of the Agreement on Agriculture.	
Mx – Soft Drinks (308) **Req. cons:** 16 March 2004	**Measures:** • Mexico's tax measures on soft drinks and other beverages that use any sweetener other than cane sugar (Ley de Impuesto Especial sobre Producción y Servicios), which include: – A 20 per cent tax on soft drinks and other beverages that use any sweetener other than cane sugar, and – a 20 per cent tax at distribution (and other stages of trade) on soft drinks and other beverages that use any sweetener other than cane sugar ("distribution tax"). **Claims:** • III of the GATT '94. In particular, – III:2, first sentence, – III:2, second sentence, and – III:4 of the GATT '94. **Mexico's defences (at the Panel AB stage):** • Mexico asked the Panel/AB to decline to exercise its jurisdiction in the case in favour of a Panel under Chapter 20 of the NAFTA. • Mexico presented a defence under XX(d) of the GATT '94 "to secure compliance with laws or regulations."	**Implemented. Mexico withdrew the measure on 27 December 2006.** • Mexico notified the implementation on 12 January 2007 (WT/DS308/16). The Federal Revenue Law for 2007 was published in the Official Journal of the Federation on 27 December 2006. • On 3 July 2006, both Parties agreed on a RPT as follows: – it will expire on 1 Jan 2007; but

Case	Subject Matter (measures / claims)	Implementation
	o Mexico requested that the Panel make a special recommendation on its report.	– if Mexico enacts legislation by 31 December 2006, repealing the measure, the RPT would expire on 31 January 2007 (this was the case as Mexico repealed the measure within this timeframe).
Mx – Customs Valuation Guatemala (298) **Req. cons:** 22 July 2003	**Measures:** • Mexican customs legislation, including *Mexico's Customs Law* and in particular Art. 84A, 86A, 144 and 158, as well as the regulations relating to that Law and subsequent supplementary provisions and/or amendments. • The Mexican regulatory framework providing for application of the mechanism of estimated prices, including: – The Resolution establishing the mechanism to guarantee the payment of duties on Goods subject to prices estimated by the Ministry of Finance and Public Credit, (Official Journal of 28 February 1994). – The Resolution containing the Annex to the Resolution establishing the mechanism to guarantee the payment of duties on goods subject to prices estimated by the Ministry of Finance and Public Credit (Official Journal of 28 February 1994), and – other rules, resolutions and supplementary provisions and/or amendments thereto. • The application of the above rules and procedures.	**Implemented.** **Mexico amended the measure.** • On 29 August 2005 Guatemala notified a MAS (WT/DS298/2). • Guatemala advised that both Parties had reached agreement on footwear and brushes. • It requested that the case be closed. • The communication does not contain any details of the agreement.

Case	Subject Matter (measures / claims)	Implementation
	Claims: • I, II, VII and X of the GATT '94; • 1, 2, 3, 4, 5, 6, 7, 8, 12, 13, 15, 16 and 22 of the Agreement on Customs Valuation and their respective Interpretative Notes as contained in Annex I to that Agreement, • the Ministerial Decision regarding cases where Customs Administrations have reasons to doubt the truth or accuracy of the Declared Value. • 4 of the Agreement on Agriculture, including its footnote. • XVI: 4 of the WTO Agreement. • XXIII:1(a) and (b) of the GATT '94, claiming a violation and non-violation case. The inconsistencies include: • These measures fix and/or apply minimum prices, minimum values or estimated prices officially established for more than 300 imported products, while also requiring the provision of a deposit or surety in order to ensure application of this mechanism, without it being possible to put an end to this practice through either the process of verification or determination of the customs value of the imported Goods or the guarantee mechanisms specified in Mexican legislation.	

Mx – Beef and Rice (295)
 Req. cons: 16 June 2003
	Measures:
	 • Definitive AD measures on:
	   – Beef (*Diario Oficial* on 28 April 2000) – the US did not challenge the measure on Beef at its Panel request; and
	   – long grain white rice (*Diario Oficial* on 5 June 2002); and
	 • Mexico's Foreign Trade Act and its Federal Code of Civil Procedure.
	 Claims:
	 • 3, 5, 6, 7, 9, 10, 11, 12 and Annex II of the ADA;
	 • 11, 12, 17, 19, 20 and 21 of the SCM; and
	 • VI of GATT.
		Implemented. **Mexico withdrew the two measures:**
		 • **Eliminated the final AD determination (*Diario Oficial de la Federación* 11 September 2006), and**

Case	Subject Matter (measures / claims)	Implementation
		• **Amended the Foreign Trade Act (*Diario Oficial de la Federación* 21 December 2006).** On 24 May 2006 (WT/DS295/12), both Parties agreed on the RPT that: • With respect to the AD investigation the RPT shall be 8 months, expiring on 20 August 2006. • With respect to Mexican law (FTA) the RPT shall be 12 months, expiring on 20 December 2006.
Mx – Beans (284) **Req. cons:** 17 March 2003	**Measures:** • The administration of the procedures set out in Official Standard 006-FITO-95 (*Diario Oficial de la Federación* 26 February 1996 and notified to the SPS Committee as G/SPS/N/MEX/44) and Official Standard 028-FITO-95 (*Diario Oficial de la Federación* 12 October 1998 and notified to the SPS Committee as G/SPS/N/MEX/68), including the refusal to furnish the SPS requirements necessary for the importation of black beans from Nicaragua; • the more favourable treatment accorded to like products originating in countries other than Nicaragua; and	**Implemented.** **Mexico amended the measure.** • On 8 March 2004 Nicaragua notified a MAS (WT/DS284/4): – Nicaragua withdrew its complaint. – The terms of the MAS were not notified.

Case	Subject Matter (measures / claims)	Implementation
	• the failure to publish the specific phytosanitary requirements for the importation of black beans from Nicaragua. • The failure to publish the rules, requirements and procedures concerning the tender for the quota allocation of black beans from Nicaragua, including but not limited to, the Public Tender No. 44/2002 for the period 2002–2003.	
	Claims: • I:1, X:1, X:3(a), XI:1 and XIII:1 of the GATT '94, and • 1.2, 1.3, 1.4(a) and 2.2(a) of the Licensing Agreement. • If the measures are SPS measures, 2.1, 2.2, 2.3, 5.1, 7 and paragraph 1 of Annex B of the SPS Agreement.	
Mx – Matches (232) Req. cons: 17 May 2001	**Measures:** • 14 Normas Oficiales Mexicanas (NOM) or Official Standarts regarding matches and dangerous substances (for the full list see WT/DS232/1). • Law on the Control of Arms and Explosives. • Federal Metrology and Standardization Law. • Regulations to the Federal Metrology and Standardization Law. • Regulations on Transport by Land of Dangerous Materials and Waste.	**Implemented.** **Mexico amended the measures.** • On 2 February 2004, Chile withdrew the complaint (WT/DS232/3).
	Claims: • 1, 2 and 5 of the TBT • 1, 3 and 5 of the Import Licensing Procedures, and • III, paragraph 4, of the GATT '94. Chile explained that: • Mexico decided in 1993 that safety matches constituted an explosive and dangerous product – due to a confusion between the chemical element "fósforo" (phosphorus) and the product "fósforos (o cerillos) de seguridad" (safety matches). Hence, they were treated as dangerous products.	

Case	Subject Matter (measures / claims)	Implementation
Mx – Transformers (216) **Req. cons:** 20 December 2000	**Measures:** • Provisional AD measure on electric transformers (of more than 10,000 KVA) exported from Brazil.	**Not implemented.** **Mexico amended the measure.**

	Claims:
	 • 5.2, 5.3 and 5.8 of the ADA because it initiated the AD investigation without evidence of dumping as defined under 2 of the ADA, of injury as defined under 3 of the ADA, and of causation of injury.
	 • 5.8 of the ADA by not terminating the investigation "promptly" when it was impossible to find dumping or injury during the period of investigation
	   – because there were no firm offers or sales or imports of the merchandise in question.
	 • 6.8 and Annex II of the ADA by using "best information available" inconsistently.
	 • 7.1(i) of the ADA because it imposed provisional measures in an investigation violating 5 of the ADA.
	 • 7.1(ii) of the ADA because it imposed provisional measures without a valid preliminary determination of dumping, in accordance with Art 2 of the ADA, because:
	   – It ignored evidence that there were neither firm offers nor sales of the merchandise in question during the period of investigation;
	   – It disregarded cost information submitted by the respondents for the establishment of normal value against 6.8 of the ADA by using "best information available;"
	   – It did not comply with Annex II, paragraph 7, of the ADA in using information presented by the petitioner as the "best information available" and it made no attempt to "check the information from other independent sources at their disposal" to ensure its accuracy and relevance.
		• Brazil never withdrew the request. Perhaps this was a hit and run violation.
		 • The provisional measure was suspended on 18 January 2001.
		 • The final determination was published on 20 March 2001 without AD duty.

Case	Subject Matter (measures / claims)	Implementation

	• 7.1(ii) of the ADA because it imposed provisional measures without a valid preliminary determination of injury, violating 3.4 and 3.7 of the ADA.
	  – It ignored evidence that the merchandise in question was not imported into, or sold to, Mexico during the period of investigation;
	  – It did not properly consider evidence relating to the factors set out in 3.7 of the ADA, but simply assumed that the evidence was false without meeting the condition established in 6.8 of the ADA for using "best information available".
	  – It accepted information presented by the petitioner as the "best information available" without meeting the conditions established in Annex II, paragraph 7, of the ADA.	

Mx – Telecoms (204) **Req. cons:** 17 August 2000	**Measures:** Mexico has: • Enacted and maintained laws, regulations, rules, and other measures that deny or limit market access, national treatment, and additional commitments for service suppliers seeking to provide basic and value-added telecommunications Services into and within Mexico. • Failed to issue and enact regulations, permits, or other measures to ensure implementation of Mexico's market access, national treatment, and additional commitments for service suppliers seeking to provide basic and value-added telecommunications Services into and within Mexico. • Failed to enforce regulations and other measures to ensure compliance with Mexico's market access, national treatment, and additional commitments for service suppliers seeking to provide basic and value-added telecommunications Services into and within Mexico.	**Implemented.** **Mexico amended the measure in two steps (1 August 2004 and 19 August 2005).** • On 1 June 2004, the Parties notified an agreement on the RPT (WT/DS204/7 amended by WT/DS204/11). They agreed to 13 months for full implementation (i.e., 29 July 2005) in two stages: – Mexico had 2 months to implement the new International Long Distance Rules,

Case	Subject Matter (measures / claims)	Implementation
	• Failed to regulate, control and prevent its major supplier, Teléfonos de México (Telmex), from engaging in activity that denies or limits Mexico's market access, national treatment, and additional commitments for service suppliers seeking to provide basic and value-added telecommunications Services into and within Mexico. • Failed to administer measures of general application governing basic and value-added telecommunications Services in a reasonable, objective, and impartial manner, ensure that decisions and procedures used by Mexico's telecommunications regulator are impartial with respect to all market participants, and ensure access to and use of public telecommunications transport networks and Services on reasonable and non-discriminatory terms and conditions for the supply of basic and value-added telecommunications Services. Annex 1 of the request for consultations contains a list of specific actions and failures to act by Mexico. ***Paragraph 7.6 of the Panel Report identifies the following measures:*** • The "Federal Telecommunications Law" ("FTL") (Ley Federal de Telecomunicaciones) of 18 May 1995. • The "Rules for Long Distance Service" (Reglas del Servicio de Larga Distancia) published by the Secretariat of Communications and Transportation ("SCT") (Secretaría de Comunicaciones y Transporte) on 21 June 1996. • The International Long Distance Rules ("ILD Rules") (Reglas para prestar el servicio de larga distancia internacional) published by the SCT on 11 December 1996.	– Then, Mexico had 13 months, from adoption, to enact regulations on purchases and sales of telecoms Services by commercial agencies. • Mexico complied on 12 August 2005. On 19 August 2005, it made a self declaration of full compliance (WT/DS204/9/ Add.8).

Case	Subject Matter (measures / claims)	Implementation
	• The "Agreement of the SCT establishing the procedure to obtain concessions for the installation, operation or exploitation of interstate public telecommunications networks, pursuant to the Federal Telecommunications Law" (Acuerdo de la SCT por el que se establece el procedimiento para obtener concesión para la instalación, operación o explotación de redes públicas de telecomunicaciones interestatales, al amparo de la Ley Federal de Telecomunicaciones) published on 4 September 1995.	
	Claims: • VI, XVI, and XVII of the GATS; • Mexico's additional commitments under XVIII as set forth in the Reference Paper inscribed in Mexico's Schedule of Specific Commitments, including Sections 1, 2, 3 and 5; and • the GATS Annex on Telecommunications, including Sections 4 and 5. Among other things, Mexico's GATS commitments and obligations require Mexico to: • provide market access and national treatment for basic and value-added telecommunications Services (GATS XVI and XVII and Mexico's Schedule of Specific Commitments annexed to the GATS); • maintain appropriate measures for the purpose of preventing a major supplier of basic telecommunications Services from engaging in or continuing anti-competitive practices, such as anti-competitive cross-subsidization (Section 1 of the Reference Paper on Pro-Competitive Regulatory Principles (the Reference Paper), which Mexico has inscribed in its Schedule of Specific Commitments as "additional commitments" pursuant to GATS XVIII);	

Case	Subject Matter (measures / claims)	Implementation
	• ensure interconnection with a major supplier at any technically feasible point in the network; under non-discriminatory terms, conditions and rates; in a timely fashion; and at cost-oriented rates that are transparent, reasonable, and sufficiently unbundled; and to provide recourse to an independent domestic body to resolve interconnection disputes within a reasonable period of time (Section 2 of the Reference Paper);	
	• administer any universal service obligation in a transparent, non-discriminatory, and competitively neutral manner that is not more burdensome than necessary for the kind of universal service defined by Mexico (Section 3 of the Reference Paper);	
	• ensure that its regulatory body is not accountable to any supplier of basic telecommunications Services and that the regulator's decisions and procedures are impartial with respect to all market participants (Section 5 of the Reference Paper);	
	• administer in a reasonable, objective, and impartial manner its laws, rules, regulations, and other measures of general application affecting trade in basic and value-added telecommunications Services (GATS VI:1); and	
	• ensure access to and use of public telecommunications transport networks and Services on reasonable and non-discriminatory terms and conditions for the supply of basic and value-added telecommunications Services and ensure that relevant information on conditions affecting access to and use of public telecommunications transport networks and Services is publicly available (GATS Annex on Telecommunications, Sections 4 and 5).	

Case	Subject Matter (measures / claims)	Implementation
Mx – Swine (203) **Req. cons:** 10 July 2000	**Measures:** • Definitive AD measure on live swine for slaughter, exported from the US (20 October 1999); • actions by Mexico in the conduct of the AD investigation resulting in this measure; and • various measures affecting trade in live swine from the US: – Import ban of certain swine (over 110 kilograms in weight). – Sanitary restrictions on the importation of swine weighing 110 kilograms or more including inspections and quarantines (excepting smaller imported swine and domestic swine) – discrimination without scientific evidence or risk assessment. – Technical regulations that are applicable to imported swine but not to domestic swine. **Claims:** • 3 and 12 of the ADA, regarding threat of material injury: – Relevant economic factors and indices on the industry; – Consequent impact of imports on domestic producers; – Causation of injury; and – Occurrence of material injury unless protective action were taken. • 6 of the ADA – Timely opportunity to exporters to prepare presentations; and – Disclosure of essential facts. • 2.2, 2.3, 3, 5.1, 5.6, 7 and 8 of the SPS; • 4.2 of the A on Agriculture; • 2 and 5 of the TBT; and • III:4 and XI:1 of the GATT '94.	**Not implemented.** **Mexico did not amend the measure.** • We considered that Mexico did not comply since it withdrew the measure more than 3 years after its imposition and did not consider the request for consultations. • The US did not withdraw the request. • Mexico withdrew the AD measure on 23 May 2003 (Diario Oficial de la Federación), (*Resolución final de la primera revisión de la cuota compensatoria definitiva impuesta a las importaciones de cerdo originarias de los EUA*). • On 20 October 1999 Mexico published the final determination with an AD duty of $0.351 USD per Kg.

Case	Subject Matter (measures / claims)	Implementation
Mx – Corn Syrup II (132) **Req. cons:** 8 May 1998	**Measures:** • The final determination the AD investigation of high-fructose corn syrup (Corn Syrup) on 23 January 1998. **Claims:** On the initiation: • 2, 4 and 5 of the ADA by determining the initiation and accepting an application without the information required; and • 12 of the ADA by not meeting the requirements. On the determination of threat of injury: • 3 and 12 of the ADA by failing to evaluate all relevant economic factors and indices and, failing to determine that injury would occur without the imposition of AD; and by failing to consider the impact of dumped imports on the full range of operations of the domestic industry producing the like product. On the determination of Dumping: • 2 of the ADA by not calculating correctly the margin of dumping for U.S.exporter Archer Daniels Midland Company. On the provisional AD measure • 7.4 of the ADA by exceeding the time provided for in the Agreement. On the Definitive AD measure • 9 and 12 of the ADA by not including in the public notice advice whether the AD duty was the full margin of dumping or less. • 10.2 of the ADA by failing to determine that the effect of the dumped imports would, in the absence of the provisional measures, have led to a determination of injury. • 10.4 of the ADA by failing to release the bonds posted by U.S. exporters. On the procedural issues: • 6 of the ADA by failing to comply with its requirements, including by:	**Implemented. Mexico withdrew the measure on 20 May 2002 (Diario Oficial de la Federación).** • We did not find any WTO reference to this implementation. • On 21 November 2001 the DSB adopted the report of the 21.5 Panel as modified by the AB. (WT/DS132/13) • There is no further DS document after the adoption of the 21.5 Panel/ AB report in this case.

Case	Subject Matter (measures / claims)	Implementation
	– failing to verify the accuracy of information provided by the domestic industry; – failing to provide exporters with opportunities to review the information and to prepare presentations on the basis of such information; – failing to advise of the essential facts under consideration which formed the basis for its decision; and – failing to require all interested Parties to provide non-confidential summaries. • 6.5 of the ADA by authorizing a representative of the domestic industry to inspect the confidential information provided by exporters, without providing the exporters with advance notice and without obtaining the specific permission to do so.	
Mx – Corn Syrup I (101) **Req. cons:** 4 September 1997	**Measures:** • The AD preliminary determination of dumping and injury in high-fructose corn syrup (Corn Syrup) from 25 June 1997. **Claims:** On the initiation: • 2, 4 and 5 of the ADA by accepting an application that did not contain the information required and that was inconsistent with these obligations. • 5.5 and 6.1.3 by not notifying the government of the exporting Member concerned "before proceeding to initiate an investigation" and by failing to provide the full text of the application "as soon as an investigation has been initiated". On procedural issues: • 6.5 of the ADA by authorizing a representative of the domestic industry to inspect the confidential information provided by US exporters, without their permission to do so. • 6.2 and 6.4 of the ADA by being extremely slow in placing relevant information, including the filings of the petitioner, in its public file.	**Not implemented. Mexico did not amend the provisional measure.** • Indeed, the US filed a new request for consultations challenging the Definitive AD measure (DS132)

Case	Subject Matter (measures / claims)	Implementation
Mx – Customs Valuation from EC (53) **Req. cons:** 27/Aug/1996	**Measures:** • Mexican Customs Law (*Ley Aduanera*), and • the Resolution establishing the general rules governing the application of the customs provisions of the North American Free Trade Agreement (*Resolución que establece las reglas de carácter general relatívas a la aplicación de las disposiciones en materia aduanera del Tratado de Libre Comercio de América de Norte – Título III: Procedimientos Aduaneros – Artículo 14*). **Claims:** • XXIV:5(b) of GATT. – On 29 December 1993, Mexico amended its Customs Law to apply CIF value as the basis of customs valuation of imports originating in non-NAFTA countries, and FOB value for imports originating in NAFTA countries. Prior to this amendment, Mexico applied FOB value for all imports.	**Not implemented.** **There is no information on implementation.** • We classified this case as abandoned. • There is no further DS document on this case beyond the request for consultations. • We did not find any information confirming that the measure had been implemented. • Due to the nature of this case, implementation would have eventually taken place when NAFTA tariffs reached zero. At that stage, there would be no further discrimination as there was no further need for valuation of NAFTA goods for customs purposes.

12. Months between Consultations and the Application of the Legal Remedy

Source: WT/DS series.

i. Mexico's Cases as Complainant

Case	Legal Remedy	Request for Consultations	Date of Implementation, MAS or Closing Date of this Work	Months from Consultations to Implementation, MAS or Closing Date of this Work
US – AD on Steel Zeroing II (344)	no legal remedy	26-May-05	1-Jan-07	19.50
US – AD on Steel Zeroing I (325)	no legal remedy	5-Jan-05	1-Jan-07	24.20
US – OCTG (282)	no legal remedy	18-Feb-03	1-Jan-07	47.10
US – CVD on Steel (280)	no legal remedy	21-Jan-03	1-Jan-07	48.03
EC – Bananas III New Request (158)	no legal remedy	20-Jan-99	1-Jan-07	96.77
EC – Bananas III (27)	no legal remedy	5-Feb-96	1-Jan-07	132.77
EC – Bananas III Old Request (16)	no legal remedy	28-Sep-95	1-Jan-07	137.10
Ecuador – Cement I (182)	no legal remedy on the provisional measure	5-Oct-99	14-Jun-00	8.43
Guatemala – Cement I (60)	no legal remedy on the provisional measure	15-Oct-96	4-Oct-00	48.33
Panama – Milk (329)	MAS *ex ante*	16-Mar-05	20-Sep-05	6.27
US – Cement (281)	MAS *ex ante*	31-Jan-03	16-Jan-06	36.03
US – Tomatoes (49)	MAS *ex ante*	1-Jul-96	1-Nov-96	4.10

Case	Legal Remedy	Request for Consultations	Date of Implementation, MAS or Closing Date of this Work	Months from Consultations to Implementation, MAS or Closing Date of this Work
Venezuela – OCTG (23)	MAS *ex ante*	5-Dec-95	6-May-97	17.27
Ecuador – Cement II (191)	compliance *ex ante*	15-Mar-00	14-Jun-00	3.03
Guatemala – Cement II (156)	compliance *ex post*	5-Jan-99	4-Oct-00	21.27
US – Offset Act (217/234)	retaliation not implemented	21-May-01	1-Jan-07	68.37

ii. Mexico's Cases as Defendant

Case	Legal Remedy	Request for Consultations	Date of Implementation, MAS or Closing Date of this Work	Months from Consultations to Implementation, MAS or Closing Date of this Work
Mx – Olive Oil II (341)	no legal remedy	31-Mar-06	1-Jan-07	9.20
Mexico – AD on Tubes (331)	no legal remedy	17-Jun-05	1-Jan-07	18.77
Mx – Olive Oil I (314)	no legal remedy	18-Aug-04	1-Jan-07	28.87
Mx – Transformers (216)	no legal remedy	20-Dec-00	20-Mar-01	3.00
Mx – Swine (203)	no legal remedy	10-Jul-00	23-May-03	34.90
Mx – Corn Syrup I (101)	no legal remedy	4-Sep-97	20-May-02	57.30
Mx – Customs Valuation from EC (53)	no legal remedy	27-Aug-96	1-Jan-07	125.97
Mx – Customs Valuation Guatemala (298)	MAS *ex ante*	22-Jul-03	29-Aug-05	25.63
Mx – Beans (284)	MAS *ex ante*	17-Mar-03	8-Mar-04	11.90
Mx – Matches (232)	MAS *ex ante*	17-May-01	2-Feb-04	33.03

Case	Legal Remedy	Request for Consulta-tions	Date of Imple-mentation, MAS or Clos-ing Date of this Work	Months from Consultations to Implementa-tion, MAS or Closing Date of this Work
Mx – Soft Drinks (308)	MAS *ex post*	16-Mar-04	17-Dec-06	33.53
Mx – Beef and Rice (295)	MAS *ex post*	16-Jun-03	21-Dec-06	42.80
Mx – Telecoms (204)	MAS *ex post*	17-Aug-00	12-Aug-05	60.70
Mx – Corn Syrup II (132)	compliance ex post	8-May-98	20-May-02	49.10

13. Country vs Country (NAFTA Chapter 20 and Like Mechanisms of other PTAs)

Source: Panel Reports. We do not cover requests for consultations that were not followed up by a request for a Panel and a Panel report.

i. Mexico as Complainant

1. US Safeguard Action Taken on Broom Corn Brooms from Mexico (USA-97-2008-01)

On 12 December 1996, Mexico imposed retaliatory tariffs on the US. According to Mexico, the US measure affected trade to the value of approximately $1.4 million in the first year.[11] The following goods were affected: fructose, wine, wine coolers, brandy, Tennessee whiskey, notebooks, flat glass and wooden furniture.[12] The decree does not have a date of expiration and we did not find information on when did Mexico stop the retaliatory tariffs.

The Other Party Involved: The US

Consultations: 21 August 1996

Report: 30 January 1998

---

11.   See the report of the Panel in USA-97-2008-01 US Safeguard Action Taken on Broom Corn Brooms from Mexico, para. 16.
12.   These goods are classified under the following HS Mexican tariff lines: 1702.40.01 12.5; 1702.40.99 12.5; 1702.50.01 12.5; 1702.60.01 12.5; 2204.10.01 20.0; 2204.21.01 20.0; 2204.21.02 20.0; 2204.21.03 20.0; 2204.21.04 20.0; 2204.29.99 20.0; 2206.00.01 20.0; 2208.20.02 20.0; 2208.30.04 20.0; 4820.20.01 10.0; 7005.29.02 20.0; 7005.29.03 20.0; 7005.29.99 20.0; 9403.30.01 12.0; and 9403.50.01 14.0.

Forum: NAFTA Chapter 20

Product: industrial Goods (Broom and Corn Brooms)

Measure and claims	Findings	Implementation
Measure: The Safeguard measure on Broom Corn Brooms (Proclamation No. 6961, 61 Fed. Reg. 64431-33 (4 December 1996) (To Facilitate Positive Adjustment to Competition From Imports of Broom Corn Brooms)).[13] **Claims:** Violation of 801(1) and 805 NAFTA, or 4 of the Safeguards Code (WTO). The "domestic industry" includes only the production of broom corn brooms and not that of plastic brooms. They are "like or directly competitive goods."	*Mexico won the four findings.* • The safeguard having been based on an ITC determination that fails to provide "reasoned conclusions on all pertinent issues of law and fact," constitutes a continuing violation of NAFTA (**MX**); and • it recommends that the US bring its conduct into compliance with the NAFTA at the earliest possible time (**MX**). **Some intermediary findings:** • Since the NAFTA (Annex 803.3(12)) and WTO versions of the rule (3.1 of the WTO Safeguards Code.) are substantively identical, application of the WTO version of the rule would have in no way changed the legal conclusion reached under NAFTA. We rely on NAFTA substantive law (**MX**); and	**The measure was implemented,** though not immediately but nine months after the Panel report. • On 12 December 1996, Mexico instituted retaliatory tariffs towards the US. According to Mexico, the trade effect of the US was approximately $1.4 million in the first year.[14] The following goods were affected: fructose, wine, wine coolers, brandy, Tennessee whiskey, notebooks, flat glass and wooden furniture. • On 8 December 1998 the Presidential Proclamation to terminate the measure was published.[15]

13. Colombia has challenged the same Presidential Proclamation 6961 in the WTO. It claimed violation of Art. 2, 4, 5, 9 and 12 of the Agreement on Safeguards and Art. II, XI, XIII and XIX of the GATT. The case was only consulted and never went to any subsequent procedural stage. See WT/DS78/1.
14. See the report of the Panel in USA-97-2008-01 US Safeguard Action Taken on Broom Corn Brooms from Mexico at p. 16.
15. See "Termination of the safeguard measure: Presidential Proclamation 7154, to terminate temporary Duties on Imports of Broom Corn Brooms, 63 Fed. Reg. 67761 (8 December 1998)."

Measure and claims	Findings	Implementation
	• the claims were properly and timely presented by Mexico (**MX**).	

2. US – Cross-Border Trucking (USA-MEX-98-2008-01)

The Other Party Involved: The US

Consultations: 18 December 1995

Report: 6 February 2001

Forum: NAFTA Chapter 20

Product: Services and Investment (Trucking Services and Investment)

Measure and claims	Findings	Implementation
Measure: • Failure to lift the moratorium on the processing of applications by Mexican-owned trucking firms for authority to operate in the US border States. **Claims:** • 1202 (national treatment for cross-border Services) and/or 1203 (most-favoured-nation treatment for cross-border Services) of NAFTA	*Mexico won the 4 findings* **The Panel unanimously found that:** The US refusal to review and consider for approval any Mexican-owned carrier applications for trucking Services violates NAFTA • Annex I (reservations), • Art. 1202 (national treatment for Services), and Article 1203 (most favoured nation treatment for Services);	**The measure has not been implemented** • On 23 February 2007, the US and Mexico started a provisional pilot programme for market access.[16] • The programme has a validity of one year. The first shipment transported by a Mexican shipper took place on September 2007.[17] • There is no one clear line of action within the US with respect to opening the market. There are internal supports for both options – opening or maintaining the market close.[18]

---

16. See http://www.dot.gov/affairs/cbtsip/dot2107.htm (consulted on December 2007).
17. See "Continuará EE.UU. implementando el programa piloto de transporte transfronterizo terrestre con México" from 7 January 2008. This information was published by *Inteligencia Comercial* (IQOM) (www.iqom.com.mx).
18. *Item.*

Measure and claims	Findings	Implementation
• 1102 (national treatment) and/or 1103 (most-favored-nation treatment) by refusing to permit Mexican investment in companies in the US that provide transportation of international cargo. Possible exceptions: • 1202 or 1203, or by some other provision of NAFTA, such as those found in Chapter Nine (standards) or by Article 2101 (general exceptions).	• an exception to these obligations is not authorized by Art. 1202 and 1203, or by the exceptions set out in Chapter Nine or under Art. 2101 (**MX**). The inadequacies of the Mexican regulatory system provide an insufficient legal basis for the US to maintain a moratorium (**MX**). The US refusal to permit Mexican nationals to invest violates: • Annex I (reservations), • Art. 1102 (national treatment – Investment), and • Art. 1103 (most-favored-nation treatment – Investment) (**MX**). **Preliminary findings:** • There was no need for a Scientific Review Board (**MX**). **Recommendation:** The US to bring its practices into compliance. In doing so the US may: • require compliance with US regulations; • require in certain cases different procedures; and • the issue of investment does not raise issues of safety as both Parties agreed.	

3. Peru – Origin of Computers from Mexico

The Other Party Involved: Peru

Consultations: 16 January 2002

Report: 11 March 2004

Forum: ALADI (ACE No 8[19])

Product: industrial Goods (computers)

Measure and claims	Findings	Implementation
Measure: The negative by Peru to grant the preferences to originated Mexican computers. **Claims:** • Art. 2, 9 and 15 of the Economic Complementation Agreement N° 8; • First and Tenth of Resolution 78; and • First and Fifteenth of the resolution 252.	*Mexico won two findings and Peru won one finding* **Findings issued by unanimity:** • The omission by Peru of informing Mexico that different certificates of origin for computers were not in light with the regimen of origin applicable is incompatible with the applicable rules of origin of the Economic Complementation Agreement No 8 celebrated between Peru and Mexico; they are contained in Art. Tenth of Resolution 78 and Art. Fifteenth of Resolution 252 (**MX**); and • The measure adopted by Peru that require the payment of import tariffs of computers from Mexico is compatible with the applicable rules of origin of the Partial Agreement of Economic Complementation between Peru and Mexico; they are contained in Art. Tenth of Resolution 78 and Art. Fifteenth of Resolution 252 (**PERU**).	**The case was automatically implemented in 2007 when the tariff applied for the product subject to the dispute became zero.** • The MFN applied tariff by Peru as of 2007 was zero with respect to the goods subject to the dispute; hence, Mexico's preferential tariff was eroded. But, we do not have information whether Mexico's exports between 2004 (report of the Panel) and 2007 were given the preference.

---

19.   See http://www.aladi.org/August 2009.

Measure and claims	Findings	Implementation
	Finding issued by majority: • The computers subject to dispute are originated in Mexico; hence, the lack of this recognition by Peru is incompatible with Art. First of ALADI's Resolutions 78 and Resolution 252, and Art. 2 and 9 of the ACE No 8 (**MX**).	

ii. Mexico as Defendant

1. Mexico – Sanitarian Registry and Access for Medicines

The Other Party Involved: El Salvador

Consultations: 18 July 2003

Report: 14 August 2006

Forum: FTA among Mexico, El Salvador, Guatemala and Honduras

Product: industrial Goods (Medicines)

Measure and claims	Findings	Implementation
Measure: Lack of Mexico's phytosanitary procedures for registering medicines. **Claims:** Art. 3-03, 15-05 and 15-10 of the FTA; and The degree of the trade effects of the measure.	*Mexico won one finding and El Salvador five findings* • The parallel letters among the FTA Parties grant Mexico a waiver of two years for its obligations under Chapter XV of the FTA (national treatment) (**MX**); • Mexico did not modify its measure to allow national treatment to producers, traders and distributors (nationals from an FTA Party) in registering medicines (**El Salvador**);	**The measure has been implemented for El Salvador** • The press in El Salvador mentioned that, based on an agreement between both Parties, Mexican legislation on the requirement to have a factory or a laboratory in Mexico will not be applied to El Salvador.[20]

---

20. See "Publica Secretaría de Salud requisitos adicionales para importar medicamentos producidos en el extranjero." from 3 January 2008. This information was published by Inteligencia Comercial (IQOM) (www.iqom.com.mx).

Measure and claims	Findings	Implementation
	• The requirement by Mexico that the factory or laboratory must be in Mexico violates national treatment, Art. 3-03, 15-05, and 15-10 of the FTA (**El Salvador**). Intermediary findings: • The claims were not extended by the complainant (**El Salvador**); • The measure was not justified under Art. XX b) of GATT (incorporated into the FTA through Art. 20-02 of the FTA). The parallel letters contemplate the registration while protecting human life or health (**El Salvador**); and • Even when the complainant did not present evidence on the trade effects, a violation cause nullification or impairment (**El Salvador**).	• On 2 January 2008 Mexico added new requirements to its legislation which already required having a factory or a laboratory in Mexico.[21]

14. NAFTA Chapter 19 Cases (Private Party vs Country on Trade Remedies)

Source: NAFTA Chapter 19 Panel reports and other information by the NAFTA Secretariat;[22] the investigating authorities from the NAFTA Parties.[23]

---

21. *Item.*
22. See http://www.nafta-sec-alena.org/August 2009.
23. For The US see:
    http://trade.gov/ia/index.asp
    http://info.usitc.gov/oinv/sunset.NSF
    http://ia.ita.doc.gov/frn/index.html
    http://www.gpoaccess.gov/fr/index.html
    For Canada see:
    http://www.cbsa-asfc.gc.ca/menu/D15-e.html
    http://www.cbsa-asfc.gc.ca/sima-lmsi/er-rre/menu-eng.html
    http://www.cbsa-asfc.gc.ca/sima-lmsi/monthly-eng.html
    http://canadagazette.gc.ca/index-e.html
    For Mexico see:
    http://www.pymes.gob.mx/upci/

i. AD/CVD Orders Imposed by the US against Exports from Mexico

1. CVD – Investigation on Leather Wearing Apparel

Date of the final determination: 10 April 1981 (46 FR 21357)

Margin of CVD at the Final Determination: not found.

Status of the order: Revoked on 9 August 1995. Amendments subsequently made revocation retroactive back to 23 April 1985.

See Federal Register: 9 August 1995 (Volume 60, Number 153)] [Notices] [Page 40568] DOC, International Trade Administration, Revocation of Countervailing Duty Orders, Leather Wearing Apparel from Mexico among them.

The DOC amended the previous revocation of this order and made the application retroactive back to 23 April 1985, rather than 1 January 1995; from that date all un-liquidated entries were to be liquidated without CVD collection, and any duty collected refunded with interest. The amendment was made in the light of the Ceramica decision (another CVD case with similar facts and also absence of injury determination). See Federal Register: 24 May 1996 (Volume 61, Number 102), DOC [C-201-001], Leather Wearing Apparel From Mexico; Notice of Termination of the Countervailing Duty Administrative Review and Amendment to the Revocation of the Countervailing Duty Order.

Parallel WTO case: None.

Measure	Date of Decisions and Findings
USA-94-1904-02 Leather wearing apparel from Mexico (DOC Final Results of Countervailing Duty Administrative Review)	**1. 20 October 1995** The Panel affirmed the determination on remand. There were no written submissions presented on the remand.

2. AD – Investigation on Cement

Date of the final determination: 30 August 1990, the DOC imposed an AD duty order on Gray Portland Cement and Clinker from Mexico, 55 Fed. Reg. 35,443.

Margin of Dumping at the Final Determination: 58.38 percent for "Cemex", 53.26 percent for Apasco, 3.69 percent for Hidalgo, and 58.05 percent for "all others."

Status of the order: In effect but with a MAS (see implementation of US – Cement Mexico (DS281))

Parallel WTO/GATT case: US – Cement from Mexico (DS281) and US – Cement (GATT case)

Measure	Date of Decisions and Findings
USA-95-1904-02 Gray portland cement and cement clinker from Mexico (DOC Final Results of AD Duty Administrative Review)	**1. 13 September 1996** The Panel affirmed the determination in the Third Administrative Review of the AD order on gray portland cement and cement clinker, 60 Fed. Reg. 26,865 (19 May 1995).
USA-97-1904-01 Gray portland cement and clinker from Mexico (DOC Final Results of the 5th AD Duty Administrative Review)	**1. 18 June 1999** The Panel affirms the decision of the DOC to refuse to revoke said order. The Panel upholds the DOC's finding that home market sales of Type II cement were outside the ordinary course of trade. The Panel upholds the DOC's decision to collapse "Cementos de Chihuahua" and "Cemex" – two producers – and calculate a single dumping margin. A Panel majority determines that bagged Type I cement should not have been included within the foreign like product and remands the issue to the DOC for a determination consistent with this opinion. A Panel majority affirms the DOC's application of its arm's-length test to the sales of Type I bulk cement to determine normal value. The Panel remands the DOC's denial of a constructed export price offset to "Cemex" and "Cementos de Chihuahua" for a detailed explanation of the questions raised by the Panel. A Panel majority affirms the DOC's difference in merchandise calculation as supported by substantial evidence and in accordance with law, but remands to the DOC for a recalculation of "Cemex's" difference in merchandise allowance with respect to only Type I bulk cement (not bagged) consistent with the Panel's majority finding regarding bulk vs bagged. The Panel affirms the DOC's allowance of a freight adjustment on bulk cement to "Cemex". The Panel affirms the DOC's adjustments to normal value for "Cemex's" rebates and for "other" adjustments for "Cementos de Chihuahua".

Measure	Date of Decisions and Findings
	The Panel affirms the DOC's normal value adjustment to "Cemex" and "Cementos de Chihuahua" of a claimed credit expense.
	The Panel affirms the DOC's normal value adjustment to "Cemex" and "Cementos de Chihuahua" of a claimed credit expense.
	The Panel affirms the DOC's determination that the Mexican indirect selling expenses should not be deducted from the constructed export price calculation.
	The Panel affirms the DOC's calculations concerning "total US expenses."
	The Panel affirms the DOC's interpretation and application of the statute with respect to movement expenses.
	Pursuant to the DOC's request, and based upon an agreement of all Parties, the Panel remands to the DOC for the correction of certain ministerial errors.
	2. 10 February 2000
	The Panel affirmed the Re-determination on Remand be affirmed.
USA-97-1904-02 Gray portland cement and clinker from Mexico (DOC Final Results of the 4th AD Duty Administrative Review)	**1. 04 December 1998** The Panel affirmed the DOC determination. The following claims were not found to be illegal: • the Exhaustion of Administrative Remedies; and • the use of best information available on the margin of 109.43 percent applied by the investigating authority to "Cemex" in the second remand of the second Administrative Review.
USA-MEX-98-1904-02 Gray portland cement and clinker from Mexico (DOC Final Results of the 6th AD Duty Administrative Review)	**1. 26 May 2005** **A. Revocation of Order** The Panel affirms the DOC's decision to refuse to revoke said Order based upon alleged defects in the initiation of the original less than fair value investigation supported by substantial evidence on the record. **B. Ordinary Course of Trade** The Panel remanded this issue: The DOC's determination that certain "Cemex's" home market sales were outside the ordinary course of trade.

Measure	Date of Decisions and Findings
	The Panel upholds the DOC's rejection of the home market sales sold from the Hermosillo plants for normal value comparison, and the use of partial adverse facts available by using sales of Type I cement produced at other Mexican plants.
	C. Collapsing The Panel affirms the DOC's decision to collapse "Cementos de Chihuahua" and "Cemex" for purposes of calculating a single dumping margin.
	D. Bulk and Bagged The Panel upholds the DOC's determination that bulk and bagged cement constituted identical merchandise for normal value comparison purposes.
	E. Terminal Charges The Panel affirms the DOC's decision regarding the treatment of terminal charges as indirect selling expenses.
	F. Differences in merchandise adjustment The Panel upholds the DOC's determination to use partial adverse facts available in calculating the difference in merchandises adjustment. The Panel remands the determination to the DOC for further analysis and explanation regarding the calculation of differences in merchandises.
	G. Classification of certain constructed export price sales The Panel remands the issue to the DOC for reclassification certain sales as constructed export price sales.
	2. 03 November 2005 The Panel: • Affirmed the recalculations made by the DOC based on the reclassification of constructed export price sales. • Remanded to the DOC for reconsideration in accordance with this opinion the ordinary course of trade determination regarding sales of Type V cement as Type V and Type II cement, and its calculation of the differences in merchandise adjustment.

Measure	Date of Decisions and Findings
USA-MEX-99-1904-03 Gray portland cement and clinker from Mexico (DOC Final Results of the 7th AD Duty Administrative Review)	**1. 30 May 2002** The Panel affirmed DOC with respect to the following findings: • "Cemex's" home market sales of cement were outside the ordinary course of trade; • an adjustment to "Cementos de Chihuahua's" US indirect selling expenses for interest allegedly incurred in financing cash deposits for AD duties was not warranted; • that resort to partial adverse facts available for "Cemex's" data from the Hidalgo plant (rather than total adverse facts available for "Cemex's" entire response) was warranted; and • that refusal to revoke the AD order based upon alleged defects in the initiation of the original less than fair value investigation was warranted. The Panel remanded the following findings: • Some of "Cemex's" home market sales were outside the ordinary course of trade; • duties should be assessed on a nationwide basis in this regional industry case; • "Cemex's" bag and bulk cement should be classified as the same like product, and that sales of "Cemex's" bag and bulk cement were at the same level of trade; • "Cemex's" and "Cementos de Chihuahua's" US warehousing expenses should be treated as indirect selling expenses; • "Cemex's" home market pre-sale warehousing expenses should not be deducted from normal value; • certain "Cementos de Chihuahua" sales to unaffiliated US customers by "Cementos de Chihuahua's" US affiliate should be classified as indirect export price sales, rather than constructed export price sales; • differences in merchandises adjustment to "Cemex's" sales for the physical differences between cement was warranted; and • an adjustment for "Cemex's" freight expenses was warranted.

Measure	Date of Decisions and Findings
	2. 11 April 2003
	The Panel affirmed DOC's Remand Re-determination with respect to the following findings:
	• "Cemex's" home market sales of Type V cement sold as Type I cement are within the ordinary course of trade;
	• sales from "Cemex's" Hidalgo plant should be included in the dumping calculation, and that partial facts available should be used to account for such sales;
	• duties should be assessed on a nationwide basis;
	• bulk and bagged cement should be treated as the same foreign like product.
	The Panel remanded to DOC's:
	• The decision to match "Cementos de Chihuahua's" US sales with "Cementos de Chihuahua's" home market sales so that DOC can make a determination whether, under the statute, "Cementos de Chihuahua's" US sales should be compared to "Cemex's" home market sales.
	3. 04 September 2003
	The Panel affirmed:
	• DOC's re-determination on remand on its application of "Cementos de Chihuahua's" sales of certain kind of Cement to "Cemex's" Hidalgo sales.
	The Panel remanded:
	• DOC's decision to apply adverse facts available to "Cementos de Chihuahua" in calculating "Cementos de Chihuahua's" importer-specific rate since it is undisputed that "Cementos de Chihuahua" fully cooperated with DOC in the seventh Administrative Review.
	4. 25 November 2003
	The Panel remanded:
	• the Third Remand Determination back to DOC and instructs DOC to strictly abide by, and implement to the letter, the remand instructions set forth in the NAFTA Panel Second Remand Decision.
	the Panel further instructs:

Measure	Date of Decisions and Findings
	• to use as non-adverse facts available for all sales at the Hidalgo plant an average of "Cemex's" prices for Type V cement sold as Type I cement; and • to apply that price to the quantity of Hidalgo sales. the Panel commented: • DOC's reasoning for failing to implement this Panel's specific instructions is disingenuous and without merit. As such, this Panel finds DOC's decision to deliberately disobey this Panel's instructions to be particularly disturbing.
USA-MEX-2000-1904-03 Gray portland cement and clinker from Mexico (DOC Final Results of the 8th AD Duty Administrative Review)	**No Decision Issued**
USA-MEX-2000-1904-05 Gray portland cement and clinker from Mexico (DOC Final Results of the Full Sunset Review of the AD Duty Order)	**No Decision Issued**
USA-MEX-2000-1904-10 Gray portland cement and clinker from Mexico (Five Year Review of the AD Duty order)	**1. 24 January 2005** The Panel denied "Cemex's" request to strike out portions of the Committee's brief. The Panel affirmed USITC's determinations regarding: • a "reasonably foreseeable time;" • the existence of a regional industry; • duty absorption; and • its decision not to cumulate imports. The Panel remanded: • the USITC to apply the "probable" or "more likely than not" standard announced by the Court of International Trade in Siderca when making its determination regarding likely volume, likely price effects, and likely impact on the industry; • on the likely volume of subject imports if the AD duty order were revoked, the USITC is to (a) explain how it is probable that subject imports would increase if the AD duty order is revoked, and (b) render a complete analysis of how the various third-country AD duty orders would affect the likely volume of subject imports to the US;

Measure	Date of Decisions and Findings
	• on the likely price effects of subject imports on the industry if the order were revoked, the USITC is to (a) explain the price implications of revocation of the AD duty order with sufficient clarity to show how the record supports the USITC findings that revocation of the order would be likely to lead to significant negative price effects on the domestic industry, (b) explain how revocation of the AD duty order would be likely to lead to significant price underselling by subject imports of the domestic product, and (c) explain how subject imports are likely to enter the US at prices that otherwise would have a significant price depressing or suppressing effect on the domestic product;
	• on the likely impact on the domestic industry if the AD duty order were revoked, the USITC is to (a) explain how it reached the conclusion that the order should remain in place in order to protect the highly-profitable, regional industry, given the continuing solid demand in the region and a substantial increase in non-Mexican cement imports; (b) explain how it reached the conclusion that the regional industry would be likely to suffer material injury, having found that the regional industry is not in a vulnerable state; and (c) explain how the decreasing market share of the regional industry, due to a substantial increase in demand, was not attributed to imports of non-Mexican cement;
	• on the USITC's conclusion that producers of all or almost all of the production in the Southern Tier region would likely suffer material injury by reason of the dumped imports if the order is revoked, the USITC is to (a) explain why producers of all or almost all of the production in the Southern Tier region would likely be materially injured if the order is revoked, (b) explain what percentage of regional production would likely suffer material injury, and (c) explain what its aggregate and individual plant analyses consisted of and what anomalies, if any, the individual plant analysis revealed; and
	• the USITC is to fully evaluate the information concerning the proposed Southdown acquisition.
USA-MEX-2001-1904-04 Gray portland cement and clinker from Mexico (DOC final results of the 9th AD duty Administrative Review)	**No Decision Issued**

Measure	Date of Decisions and Findings
USA-MEX-2002-1904-01 Gray portland cement and cement clinker from Mexico (USITC final results of the Five Year Review of the AD duty order) (USITC Dismissal of a Request to Institute a Section 751(b) Investigation)	**No Decision Issued**
USA-MEX-2002-1904-05 Gray portland cement and clinker from Mexico (DOC final results of the 10th AD Duty Administrative Review)	**No Decision Issued**
USA-MEX-2003-1904-01 Gray portland cement and clinker from Mexico (DOC Final Results of the 11th AD Duty Administrative Review)	**No Decision Issued**
USA-MEX-2003-1904-03 Gray portland cement and clinker from Mexico (DOC Final Results of the 12th AD Duty Administrative Review)	**No Decision Issued**
USA-MEX-2004-1904-03 Gray portland cement and clinker from Mexico (DOC Final Results of the 13th AD Duty Administrative Review)	**No Decision Issued**
USA-MEX-2006-1904-03 Gray portland cement and clinker from Mexico (DOC Final Results of the 14th AD Duty Administrative Review)	**No Decision Issued**
USA-MEX-2007-1904-02 Gray portland cement and clinker from Mexico (DOC Final Results of the AD Duty Administrative Review)	**No Decision Issued**

3.   AD – Investigation on Flowers

Date of the final determination: 23 April 1987, the AD Duty Order on Certain Fresh Cut Flowers from Mexico was published in the Federal Register 52 Fed. Reg. 13491 (1987).

Margin of Dumping at the Final Determination: not found.

Status of the order: revoked.

For Rancho del Pacifico on 14 May 1998 (Volume 63, Number 93, DOC, International Trade Administration, [A-201-601], Certain Fresh Cut Flowers From Mexico; Notice of Final Results of AD Duty Administrative Review, and Revocation of AD Duty Order in Part)

On 3 September 1999, the DOC published notice that it was revoking the orders because the domestic interested parties had withdrawn, in full, their participation in the ongoing Sunset Reviews (64 FR 48346 and 48347).

Parallel WTO case: None.

Measure	Date of Decisions and Findings
USA-95-1904-05 Fresh cut flowers from Mexico (DOC Final Results of AD Duty Administrative Review)	**1. 16 December 1996** The Panel upheld: • The DOC's finding that each complainant (Mexican exporters) made evasive and misleading statements with respect to its obligations to file tax returns for the years covered by the period of review. The Panel upheld: • The DOC's finding to use "best information available" as supported by substantial evidence on the record and otherwise in accordance with the law. The Panel remanded: • The Final Determination to the DOC with instructions to assess the second-tier best information available rate of 18.20 percent for each complainant (Mexican exporters) given that there is evidence in the administrative record that each of the Ranches made efforts to cooperate with the DOC's investigation.

4. AD – Investigation on Non-Alloy Steel Pipe and Tube

Date of the final determination: 2 November 1992.

See Certain Circular Welded non-Alloy Steel Pipe from Brazil, the Republic of Korea (Korea), Mexico, and Venezuela, and Amendment to Final Determination of Sales at Less Than Fair Value: Certain Circular Welded Non-Alloy Steel Pipe from Korea, 57 FR 49453 (2 November 1992).

Margin of Dumping at the Final Determination: not found.

Status of the order: In effect.

Parallel WTO case: None.

Measure	Date of Decisions and Findings
USA-97-1904-06 Circular welded non-alloy steel pipe and tube from Mexico (DOC Final Results of the AD Duty Administrative Review)	**No Decision Issued**
USA-MEX-98-1904-05 Circular welded non-alloy steel pipe from Mexico (DOC final scope ruling – AD order)	**1. 19 November 2002** The Panel remanded: • The Scope Ruling for action not inconsistent with this decision. DOC should have began its analysis of the Order's scope with the refutable presumption that mechanical tubing – the merchandise subject to the Scope Ruling – is outside the scope of the Order and then consider such record evidence as may demonstrate that specific mechanical tubing products are covered by the Order. Yet, it adopted the opposite approach and expanded the Order beyond its original scope. In addition, it did not explain its analysis. **2. 16 May 2003** The Panel remanded: • the Scope DOC with instructions to determine based on record evidence whether the Order applies to the specific mechanical tubing products intended to be exported by Galvak. **3. 18 December 2003** The Panel remanded: • The Scope Determination to the DOC with instructions to apply its definition of mechanical tubing to the record evidence, including Galvak's 11 August 1998 submission, and to fully explain its reasoning in support of its conclusions. **4. 07 January 2004** The Panel affirmed the re-determination: • The DOC's Third Re-determination on Remand is reasonable and adequately supported by evidence in the administrative record. Galvak is free to file future scope ruling requests with respect to specific products that meet both standards.

5.   AD – Investigation on OCTG

Date of the final determination: 11 August 1995, DOC [A-201-817] AD Duty Order: Oil Country Tubular Goods from Mexico 60 FR 41056, Number 155.

Margin of Dumping at the Final Determination: 23.79 percent

Status of the order: Expired on 25 July 2006

The revocation decision was published on 22 June 2007 and it was made retroactive to 25 July 2006. See Oil Country Tubular Goods from Argentina, Italy, Japan, Korea, and Mexico; Revocation of AD Duty Orders Pursuant to Second Five-year (Sunset) Reviews from 22 June 2007, 72 FR 34442, Number 120.

Parallel WTO case: US – AD Measures on Oil Country Tubular Goods (OCTG) from Mexico (DS282) and US – AD Administrative Review on Oil Country Tubular Goods from Argentina (DS346), and US – Sunset Reviews of AD Measures on Oil Country Tubular Goods from Argentina (DS268).

Measure	Date of Decisions and Findings
USA-95-1904-04 Oil country tubular goods from Mexico (DOC Final Determination of Sales at Less than Fair Value)	**1. 31 July 1996** The Panel upheld: • The DOC's calculation of TAMSA's financial expense on the basis of best information available and on the alternative basis that the 1993 financial data was not representative of the financial expenses incurred during the period of investigation. • The DOC's rejection of TAMSA's non-standard cost allocation method and its substitution of an allocation method based on standard costs. The Panel also granted the DOC's request for a remand to re-calculate the nonstandard cost allocation for a particular subset of TAMSA's sales. The Panel remanded: • Final Determination to the DOC for a detailed explanation of the reasons for its rejection of the 1993 financial data as non-representative of the general and administrative expenses incurred during the period of investigation. The Panel determined: • That the challenge by TAMSA to the Final Determination, based on a statement made by the DOC in the Team Concurrence Memorandum, is not ripe for consideration.

| USA-MEX-2001-1904-03 Oil country tubular goods from Mexico (DOC Final Results of the Full Sunset Review of the AD Duty Order) | **1.   11 February 2005**

The Panel remanded with the following instructions:

• The DOC is directed to determine whether the "other factors" raised by TAMSA in its "substantive response" to the initiation of the Sunset Review are "relevant" to the DOC's "likelihood" determination. If the DOC considers that they are not, it is directed to explain the reasons leading to that decision.

• As needed to consider its "likelihood" determination, the DOC is directed to reopen the record for the limited purpose of investigating and fact-finding concerning the relevance and bearing of TAMSA's "other factors" on the DOC's determination of whether revocation of the AD duty order would be likely to lead to continuation or recurrence of dumping.

• The DOC is further directed to complete its investigation and fact-finding of TAMSA's "other factors", to determine their relevance and their effect on the DOC's "likelihood" determination, and to issue the DOC's "likelihood" determination within thirty days from the date of this Panel decision. |
| | **2.   08 February 2006**

The Panel remanded with the following directions:

• The DOC is directed to determine whether the decrease in the magnitude of TAMSA's foreign currency denominated debt in the Sunset Review period outweighs the "likelihood" presumption that results from the decrease in TAMSA's post-order exports.

• If the DOC determines that the lower level of TAMSA's foreign currency denominated debt does not outweigh the "likelihood" presumption that results from the decrease in TAMSA's post-order exports, the DOC is directed to explain the reasons leading to its determination.

• If the DOC determines that the lower level of TAMSA's foreign currency denominated debt in fact outweighs the "likelihood" presumption that results from the decrease in TAMSA's post-order exports, the DOC is directed to enter a finding of no likelihood of continuation or recurrence of dumping. |

3.   28 July 2006

The Panel remanded with the following directions:

* The DOC is directed to reconsider its likelihood determination and either issue a determination of no likelihood or give a reasoned analysis to support a conclusion that TAMSA's dumping is likely to continue or recur. In particular, the DOC is directed to explain why TAMSA's high financial expense ratio is likely to recur considering the decrease in TAMSA's foreign currency denominated debt during the Sunset Review period as evidenced by the actual financial expense ratio established in the record of this proceeding.

The Panel further explained:

* Notwithstanding DOC's own determination that TAMSA has shown good cause for the consideration of "other factors," the DOC has failed to support its likelihood of continuation or recurrence of dumping determination in light of the "other factors" presented. DOC's Second Re-determination on Remand has failed to consider the decrease in TAMSA's foreign currency denominated debt during the Sunset Review period as evidenced by the DOC's consideration of a fictitious financial expense ratio in place of its consideration of the actual uncontested financial expense ratio in the record.

4.   17 January 2007

The Panel remanded with the following directions:

* Reconsider its likelihood determination and either issue a determination of no likelihood or give a reasoned analysis to support the conclusion that TAMSA's dumping is likely to continue or recur on revocation of the AD duty order.

In the event that the DOC reissues a likelihood determination:

* To explain in detail why the elimination of TAMSA's foreign debt does not outweigh the likelihood presumption derived from the post-order reduction of TAMSA's exports. In its evaluation of TAMSA's "other factors," the DOC is directed to utilize the actual financial expense ratio established in the record of this proceeding. The DOC is also directed to provide an explanation supported by Sunset Review law indicating why TAMSA's zero margin calculations have no predictive value.

	The Panel emphasized: • That it will not affirm the DOC's Fourth Re-determination if the DOC continues to be disrespectful of the Panel's review authority under Chapter 19 of the NAFTA by issuing affirmative remand determinations which cannot be supported by the record and that continue to rely on evidence that the Panel has already held to be insufficient.
	5. 01 June 2007 The Panel remanded: • For the DOC to make a determination consistent with the decision of this Panel to the effect that the evidence on the record does not support a finding of likelihood of recurrence or continuation of dumping upon revocation of the AD duty order, and to make that determination within ten days from the date of this Fifth Panel Decision. The Panel explained that: • DOC has proven that remanding once again would be a futile attempt to get the DOC to issue a determination supported by the evidence on the record and in accordance with US AD law. • Its repeated attempts at evading an analysis substantiated by the facts of the case and US law, together with the evidence on the record, lead the Panel to assume that DOC cannot issue a reasonable affirmative likelihood of recurrence or continuation of dumping determination.
USA-MEX-2001-1904-05 Oil country tubular goods from Mexico (DOC Final Results of the 4th AD Duty Administrative Review and Determination Not To Revoke)	**1. 27 January 2006** The Panel upheld: • The DOC's determination that TAMSA did not meet the commercial quantity threshold for revocation of the AD order. • The DOC's rejection of the argument that zeroing is contrary to US law. • The DOC's inclusion of the cost of export credit insurance as a direct cost of sale. The Panel remanded: • The Final Determination to the DOC with instructions to recalculate the cost of production of the two sizes of pipe by averaging the costs and recalculating the constructed value. • The Final Determination to the DOC with instructions for recalculating the amount of packing costs included in the calculation of constructed value.

	2. 11 August 2006 The Panel remanded: • The DOC to reconsider its determination that Hylsa did not ship in commercial quantities consistent with the findings of this Panel. The Panel explained: • It is our conclusion that the DOC acted in an arbitrary and capricious fashion when it failed to adequately justify its determination that Hylsa did not ship the subject matter goods in commercial quantities during the periods of review in question. We therefore are remanding the matter to the DOC for further consideration, in light of the issues raised by the Panel. This is necessary because of our decision that the results of the ninth Administrative Review cannot be taken into account by the DOC in its decision in the Fourth Review, leaving the commercial quantities determination the sole basis for its refusal to revoke the AD order against Hylsa.
	3. 16 January 2007 The Panel affirmed: • The DOC's determination that Hylsa did not ship in commercial quantities and that its determination not to revoke the AD order is upheld. The Panel explained: • It is our conclusion that the DOC acted within its discretion and has satisfied their burden in using an "absolute" standard in this particular case for assessing whether shipments occurred in commercial quantities. The DOC has adequately justified their determination that Hylsa did not ship the subject matter goods in commercial quantities during the periods of review in question and thus does not qualify for revocation of the AD order.
USA-MEX-2006-1904-06 Oil country tubular goods from Mexico (DOC Final Results of AD Duty Administrative Review)	**Active No Decision**
USA-MEX-2001-1904-06 Oil country tubular goods from Mexico (USITC Dismissal of a Request to Institute a Section 751(b) Investigation)	**1. 22 March 2007** The Panel affirmed the determination in all respects.

6. AD – Investigation on Porcelain-on-Steel Cookware

Date of the final determination: 2 December 1986, DOC, International Trade Administration, AD duty order on Porcelain-on-Steel Cooking Ware from Mexico, 51 Fed. Reg. 43,415 (1986).

Margin of Dumping at the Final Determination: Not found.

Status of the order: revoked as of 1 December 1995 (as stated by the determination dated 22 April 2002).

From 1 December 1995 (from that date all un-liquidated entries were to be liquidated without AD collection, and any duty collected refunded with interests). The AD measure was, however, still in force during the period from 1 December 1995 to 30 November 1999 when ongoing litigations with respect to reviews of the order were dismissed.

See DOC, International Trade Administration, [A-201-504], Porcelain-on-Steel Cookware from, Mexico: Final Results of Changed Circumstances AD Duty Administrative Review, Revocation of the AD Duty Order, and Rescission of Administrative Reviews, Federal Register/Vol. 67, No. 77/Monday, 22 April 2002.

Parallel WTO case: None.

Measure	Date of Decisions and Findings
USA-95-1904-01 Porcelain-on-Steel cookware from Mexico (DOC Final Results of AD Duty Administrative Review)	**1. 30 April 1996** The Panel affirmed the DOC's determinations with respect to all issues. But, the Panel remanded: • The issue concerning the error associated with product number 10158 for further proceedings not inconsistent with this opinion; and • the issue of the appropriate adjustment for rebated or uncollected value-added taxes with instructions for the DOC to apply the tax neutral methodology approved by the Court of Appeals for the Federal Circuit in Federal Mogul v. US, 63 F.3d 1572 (Fed. Cir. 1995).
USA-96-1904-01 Porcelain-on-Steel cooking ware from Mexico (DOC Final Results of the 6th AD Duty Administrative Review)	**No Decision Issued**

Measure	Date of Decisions and Findings
USA-97-1904-05 Porcelain-on-Steel cookware from Mexico (DOC Final Results of the 8th AD Duty Administrative Review)	**No Decision Issued**
USA-97-1904-07 Porcelain-on-steel cookware from Mexico (DOC Final Results of the 9th AD Duty Administrative Review)	**1. 30 April 1999** The Panel affirmed: • The decision of the DOC in all respects. But, it remanded: • The use of the global ratio in calculating Yamaka's indirect selling expense to determine whether its calculation was in fact a clerical error. It instructed that if so, the error be corrected and the basis of the correction be explained in detail, with specific comments addressed to the proper calculation.
USA-MEX-98-1904-04 Porcelain-on-Steel cookware from Mexico (DOC Final Results of the 10th AD Duty Administrative Review)	**No Decision Issued**
USA-MEX-99-1904-05 Porcelain-on-Steel cookware from Mexico (DOC Final Results of the 11th AD Duty Administrative Review)	**No Decision Issued**
USA-MEX-2000-1904-04 Porcelain-on-Steel cookware from Mexico (DOC Final Results of the 12th AD Duty Administrative Review)	**No Decision Issued**
USA-MEX-2001-1904-02 Porcelain-on-Steel cookware from Mexico (DOC Final Results of the 13th AD Duty Administrative Review)	**No Decision Issued**

ii. AD/CVD Orders Imposed by Canada against Exports from Mexico

1. AD Investigation on Hot Rolled Carbon Steel Plate

Date of the final determination: 27 October 1997.

See inquiries (Section 42), Findings and Reasons, Certain Hot-Rolled Carbon Steel Plate from Mexico, China, South Africa and Russia, Inquiry No. NQ-97-001.

Margin of Dumping at the Final Determination: 26.2 percent.

Status of the order: Revoked on 10 January 2003.

The Canadian authority rescinded its finding concerning certain hot-rolled carbon steel plate originating in, or exported, from Mexico on 10 January 2003. See Expiry Reviews (Section 76.03) – Final Certain Hot-Rolled Carbon Steel Plate Originating from Mexico, China, South Africa and Russia, Expiry Review No. RR-2001-006. This decision was published in Vol. 137, No. 3 of the Canada Gazette on 18 January 2003.

Parallel WTO case: None.

Measure	Date of Decisions and Findings
CDA-97-1904-02 Certain hot-rolled carbon steel plate, originating in or exported from Mexico (Canadian International Trade Tribunal Injury Finding)	**1. 19 May 1999** The Panel remanded: • This matter to the Canadian International Trade Tribunal and instructed it to determine whether, under section 43 (1.01) of the Special Import Measures Act, a separate order is required in respect of Mexico and further, whether separate reasons are also requisite. The Panel explained: • The matter was remanded given that the interpretation of the Special Import Measures Act is within the jurisdiction of the Canadian International Trade Tribunal and that it is charged with the duty to interpret and apply this law, including section 42, in a reasonable manner.
	2. 15 December 1999 The Panel affirmed: • The Tribunal allowance on the late disclosure or non-disclosure of certain interrogatory material, given the

Measure	Date of Decisions and Findings
	Canadian International Trade Tribunal's broad powers with respect to the conduct of the hearing and the Complainant's inability to specify the resultant prejudice.
	The Panel affirmed:
	• The Determination with respect to not issuing separate reasons for AHMSA.
	The Panel affirmed:
	• The determination with respect to cumulation, since the decision under these circumstances was unreasonable.
	The Panel affirmed:
	• The determination with respect to not excluding AHMSA.
	This Panel affirmed the findings:
	– Deference to the Tribunal. – The Standard of Patent Unreasonability. – Downward Trend in Industry Prices. – Price Gap increasing. – Delivery System Details. – Further increases in imports and displacements. – Price Erosion and Suppression. – Causation.
CDA-MEX-99-1904-01 Certain hot-rolled carbon steel plate, originating in or exported from Mexico (Canadian International Trade Tribunal Injury Finding – Corrigendum to the Finding of 27 October 1997)	**No Decision Issued**

iii. AD/CVD Orders Imposed by Mexico against Exports from the US and Canada

1. AD – Investigation on Bovine Carcasses and Half Carcasses, Fresh or Chilled from the US

Date of the final determination: 28 April 2000.

See *Resolución final de la investigación AD sobre las importaciones de carne y despojos comestibles de bovino, mercancía clasificada en las fracciones arancelarias 0201.10.01, 0202.10.01, 0201.20.99, 0202.20.99, 0201.30.01,*

0202.30.01, 0206.21.01, 0206.22.01 y 0206.29.99 de la Tarifa de la Ley del Impuesto General de Importación, originarias de los Estados Unidos de América, independientemente del país de procedencia.

Margin of Dumping at the Final Determination: From 0.03 $USD per Kg to 0.80 $USD per Kg.

Status of the order: In effect (five years from 28 April 2005).

See Sunset Review's final determination published on 24 April 2006.

Parallel WTO case: Mexico – definitive AD measures on beef and rice (DS295): The US only challenged the AD measure on Beef at consultations stage and did not pursue to the Panel/AB.

Measure	Date of Decisions and Findings
MEX-USA-00-1904-02 Bovine carcasses and half carcasses, fresh or chilled originating in the US (SECOFI Final AD Duty Determination)	1. **15 March 2004** **On general issues** The Panel upheld: • The application of a final AD duty based on a sample; since, there is no injury to Packerland Packing Company, Inc., because its right was recognized by the investigating authority. The resolution indicates that the company can request that the investigating authority determines an individual margin of price discrimination for it, upon the presentation of the appropriate information. The Panel dismissed: • The claims on the competence of the Deputy Director of Legal Affairs of the Secretariat of Commerce and Industrial Development; since, they lack of legal grounds. • The claims on Illegal receipt of the official questionnaires, evidence, and arguments presented beyond the legal time limit; since, the issues became moot when the interested parties did not proceed in their claim. The Panel remanded: • The determination of a relevant market, as well as the establishment of the classification certificate and of useful shelf life; so that this issue is corrected in accordance with this resolution. • The determination on a AD duty greater than the margin of dumping calculated for each one of the products subject of the investigation; so that this issue is re-determined in accordance with this resolution.

Measure	Date of Decisions and Findings
	• The determination on the application of the methodology used to calculate the margin of dumping to determine the AD duties for broker companies as it is incorrect; so that the investigating authority adopts the measures in conformity with this resolution. The Panel abstained to rule on: • The determination on extension of the deadline for the preliminary AD duties; since, it lacks the authority to review preliminary measures issued during the investigation. **On the threat of injury to the national production of meat in carcasses, fresh, chilled, or frozen:** The Panel affirmed: • That each factor considered should be satisfied to find a threat of injury. • The modification of the methodology to use real prices in Mexican pesos. • The projection of a future increase in the relevant imports. • The determination in relation to the export prices. The Panel Remanded with the following instructions: • Not to include the totality of the imports in its consideration of the rate of increase and; • to properly analyze the available and not used capacity of all the exporters from the US following this resolution. **On the injury to the national production of meat in boneless cuts and with both, fresh, chilled or frozen:** The Panel Upheld: • Some findings challenged on the determination of injury. • The decision with regards to the change of methodology. • The decision to limit the consideration of installed capacity in the Mexican Federal Inspection Type slaughterhouses. • The decision of not considering the information presented by PM Beef Holding, LLC, for the determination of an individual margin of dumping. The Panel Remanded with the following instructions: • To reach a finding of injury, carrying out the causality analysis required by Article 41 of the Foreign Trade Act.

Measure	Date of Decisions and Findings
	The Panel did not decide on:
	• The determination that the national production of tongues, liver, and other eatable offal do not supply the same markets and the imported products; since, the national production abandoned the review.
	2. 11 May 2007
	The Panel Affirmed the remanded determination.

2. AD – Investigation on Sodium Hydroxide (caustic soda) from the US

Date of the final determination: 12 July 1995

See *Resolución final de la investigación AD sobre las importaciones de sosa cáustica líquida, mercancía comprendida en la fracción arancelaria 2815.12.01 de la Tarifa de la Ley del Impuesto General de Importación, originaria y procedente de los Estados Unidos de América.*

Margin of Dumping at the Final Determination: product below the reference normal value of 147.43 $USD per metric ton, would pay the difference between the export price (Ex-Works) and the reference normal value, with a ceiling of 38.89 $USD per ton.

Status of the order: In effect (five years from 13 July 2005).

See Sunset Review's final determination published on 6 June 2006.

Parallel WTO case: None.

Measure	Date of Decisions and Findings
MEX-USA-2003-1904-01	Active
Imports of sodium hydroxide (caustic soda) originating in the US (Secretaría de Economía Final AD Determination of the Sunset Review)	**1. 13 July 2006**
	The Panel decided, by majority, that it lacked competence to review the final determination of the Sunset Review (based on Based on NAFTA Article 1904, Annex 1911, and Articles 59, 68, 70, 89, 89(A), 89(B), 89(D) and 89(F) of the Foreign Trade Act).
	The Panel emphasized:
	• That this decision concluded the bi-national Panel's task. Consequently, the decision was final and definitive.
	The Panel explained:
	• That Sunset Reviews are not included in the treaty on the list of Mexico's definitions of the final determinations subject to bi-national Panel review. It found no ambiguity, obscurity, or absurdity in this plain reading of the literal language of the treaty.

3.   AD – Investigation on Cut-to-Length Plate Products from the US

Date of the final determination: 2 August 1994.

See *Resolución definitiva de la investigación AD sobre la importación de placa en hoja; mercancia comprendida en las fracciones arancelarias 7208.32.01, 7208.33.01, 7208.42.01 y 7208.43.01, de la Tarifa de la Ley del Impuesto General de Importación, originaria y procedente de los EE.UU.*

Margin of Dumping at the Final Determination: From 3.86 percent to 78.46 percent.

Status of the order: Revoked on 22 October 1999.

See Sunset Review's final determination published on 21 October 1999.

Parallel WTO case: None.

Measure	Date of Decisions and Findings
MEX-94-1904-02 Imports of cut-to-length plate products from the US (SECOFI Final AD Duty Determination)	**1. 30 August 1995** The Panel Remanded with the following instructions: • To recalculate or clarify the calculations of freight adjustments with respect to both the US and Mexican price determinations, and • to determine injury without resort to the expert consultant's report on injury, unless opposing counsel had the opportunity to comment on the report as well as on the possible bias of the consultant.

4.   AD – Investigation on Fructose Corn Syrup from the US

Date of the final determination: 23 January 1998.

See *resolución final de la investigación AD sobre las importaciones de jarabe de maíz de alta fructosa, mercancía clasificada en las fracciones arancelarias 1702.40.99 y 1702.60.01 de la tarifa de la ley del impuesto general de importación, originarias de los Estados Unidos de América, independientemente del país de procedencia.*

Margin of Dumping at the Final Determination: From 55.37 USD to 175.85 USD per metric ton.

Status of the order: Revoked on 21 May 2002 through the Resolution published on 20 May 2002.

See *resolución por la que se da cumplimiento a la decisión final del Panel binacional del 15 de abril de 2002, encargado de la impugnación al informe de devolución de la autoridad investigadora del 23 de noviembre de 2001, del caso MEX-USA-98-1904-01, revisión de la resolución final de la investigación AD sobre las importaciones de jarabe de maíz de alta fructosa, mercancía clasificada en las fracciones arancelarias 1702.40.99 y 1702.60.01 de la tarifa de la ley del impuesto general de importación, originarias de los Estados Unidos de América, independientemente del país de procedencia, emitida por la ahora Secretaria de Economia, y publicada en el Diario Oficial de la Federación el 23 de enero de 1998.*

Parallel WTO case: Mexico – Corn Syrup II (DS132); and Mexico – Corn Syrup I (DS101)

Measure	Date of Decisions and Findings
MEX-USA-98-1904-01 Imports of high-fructose corn syrup originating in the US (SECOFI Final AD Duty Determination)	**1. 03 August 2001** This Panel remanded with the following two options: • That because the investigating authority has failed to prove threat of injury, the investigating authority promptly terminate the AD duties and refund the duties collected since its imposition; or • Should the investigating authority wish to re-evaluate what basis and justification -if any- there is for its finding of threat of injury, consistent with the findings of this Panel, and in light of the multiple proceedings already completed, it proceed accordingly. The Panel noted, among others: • The investigating authorities expressly revised its reasoning in response to a WTO Panel that found violation on the threat of injury analysis; • the investigating authority has conducted two public inquiries concerning the alleged threat of injury to the domestic sugar industry and issued two essentially identical determinations of threat of injury; and • this Panel has found that in the investigating authority's Revised Determination was still no support for its conclusion that there existed threat of injury.
	2. 15 April 2002 This Panel remanded ordering the investigating authority to • Take action consistent with our decision that the duties have been imposed and collected contrary to law, no later than 30 days following the entry of this decision.

Measure	Date of Decisions and Findings
	The Panel noted that: • The investigating authority has had multiple opportunities to both review the material and to expand upon it as a result of the first WTO Panel; • it has twice failed to demonstrate to this Panel that the administrative record supports its conclusion on threat of injury; • That there exists no support in the combined record on threat of injury; and • This Panel also found ADD had been and continue being inconsistent to international provisions and applicable laws.

5. AD – Investigation on Polystyrene and Impact Crystal from the US

Date of the final determination: 11 November 1994.

See *Resolución definitiva de la investigación AD sobre las importaciones de poliestireno cristal e impacto, mercancía clasificada en las fracciones arancelarias 3903.19.02, 3903.19.99, 3903.90.05 y 3903.90.99 de la Tarifa de la Ley del Impuesto General de Importación, originarias de la República Federal de Alemania y de los Estados Unidos de América, independientemente del país de procedencia, mediante la cual se determinaron diversas cuotas compensatorias, únicamente a las importaciones de poliestireno cristal originarias de los Estados Unidos de América, exceptuando del pago de las mismas, a las importaciones provenientes de la exportadora estadounidense The Dow Chemical Company.*

Margin of Dumping at the Final Determination: From 11.82 percent to 44.32 percent.

Status of the order: Revoked as of 11 November 1999.

See Resolution published on 23 March 2001.

Parallel WTO case: None.

Measure	Date of Decisions and Findings
MEX-94-1904-03 Polystyrene and Impact Crystal from the US (SECOFI Final AD Duty Determination)	**1. 12 September 1996** The Panel affirmed the final determination.

6. AD – Investigation on Flat Coated Steel Plate from the US

Date of the final determination: 2 August 1994.

See *Resolución definitiva de la investigación administrativa en materia de prácticas desleales de comercio internacional, en su modalidad de dumping, sobre las importaciones de aceros planos recubiertos, mercancía comprendida en las fracciones arancelarias 7210.31.01, 7210.31.99, 7210.39.01, 7210.39.99, 7210.41.01, 7210.41.99, 7210.49.01, 7210.49.99, 7210.70.01 y 7210.70.99 de la Tarifa de la Ley del Impuesto General de Importación, originarias y procedentes de los Estados Unidos de América.*

Margin of Dumping at the Final Determination: 38.21 percent.

Status of the order: Revoked as of 2 August 1999.

See Resolution dated 27 October 1999.

Parallel WTO case: None.

Measure	Date of Decisions and Findings
MEX-94-1904-01 Import of flat coated steel products, in and from the US (SECOFI Final AD Duty Determination)	**1. 27 September 1996** The Panel upheld the Final Determination in all respects, except as remanded. The Panel Remanded: **Competence and Formality Requirements** • The Panel declares illegal all administrative determinations that concern "Inland" and with no legal effect. It instructs (a) to consider the evidence presented, (b) to give "Inland" further right with respect to evidence, (c) to make new administrative determinations taking into account the evidence "Inland" has presented, and/or (d) to take any other action permitted by applicable law. **Dumping Issues** • Instructs the investigating authority (a) to determine standard values for exports of "New Process" (one of the exporters); (b) to use the cost data submitted by New Process; (c) to use the export prices provided by New Process in determining any price discrimination margins; (d) to compute new price discrimination margins for New Process; and (e) to determine injury or threat of injury with the new margin of dumping.

Measure	Date of Decisions and Findings
	• Directs the Investigating Authority to give "Inland" an opportunity to present additional evidence.
	• Instructs, for "USX," the Investigating Authority (a) to determine an overall profit for sales of a "general category" of products; (b) to determine a reasonable amount of profit that is no higher than this overall profit on domestic sales of products in this general category, unless it determines that there has been no overall profit for this general category; (c) to recalculate the reconstructed value for "USX" based on this recalculated profit component; (d) to use the bank finance charge proposed by "USX" in computing the export price on the sale involving that finance charge; (e) to recalculate the price discrimination margins for "USX" Corporation based on the above; and (f) based on any price discrimination margins, to determine if exports by "USX" caused injury or threat of injury.
	• The Panel declares that the determination of the freight adjustment on the export prices for "Bethlehem," and the allocation of restructuring expenses to the reconstructed value for "Bethlehem," were illegal under Mexican law.
	Injury Issues
	• Directs the investigating authority to consider the comments of the interested parties on the contents of the "dictamen técnico" and to maintain the confidentiality of the identity of the consultant who prepared the dictamen técnico.
	• Directs the investigating authority to consider the additional views of the interested parties on whether products included in the "Nota Nacional" should be excluded in determining a threat of future injury; and to make a new determination about threat of future injury after considering these additional views.
	• Directs the investigating authority to assure interested parties an appropriate opportunity to comment on the post-period 1992 data used for the threat of future injury determination.
	• Directs the investigating authority to consider the additional views of the interested parties on whether the "product mix" methodology used distorted the price comparisons, and to make a new determination about threat of future injury after considering these additional views.

Measure	Date of Decisions and Findings
	2. 15 September 1997
	The Panel affirmed:
	• The allocation of raw material costs of "New Process" (one of the exporters).
	The Panel remanded:
	• Fully inform "New Process" of all missing information and of all needed clarifications regarding proposed calculations of hand labor cost, overhead expense, profit and credit expense for "New Process," and regarding product exclusions for "New Process;"
	• give "New Process" an opportunity to provide additional information and to make clarifications regarding proposed calculations of hand labor cost, overhead expense, profit and credit expense, and regarding product exclusions; and
	• based on the above, make new dumping calculations for "New Process" and for "Inland."
	3. 13 April 1998
	The Panel affirmed the second remand report by the investigating authority.

7. AD – Investigation on Urea from the US

Date of the final determination: The final determination was published on 17 April 2000 without AD duties but revoked in compliance with a 1904 Panel report. A new resolution was issued (the re-determination) published on 18 October 2002 and it imposed AD duties to be applied subject to certain conditions.

See *Resolución (published on 17 April 2000) final de la investigación AD sobre las importaciones de urea, mercancía clasificada en la fracción arancelaria 3102.10.01 de la Tarifa de la Ley del Impuesto General de Importación, originarias de los Estados Unidos de América y de la Federación de Rusia, independientemente del país de procedencia".*

See *Resolución (re-determination) por la que se da cumplimiento a la decisión final del 23 de mayo de 2002 del Panel binacional del caso MEX-USA-00-1904-01, encargado de la revisión de la resolución final de la investigación AD sobre las importaciones de urea, mercancía clasificada en la fracción arancelaria*

3102.10.01 de la Tarifa de la Ley del Impuesto General de Importación, originarias de los Estados Unidos de América y de la Federación de Rusia, independientemente del país de procedencia, por lo que respecta únicamente a las importaciones estadounidenses, emitida por la Secretaría de Comercio y Fomento Industrial, ahora Secretaría de Economía, y publicada el 17 de abril de 2000; y por la que se revoca la resolución final referida por lo que respecta a las importaciones rusas y en consecuencia se emite una nueva determinación (published on 18 October 2002).

Margin of Dumping at the Final Determination:

For Urea from the US:

- Imports below 160 USD per metric ton would pay the difference between the import value and the reference price with a ceiling of 52.75 USD per metric ton if they are from the US. If the import price is over this reference price, no AD duty was payable.
- The petitioner stated that it would resume production on 15 January 2003. Hence, the AD duties were to start on 16 April 2003 if "AGROMEX" restarted domestic production, or 3 months after domestic production had restarted. "AGROMEX" had had until October 2003 to restart domestic production.

Status of the order: There was no AD duty applied. Mexico notified that the petitioner did not restart domestic production by 31 October 2003. This was a prerequisite for the application of AD duties.

See *Communication published on 18 March 2004: COMUNICADO Oficial en alcance a la Resolución por la que se da cumplimiento a la decisión final del 23 de mayo de 2002 del Panel binacional del caso MEX-USA-00-1904-01, encargado de la revisión de la resolución final de la investigación AD sobre las importaciones de urea, mercancía clasificada en la fracción arancelaria 3102.10.01 de la Tarifa de la Ley del Impuesto General de Importación, originarias de los Estados Unidos de América y de la Federación de Rusia, independientemente del país de procedencia, por lo que respecta únicamente a las importaciones estadounidenses, emitida por la Secretaría de Comercio y Fomento Industrial, ahora Secretaría de Economía, y publicada el 17 de abril de 2000; y por la que se revoca la resolución final referida por lo que respecta a las importaciones rusas y en consecuencia se emite una nueva determinación, en concordancia con la decisión final del 29 de enero de 2004 del Panel binacional encargado de la revisión al informe de devolución de la autoridad investigadora del 14 de octubre de 2002.*

Parallel WTO case: None.

Measure	Date of Decisions and Findings
MEX-USA-00-1904-01 Imports of urea originating in the US (SECOFI Final AD Duty Determination)	**1. 23 May 2002** The Panel remanded with the following instructions: • To issue the corresponding final determination to be consistent with this Decision, particularly with the alleged change of the legal standing of the complainant and the alleged lack of analysis to allegations and evidence submitted by the complainant; in general, it has to adopt any measures not incompatible with this Decision.
	2. 29 January 2004 The Panel affirmed: • The Determination on Remand of the investigating authority with respect to imports of urea original from the US, regardless of the exporting country.

8. AD – Investigation on Rolled Steel Plate from Canada

Date of the final determination: 28 December 1995.

See *Resolución final de las investigaciones AD y antisubvención sobre las importaciones de placa en rollo, mercancía clasificada en las fracciones arancelarias 7208.10.02, 7208.25.99 y 7208.37.01 de la Tarifa de la Ley del Impuesto General de Importación, originarias de la República Federativa de Brasil, República de Venezuela y Canadá, independientemente del país de procedencia, mediante la cual se impusieron cuotas compensatorias que van de 84.05 a 14.15 por ciento.*

Margin of Dumping at the Final Determination: 31.08 percent.

Status of the order: Revoked as of 29 December 2000.

See Resolution published on 30 January 2001.

Parallel WTO case: None.

Measure	Date of Decisions and Findings
MEX-96-1904-02 Rolled steel plate originating in or exported from Canada (SECOFI Final AD Duty Determination)	**1. 17 December 1997** The Panel remanded with the following instructions: **Regarding "Titan"** • Establish, based solely on the information contained in the administrative record, whether "Titan" was the only exporter of Canadian made rolled steel "plate" to Mexico in 1992;

Measure	Date of Decisions and Findings
	• establish definitively the volume of rolled steel plate exports attributable to "Titan" during 1992 and indicate how much, if any, were second quality goods;
	• assess, based on the analysis resulting from the new analysis, whether the total imports from "Titan" were significant for the purposes of accumulation in accordance with Mexican law;
	• evaluate, based on the new results, the injurious impact of "Titan's" 1992 exports from Canada on producers in Mexico; and
	• substantiate the new conclusions respecting points through the identification of the relevant supporting evidence in the administrative record.
	• based on the new analysis, to establish, if appropriate, a specific margin of price discrimination in respect of imports from "Titan."
	Regarding Canadian Exporters other than "Titan"
	• All the evidence indicates that "Titan" was the sole supplier of these goods to Mexico during the period of investigation. Accordingly, we order that the countrywide price discrimination margins against Canadian producers must be reassessed.
	2. 03 August 1998
	The Panel upheld the determination on remand except as remanded.
	The Panel Remanded:
	With respect to "Titan"
	• The price discrimination margin of 108 percent applied to "Titan" within the Determination on Remand and orders not to give it any legal effect; and
	• instructs (a) to allow "Titan" to present evidence to be treated as an independent trading company; b) to allow "Titan" to comment on the analysis of the evidence, (c) to calculate a new dumping margin for "Titan" taking into account any evidence presented and (d) to take any other action permitted by applicable law.

Measure	Date of Decisions and Findings
	With respect to all other Canadian Exporters
	• The price discrimination margin of 108 percent applied to all other Canadian exporters within the Determination on Remand and orders not to give it any legal effect; and
	• instructs to determine a rate of price discrimination not higher than 31.08 percent for Canadian exporters other than "Titan," based on the data available in the record.

9. AD – Investigation on Hot-Rolled Steel Sheet from Canada

Date of the final determination: 30 December 1995.

See *Resolución final de las investigaciones administrativas AD y antisubvención sobre las importaciones de lámina rolada en caliente, mercancía comprendida en las fracciones arancelarias 7208.13.01, 7208.14.01, 7208.23.01 y 7208.24.01 de la Tarifa de la Ley del Impuesto General de Importación originaria de la República Federativa de Brasil, República de Venezuela, República Federal de Alemania, Canadá, República de Corea y el Reino de los Países Bajos, independientemente del país de procedencia.*

Margin of Dumping at the Final Determination: From 15.37 percent to 45.86 percent.

Status of the order: Revoked as from 16 August 1997.

See Resolution published on 15 August 1997.

Parallel WTO case: None.

Measure	Date of Decisions and Findings
MEX-96-1904-03 Hot-rolled steel sheet originating in or exported from Canada (SECOFI Final AD Duty Determination)	**1. 16 June 1997** The Panel remanded with the following instructions: **A. Regarding "Titan:"** • Accord to the imports coming from "Titan" and supplied by "Dofasco" the same treatment as for the imports from "Dofasco" set out in paragraph 581 D of the Final Determination. • Assess for imports from "Titan" supplied by Canadian manufacturers other than "Dofasco" AD duties that are specific to each of those suppliers. Prior to doing this, it shall:

Measure	Date of Decisions and Findings
	– Evaluate the impact of the exclusion of the imports coming from "Dofasco" on the total volume of imports from Canada.
	– Assess whether the resulting total volume of exports from Canadian companies other than "Dofasco" is still significant and, therefore, justifies its accumulation with the imports from Brazil, Korea, Germany, the Netherlands and Venezuela in the analysis of injury and cause and effect.
	• In the event that the volume of imports from Canada referred to in the above paragraph were found to be significant, undertake an analysis of injury and cause and effect for each of the suppliers of "Titan" other than "Dofasco."
	• In either of the situations described above, calculate for, each of "Titan's" suppliers other than "Dofasco," the corresponding AD duty to be applied to imports by "Titan" separate from those incoming from "Dofasco."
	B. Regarding "Algoma" and "Stelco:"
	• Whereas the investigating authority maintained that this was an INJURY and not a THREAT OF INJURY investigation, and whereas under the applicable legal provisions and, as demonstrated by the evidence in the Administrative Record, the Canadian companies, "Algoma" and "Stelco" did not export any Hot Rolled Steel Sheet to Mexico during the investigation period, and whereas both companies did provide the required information to the investigating authority during the investigation, the investigating authority shall act on the basis that the legal requirements for the imposition of AD duties for injury were not met.

iv. Extraordinary Challenge Committee Cases

1. US Imposition of AD on Cement from the Mexico

Measure	Date of Decisions and Findings
ECC-2000-1904-01USA Gray portland cement and clinker from Mexico (Extraordinary Challenge Committee (ECC) Proceeding relating to USA-97-1904-01 Panel Review)	**1. 30 October 2003** The ECC concluded that the petitioners (the US and the Southern Tier Cement Committee) had failed to demonstrate either that the Bi-national Panel had "manifestly exceeded its powers, authority or jurisdiction" or that the Panel's determination on the

Measure	Date of Decisions and Findings
(Extraordinary Challenge Committee unanimously denied the petition of the Government of the US and affirmed the 18 June 1999 decision of the Bi-national Panel.)	single issue raised in the petition "threatens the integrity of the Bi-national Panel review process." Inasmuch as these criteria were not met, the petition was denied and the 18 June 1999 decision of the Bi-national Panel left unaltered.

Bibliography

Appleton, Barry. *Navigating NAFTA: A Concise User's Guide to the North American Free Trade Agreement.* Rochester, NY: Carswell, 1994.

Bhala, Raj. *International Trade Law: Interdisciplinary Theory and Practice,* 3rd edn. Newark, NJ: LexisNexis, 2008.

Clyde-Hufbauer, Gary & Ben Goodrich. *Lessons from NAFTA: Free Trade Agreements, US Strategies and Priorities.* Washington, DC: Institute for International Economics, 2004.

Czako, Judith, Johann Human & Jorge Miranda. *A Handbook on Anti-Dumping Investigations.* New York: Cambridge University Press, 2003.

Enders, Alice. *Dispute Settlement in Regional and Multilateral Trade Agreements: Regional Integration and the Global Trading System.* London: Harvester Wheatsheaf, 1993.

Gantz, David. 'Dispute Settlement under the NAFTA and the WTO: Choice of Forum Opportunities and Risks for the NAFTA Parties'. *American University International Law Review* 14 (1999): 1025.

Hudec, Robert E. *Enforcing International Trade Law: The Evolution of the Modern GATT Legal System.* Salem: Butterworth Legal Publishers, 1993.

Jackson, John H. *The Jurisprudence of GATT and the WTO.* Washington, DC: Cambridge University Press, 2000.

Jackson, John H., William J. Davey & Alan O. Sykes. *Cases, Materials and Texts on Legal Problems of International Economic Relations.* St. Paul, MN: West Group, 2001.

Kennedy, Kevin C. *Parallel Proceedings at the WTO and under NAFTA Chapter 19: Whither the Doctrine of Exhaustion of Local Remedies in DSU Reform? George Washington International Law Review* 39 (2007): 47.

Mavroidis, Petros C. *Trade in Goods: The GATT and Other Agreements Regulating Trade in Goods.* New York: Oxford University Press, 2007.

Nottage, Hunter & Thomas Sebastian. 'Giving Legal Effect to the Results of WTO Trade Negotiations: An Analysis of the Methods of Changing WTO Law'. *Journal of International Economic Law* 9, no. 4(2006): 989–1016.

Palmeter, David & Petros C. Mavroidis. *Dispute Settlement in the World Trade Organization.* Cambridge, UK: Cambridge University Press, 2004.

Pauwelyn, Joost. *Conflict of Norms in Public International Law.* Cambridge, UK: Cambridge Studies in International and Comparative Law, 2003.

Pauwelyn, Joost. 'Adding Sweeteners to Softwood Lumber: The WTO-NAFTA "Spaghetti Bowl" Is Cooking'. *Journal of International Economic Law* 9, no. 1 (2006): 197–206.

Perezcano-Diaz, Hugo. *El Arbitraje a Nivel Internacional y Dentro del Marco del TLC: El Arbitraje en las Relaciones de Consumo.* Mexico City, Mexico: Procuraduría Federal del Consumidor, 1997.

Schwartz, Warren F. & Alan O. Sykes. 'The Economic Structure of Renegotiation and Dispute Resolution in the World Trade Organization'. *The Journal of Legal Studies* 31 (January 2002): 179–204.

Vermulst, Edwin & Folkert Graafsma. *WTO Disputes: Anti-Dumping, Subsidies and Safeguards.* London: Cameron May, 2002.

Index

GLOBAL TRADE LAW SERIES

1. Emmanuel T. Laryea, *Paperless Trade: Opportunities, Challenges and Solutions*, 2002 (ISBN 90-411-9897-0).
2. Xiang Gao, *The Fraud Rule in the Law of Letters of Credit: A Comparative Study*, 2002 (ISBN 90-411-9898-9).
3. Yuwa Wei, *Comparative Corporate Governance: A Chinese Perspective*, 2003 (ISBN 90-411-9908-X).
4. Ross P. Buckley (ed.), *The WTO and the Doha Round: The changing Face of World Trade*, 2003 (ISBN 90-411-9947-0).
5. Bradley J. Condon, Joyce C. Sadka, Tapen Sinha (eds), *Insurance Regulation in North America: Integrating American, Canadian and Mexican Markets*, 2003 (ISBN 90-411-2301-6).
6. Jan Hoogmartens, *EC Trade Law Following China's Accession to the WTO*, 2004 (ISBN 90-411-2301-6).
7. Yang Guohua, Bryan Mercurio, Li Yongjie, *WTO Dispute Settlement Understanding: A Detailed Interpretation*, 2005 (ISBN 90-411-2361-X).
8. Jan Job de Vries Robbé, Paul U. Ali, *Securitisation of Derivatives and Alternative Asset Classes, Yearbook*, 2005 (ISBN 90-411-2375-X).
9. Markus W. Gehring, Marie-Claire Cordonier Segger, *Sustainable Development in World Trade Law*, 2005 (ISBN 90-411-2366-0).
10. Yann Aubin, Arnaud Idiart. *Export Control Law and Regulations Handbook: A Practical Guide to Military and Dual-Use Goods Trade Restrictions and Compliance*, 2007 (ISBN 90-411-2601-5).
11. Henry Kibet Mutai, *Compliance with International Trade Obligations: The Common Market for Eastern and Southern Africa*, 2007 (ISBN 978-90-411-2664-1).
12. Yong-Shik Lee, *Economic Development through World Trade: A Developing World Perspective*, 2007 (ISBN 978-90-411-2681-8).
13. Yanning Yu, *Circumvention and Anti-Circumvention Measures: The Impact on Anti-Dumping Practice in International Trade*, 2007 (ISBN 978-90-411-2686-3).
14. Ross Buckley, Vai Io Lo, Laurence Boulle, *Challenges to Multilateral Trade: The Impact of Bilateral, Preferential and Regional Agreements*, 2008 (ISBN 978-90-411-2711-2).
15. K.D. Raju, *World Trade Organization Agreement on Anti-dumping: A GATT/WTO and Indian Jurisprudence*, 2008 (ISBN 978-90-411-2780-8).
16. Xiaochen Wu, *Anti-dumping Law and Practice in China*, 2008 (ISBN 978-90-411-2790-7).
17. Amin Alavi, *Legalization of Development in the WTO: Between Law and Politics*, 2008 (ISBN 978-90-411-2795-2).
18. Henrik Andersen, *EU Dumping Determinations and WTO Law*, 2009 (ISBN 978-90-411-2827-0).

19. Sherzod Shadikhodjaev, *Retaliation in the WTO Dispute Settlement System*, 2009 (ISBN 978-90-411-2811-9).
20. Yi Shin Tang, *The International Trade Policy for Technology Transfers: Legal and Economic Dilemmas on Multilateralism versus Bilateralism*, 2009 (ISBN 978-90-411-2825-6).
21. Reem Anwar Ahmed Raslan, *Antidumping: A Developing Country Perspective*, 2009 (ISBN 978-90-411-3128-7).
22. Pietro Poretti, *The Regulation of Subsidies within the General Agreement on Trade in Services of the WTO: Problems and Prospects*, 2009 (ISBN 978-90-411-3162-1).
23. Esther Lam, *China and the WTO: A Long March towards the Rule of Law*, 2009 (ISBN 978-90-411-3144-7).
24. Jorge Alberto Huerta-Goldman, *Mexico in the WTO and NAFTA: Litigating International Trade Disputes*, 2010 (ISBN 978-90-411-3169-0)

Due Date	Date Returned
APR 1 7 2013	APR 0 9 2013
www.library.humber.ca	